Operations Management

Operations Management

A Systems Approach through Text and Cases

C. J. CONSTABLE

Professor of Operations Management,
Cranfield School of Management

and

C. C. NEW

Lecturer in Production and Operations Management,
London Graduate School of Business Studies

A Wiley—Interscience Publication

JOHN WILEY & SONS

Chichester · New York · Brisbane · Toronto

Copyright © 1976, by John Wiley & Sons Ltd.

Reprinted May 1978
Reprinted January 1982
Reprinted May 1983

Library of Congress Cataloging in Publication Data:

Constable, Charles John.
  Operations management.

  'A Wiley—Interscience publication.'
  1. Production management. 2. Production management—Case studies. I. New, Colin, joint author.
II. Title.
TS155.C635   658.5   75-37667

ISBN 0 471 01651 9 (Cloth)
ISBN 0 471 01758 2 (Paper)

Typeset in IBM Journal by Preface Ltd, Salisbury, Wilts
and printed in Great Britain by The Pitman Press, Bath

Preface

This book is based on the material used on Operations Management programmes at Cranfield School of Management and the London Graduate School of Business Studies, for both practising managers and students taking masters degrees in Business Administration. Many of the participants in these programmes are neither practising operations managers nor future operations managers, but are concerned with the role of operations in the whole company. It is, therefore, expected that the book will be of value to post-graduate management students, practising managers and management students following part-time and full-time programmes in technical colleges, whatever their specialization.

The study of operating systems, whether they be manufacturing, hospital administration, distribution networks or airline management is characterized by a need to examine the system as a whole rather than concentrating attention on particular system elements. Approaches to the teaching of operations management seem to have polarized into the study of analytical techniques and the study of total systems, usually through case-discussion. It is a pity that so much energy has been wasted in the debate between the 'case-teacher' and the 'techniques-teacher' as to the relative merits of each approach. Our view is that the basic skills of successful operations management lie in the diagnosis of existing problem areas, the development of action programmes taking account of the interaction of the system elements and the implementation of system changes. It is therefore essential to be aware of the analytical tools available to the operations manager and also to be able to carry out satisfactory synthesis of the operations system. The first requirement favours a 'techniques' approach, the second a 'systems' approach. Development of the skills necessary for the satisfactory analysis and synthesis of operating systems is very difficult to achieve solely through the more traditional learning vehicles of direct lectures and worked exercises or examples. Case discussion provides one means of exposing the student to a range of different business situations which it would take many years to experience in practice. The development of individual diagnostic abilities in such situations is achieved through the need to devise, during case preparation, specific proposals which the student must be prepared to defend in group discussion.

However, development of the skills of analysis and synthesis cannot be achieved through an arbitrary set of cases. The cases must enable the student to come to grips with the operating system and to define the problems. He must identify the possible courses of action and the methods by which they could be implemented. The cases must therefore contain sufficient data (of the kind normally available to an Operating Manager) to enable the student to support proposed courses of action with quantitative analysis tempered with judgement and intuition. Cases which are mere descriptions of operating systems cannot provide such a learning experience, nor can artificially simplified examples designed to illustrate the application of particular quantitative techniques, though these may be useful as further exercises.

The text of this book, therefore, provides a basic analytical framework within which to study the operating systems presented in the case section. It cannot and will not be all things to all people. Many teachers will choose to supplement the text material with more detailed references and we have made a number of suggestions at the end of each chapter with this in mind. Many teachers will use additional case material with which they are particularly familiar or which extends study in a particular area.

The cases included should, however, provide sufficient material to cover the major areas of operating systems in a single course. They are not a substitute for the traditional teaching of the 'techniques of Operations Management' such as work study, quality control methods and inventory control, but provide a necessary complement which is particularly beneficial for use with students aspiring to general management positions. The techniques may be learned either side by side, or through prior course work or only after the need for analytical techniques has been identified from discussion of the case situation. The tutor will wish to develop his course to suit the particular needs of his student group. For this reason we have not grouped the cases by chapter. In fact, each one touches on several chapters. However, for the guidance of tutors preparing course plans, the front table relates the cases to the chapters to which they are most relevant.

Particularly in manufacturing industry, there seems to be a tendency to regard production operations as a necessary evil — a cost sink rather than a profit source. However, manufacturing is a strong competitive weapon in the corporate armoury and the efficient management of the enterprise depends on the development of a manufacturing policy which reflects corporate objectives through to the operating levels. Only through the study of a company's operating system, market environment and other external pressures is it possible to develop such a consistent set of policies

The case approach is probably the most efficient way of developing the skills and insights which will enable the student to take this broad view. Most of the cases are set in European business environments, in a wide range of industries. A significant proportion are set in non-manufacturing operations. All the cases included here have been used with groups of business executives and graduate students both inside and outside graduate business schools and all have proved to be excellent learning vehicles. Neither the case information nor the actual analysis provide the major learning experience, though practical application of analytical techniques provides a useful spin-off. The cases merely provide the means by which the student may develop his skill in the diagnosis of operating systems.

For the teacher the preparation of case material for class discussion can be very time consuming. As an aid to such preparation a 'teachers manual' is available to *bona fide* teachers considering adoption of this text. This includes suggested course outlines and case assignments and notes on the analysis of the individual cases as a guide for class discussion. Enquiries should be directed to the Case Clearing House of Great Britain and Ireland, Cranfield Institute of Technology, Cranfield, Bedford, England.

To The Student — Before We Start

For many students, initial exposure to case analysis is a traumatic experience, particularly if it follows on from courses in techniques and quantitative analysis which are much less open-ended. What follows is an attempt to relieve the trauma.

Each case should be approached with a determination to specify as clearly as possible:

(1) The objectives to be achieved.
(2) The alternative courses of action available.
(3) How you would choose between them.
(4) How you would implement your chosen course of action.

Sometimes, the emphasis given in the case to overt problems will obscure the most important issues. Here diagnostic skill is essential; the manager usually sees the symptoms not the disease. You should be prepared to question all the information given in the case. What is the source of this data or opinion? How reliable is it likely to be? Is the analysis correct? Only by delving below the surface will you discover many of the most important points.

Intuition, imagination and creative thought are as much a part of case preparation as quantitative analysis of the data available. However, wherever it is possible to support your judgement and intuition with quantitative analysis, you should do so.

As a practical guide to the preparation of cases the student will probably find that the best plan is to begin by reading fairly quickly through the whole case, next study the type and form of any data available and then go back to examine the material in detail. The best method of assessing whether or not you have any firm conclusions is to try to write down, on one side of paper, your views and supporting evidence. If you cannot do this then you are not really ready to discuss the case with other students. The time taken to reach this stage will, of course, depend on your experience of case analysis and the scope of the case. As a rough guide it will usually be a minimum of two hours, on average about three hours. We are sure you will find the time well spent.

Acknowledgements

Many individuals and organizations have helped in providing material for this book. We are most grateful to the companies, both those identified and those wishing to remain anonymous, which permitted us to write case studies. Particular thanks must to to Malcolm Dodman and Martyn Pitt, Research Associates at the Cranfield School of Management, who assisted in the writing of many of the cases. We would like to express our appreciation to the following individuals and Institutions for permission to reproduce their cases.

Professor J. R. M. Gordon and L'Institut pour l'Etude des Methodes de Direction de l'Enterprise (IMEDE), Lausanne for Great Northern Fluids Ltd.; the President and Fellows of Harvard College for the Winton Shirt Company; P. Mayer and P. Clugnet and Centre d'Enseignment Superieur des Affaires de Jouy-en-Josas (CESA) for Sonimage; B. Fielden of the Cranfield School of Management for the Whitehaven Steel Co. Ltd.; Dr. L. G. Franko and Centre d'Etudes Industrielles (CEI), Geneva for Bell Schönheitsprodukte GmbH; Professor T. A. J. Nicholson of the London Graduate School of Business Studies for Parsons Peebles Ltd. (A); and Professor Karl M. Ruppenthal of the University of British Columbia for Trans World Airlines.

Elisabeth Constable provided much practical guidance on style and corrected many drafts. Veronica Wright patiently typed and retyped the drafts and Diana Radford typed a number of the cases. We greatly appreciate all their efforts.

Finally, we would like to thank our respective Institutions, The London Graduate School of Business Studies and the Cranfield School of Management for enabling us to have the time and facilities to complete this book.

Contents

4 Managing the Materials System (1) 42

5 Managing the Materials System (2) 64

6 Managing Quality and Reliability 78

Cases

CLASSIFIED CASE LIST — BY MAJOR TOPIC COVERAGE AND CHAPTERS

CASE	1 & 2 Analysis of Operations Systems	3 Managing the Labour Force	4 & 5 Managing the Materials System	6 Managing Quality and Reliability	7 Production Planning and Control	8 Managing Continuous Systems	9 Managing Assembly Processes	10 Managing Job and Batch Production	11 Managing Large Scale Projects	12 Managing Service Operations	13 Measuring Manufacturing Performance	14 Establishing Manufacturing Policy
Anglia Metals	x				x							x
Arctcraft (A)	x		x		x							
Barwick Switch					x							x
Bell Schonheitsprodukte												x
Berger Paints (Dist)			x							x		
Berger Paints (Prod)			x		x							

	1	2	3	4	5	6	7	8	9	10	11
Bridge Electric (A)						x					x
Bridge Electric (B)											x
Great Northern Fluids	x	x			x						
Lemont (B)				x			x				
Midwich Hospital		x	x								x
Parsons Peebles		x			x			x			
Peterborough M.C.					x						x
Production Control Short Cases								x			x
Sonimage						x				x	
Special Chemical Co.							x		x		x
Trans World Airlines	x		x								x
Whitehaven Steel				x							x
Winton Shirt						x			x		x

CHAPTER 1

Analysis and Synthesis in Operations Management

What is Operations Management?

Operations management is concerned with the management of the physical resources required for production, whether the product be a manufactured item or a service. In a pure manufacturing context, operations management will include production management but may also be concerned with distribution and with supplies management. Operations management is principally concerned with the management of currently available facilities (labour, capital etc.) in order to ensure that they meet current market requirements. It is also concerned with the original design or extension of these facilities in so far as this affects the operating system. In service functions like banking, insurance and catering, operations management is again concerned with meeting current market demand for the 'product', i.e. banking facilities, a hotel bedroom etc., using the currently available resources. Managing a service is far more akin to managing production than is generally appreciated; the principal distinction is the highly perishable nature of the product, there being few more perishable products than a hotel bedroom or an airline seat.

The Importance of Operations Management

The efficient management of the physical operations of an enterprise is important for a number of reasons:

(1) The number of people employed in these areas far outweighs the number employed in other functions. As a consequence:
(2) A major proportion of total revenue is spent on operations.
(3) In most manufacturing companies, about 80% of the total capital investment expenditure will be in the operations area.

On a national level, the importance of the manufacturing sector of the economy is clear: it employs some 44% of the total UK labour force, produces 43% of the GDP (1972) and 86% of all exports. Out of a total working population of around 23 million, eleven million people are employed in this sector and some three million of these are employed in the production of engineering and electrical goods. These

EMPLOYMENT	% OF LABOUR FORCE EMPLOYED			
	UK	USA	FRANCE	GERMANY
Primary (extractive)	2	4	13	8
Secondary (manufacture)	44	31	40	50
Tertiary (services)	54	65	47	42
GDP	% CONTRIBUTION TO TOTAL GDP			
Primary	3	3	6	3
Secondary	43	34	48	52
Tertiary	54	63	46	45

Source: ILO and OECD Statistics.

Figure 1   Distribution of employment and origin of GDP (1972)

alone produce 60% of total UK exports. A very high proportion of the people employed in the manufacturing sector are involved directly in 'operations'. Moreover, a considerable proportion of the employees in the very diverse service sector are also involved in operations. In most of the 'developed' economies, the service industries are growing far more quickly than manufacturing industry and already account for almost two-thirds of the total US labour force and over half of UK employment (see Figure 1).

The relative importance of some of the sectors within manufacturing is illustrated in Figure 2 which shows the total output by sector and the proportion of output exported. It is not just the value of exports by sector which is important here but also their content. If one examines the value per tonne of the goods exported from the UK and the trade balance at various levels, (Figure 3), it is clear that the goods exported have relatively low value per tonne compared with the goods imported. This is confirmed by comparative data for other advanced industrial economies as illustrated in Figure 4. This figure shows that although the UK situation improved somewhat between 1969 and 1972, the value per tonne of imports was still considerably higher than the value per tonne of exports. This is not a direct relationship, but it would appear that the UK exports relatively low technology products – products which the 'semideveloped' nations may soon be able to produce for themselves. The need for the UK to create effective manufacturing systems making advanced technology, high value goods is readily apparent. Such systems will require able, well trained operations managers.

Operations Management Problems

The management problems in operating systems arise from two decision processes: the initial design of the operating system in order to achieve certain eventual output, and the efficient running of the operating system in terms of current performance objectives. The design of the operating system will necessitate examination of plant layout, manufacturing processes, information systems and

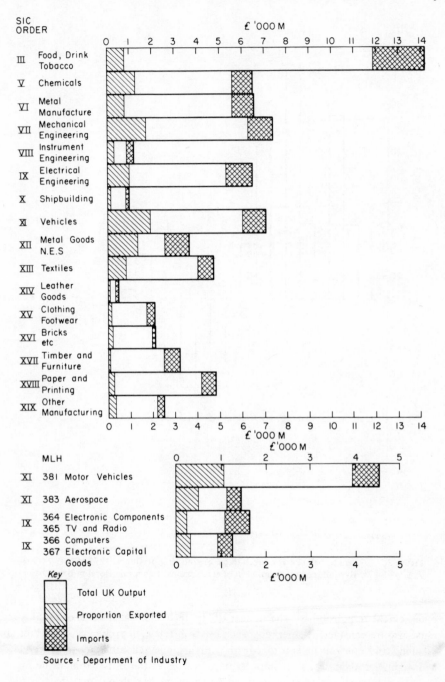

Figure 2   UK output for selected manufacturing industries (1973) showing proportion exported and total imports

4

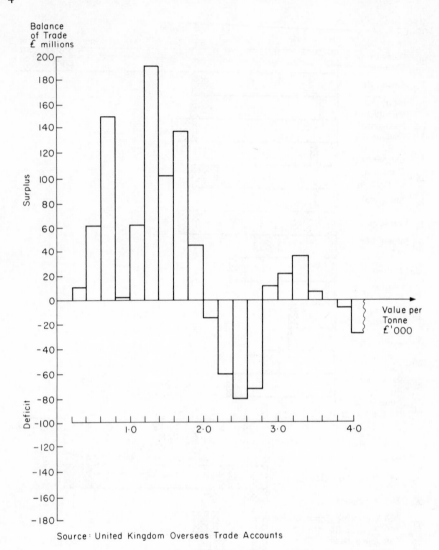

Source: United Kingdom Overseas Trade Accounts

Figure 3   UK trade balance for mechanical engineering products, 1973 (SITC 71 less 711. 4—5—7). Reproduced by permission of the National Economic Development Office

management responsibility. The impact of the technological systems on employees must also be considered. Operating decisions will relate to problems of production planning and control, inventory control, quality and reliability, customer service and employee relations. It is important to realize at the outset that while many operating systems (be they in banking or chemical processing) may have a high 'technological' content which is specific to the industry, it is not usually necessary to be completely familiar with the technology in order to assess the efficiency of the operating system. It is, however, essential to be able to identify the effects of

| | Value per tonne $ | | | | Ratio of imports value/tonne to | |
| | Exports fob | | Imports cif | | Exports value/tonne | |
	1969	1972	1969	1972	1969	1972
Sweden	2709	3705	2269	3128	0.84	0.84
West Germany	2589	3966	2556	3379	0.99	0.85
France	2333	2907	2559	3323	1.10	1.14
Italy	2339	2996	2791	3699	1.19	1.23
UK	2040	2841	3808	3731	1.87	1.31

Note: The product coverage for this table is for SITC 71 less 711. 4—5—7 (aircraft engines, internal combustion engines and nuclear reactors)
Source: United Nations Trade Statistics

Figure 4   The relation of the value per tonne of imports to the value per tonne of exports in mechanical engineering products 1969 and 1972. Reproduced by permission of the National Economic Development Office

the required technology in terms of, for instance, processing restrictions, quality requirements or yield rates. Moreover, the study of the physical system must be undertaken with an appreciation of how the people involved in the operating system behave and are likely to react to any changes proposed.

The Systems Concept in Operations Management

A system is defined as 'anything formed of parts placed together or adjusted into a regular and connected whole; a set of things considered as a connected whole'. Hence, the concept of the circulatory 'system' of blood in the human body, or of the respiratory 'system'. Note, however, that each of these systems:

(1) consists of a set of interacting sub-systems, and
(2) is itself a sub-system of a larger system (the human body).

In an exactly analogous way, the operating 'system' of a manufacturing or service organization consists of a set of highly interactive sub-systems and is itself a sub-system of the total enterprise interacting with the marketing system, the financial system, etc.

An operations manager must be aware of the total system and recognize that it includes a number of interacting objectives. Theoretically, he should study any variable which affects the achievement of these objectives. However, because the problems of the total system are usually too complex to handle, he will probably divide the operations system into a set of manageable sub-systems and treat these as independent. Decisions in one sub-system, e.g. quality control, will of course affect the operation of other sub-systems, e.g. production control, employee motivation etc. The manager must be able to assess the effects of such interactions on the total system performance. It should be apparent therefore that the performance of the system depends on the performance of the manager, since the multiple interactions between sub-systems are his main responsibility.

The interrelationships between sub-systems may be illustrated through two simple examples:

(1) If, as a result of customer complaints, the manager of a factory producing garments raises the quality control standards, he may cause lower output (and lower short term profits) due to more rejects, lower earnings for operatives (who have to carry out more rework) and more production control problems because of the recycling of work. This may, of course, still be the 'best' course of action for the long term market and profit objectives. The important point is that the manager must be aware of all of the effects of such a decision if he is to weigh them rationally.

(2) A restaurant chain may decide to redesign its franchised outlets in such a way that they can only cope with a specific limited range menu in order to achieve highly efficient service. Any change in eating habits or in the cost structure of the menu will render such a design partially ineffective because of its inflexibility; also re-equipping may be very expensive.

Thurston (1963) defines a production system as a system for changing materials as they flow through one or more process stages. In order to achieve efficient materials flow, it is of course necessary to define the design of the product and the design of the process through which the flow is to take place. We therefore have three basic elements:

(1) Product design
(2) Process design
(3) Material flow

A multiplicity of factors affect these elements. Figure 5 illustrates these in a graphical form and also shows the other major systems with which the production system itself interacts. The central nature of production in the diagram does not imply that this is necessarily the most important functional area but only that it is the area with which we are most concerned here. Whether production, finance or marketing is the most important functional area of a business is a largely sterile question since in general, all are equally essential to survival. Their importance relative to each other will depend on the nature of the product market, the industrial sector and the economic climate, all of which are subject to change.

Towards a General Theory of Operations

While the elements defined above and the operating factors shown in Figure 5 exist in all production systems and, in modified form in all service systems, their relative importance in particular situations will vary enormously. The task of the operations manager is to assess the relative importance of the factors to a particular decision, to judge the interrelationships which exist and to balance the advantages and disadvantages of various possible courses of action. Moreover, the relative

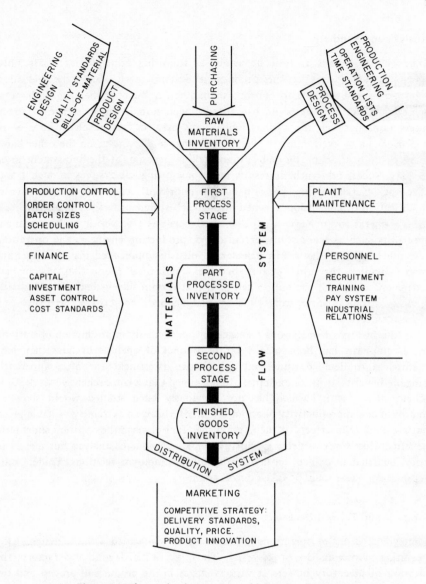

Figure 5   The production system and interrelated systems

importance of the various factors not only differs from company to company but also differs from time to time within a company, depending on the environmental pressures acting on the production system (e.g. economic constraints, competitive manoeuvres etc.). Many of the case studies in this book can be used to develop the operations management skill of analysing a particular situation, judging the relative importance of the factors involved, identifying the relationships between the various sub-systems and reaching and implementing a programme of action.

Analysis and Synthesis

Starr (1972) defines analytic behaviour as following principles of disassembly. Using analysis, we take the production system apart, study the individual sub-systems and attempt to improve them, then reassemble them in the hope of achieving a better system. As has already been noted, the existence of strong interactions between the various sub-systems may, in fact, result in little or no improvement or even in lower overall performance. Synthesis, on the other hand, involves unification of the sub-systems taking account of the sub-system inter-actions. Successful synthesis results in reconstituting sub-systems in such a way that the overall system performance is improved. This will usually involve modification of conclusions reached through sub-system analysis. The essential task of the operations manager is not so much analysis (for which he has technical specialists such as work study practitioners, production engineers and operations researchers) but synthesis. In particular, it must be appreciated that the larger and more complex the total system becomes (and total production systems are extremely complex), the more likely it is that certain sub-systems will necessarily have to operate in an apparently sub-optimal manner if good overall performance is to be achieved.

In the history of operations management, particularly in production operations, much emphasis has been placed on techniques of analysis because they lend themselves to detailed study and quantitative assessment and offer apparently tangible benefits. It is, for example, often claimed that a comprehensive work study scheme in a factory which has not previously been studied would show an improvement in productivity of about one-third. This is an extremely valuable prize, but the long term effects of such action may far outweigh the apparent short term benefits. This is not to decry work study as a technique of analysis but merely to point out that its effects on labour flexibility, employee relations, Trade Union organization etc. should be taken into account.

Strategic and Tactical Decisions

Strategic decisions of operations management are concerned with the design of the operating system in the broad sense. Thus, the initial layout of a factory, the location of inventory buffers at various stages in the production process and the degree of automation to be built into the production system are all major strategic decisions. Those decisions which relate mainly to the running of the operating system are at a tactical level, for example the level of inventories to be held and the scheduling of orders to be completed are tactical decisions. These decisions relate to the choice of alternatives for implementing a strategic decision. Starr (1972) distinguishes between strategic decision alternatives involving system effectiveness and tactical decisions involving system efficiency. Tactical decisions will, through sub-system interactions, affect the system's overall performance. Strategic decisions will change the relationships between all sub-systems and cause changes in the equilibrium of the total system. In other words, system effectiveness is concerned with the achievement of the desired end results for the whole system, while efficiency is mainly concerned with the achievement of sub-system goals.

The analytical approach to operations management stresses the need to improve efficiency but gives little consideration to the question of system effectiveness. A very limited choice of strategies is studied but enormous effort is put into efficient implementation of the strategy chosen by considering as many tactical alternatives as possible.

The growth of the organization usually found in engineering machine shops is typical of such restrictive decision making. Under functional layout, all machines of a certain type are grouped together in one or more functional areas (departments); for example, all turret lathes are in one section, all vertical milling machines in another. It is relatively easy to trace the growth of such an organization through the craft apprenticeship system and functional specialization. An enormous amount of effort has been put into trying to improve the efficiency of such production systems through close control of work time (method and time studies), sophisticated scheduling and production control systems (particularly in recent years, large computer based systems) and a highly structured work environment. Nevertheless, in even the most efficiently managed functional systems, jobs spend considerably more time waiting than actually being worked on. Since a prime objective of such systems is that throughput time should be as short and as reliable as possible, it can be seen that the relative effectiveness achieved is low. In order to achieve performance objectives, there is growing evidence to support a strategic change involving total reorganization of the production facilities into group layout, with the essential concomitant changes in system management. This may considerably increase the effectiveness of the production system. It appears that by concentration on increasing the efficiency of an existing system, opportunities to increase effectiveness of the total system have been ignored. The possibility for such a basic change does not arise only when a new production system is set up. It is true that if there has been an expensive commitment to a particular strategy there is a strong tendency to 'stay with it' and concentrate on efficiency. However, as time goes by, commitment is reduced and it is possible to try a strategic alternative. In fact, although the change to group organization requires little investment in money terms (relocation expenses and, possibly, some capital investment), it will require a great deal of management time.

The Systems Concept and Organizational Structure

A true systems view of operations management embraces all factors which affect the operations manager's achievement of his objectives. This means that all the relevant relationships between the various sub-systems must be considered and the operating system must be viewed in relation to the other sub-systems of the corporate system. In practice, an operations manager cannot and should not take decisions on the basis of the operating system alone but must also consider marketing, financial and personnel factors. The same point does of course apply to

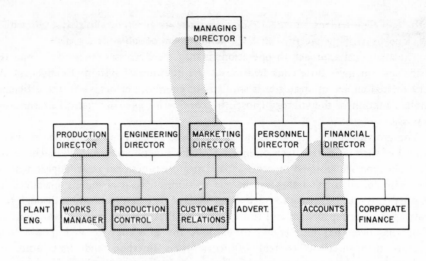

Figure 6   The systems view and organizational structure

the other corporate sub-systems; while it is a sin to make something you cannot sell it is also a sin to sell something you cannot make!

The traditional view of a functionally organized company as represented by a formal organization chart, tends to obscure this systems view since it implies system boundaries which do not exist. Figure 6 illustrates the point that the systems view requires that all factors relevant to a decision must be included in the decision sub-system. In this case, the decision might concern, for example, the revised delivery date for a customer order. Marketing will be affected because of customer relationships, finance may be affected because of delayed payments or default penalties, and so on.

At least one large UK company has recognized the multifunctional role of operations management by appointing an operations manager in addition to the existing management structure of production manager, marketing manager etc. Whether such an approach is generally viable is questionable since the role implies responsibility without authority; the operations manager is not a 'line' appointment and he cannot directly require production or marketing to modify their decisions for the good of the whole system.

It is, or course, relevant to ask at this stage why, if the whole company is based on a systems philosophy, there should be any problem in reconciling the views of marketing and production or finance and production etc. If each functional area operated within the same decision sub-system and with a single company viewpoint, then no disagreement should exist. The problem, of course, is that neither of these conditions generally applies. Each manager may have a slightly different decision sub-system and may interpret qualitative data in a different way with a different value system. Also, individual managers may have conflicting objectives, or an individual manager may have objectives which conflict with company policy. Such conflicts of interest are also present in the relationships between management and the workforce. The unitary view is that management and workforce have the same objectives and can work towards common ends, hence the notion of developing 'team spirit' and 'corporate identity'. The pluralistic view is that management and workforce objectives diverge in some fundamental respects and that to assume otherwise undermines the importance of bargaining strategy and negotiation.

The Study of Operating Systems

None of what we have said negates the need for analysis and appraisal of sub-system performance, but in carrying out such analysis we must remain aware of the total operating system and its place in the corporate system. We must learn to evaluate the effect of sub-system changes on the total system performance and appreciate that optimization of a particular sub-system, e.g. inventory control, will often result in sub-optimal performance at the system level. It will often be essential to design sub-systems to operate deliberately at a lower performance than that which they are capable of in order to achieve better overall performance. The study of operating systems therefore requires a knowledge of the techniques of analysis, an appreciation of their relevance to particular situations and the development of the skills of synthesis required to understand total systems performance.

Conclusions

Operations management is of vital importance to an organization because, typically, it employs the great proportion of the workforce and is responsible for the deployment of most of the capital. The operations system is a set of interacting sub-systems which must all be coordinated in order to achieve good performance. The relative importance of particular sub-systems will vary from one organization to another. Similarly, the importance of the operating system will vary within the total corporate system. Traditionally, techniques of analysis have been used to 'improve' individual sub-systems, possibly with detrimental effects on the system as a whole. Successful synthesis is beginning to be recognized as the prime function of the operations manager.

References

Starr, M. K. (1972) *Production Management, Systems and Synthesis*, Prentice-Hall Inc., New Jersey (Second Edition).

Thurston, P. M. (1963) 'The Concept of a Production System', *Harvard Business Review*, November—December 1963.

CHAPTER 2

Classification of Production Systems

The earliest attempt at a formal classification of production systems which related to the actual operations of the company is probably that of Woodward (1958, 1965). This study was mainly concerned with the organizational structure which resulted from operating in a particular way. Three types of production 'system' were identified:

(1) Small batch and unit production.
(2) Large batch and mass production.
(3) Process production.

These were compared in their effect on:

(1) The span of control of the first line supervisor.
(2) The number of levels of authority in the management hierarchy.

Woodward's results showed that companies using process production had most levels of authority (6) and the smallest span of control of the first line supervisor (15 subordinates); this may reflect the high technology of these systems and the relatively small labour force required to run them. The span of control was greatest in mass production firms (the median firm supervisor had 45 subordinates); unit production firms had a median of about 25 subordinates. Mass production firms also tended to have more levels of authority (4) than unit production firms (3).

Woodward's work is useful but limited. It concentrates on the internal technological factors in a company's operation rather than on the market environment. Burbidge (1968) also suggested an internal classification based on the material flow characteristics of the production process and Ingham (1971) suggested a combined sales/production classification based on the degree to which a company specifies its own product line.

There is little point in classification for its own sake, but certain characteristics of production systems do have a considerable impact on the type of operations problems encountered and on the freedom of action of the operations manager. It is therefore useful to attempt a classification based on characteristics which directly affect the operations system. This means that both the internal manufacturing system and the external market environment must be examined. Companies usually will not fall neatly into specific categories. It is important too, to look at the problems arising from the mixing of widely different systems.

We define three basic characteristics of an operations system:

(1) The nature of the product structure.
(2) The organization of the physical flow system.
(3) The nature of customer orders.

These are examined below.

The Nature of the Product Structure

It is first necessary to divide the company's products into those the customer regards as single items and those he regards as multi component assemblies. In practice, few companies do produce single item products when packaging is taken into account. The only extensive cases are subcontractors who produce components for someone else to assemble or producers of bulk chemicals. Note, however, that if one takes raw materials into account, most chemical products are actually 'assemblies'. The great bulk of production in the engineering, electronics, furniture and similar industries is concerned with assemblies of components which are either manufactured within the company or purchased from outside. This is important because the production system is often split (as in Figure 7), with the physical system required to produce components being separate from that used for product assembly.

Organization of the Physical Flow System

Figure 8 shows the form of the three basic organizational structures: line, functional and group. As we have already pointed out, component manufacture and assembly are often organized in different ways, the most common combination being:

COMPONENT		PRODUCT
MANUFACTURE		ASSEMBLY
UNDER	→	UNDER
FUNCTIONAL		LINE
ORGANIZATION		ORGANIZATION

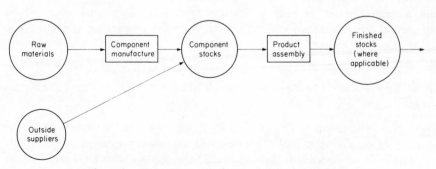

Figure 7   Component manufacture and product assembly

Functional Organization   Under functional organization, the production facilities are grouped together by function or type; for example, in a furniture factory all the drilling machines would be grouped together in one area, all the sanding and finishing machines in another. Production orders are routed through the functional departments required to perform each operation and the order passes from department to department.

While functional organization may have benefits in terms of 'collective expertise', the individual operator is far removed from the finished item, carrying out a small task in the total production cycle on only a few components of the final product. The main advantage of such an organization is its extreme flexibility; it can produce a very wide range of products.

Line Organization   Manual assembly lines are commonly used for product assembly. Line organization, however, also includes 'transfer machines' (transfer lines) for the production of components and continuous process plant. The essential characteristics of line organization are:

(1) That the material flow system through the manufacturing facilities is unidirectional, and
(2) that any product flowing along the line usually requires all the facilities on the line.

For technological reasons, transfer lines and continuous process machinery can only process one product type at a time. They may be devoted entirely to that one product though more often they produce a small range of very similar items. When the product type is changed, complex resetting is usually necessary. Manual assembly lines impose less stringent constraints and often operate as mixed-model lines processing a mix of similar products simultaneously. Vehicle final assembly lines usually operate in this way.

Continuous process systems, in particular, are plant dominated. The operation of the system is defined almost completely when the plant is designed. It is usually dedicated to the processing of one particular product or product group. Constant control of the process will be necessary for the efficient operation of the plant but all the necessary control operations (for instance the ability to adjust temperatures and pressures), must be built in intially. Such plant dominated systems have completely different management problems from other operating systems. These are discussed in Chapter 8.

Group Organization   Group organization is somewhat similar to line organization except that:

(1) A particular group or cell of facilities processes a range of items with similar facility requirements. All the items will not usually need all the facilities. Although processed by the same cell, the items themselves may not be physically very similar.

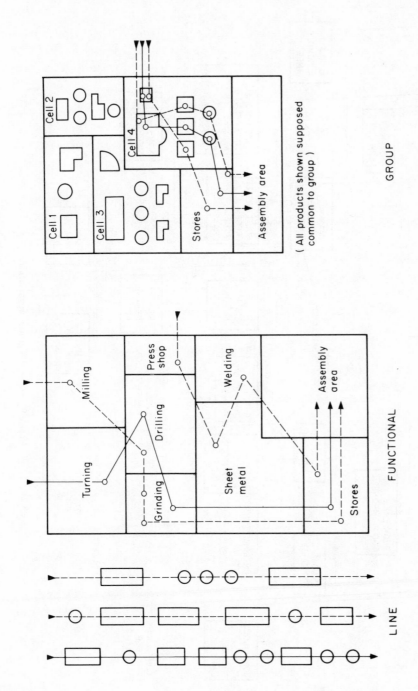

Figure 8   Organizational structures for the physical flow system

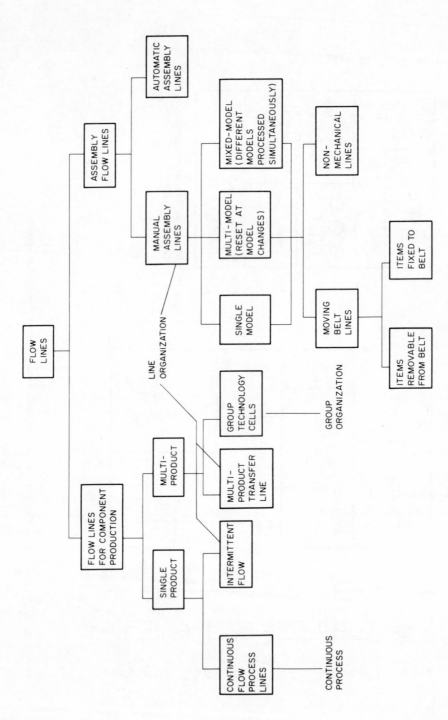

Figure 9   Line and group organization

(2) Different facilities within the group will usually be working on different items. This is not possible on a non-manual transfer line.

(3) Some degree of resetting (as little as possible) may be required each time a new item or batch of items arrives at a facility in the group.

As under line organization, the principal characteristic of group organization is that material flow should be unidirectional as far as possible. Figure 9 shows the general relationship of line and group organization.

The Nature of Customer Orders

The market variable which has most effect on the operation of the production system is the degree to which the link between manufacturer and customer is direct or indirect. We distinguish between the situation where products are made to customer order and that where they are made for stock. However, where products are made to order, many different degrees of 'dependence' may be identified.

Make to Customer Order   If it is possible at some stage of production to identify a particular work-in-process order as being exclusively for a particular customer, then the company operates in a make-to-order market. One fairly direct way of determining this is to examine orders on the shop floor. If the order document specifies a customer, then it is a make-to-order situation. This does not necessarily mean that such correspondence exists throughout the production process. For example, most components may be made for stock, customer orders only being identified as the assembly stage. The degree to which manufacture may proceed prior to receipt of a customer order depends mainly on whether the customer controls design of the order. Possible systems include:

(1) JOBBING PRODUCTION. The company manufacturers many small orders for a wide range of customers and each order has its own individual design features. Order quantities are generally small and few components are common to more than one order. As a result, little work can be carried out prior to order receipt.

(2) CONTRACT WORK. The customer design is usually specified only in broad outline and the order involves considerable detailed design work. The products are usually large, complex and expensive, for example, chemical plant or specialist machine tools.

(3) REPEAT ORDER OR BATCH PRODUCTION. A standard range of products is offered, usually consisting of various combinations of standard modules. Component manufacture is often for stock and assembly programmes may proceed on the basis of a forecast order mix or only against firm orders. The promised delivery date will depend on the current backlog and the customer allocation of the current mix being processed. it is possible to end up with short term finished stocks if the forecast sales mix is in error but these are not planned stocks.

(4) CALL-OFF SCHEDULES. This is a particular case in which the customer specifies quantities to be delivered over future periods. The product may be

specific to this customer or sold to several customers, or the supplier company may choose to 'make-for-stock' against firm customer commitments. Supplies to the motor industry often operate against 'call-off'.

Make for Stock   A make for stock company offers 'off-the-shelf' service to its customers for a range of standard products. The customer is often not the final consumer; for instance, in food manufacture, the manufacturing organization has little, if any, contact with the eventual customers. The production system is geared to the replenishment of finished goods stocks on the basis of a forward plan with consequent modifications in the light of market demand. In practice, many companies operate a mixture of making-to-customer order and making-for-stock. One survey indicated that while 11% of respondent companies made only for stock and 17% only to order, the other 72% were mixed. This raises considerable problems because the production planning and control system and organizational requirements for the two cases are often in conflict.

Comparing the Physical Organizations

A particular line or group will be responsible for the production of complete items (though not necessarily complete products). They are therefore 'product oriented' systems, whereas a functional organization is, by definition, 'process oriented'. Manual assembly of products for stock in relatively high volume is commonly associated with line organization because:

(1) It is possible to use relatively unskilled labour.
(2) It requires low work-in-process inventories.
(3) It reduces training time.
(4) It facilitates 'efficient' work design.

These points are examined in more detail in Chapter 9. On the other hand, unit assembly by a small group or even an individual is more likely to be suitable for making-to-order in small batches or for jobbing work.

Component manufacture is, however, rarely based on line organization because the volume required to support the necessary investment in transfer lines is rarely large enough, even in the 'mass production' industries. Many component parts for cars, for example, are produced in batches under functional organization. The problem here centres round the provision of expensive locating devices at the machine stations and the relative inflexibility of machine cycle times. Since the output rate is governed by the longest cycle time, the result is low utilization of many facilities.

Functional organization is, without doubt, the most flexible structure available. However, this flexibility is only achieved at the cost of the high work-in-process inventories which are necessary to stabilize the very uneven flow of work through such systems. By comparison, line organizations are very inflexible but permit very efficient throughput rates with low working inventories. Group organization has the advantage of preserving the throughput efficiency of line organization (mainly due to the unidirectional flow of materials in such systems), while giving up relatively little in terms of overall flexibility. Only 'standard' facilities are used and they can be used for 'out-of-group' work when not required.

If work-in-process inventories were the only cost of functional systems, the situation would not be so serious. However, the implications of this for the total throughput time for orders is immense. Suppose an order requires 10 operations with a total work content time for the batch of 20 hours. It is by no means unusual to find inventory levels in functional organization of at least two days work at each work centre. The order would therefore take something like 3 weeks (10 x 2 = 20 days) to have only 20 hours' work done on it. If we define the 'throughput efficiency' of a production system (or part of a system) as

$$\text{Throughput efficiency (TE)} = \frac{\text{total work involvement time for the batch}}{\text{total time in system}} \times 100\%$$

then a typical functional organization would have a TE of around 10—20%, rarely higher than 40%. In contrast, a line organization often necessarily has an efficiency approaching 100% because of the physical characteristics of the line flow. Group organization is often capable of a TE of up to 70—80%. A company using functional organization for component manufacture and line organization for assembly will have a 'mixed' efficiency; however, the assembly time is usually so short that the overall efficiency remains very low.

Key Operating Problems in the Make-to-order and Make-for-stock Situation

The Controllable Variables
In general terms, the production problem may be viewed as one of balancing a number of interacting variables. The principal variables are:

(1) Capacity (output rate).
(2) Finished stock levels (inventory investment).
(3) Customer delivery times.

For a given quality/price structure, these are the variables the operations manager must manipulate. The make-for-stock company preselects variable (3) as 'off-the-shelf' and this reduces the major problem to one of balancing production plans against demand patterns through the building of anticipation inventories. The make-to-order company usually preselects variable (2) as zero and must balance capacity against customer delivery times. With stable uniform market demand, there would be relatively little problem in balancing these variables. However, typically, the make-for-stock company operates in a seasonal market, e.g. food products, and the make-to-order company produces capital goods which follow the general trade cycle of demand.

Thus, the make-for-stock company is faced with a short term problem of manipulating both production rates and stock levels in an effort to meet market demand. The make-to-order company faces the long term problem of balancing production capacity against customer delivery promises in order to meet market demand. In neither case will it usually be practicable or economic to attempt to match output capacity with the actual demand pattern.

The Make-for-stock Company

Figure 10 illustrates the typical problem of the make-for-stock company. A feasible production plan must be chosen for each product so that:

(1) All the sales forecasts/distribution requirements can be met, and
(2) The production facilities are not overloaded. (Figure 10 shows two possible plans (A) and (B) for a single product, X.)

Moreover, as the year progresses the actual sales data will not match the plan. A reallocation of available production capacity must be made to increase production of some products and reduce production of others. At intervals, data must be assessed to decide:

(1) Whether demand has deviated enough to warrant changing the plan.
(2) If it has, has the total demand for the product increased or is it a case of redistribution over the year?
(3) In what ways the plan should be changed in relation to other product plans so that balance is maintained across the total capacity.

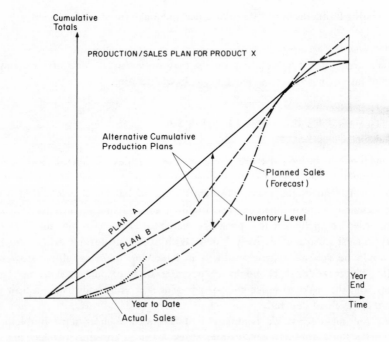

Figure 10   Balancing sales and capacity in the make-for-stock company

It should be clear that in the make-for-stock company, sales forecasting and production planning are crucial to the production operation as well as to marketing, although production is one stage removed from the market place through the finished goods inventory. Also, such companies produce standard products on a repetitive basis. There is therefore a need for firm cost control, probably through fairly sophisticated standard costing procedures.

The Make-to-order Company

The major operating problem of the make-to-order company is concerned with offering competitive delivery lead times and completing orders by promised delivery dates. Since the demand level usually follows the economic cycle and stocks can rarely be built except at high cost and great risk of technological obsolescence, this task centres round controlling the physical orders on the factory by means of an 'order book'. As demand increases, slack is taken up in the available capacity until a backlog of orders builds up. Delivery lead times are extended and this continues until demand falls off again and lead times are reduced. It is here that we see the crucial problem of functional organization; long delivery lead times even before a backlog builds up.

The method used to control the intake of jobs to the manufacturing facilities is of great importance and we shall return to it in Chapter 10. For the moment, we note that the major operating problems of the make-to-order company are those of controlling the flow of orders through the production system in order to meet delivery promises.

Figure 11 compares the main features of the make-for-stock and make-to-order situations. The essential difference is seen in the relative ranking of the key performance variables. Note that the low ranking of, for instance, customer service

	Make-to-customer-order	Make-for-stock
Product Characteristics	Customer specified large range expensive	Producer specified small range inexpensive
Production facilities	General purpose	Often special purpose
Key performance variables	1) Delivery lead times 2) Delivery performance 3) Quality 4) Cost 5) Plant utilization	1) Cost 2) Quality 3) Utilization 4) Customer service
Main operating problem areas	Control of operations once started. Commitment control.	Planning production. Forecasting. Responsiveness.

Figure 11   Comparison of the make-to-order and make-for-stock situations

in the make-for-stock case does not indicate that it is itself unimportant, but that by virtue of the way the system operates it will be satisfactory most of the time. The major problem of the make-to-order company is one of control. The major problem of the make-for-stock company is one of planning.

It has already been mentioned that additional problems exist for companies operating a 'mixed mode' system for reasons which should now be apparent. If operating systems are efficient at controlling the multiple interactions of many customer orders with different due dates, they are unlikely to achieve maximum output at low unit cost for stock item orders competing for the same facilities. Any attempt to operate make-for-stock and make-to-order on the same facilities is bound to run into trouble. Either delivery performance will be bad or cost effectiveness on stock orders will be low. More likely, both will suffer. Nevertheless, the prospect of using make-for-stock orders to 'fill in' when customer orders are low is extremely attractive, hence the number of companies reportedly operating in this way. two points arise here. Firstly, when customer orders are low, 'off-the-shelf' orders will also tend to be low. 'Fill-in' will, therefore, involve the expense of building finished goods inventory. Secondly, the use of a functional organization for component production effectively rules out any real hope of dual use of facilities. The problems of relative priorities and long lead times are too great. The use of group organizations offer some hope for the future of such mixed systems.

Conclusions

We have presented a classification system for operating systems based on three factors:

(1) The nature of the product structure, whether it be a one piece product or an assembly structure.
(2) The organization of the physical flow system, whether it be functional, line or group.
(3) The nature of customer orders, whether it be make-to-order or make-for-stock.

The effect of the product structure is seen mainly in the degree of coordination required to bring together the items required for assembly. Organizational structure has a major impact on the level of work-in-process in the system and hence on customer delivery times and throughput efficiency. Finally, the nature of the customer order often determines the key performance variables of the operating system. A make-to-order company is more likely to emphasize delivery performance while the make-for-stock company will emphasize cost effectiveness. The different planning and control requirements for achieving good performance on either of these variables often conflict. Since many companies do operate with mixed systems, both objectives often suffer. However, this may be acceptable if it achieves some degree of load levelling.

References

Burbidge, J. L. (1968) *The Principles of Production Control*, Macdonald and Evans Ltd., London (Second Edition).

Ingham, H. (1971) *Balancing Sales and Production*, Management Publications Ltd., London.

Woodward, J. (1958) *Management and Technology*, HMSO, London.

Woodward, J. (1965) *Industrial Organisation — Theory and Practice*, Oxford University Press.

CHAPTER 3

Managing the Labour Force

Introduction

The human resource is one of the major assets available to the operations manager. In broad terms, the managerial task is to ensure that the right human skills are available in the right quantity when required and are used both effectively and efficiently. The vast majority of the labour force in both manufacturing and non-manufacturing organizations is employed on operational tasks. In practice, it is normally difficult to make rapid alterations either to the size of the work force or its inherent skills. The flexibility of the labour force is also often limited, either by limited skills or restrictive practices.

Traditionally, labour has been viewed as a cost rather than an asset, and as an infinite resource, rather than a limited commodity. Some organizations are perhaps now aware of the limitations of their labour force as a resource, but they still tend to view labour as a cost rather than an asset to be effectively deployed. The significance of labour in cost structures varies greatly. In service industries, labour may be as much as 80% of the total cost. In manufacturing, labour is rarely more than 50% of the total cost and more commonly between 10% and 30%.

The breakdown of labour costs within organizations varies greatly. In manufacturing, workers are usually divided into direct and indirect labour. Direct labour is normally defined as that part of the labour force actually employed on the production of the end product; all other categories of labour are indirect. The dividing line however may vary; in some organizations, for instance, inspection and quality control personnel and progress chasers are classified as direct and in others as indirect.

Indirect personnel can be divided into two further groups for costing purposes. Those associated with manufacturing (for example, the production control office or the maintenance organization), can be classified as factory overhead; other indirect personnel (for example, computer and purchasing staff), can be classified as general overhead. It is important to realize that even in direct labour intensive manufacturing, there is normally at least one indirect worker for every direct worker. In advanced technology manufacturing, there may be as many as four indirect workers for every direct worker on the shop floor.

In management education, the study of the management of people tends to be divided between the teaching of organizational behaviour and industrial relations.

These are separate and important areas of specialization but do not preclude the need for study of the labour force in the context of operations management. Specialists in organizational behaviour and industrial relations fulfil staff roles in relation to the man responsible for managing the operation. We believe, therefore, that emphasis should also be placed on defining and understanding the management of the labour force within the study of operations management.

The Historic Traditional View

For many centuries, the management of labour was based on the belief that men and women were motivated by financial reward for work done and by fear of the loss of that reward. Human labour provided physical effort and there was usually a surplus of labour available. The case with skilled craftsmen was different; it was common practice for them to protect the value of their labour by placing restrictions on the numbers allowed to enter their trade. Extended apprentice periods with little or no remuneration were used to control numbers.

The new manufacturing techniques of the Industrial Revolution resulted in the concentration of manufacturing into factory units. As the use of machinery increased, so of course did capital investment, and this led to concern about the utilization of these capital assets. The effective use of the human resource became the most important factor in achieving the maximum output from the new technologies. The basic framework of what came to be called industrial engineering was developed in the late nineteenth century. Much of the pioneering work was done by F. W. Taylor in the USA. He appreciated that most work methods could be greatly improved by careful study and analysis and that control of machinery utilization and labour could only be achieved if it was preceded by careful measurement. His ideas and techniques came to be known as 'Scientific Management'. His methods were widely adopted by American industry. However, from the outset, many questioned his ideas on the grounds that they were 'inhuman'. In the end, such charges led to an investigation by a Special Committee of the House of Representatives in 1911.

Between 1900 and 1930, much more pioneering work was done in industrial engineering, particularly in method study. However, industrial engineering was little practiced in England until after the second world war. Then, in the late 1940s and all through the 1950s its use spread. It was widely introduced, usually to promote productivity, particularly manpower productivity. Its introduction into an organization was often effected by external consultants, and was often associated with changes in payment systems. There might be a change from one type of piecework system to another (supposedly more rational) or the introduction of a piecework scheme where none had existed. The new systems were often ill conceived or too quickly compiled. Frequently management did not have the necessary skills to implement the schemes effectively, when the external consultants had left. Misapplication, coupled with initial mistrust by many traditional trade unionists, has made work study unfashionable; it is considered irrelevant for the 1970s and future decades. This view, however, may be an overreaction.

The Environment of Work

The work environment involves people and manmade physical facilities. Frequently, people have been seen as the flexible element within this total system. There has been great emphasis on creating machines and layouts with ever greater production capacity. People have been expected to adapt and adjust to changes in the physical part of the system. Consideration of the human role in the system has often been secondary.

This approach has been adopted in an age of great technological advance. These advances have produced much increase in material wealth which has greatly benefitted the people within the advanced technological societies. Terms and conditions of employment have greatly improved since the start of the industrial revolution. However, these improvements have rarely been objectives in themselves when new manufacturing facilities have been created. Indeed, these improvements have not prevented the introduction of many millions of jobs in the advanced industrialized societies which fail to utilize the human physical and mental capabilities satisfactorily. Tedium and monotony lead to boredom. Underutilization and lack of challenge lead to disenchantment. Lack of responsibility and tight control leads to withdrawal of commitment. All too often, a job becomes merely a means of acquiring the money necessary to exist in our supposedly advanced society. People live for their leisure time only and work becomes an increasing drudge. One of the greatest challenges facing the operations manager is that of putting interest back into work.

Although there has been much theorizing about motivation and work satisfaction, there have been relatively few experiments on any scale. The most publicized to date have been those in the Scandinavian automobile industry. Here attempts have been made, it is claimed, to adapt factory work to people rather than people to machines. The concept of job enrichment is discussed in the chapter on 'Managing the Process — Assembly Lines'. Automation of operations is discussed in the chapter on 'Managing the Process — Continuous Systems'.

The Organization and Control of Work

Although the work environment in many operations systems is in urgent need of improvement this does not mean that techniques developed over the past decades are now irrelevant. The fundamentals of work study are as valid and useful today as ever they were. Rarely are work methods incapable of improvement and method study is still the process by which that improvement is achieved. This involves selecting the job to be studied, defining and then improving the existing method, installing the new method and then maintaining its application. The task facing the operations manager today is to train every member of the work force to be an effective method study analyst. He must also prevent restrictive practices, eliminate fears of redundancy and avoid ill-conceived payment systems which might prevent the implementation of method improvement.

Taylor's view, that measurement is necessary before control can be established, is certainly as valid today as it was 90 years ago. But the problem in many companies is that work measurement is associated with a desire by management to alter the payment system to the detriment of the work force. While work measurement may play some role in determining levels of payment, it is vital to recognize that it has a number of other more important functions.

Knowledge of the time required to carry out work is fundamental data necessary for all forms of operations planning. This type of data is required for:

(1) Estimating for future possible contracts. Any organization which bids for contracts requires a data bank to assess manpower time requirements for prospective work.

(2) Costing. This is similar to the estimating process. It is, however, a more continuous activity since both product characteristics and work methods are frequently changed thus requiring revisions of the cost analysis.

(3) Planning facility requirements. The process of interpreting a sales forecast into a manufacturing plan requires data on the work content contained in a given product or class of products. One of the most critical decisions made by the operations manager is that of determining the future capacity of the system. Capacity does, of course, consist of both machinery and manpower.

(4) Scheduling existing facilities. Converting a short term demand into an organized load on a manufacturing facility requires detailed information, both about the capacity available and the work content of the forecast. This data is expressed in man hours and machine hours and is derived from work measurement.

(5) Balancing the sections of the manufacturing facility with each other. Lack of balance between the parts of a system leads to idle machinery and under utilization of manpower. Planning for balance between various sections and achieving balance in operation both require detailed data on the work content of the jobs to be carried out.

(6) Determining remuneration levels. Even though the incidence of piece work is declining throughout manufacturing industry, there are still some industries where it is widely used, e.g. the clothing industry. However, the abandonment of piecework for measured day wage systems does not imply that work measurement is no longer required to establish wage rates. Measured day wage implies that an acceptable and fair rate of output will be established for the guaranteed wage offered.

The level of accuracy required in work measurement data for the various activities listed above varies considerably. To interpret an annual sales forecast into a manufacturing facility requirement will probably require data aggregated at the product group level and by major activity classifications, e.g. total machine hours required to manufacture parts for product group A, man hours required for sub-assemblies for product group B, etc. At the other end of the scale, work measurement used to derive piecework standards needs to be extremely accurate. If an individual's earnings depend on the accuracy of the work measurement data, he or she is going to be extremely concerned about an error in the data of as little as

5% if that error reduces wages. (The process of deriving work standards is explained in the appendix at the end of this chapter.)

Herein lies the cause of the problem which has surrounded work measurement. The measurement of work is a relatively inaccurate process. There are a number of causes for this. Firstly, the wide variety of jobs which go through most systems make it impossible to measure every variation individually. Thus, some averaging inevitably takes place. Even if the averaging is correct at the outset, changes in overall product mix and different mixes from one time period to another often mean that wages calculated on the original data are incorrect. The second major cause of inaccuracy is human variability. Although it is always stated that work measurement involves measuring the work content of a job and not the individual person carrying out the job, the fact remains that the data recorded is influenced by the particular person doing the work. The industrial engineer is expected to adjust the actual time observed depending on whether the person observed is fast, average or slow at the work. This process is known as performance rating. In an organization where work study is well organized, untrained people would not be measured and industrial engineers would be skilled in recognizing different rates of work. Nonetheless, the process of performance rating is an uncertain one. Experiments have shown that skilled analysts are relatively accurate in assessing rates of work within plus or minus 30% of the average, but accuracy declines considerably when more extreme paces of work are observed. The implication is, therefore, that work measurement is often not sufficiently accurate to withstand the detailed focus placed on it in direct incentives schemes. This fact has been exposed time and time again in countless organizations.

Measuring Labour Performance

Measuring performance implies that the actual rate of work can be compared against a standard.

Indices of labour performance reflect two factors. The first is efficiency while carrying out measured work. This is expressed as a ratio of standard hours of work produced and the actual time required to perform that work. The second ratio measures overall labour effectiveness. It takes into account work carried out for which no standards exist. This work is generally credited at a pre-agreed rate. It also takes account of idle time caused, for example, by lack of work availability or machine breakdown. Thus the effectiveness index is calculated by dividing the standard hours of work produced plus appropriate credits for unmeasured work by the total time spent at work by the labour force. An example of the calculation of these two indices for a section of 15 people is given below.

Standard hours produced (a)   = 620

Credited non-measured activities (b) = 104

Time spent on measured work (c)   = 470

Time spent on non-measured work (d) =   90

Idle time (e)   = 40

Total hours at work (c + d + e)   = 600

Efficiency while working on measured work = $\dfrac{\text{Standard hours produced}}{\text{Time spent on measured work}}$

$$= \frac{620}{470} \times 100 = 132$$

Overall labour effectiveness = $\dfrac{\text{Total output credited } (a + b)}{\text{Total hours worked } (c + d + e)}$

$$= \frac{724}{600} \times 100 = 121$$

Labour performance indices can be calculated for individuals or for groups. They can be calculated and reported on a daily, weekly or monthly basis. The degree of detail reported often varies for different levels of management. For example, the foreman may require individual performances on a daily basis. The plant manager may require the performance of each section as a group on a weekly basis. Finally, the divisional general manager may require the labour performance for each plant on a monthly basis.

Learning Curves

When work measurement data is derived and used to give labour performance indices, it is presumed that the personnel involved have the appropriate skills and are fully trained in the particular jobs. Inevitably, there are periods of time when jobs are being learned. Work measurement carried out during such periods would produce inaccurate data since as experience grows, speed will improve.

This can present a difficult problem, particularly when accurate data is required early in the life of a new job or in the manufacture of a new product. Such data may be required to derive accurate product costings, to assess the amount of labour or machinery necessary for a given volume of output (recruitment and purchasing lead times may be lengthy) or to establish wage rates. A concept has been developed which helps to predict the labour time which will be required to produce large volumes of an item on the basis of the time taken to make the initial items. The concept is known as a learning curve. The theory involved is that there will be a constant improvement factor in the time required with each doubling of output. Thus, if the improvement factor is 0.9 the time required would be as follows:

Item	Time Required
1st	1
2nd	1 x 0.9 = 0.9
4th	0.9 x 0.9 = 0.81

Item	Time Required
8th	0.81 x 0.9 = 0.73
16th	0.73 x 0.9 = 0.67
32nd	0.67 x 0.9 = 0.60
64th	0.06 x 0.9 = 0.54 (i.e. the 64th item would require only 0.54 of the time taken for the first item)
etc.	

The learning curve is clearly based on geometric progressions. Tables have been drawn up for different improvement factors which permit the prediction of the time future items will take if the time is known either for the first item or for an initial batch.

Improvement takes place in virtually every activity as learning takes place. The extent of the improvement will depend on such factors as familiarity with the type of work and the extent to which the time cycle is machine paced. Usually, it falls within the range of 0.95 to 0.8. Ideally, an organization should carry out empirical research to establish the level of improvement factor which should be applied to different types of job. As well as establishing the appropriate factors, such research may show that improvement levels off after a given volume of output.

The Control of Indirect Labour

Work measurement was originally introduced in the context of the shop floor labour force. Now, for most organizations, this represents a minority of personnel employed. Thus the cost of indirect labour generally far exceeds that of direct labour. However, many organizations continue to place emphasis on measuring and controlling direct labour while ignoring the need for control of indirect labour. Often, some of the work carried out by the indirect labour force is complex, and therefore difficult to measure and control. However, not all indirect work falls in this category. Much of it is repetitive and routine. Discrepancies between the levels of control of the direct and indirect parts of the workforce can become a major source of dissatisfaction.

Conventionally, control of indirect labour is based on an annual manpower budget. Each group or department head states the labour requirements for the coming year. However, it is generally well recognized that all estimated requirements will be cut back in the review process. The shrewd department manager therefore estimates the extent of the cut back and increases his budget accordingly. If on-going control is considered necessary, it is exercised either through a total ban on new recruits, or if circumstances are more desperate, through a percentage cut across all departments. Both these approaches again encourage managers to build up surplus labour. Thus they can survive economy measures. Such control mechanisms discriminate against the manager who attempts to run his department with the minimum necessary labour. Often, the final organizational discouragement to operating with minimum labour is that a manager's status is measured by the number of people in his department. This does not encourage suggestions which might halve labour requirements.

More logical control could be exercised if the work volume were measured and expressed as a labour time requirement. For this to be possible the following conditions must exist:

(1) The work to be controlled must produce definable, countable units of output.
(2) The average time per unit of output, taken across all the units produced in each control period, must be reasonably consistent.
(3) The count of the volume of output must be a reasonable reflection of the amount of work effort required during the control period. For example, to state that an accounting department produces one monthly budget per month has little value for control purposes.
(4) The nature of the work passing through the department must not be subject to constant change.
(5) The cost of installing and maintaining the control system must not exceed the benefits which can be derived from establishing better control. These benefits can obviously only be derived from reducing the level of manpower required to carry out a given volume of work.

Attempts to apply more rational control over indirect labour have been made by a number of organizations during the past ten years. Unfortunately, many of these attempts have been ill-conceived. All too frequently, they have led to trade union opposition and have eventually been abandoned. Closer control is often opposed because it is associated with attempts to reduce the labour force. However, the introduction of control programmes at times of expansion rather than contraction, and the use of natural labour wastage can minimize opposition.

Control should be established for groups of people rather than for individuals. The control period should be between a week and a month. Control operated in this form does not require accurate work measurement. Carrying out the necessary work measurement and operating such control schemes is very dependent on the collaboration of the group of people involved. Frequently, the best method of measuring the work is for the work group to record units of output produced and time taken. When other methods of measurement are used, personnel may have to record output during the measurement stage. This recording may be reduced when the ongoing system is in operation but collaboration and cooperation will still be required to produce output data. Control programmes can therefore be disrupted by refusal to cooperate in the reporting process or by deliberate misreporting. It is often necessary to offer basic assurances and some form of additional reward for assisting in the implementation of a control programme. The minimum basic assurances can be:

(1) that no redundancy results from the programme, and
(2) that no individual receives a reduction in earnings as a result of a transfer caused by the programme.

Both these conditions should be relatively easy to meet if the programme is installed at a time of expanding activity and at a pace related to natural labour wastage. It is important, however, to resist:

(1) Introducing direct incentives in the indirect areas being placed under control.
(2) Paying a permanent bonus based on the wage savings which appear to arise through better control.

The measurement is rarely accurate enough to be used for direct incentive purposes. Even if precise work measurement has been carried out and direct incentives seem applicable, great caution should be exercised. The implications of introducing direct incentives in indirect areas must be considered in a total context rather than within the context of a single department. While the scheme might be suitable and have beneficial results in a specific department, it will probably cause considerable disruption in other surrounding departments. The increased earnings likely to result from the incentive scheme will lead to demands for similar 'treatment' in other departments. This may force management to instal incentive schemes in areas where they are most unsuitable.

Paying a proportion of the savings derived from implementing the control programme as a permanent bonus also has pitfalls. It may be relatively straightforward to calculate the savings resulting from the better control for one or even two years after implementation, but the calculation becomes more and more uncertain as time goes by. There will be changes in the nature of the work carried out and improvements in working methods. Both may result in real savings which may be credited to the group although they do not reflect any increased effort. This may lead either to paying out part of an imaginary saving or to a dispute with the group about the size of the saving being achieved. Thus, although implementation may be helped by sharing out the apparent savings, in time this can become a source of contention.

The best way of ensuring the implementation of better control is to establish a sound job evaluation system and wages structure. Indeed, it can be advantageous to introduce job evaluation and revised wage grading at the same time as the control programme. The control programme is also likely to expose the need for greater job flexibility and a wider range of skills for individual members of the workforce. Such changes are often necessary to permit existing idle time to be utilized effectively.

Rewarding the Labour Force

The detailed design of the reward structure is usually controlled by the personnel department. The consequences of the reward structure, however, are faced daily by the operations manager. It is important, therefore, that he understands the objectives of the reward system and influences changes within it.

Management objectives in the design of the reward system may include:

(1) Effective control of costs.
(2) The maximum flexibility in the use of labour.

(3) Maintenance of an orderly wage structure with the avoidance of leap-frogging differential problems.

(4) The ability to increase productivity.

(5) Assisting the first line supervisor in avoiding industrial relations problems.

(6) The prevention of fluctuations and instability in wage levels which may create tensions in the workforce.

The trade unions and workforce may also have objectives in relation to the reward structure which may not correspond with those of management. These may, for instance, include:

(1) The ability to create a constant upward pressure on wage levels.

(2) The provision of a stable, reliable wage.

(3) The ability of the work group to control both the work situation and the pay system.

(4) The provision of a means of building up union power. For example, 'payment by results' systems may create worker solidarity and thus assist trade unions in building up their membership.

Factors Influencing the Choice of Payment Systems

Care must be taken to link the nature of the production system with the payment structure. There is little point in introducing direct incentives to jobs which are largely machine controlled. Similarly, for a company specializing in one-off production, a direct incentive scheme will damage industrial relations. It would entail shop floor bargaining between a rate fixer and a shop steward for every item produced. The following factors should be considered:

(1) The amount of fluctuation in the work load. This may be caused by varying run lengths or seasonal fluctuation.

(2) The frequency with which discontinuities occur. New processes and technologies may suffer from high breakdown frequencies.

(3) The relative importance of quality, quantity, accuracy and consistency.

(4) The extent to which worker effort and machine effort affect productivity.

(5) The ease or difficulty of measuring work output.

(6) The availability and nature of first line supervision.

When analysing an existing wage system, it is important to consider the following factors:

(1) The number of wage rates.

(2) The type and nature of differentials.

(3) The existence of special payments.

(4) The significance of overtime payments.

(5) Labour turnover and absenteeism.

It must be remembered the wage structure will affect the attitude of the workforce to the company. It will also affect the company's ability to attract the required labour skills. It is vital to establish whether labour costs are increasing at a greater rate than labour productivity. A careful definition of objectives and a recognition of the relationship between the nature of the operations system and the payment structure should lead to the identification of the best type of reward structure. A wide range of wage systems are currently in use and these are discussed briefly below.

Payment Systems

Time Rates

This is the simplest type of payment system. A fixed hourly, weekly or monthly rate is paid. It is simple to administer but does not provide any form of financial incentive to the workforce.

Payments by Results

Payment by results systems have many variations. The simplest form is where payment is directly related to output. The word 'piecework' originated from this type of system since payment was by the piece, i.e. each unit of output. Most payment by results systems are more complex than this. Almost invariably, a minimum guaranteed wage exists. This means the incentive only becomes operative after a certain level of output has been reached. The bonus may then be directly related to output on a straight line basis no matter what the volume, or it may operate at different rates depending on the amount of extra output. The movement of the bonus may be upwards or downwards depending on the philosophy of the wage system.

Payment by results can undoubtedly provide a major incentive, particularly where considerable physical effort is involved. Theoretically, output should be increased and unit costs reduced. However, it is now recognized that many disadvantages are associated with such schemes. The fixing of fair bonus rates presents problems. Bonus rates are a source of constant contention and can lead to endless industrial disputes. In practice, it can be difficult to keep wages under control and steady wage drift is usually associated with payment by results. Earnings fluctuate widely through no fault of the employee. Since employees naturally wish to even out their earnings, there is a tendency to misreport the actual volume of work carried out in any given week. This can lead to confusion in planning and control systems. Employees may also seek to achieve earnings without undue effort by qualifying for special allowances, avoiding what are considered to be poorly rated jobs and embarking on slow-downs during periods when rates are being fixed. Direct incentives may pose problems of integrating employees into the wage structure, reduce the mobility of labour, lead to declining quality of output and create a climate of resistance to methods improvement. It is also possible that the incentive scheme will actually restrict rather than increase output. Maximum earnings may be established by group norm. The work group may decide that no one should earn more than this level of wage because they believe that management will then seek to reduce the piecework rate. Unfortunately, this belief may be a result of bitter past experience.

In the operation of direct incentive schemes, management is frequently not in control of production. It is not uncommon for supervisors to earn less than their subordinates and for skilled employees to earn less than semiskilled. The final disadvantage of such schemes is that the cost of administering the wage system can be extremely high. *Undermines role of 1st line supervisor*

Measured Day Work

The basic concept of measured day work is that the incentive element of a wage is compounded with the basic day rate, thus giving a high non-fluctuating weekly wage. The philosophy of the system assumes that the workforce will accept a moral obligation to maintain a high rate of work output. The term 'measured day work' implies that a rate of output will be fixed on the basis of some form of work measurement.

Again, many variations exist. The simplest system involves a fixed daily wage for which an anticipated and agreed level of output will be maintained. This is common where the workforce have little influence over the pace of work, for example on a car assembly line. Variations include systems such as premium pay plans. Here, graded steps of wages are paid according to the pace of working. An individual or group of workers contract to work at a particular pace. If the pace is not maintained over an agreed period, usually several weeks, the individual or group must move down to the next lower rate of pay. Conversely, if an ability to work faster than the agreed rate is demonstrated, then the individual or group may move up to the next stage. This relatively simple system offers the advantage of a degree of financial incentive coupled with a stable and known rate of wages.

With measured day work systems the onus for ensuring a flow of work rests entirely with management. The workforce does not suffer any loss of pay if work is not available. A high level of first line supervision is required to ensure good work flow and proper organization of the work group. Organizations moving from payment by results to measured day wage systems find that the role of the first line supervisor differs radically between the two systems. In the former, the wage system tends to become the control mechanism and first line supervision becomes relatively powerless. In the latter, able supervision is required. A vital ingredient of change from payment by results to measured day work must be careful retraining of first line supervisors to assume their proper roles.

Plant Wide Incentives

This type of scheme can range from a simple profit sharing plan based on annual profits to much more complex schemes based on changes in labour productivity. The latter schemes involve establishing a norm on the basis of historic results and then sharing improvements above this norm between the company and the workforce. Two well known schemes are the Scanlon and Rucker plans. Both are based on determining improvements in added value and sharing the gain between the company and the workforce.

Well-organized schemes of this sort can result in greatly increased cooperation between all levels of employees. A carefully planned committee structure can ensure participation of the workforce in the running of the company. Bonuses are only paid when they can be afforded. The disadvantages of such schemes are that they are plant wide and the bonuses are only paid at infrequent intervals. This may result in little incentive for the individual worker. The level of bonus can be affectd by circumstances totally outside the employees' control, for example a poor product line or poor marketing, and trouble may ensue when bonuses decline, particularly after a long period when they have been rising.

Job Evaluation

Job evaluation is defined by the International Labour Office as 'an attempt to determine and compare the demands which the normal performance of particular jobs makes on normal workers without taking account of the individual abilities or performance of the workers concerned'. Hence, job evaluation is concerned with rating the job rather than the person performing it. It also considers the relative worth of jobs, but although it provides information which assists pay structures, it does not determine the actual rates of pay. This is a separate exercise. It must also be appreciated that job evaluation is not a scientific process. Its application involves making judgements which inevitably contain subjective elements. Nonetheless, it is a systematic and impersonal approach and may be preferable to the haphazard methods commonly used.

All methods of job evaluation involve comparison. At the simplest level, one job is compared with another and a decision made as to which is of higher value. Once jobs have been ranked, they can be grouped together in grades thus simplifying overall pay structures.

Job evaluation can become both more complex and potentially more precise; the various aspects of a job can be analysed and points allocated to each aspect depending on its significance. For example, a job might be broken down into four main areas, skill, effort, responsibility and job conditions. Further subdivision might take place. For example, skill could be subdivided into

(1) education required,
(2) previous experience necessary, and
(3) initiative needed.

Each of these sub-factors could be allocated a maximum number of possible points although the maximum may not be common to each sub-factor. A job would then be analysed into the sub-factors and points allocated depending on the requirement of the job in that sub-factor. The sum of the points for the job would represent the overall evaluation.

A carefully thought out job evaluation scheme should ensure that jobs are correctly ranked one with another. If the scheme is applied effectively, involvement of the work force should ensure that they accept the fairness of the evaluation. If appropriate payment scales are then allocated to the different grades of job, problems of differential payments between different types of job should be minimized.

The difficulties in job evaluation arise when comparing very dissimilar jobs. An important factor in one job, perhaps deserving a high possible maximum of points, may be a relatively insignificant factor in another job. Thus, if both are evaluated on the same points allocation, an unfair result might be obtained. Job evaluation may give the appearance of precision, but it involves many subjective judgements. For example, deciding which sub-factors to include, deciding the maximum possible point allocations and the allocation of points from that maximum for a given job are all subjective judgements. Ideally, though, these are informed subjective judgements.

This brief review of possible wage structures indicates that a range of alternatives exists. Each is not mutually exclusive; for example, job evaluation might be combined with some form of measured day work scheme. An organization may wish to use more than one type of payment system within the total organization. This may well be necessary when differing types of work are involved. However, care must be taken to ensure that differing types of wage payment systems are not potential sources of unrest amongst the labour force.

Conclusions

Ever increasing demands will be placed on the operations manager to create systems which give design priority to the human rather than the mechanical element of the system. This will involve spending capital on humanizing the working environment. There will be a growing emphasis on applications of the behavioural sciences in the management of operations. Such applications will become required practice for future industrial engineers. Responsibility for work place decisions is likely to shift more and more to those carrying out the work. This will pose severe problems for those responsible for designing and implementing scheduling systems. It could also result in a change in the role of first line supervision or possibly even the elimination of this level of supervision in a formal sense. Work groups will develop leaders who may wish to remain part of the group rather than become the first level of the management structure. Although payment systems will continue to move away from direct personal incentive schemes, there will be a need for some element of incentive in the pay structure for some time to come. Control of the labour force will still be needed. However, control systems should be more evenly spread over the whole body of the workforce and should place less emphasis on individual performance and more on group performance.

APPENDIX

Derivation of Work Standards

Introduction

Work standards can be derived by:

(1) Direct observations by a work study analyst. This includes time studies and work sampling techniques.
(2) Using data derived from observations on similar jobs.
(3) Reported information compiled by the people performing the work.

It is important to realize that all methods involve a sampling process. A time study (i.e. a period of observation by a work study analyst) may be continuous over a period but that period is only a sample from the total time during which the job is carried out. Work sampling is by definition a sampling process. Using predetermined data involves relying on the sample used to construct the data. This in practice is usually large. Reported information is a sample in the same sense that a time study is a sample. However, the sample here is usually over an extended time period. Theoretically, work measurement should only involve properly trained personnel working under standard conditions. In practice, both people and conditions vary. Variation in people, i.e. speed at which they work, is theoretically adjusted by the process known as performance rating. The problems associated with this have already been discussed in this chapter. Thus the data should be collected through observations on a typical cross section of people and under the full range of possible working conditions. The sample size is also affected by the variation that can occur in the time required for the job and the level of accuracy required in the time standard. A job which can vary from two minutes to two hours will require many more cycles to be observed than one which varies between eight and nine minutes. As pointed out in the chapter, the accuracy required in time standards depends on the purpose for which they are to be used.

Each type of technique has advantages and disadvantages. Direct observation by a work study analyst ensures that the work for which standards are required is actually observed by a person who should be impartial. For repetitive short cycle jobs it can be the cheapest way of deriving standards. But the presence of someone with a stop watch is unacceptable in some organizations. The very presence of the analyst can create untypical conditions. The people observed may slow down to obtain 'slack' standards or speed up to impress. Although performance rating should take account of this, in practice some jobs are very difficult to rate accurately, particularly when only one person does the job and no comparison is available.

The use of predetermined data can raise doubts about the applicability of the data, except where the most routine jobs are involved. Where jobs are not straightforward, much time may be required to analyse the job into its constituent elements in order to permit the application of the predetermined data. However, its use does dispense with the need for any form of direct personal timing. This can be an overriding factor. To obtain reported information from a work group requires cooperation and honesty. Such a system removes the stress created by direct observation of a work study analyst. Data can be collected cheaply over extended time periods. Where job cycles are long and variable this may be the only economic way of establishing standards. The method is open to error in recording which may be either accidental or intentional; errors can occur both in times recorded and output counts. Another difficulty is that it is impossible to apply any form of performance rating with any level of confidence.

Establishing the Basic Time

Depending on the work measurement method, the job may be broken down into elements. The purpose of the work measurement is to record the time taken for a sufficiently large number of occurrences to give a reliable average time. If performance rating is being used, the observed time is adjusted by the performance rating. Several rating scales exist. Unfortunately, the approach adopted by the British Standard Institution (BSI) is different from the rating scales derived from American work study practice. These latter scales are established by two points. The first represents the speed at which a fully-trained person will work at a job throughout the whole day under non-incentive conditions. The second represents the speed at which such a person would have to work to earn the expected bonus level under incentive conditions. The second point is one third higher than the first. The three common scales are known as 60–80, 75–100 and 100-133 scales, Thus, in a time study where the following times and ratings using the 100-133 scale were recorded, the basic time would be calculated as shown below.

Element	Observed Time (minutes)	Rating (100–133 scale)	Basic Time (observed time x Rating/100)
A	.26	90	.23
B	.74	110	.81
C	.12	100	.12
D	1.35	125	1.69

It can be seen that the times are adjusted to represent the time that would be taken by a person defined as working at a non-incentive pace. The BSI scale defines a single point, 100%, as equivalent to the pace a fully trained person should work to earn the expected bonus, i.e. the 80, 100 and 133 points on the 60–80, 75–100 and 100–133 scales respectively. Rating on the BSI scale is expressed in percentage terms whereas the other scales are absolute numbers. However the most important difference between the use of the BSI scale and the other scales is the way in which basic minutes are calculated. Using the BSI scale, basic minutes are calculated by converting to a 100% performance rate, i.e. to an incentive-based work rate. This is in direct contrast to the other systems where basic minutes are equated to a day wage, non incentive rate of work. The regrettable conclusion is that basic minutes and hence standard times for the same job are not standard but depend on the performance rating scale used. Using the BSI scale the basic time would only be three quarters of that calculated using the other performance rating scales. It can also be seen that the process of performance rating relates measuring work to the concept of incentive payments. This does not help in establishing that work measurement is not primarily concerned with incentive payments.

Establishing the Standard Time

When sufficient observations have been taken to ensure reliable averages for the basic times, two further additions are made to calculated standard times. The first addition is designed to take account of the non-routine events which occur in virtually all jobs, for example instructions from the supervisor, answering the telephone, rethreading a sewing machine. The percentage of work time taken up by such events is determined from observations and a common figure may be derived for a department or section based on all the work measurement undertaken. The second addition makes allowances for relaxation requirements. The amount of relaxation built into standard times depends on the type of work and working conditions involved. Heavy physical work requires more rest than sedentary work; monotonous work more than variable work; work in noisy conditions more than work in peaceful surroundings. Standards for relaxation allowances have been developed and are given in most texts on work study. No allowance should be less than 10% of working time. For very heavy physical work under adverse conditions the allowance can be as high as 50% of working time, that is equivalent to one third of total time. Most jobs fall within the range of 12 to 20% of working time. Typically, this is equivalent to about one hour in the working day.

Thus for the four element job for which basic times were calculated, with an interruption allowance of 6.5 percent and a relaxation allowance of 14 percent, the standard time would be calculated as shown below.

Element	Average Basic Time (a)	Basic Time & Interruption Allowance (b) = 1.065 x (a)	Rest Allowance (c) = (b) x 0.14	Standard Time (b) + (c)
A	.27	.29	.04	.33
B	.76	.81	.11	.92
C	.17	.18	.03	.21
D	1.48	1.58	.22	1.80
			TOTAL	3.26

It is important to understand that standard times already contain the allowance described above. By doing this, standard times can be used directly for planning and performance calculation purposes. Thus, if someone completed 192 cycles of the job made up of elements A, B, C and D in an eight hour day their performance for that day would be:

$$\frac{192 \times 3.26}{480} \times 100 = 131$$

This performance level would be equivalent to 99% on the BSI scale.

Further Reading

Aitken, H. G. J. (1960) *Taylorism at Watertown Arsenal*, Harvard University Press, Cambridge, Mass.

Constable, C. J. and Smith, D. A. (1966) *Group Assessment Programmes: The Measurement of Indirect Work*, Business Publications, London.

Currie, R. M. (1963) *Work Study*, Pitman, London (2nd Edition).

Dudley, N. A. (1968) *Work Measurement: Some Research Studies*, Macmillan, London.

International Labour Office (1964) *Introduction to Work Study*, I.L.O., Geneva.

Lupton, T. (Editor) (1972) *Payment Systems: Selected Readings*, Penguin, Harmondsworth.

Lupton, T. and Gowler, D. (1969) *Selecting a Wage Payment System*, Kogan Page, London.

Norman, R. G. and Bahiri, S. (1972) *Productivity Measurement and Incentives*, Butterworths, London.

CHAPTER 4

Managing the Materials System (1)

Introduction

The materials control system is of major importance to a manufacturing company. Its efficient operation affects not only the level of inventories carried, and hence the working capital required, but also the whole flow of orders through production. We identify and examine three major 'operating areas' within the materials system:

(1) Purchasing
(2) Inventory planning and control
(3) Distribution

Purchasing

The fundamental functions of purchasing are:

(1) Buying the required products and services.
(2) Ensuring that these are available at the appropriate time.
(3) Securing adequate supplies.
(4) Paying the proper price.

The importance of purchasing in manufacturing companies is illustrated in Figure 12 which shows the proportion of total factory costs attributable to bought-out items for a number of UK companies. These companies were drawn from a wide variety of industries and the results illustrate the spread of relative dependence on the purchasing function. Nevertheless, almost 50% of the companies had over half the total factory cost as bought-in materials and 80% of the companies had more than 30% of total factory cost as materials input. It is usual for industries like food processing and fertilizer production to have a very high material proportion. By contrast, highly engineered goods generally have a relatively low proportion. In a major food group where the total company turnover (less profit) is of the order of £5,000 million p.a., some £3,500 million or 65–70% is spent on items purchased by about 400 buyers; this represents a purchasing power of some £10 million per year per buyer.

% of total factory cost attributable to purchased items	% of companies in this range (Sample size 105, 8 non-respondents)	Cumulative % (% of companies in this category or below)
Less than 30%	12	12
30—40%	16	28
40—50%	18	46
50—60%	28	74
60—70%	9	83
70—80%	9	92

Figure 12   The importance of purchasing in UK manufacturing companies (from J. M. Stevens, M.A. thesis, Liverpool University 1973; reproduced with permission)

Purchasing and Production

In most manufacturing organizations, the provision of goods for production is the principal role of the purchasing function. Production must rely on purchasing to supply the right goods at the right time, while purchasing must rely on production for adequate information concerning current and future needs. Purchasing must be actively involved in recommendations for new products and quality changes; it must initiate long term forward supply contracts and changes in order quantities. Moreover, since purchasing personnel are actively engaged in the market for goods, the company must rely on them to anticipate trends and advise on methods of avoiding shortages or disruption of production.

Purchasing and Product Design

A new product can be designed with specifications outside normally accepted commercial standards. This can occur when the designer is unaware of the range and quality of raw materials and parts which can be readily supplied. In such cases, purchased items have to be specially commissioned, probably from a restricted set of suppliers. Costs will be higher, supplier dependence greater and quality more difficult to maintain. Value engineering and value analysis aim to achieve a cooperative effort between purchasing and design, thus ensuring that practical design standards are specified. This will reduce costs without substantially affecting the desired design characteristics. (See Chapter 6.)

Purchasing and design personnel should also be concerned with systematic standardization and product simplification. Their aim should be to save money by reducing the variety of items purchased, and to eliminate unecessary differences between items. Again, purchasing personnel should keep the design department in touch with the market situation so that they are always aware of prices and the availability of raw materials. If the design department is well informed, new products will incorporate the latest materials and modifications to old products will give greater cost effectiveness.

The Make or Buy Decision

Deciding whether an item should be made within the company or bought in is rarely the sole responsibility of the purchasing department. It will almost always involve the production department and may well involve production control and engineering.

The make or buy decision may be taken at different levels in the organization depending on the following circumstances:

(1) The company could make the item on existing facilities and has capacity to do so.
(2) The company could make the item but would require additional capacity to do so.
(3) The company has no experience of manufacturing this type of item and would require new investment in plant to do so.
(4) The company has no experience of manufacturing this type of item and entering into its manufacture would amount to a move towards vertical integration as, for instance, in raw material production.

The decisions involved in (3) and (4) are obviously at a policy level and are such that purchasing would have relatively little say in the matter. The purchasing department is mainly concerned with the strategic decisions involved in deciding how to use the company's existing technical resources, that is (1) and (2) above.

In theory, every purchased item is a potential candidate for manufacture and every manufactured item is a potential candidate for purchase. However, in practice, items like basic raw materials could not be manufactured without a radical change in the compnay business; and the manufacture of service items like stationery, lubricating oils, etc. would also involve major changes. Similarly, the purchase of key components of a company's product might so change the nature of its business as to be unacceptable at a policy level.

There remains, therefore, a subset of items which could be either made-in or bought-out without significantly affecting the nature of the business. The simplest way to decide which option to take is to choose the cheapest. The problem, however, is how to decide which factors should be included in the cost figures and to estimate the time span of the costs involved. The two basic considerations are cost reduction and capacity balancing.

Cost Reduction

Make or buy decisions must be made on the basis of incremental rather than full cost comparisons. One often hears it said that 'we can buy them cheaper than we can make them' and although this may be literally true under a 'full cost' accounting system, it has no relevance to the decision. We must ask of currently purchased or manufactured items: 'What additional costs will be incurred and what costs will be truly avoided if a change is made?'. There may be many reasons why the vendor is able to offer the item at a lower price than the production 'cost' and yet still make a profit himself: he may, for instance, have a high production volume, low factory overheads or lower administration costs. However, it may well not be profitable to purchase the item. If the factory overheads and the general and administrative overheads will be incurred anyway, then the only avoidable costs in manufacturing the item are the direct costs and variable overheads. It is these which must be compared with the purchase price.

Capacity Balancing

Where demand for a firm's products varies substantially, management may either build items for stock in periods of low demand (but note that this is only possible for companies which make fairly standard products) or accept a highly fluctuating production load. Since it is internally difficult to cope with large load fluctuations, companies often maintain an internal capacity which meets the base load and use outside suppliers to meet the variable load. In these cases, many items may be made simultaneously both internally and externally, or components may be bought out during a busy period and made during a slack one. The company is, in fact, buying capacity rather than items. The economic factors to be taken into account are the longer term costs of hiring, redundancy, capacity utilization and operator training.

Other considerations which affect the make or buy decision are problems of quality control and multisourcing of supplies. A company may not be able to find a supplier who can easily meet its quality requirements or, conversely, may prefer to avoid the manufacture of precision items such as bearings. Many companies use several suppliers in preference to a single one in order to avoid shortages resulting from labour disputes or production difficulties. The requirements for critical items may be met partly by internal manufacture as a matter of policy.

Subcontracting of Work

The distinction between purchasing and subcontracting is often ill-defined, particularly where the company is buying capacity rather than components. In some cases, the distinction is clear. If an item is sent out for only some of its production operations, this is clearly subcontract work; general items bought from a suppliers' stock are clearly purchased items. However, many items may be completely manufactured by the supplier especially for the purchaser, and these may be regarded as either purchased or subcontracted. The subcontract decision is identical to the make-or-buy decision except that a company may only be subcontracting certain operations. For example, if the forward load on a machine shop indicates an overload in the drilling section over the next six months, then some drilling work will have to be subcontracted unless either drilling capacity is increased or orders are delayed. If the situation is of a temporary nature, then capital expenditure on capacity expansion will rarely be justified. The extra revenue costs of the subcontract work may be regarded as the savings achievable through the capital expenditure and a rate-of-return calculated. However, such a decision may affect the viability of future capacity expansion because of space restrictions etc., and this is not easily quantified.

The Right Quantity at the Right Time

What is the right quantity to buy? If a firm needs 100 per week of a particular item, then obviously the buyer has to obtain 100 per week. But this will probably not be the purchase quantity. The buyer could place one order every ten weeks for 1,000 items, thus cutting down on purchasing while piling up stocks. Alternatively he could place a schedule order every twenty weeks, scheduling deliveries at the rate of 200 a fortnight, thus cutting down on stock as well as on purchasing work.

The supplier also has an interest in this question. Naturally, he prefers large orders. Consequently, lower prices are quoted for large quantities as an inducement to buy. The supplier may also use a complex discount system to encourage purchasing during seasonal troughs in demand, or to encourage scheduled orders over long periods. It may or may not be advantageous for the purchasing company to utilize such discounts.

The internal factors to be considered in deciding the order size, are:

(1) The quantity required.
(2) Whether an order is likely to be unique, infrequent, seasonal or regular.
(3) Item shelf life and obsolescence.
(4) Storage space.
(5) Finance.

The external factors to be considered in ordering are:

(1) Trade customs (order units of 10, 12, 100, 144, 1,000 etc.).
(2) Delivery periods.
(3) Expected changes in delivery and price.
(4) Quantity discounts.
(5) Market characteristics and price savings.

For unique/infrequent needs, the right purchase quantity is usually the quantity requisitioned. Hence, it is settled outside the purchasing department and it would be unusual for commercial considerations to affect the quantity.

For seasonal needs, a purchase programme has to be worked out. This depends on the production programme and the sales forecast, as well as on external considerations. Usually, it is settled jointly by the purchasing department and the other departments involved. The fruit packing industry's demand for tin cans is a good example of seasonal need. Varying discounts are offered by the can manufacturers depending on how far in advance of the season, within a limit of three months, cans are taken. The value of these discounts has to be considered in relation to the available storage space and the current financial situation.

When supplies are bought in a fluctuating price market, the size and timing of orders is critical. The buyer dictates the quantity to buy and he must time his orders to the best advantage of his firm. Nevertheless, management must control what he is doing. Usually, this is done by limiting finance or by controlling the time period for which he can buy forward. The buyer must obtain permission to commit more than his authorized funds, or to cover ahead for more than his authorized time. This method of purchase is generally used in the commodity market dealing in spot or futures for copper, tin, wool, etc. The large losses incurred by Rowntree's on the 1973/74 cocoa market indicate the risks of inadequate control.

When regular requirements are bought in stable markets, the purchase methods may include:

(1) Period contracts which specify delivery times and quantities.
(2) Period contracts giving the total quantity but not specifying the timing of deliveries. This is detailed by a series of releases against the order.
(3) Individual orders for purchase quantities chosen to balance savings from large orders against savings from low stocks; i.e., Economic Order Quantities.

Purchasing is obviously a vital element in the financial performance of the company, yet it remains relatively neglected by senior management. Purchasing is often delegated, in practice if not in theory, to very junior clerks. Consider a company whose purchase content of factory cost is 50% (the mode from Figure 12 is 50—60%). A breakdown of the finished price might be:

Purchased materials etc.	40% (50% of factory cost)
Direct Labour costs	15%
Variable overheads	10%
Fixed overheads	15%
Selling expenses	10%
Profit	10%
	100%

Then a 1% reduction in purchase cost (0.40%) increases profit by 4%. A 1% reduction in direct labour cost, which would almost certainly be much more difficult to achieve, would only increase profits by 1.5%. The high 'leverage' of such purchased items should encourage more attention to be paid to purchasing.

Inventory Policy, Management, Control and Operation

There is much confusion over the terms 'stock control', 'inventory control', 'inventory policy', 'inventory management' etc. and it is worthwhile to attempt at least a self-consistent understanding of these terms. We treat the terms 'stock' and 'inventory' as interchangeable in a technical sense, and deal with four levels of decision making:

(1) Inventory policy.
(2) Inventory management.
(3) Inventory control.
(4) Inventory operation.

Inventory policy

Inventory policy is concerned with decisions at a policy level which affect the operations of the production/inventory system. In particular, it is concerned with the stages in the system at which inventory is held. These are, for instance, inventories of components and finished goods. Inventory policy is also concerned with the treatment of common components and the choice between the use of a dependent demand based system and an independent stock point system (see below). Inventory policy will affect customer's delivery promise dates, the quality of service and also the production planning and control system.

Inventory Management

Inventory management is concerned with decisions at a strategic level within the framework of the specified inventory policy. For the independent demand case (see below), the strategic decisions are concerned with the type of system to be operated. There are four main systems:

(1) A re-order level/re-order quantity system
(2) A re-order level/order-up-to level system
(3) A review period/order-up-to level system and
(4) A review period/re-order quantity system

The choice will depend on the operating constraints, the system characteristics and the relative costs involved. The costs can be gauged by examining the expected impact of the inventory control decisions. The dependent demand case (see below) permits the following alternatives;

(1) A regenerative material requirements planning (MRP) system, which re-generates all demand schedules in each time period through product explosion.
(2) A net-change MRP system, which maintains a continuously updated status, processing only the changes reported.

Inventory Control

Inventory control is concerned with decisions at the tactical level using the existing control system in order to meet current objectives over the whole inventory. The inventory control system is concerned with the process used to set the control variable values, for instance, the re-order level and the re-order quantity. The objective is to select values which, when used in the operating system, will produce results in line with management objectives for the whole inventory system. The relevant performance criteria are:

(1) Investment in working capital required.
(2) Customer service.
(3) The running costs of the system.

In an MRP system, such control variables will include safety stock factors, batching methods and inventory cost factors.

In practice, the choice of system control parameters must be based on the trade off ('exchange') curves for the various performance criteria. Thus, batching must consider the trade off between set-up/order costs and inventory investment; safety stocks must consider the trade off between customers service levels and inventory investment. These are discussed in more detail in Chapter 5.

Inventory Operation

Inventory operation is concerned with the implementation of the control parameters. It involves the day-to-day operating system which:

(1) records stock availability and outstanding orders,
(2) processes stock transactions, and
(3) generates replenishment orders.

Such operations may be based on computer processing, manual records or on the physical stock itself.

Thus, we see that the inventory system must be examined at all levels and that it has a critical impact on the manufacturing system. Despite the fact that inventory appears as an asset on the balance sheet, few managers regard it as such; it is more often regarded as a necessary evil which should be minimized for efficient operation. Such a view must be resisted. It is doubtless true that many companies do carry excess inventories, but this is usually because they are inventories of the wrong items, for instance, slow moving inventories of almost obsolete designs. Inventory reduction programmes across the board usually have negligible effect on the slow-movers but often reduce service on other items. This may be acceptable in, for instance, a cash flow shortage, but the effects of inventory reduction must always be fully understood.

The Importance of Inventory Policy

The prime function of inventories anywhere in the production/distribution system is to 'uncouple' the links in the chain. A good inventory system will make it possible to allow for infrequent replenishment and to cater for uncertain rates of use. Inventories may be held at various points in the system as:

(1) Raw materials.
(2) Work in process.
(3) Part processed items (including component stocks).
(4) Finished goods.
(5) Distribution depot stocks etc.

At each point, the inventory provides a buffer between stages, for instance raw materials between production and the supply market, work-in-process between production facilities etc. (see Figure 13).

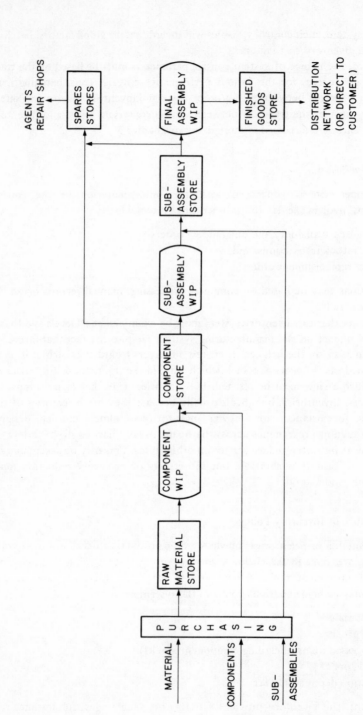

Figure 13   The general form of the production/inventory system

There are four principal types of inventory:

(1) The anticipation inventory. This is built during a low sales season to cover high season sales when demand exceeds company capacity (for instance, in ice cream manufacture).
(2) The lot size inventory. Production (or purchasing) may choose to make (buy) more of a particular item than they require for immediate use in order to spread the set-up (ordering) costs across more items.
(3) The fluctuation inventory. Some part of the inventory may be held solely as a buffer against uncertain demand in order to maintain continuity of supply, for example safety stocks of finished goods and work-in-process inventories.
(4) The distribution inventory. Transportation logistics necessitate inventories in the distribution system.

As we have seen in Chapter 2, the type of market in which the company operates will have a considerable effect on possible inventory policy. The make-to-order firm, for instance, will rarely be able to build anticipatory inventories.

Inventory policy is of crucial importance to the firm since it has a direct impact on:

(1) Customer service, either through the ability to supply 'off-the-shelf' or through the delivery lead time.
(2) Working capital requirements. A large proportion of working capital is usually tied up in inventory investment.
(3) The efficiency with which the production system operates.

In particular, inventories of part-processed items or finished components are very important in the make-to-order company. In such companies, inventory policy directly determines delivery lead time. If orders have to be started at the raw material stage, the shortest lead time will be the full manufacturing cycle time; if orders can be built up mainly from component inventories, the delivery time will be governed solely by the assembly time.

The costs of holding inventories must be weighed against their potential advantages. Working capital will be tied up and there are other costs to consider. These might result from:

(1) Extra storage space required.
(2) The increased risk of losses through obsolescence.
(3) Deterioration of items in storage.
(4) Clearing old inventory when product line changes are made. This will impede rapid response to competitive pressure.

The Nature of Inventory Control Decisions

The inventory control system is ultimately the trigger mechanism which initiates production orders. This role is of far greater importance to the company than the traditional 'cost-centred' view of inventory management since it affects directly:

(1) the load level on the production facilities,
(2) the maintenance of correct relative priorities on jobs to be done,
(3) the provision of adequate supplies of the various component parts of an assembly, i.e. 'the right bits at the right time'.

It is important, therefore, to understand that there are two fundamental classes of inventory control system and that these are based on quite different assumptions about the demand patterns to be met.

The Dependent/Independent Demand Principle

An item is subject to an independent demand pattern if its rate of use does not depend directly on the rate of use of any other item. Thus, in general, the demand for finished goods can be regarded as independent as far as the company is concerned. It may be forecastable on the basis of the sales of other items (e.g. the demand for spares of a particular model of car is presumably related to the number of cars of that model sold) but there is no direct relationship between these items. On the other hand, if a company builds motor cars at the rate of 100 per week and each car has 5 wheels and 1 gear box, then the demand for wheels for car assembly (500 per week) and gearboxes (100 per week) is clearly directly related to the number of cars built. There may in addition be some independent demand for spare gearboxes, but as far as car assembly is concerned, the demand for gearboxes depends on the demand for cars. It should be clear that for dependent demand items, it is quite wrong either to make independent forecasts of future demand or to use past sales as a guide to the future. Only one forecast is necessary for such items. It must be made at the highest level and all other demand should be inferred from this.

Inventory Control Systems for Independent Demand Items

Such systems usually rely on past demand data to forecast future sales rates, though modifications which consider planned sales are possible. These systems are only concerned with a single replenishment decision.

The main features of an inventory control system are illustrated in Figure 14. Three fundamental decisions are involved:

(1) When should an order be raised?
(2) How many items should be made?
(3) What safety stock is required to provide for uncertainties?

In Figure 14, the trigger mechanism is the re-order level, i.e. the stock level at which a new order is initiated. This is the simplest trigger mechanism. The system policy requires the generation of an order of fixed size (the re-order quantity) each time stock falls to the re-order level. Such a system does, of course, require stock levels to be monitored continuously. An alternative to the re-order level system is the

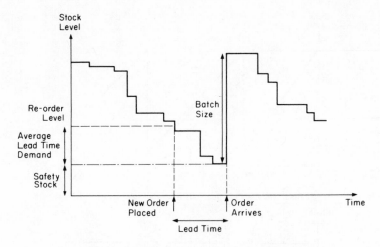

Figure 14   Main features of a stock control system

periodic review system in which stock levels are reviewed at a predetermined interval, the review period. If the stock level is below a minimum an order is placed which is sufficient to bring stock up to a predetermined level, the maximum stock. Under a re-order level (ROL) system, the ROL must be sufficient to cover both demand within production lead time and any safety requirements. Under a periodic review system, the minimum stock level must be sufficient to cover demand within the lead time plus the review period and any safety requirements. Most computerized stock control systems use a periodic review system since this fits in well with, for instance, weekly computer runs.

Under a re-order level system, the 'trigger point' is controlled by the ROL given by:

$$\text{ROL} = \left\{ \begin{array}{l} \text{forecast of demand} \\ \text{within production} \\ \text{lead time} \end{array} \right\} + \left\{ \begin{array}{l} \text{Safety stock to} \\ \text{cover uncertainty} \end{array} \right\}$$

It is the method often used to forecast demand within lead time which raises problems with 'dependent demand' items. The most common forecast is one based on past demand and such a forecast is likely to cause large excess inventories for dependent demand items. Moreover, such a system assumes that it is past demand (that which depleted stock to the re-order level) which governs when a new order is to be initiated. If the rate of use is uniform this is reasonable, but if stock withdrawals are made in large discrete lumps then, again, excess inventories will be generated. Figure 15 shows the behaviour of a ROL system for large 'discrete' withdrawals. Each time the stock is withdrawn, the ROL is broken and a new order is initiated, but the order arrives considerably before a new issue is required. The dotted curve of Figure 15(b) would give a much lower average stock level. Implementing such a policy requires consideration of both the quantity and timing

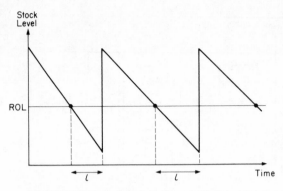

(a) Small independent demands from multiple sources

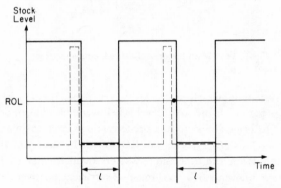

(b) Large discrete batch size withdrawals - a typical dependent demand item

Figure 15   The effect of re-order point control on dependent demand items

of stock withdrawals and this cannot be done through the backward looking ROL system.

An additional problem of customer service arises when stocks of dependant demand items are controlled independently. If an independent demand system is used to control the inventories of component parts on the basis of providing say a 95% service to the assembly area, then this implies that 95 times out of 100 an individual item will be available. If an assembly consists of 10 items, the total service level is, however, only $(0.95)^{10} = 0.60$, that is 60%. This service level would effectively prevent such systems from operating at all, even for assemblies of relatively few components. The result is usually that the formal inventory control system (and with it the load forecasts and scheduling plans based on it) is discarded and the assembly department controls component manufacture through shortage lists and personal intervention.

Allocation Stock Control

Simple stock control systems can be modified so that future demand is forecast on the basis of known requirements for product assembly, i.e. it takes account of the dependent nature of the demand. We have:

$$\begin{Bmatrix} \text{Free} \\ \text{Stock} \end{Bmatrix} = \begin{Bmatrix} \text{Current} \\ \text{Stock} \\ \text{Level} \end{Bmatrix} + \begin{Bmatrix} \text{outstanding} \\ \text{orders on} \\ \text{production} \end{Bmatrix} - \begin{Bmatrix} \text{predicted} \\ \text{requirements} \\ \text{during lead} \\ \text{time and} \\ \text{review period} \end{Bmatrix}$$

Stock is then controlled on the basis of the free stock level. If the forecast of the free stock level at the end of:

(replenishment lead time) + (stock review period)

is greater than the desired 'safety stock' level then no action need be taken. Such a system caters well for changing demand patterns, but the problems of coordinating the timing of replenishment and sales is still largely ignored. The clerical implementation of such a system raises considerable problems, because planned and unplanned stock issues have to be treated differently and because dual stock records are required (physical stock and free stock). A detailed discussion of a wide variety of inventory control systems may be found in Corke (1969).

Inventory Control Systems for Dependent Demand Items

The correct development of demand schedules for dependent items relies on the use of parts explosion. This means the extrapolation of demand for components from the demand for the finished products by using lists of parts and 'number required' data.

The principle of such *material requirements planning* is that a time phased schedule of requirements (over a predetermined planning horizon) is generated for each component/sub-assembly/raw material on the basis of independent forecasts of demand at the highest level (the master schedules). In a full requirements planning system, such schedules of component demand will take account of:

(1) Consolidation of demand for common components,
(2) Existing physical stock levels,
(3) Production/procurement lead times,
(4) Production batching policy.

The generation of requirements schedules for component items is illustrated in Figure 16 which is largely self-explanatory. Such a cycle will be repeated at various levels of sub-assembly and would also normally include an offsetting procedure for existing system stocks (finished items and work-in-process). Figure 18 shows how the time phased requirements planning schedule for sub-assemblies A1 and B1 and

56

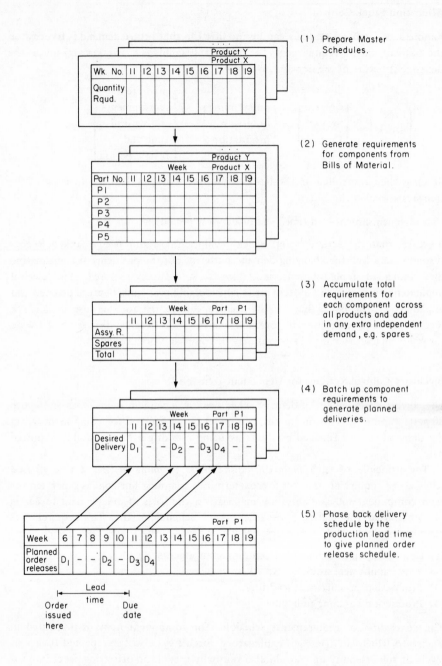

(1) Prepare Master Schedules.

(2) Generate requirements for components from Bills of Material.

(3) Accumulate total requirements for each component across all products and add in any extra independent demand, e.g. spares.

(4) Batch up component requirements to generate planned deliveries.

(5) Phase back delivery schedule by the production lead time to give planned order release schedule.

Figure 16   The generation of component requirement schedules

(a) The BOM structure

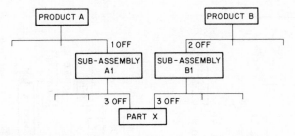

(b) Demand forecasts:
time-phased forecast
of stores withdrawals

Week number	8	9	10	11	12	13	14	15	16	17	
Product A	10	10	10	10	10	10	10	10	10	10	etc
Product B	20	20	20	20	20	20	20	20	20	20	etc

(c) Production Lead Times
Assembly lead time (time to assemble products A and B from sets of components)
= 2 weeks
Manufacturing lead time for subassembly A1 = 2 weeks
Manufacturing lead time for subassembly B1 = 3 weeks

(d) Existing stocks

Item number	Stock Work-in-progress	Finished
A	15	30
B	30	20
A1	15	7
B1	50	80
X	–	200

(e) Batching
Product A is assembled in 20s
Product B is assembled in 30s
Sub-assembly A1 is assembled in 30s
Sub-assembly B1 is assembled in 100s

Figure 17   Data required to determine the net requirement schedule for part X (adapted from C. New, Requirements Planning, Gower Press, London 1973, reproduced with permission)

for part X of Figure 17, are generated. Account is taken of stocks, batching, lead time offsetting and the quantity required. The resulting schedule represents the *net requirements schedule* (NRS) for component X which details the necessary minimum inputs to stores required to meet higher level demand. The *gross requirement schedule* (GRS) also shown represents the time phased withdrawal pattern from the stores. The distortion of the master schedules at the component level is primarily due to the batch sizes used. This can have a very serious impact on the resulting production plans. (Chapter 5 returns to the problem of batching.)

Diagram (product structure):

- PRODUCT A — 1 OFF — S/A A1 — 3 OFF — PART X
- PRODUCT B — 2 OFF — S/A B1 — 3 OFF — PART X
- PART X

Week number	8	9	10	11	12	13	14	15	16	17
Assembly Level										
Product A GRS	10	10	10	10	10	10	10	10	10	10
Less stock gives NRS	–	–	–	10	10	10	10	10	10	10
Less WIP	–	–	–	–	5	10	10	10	10	10
Batch	–	–	20	20	20	–	20	–	20	–
GRS for assembly A1	–	–	20	20	20	20	20	20	20	20
Product B GRS	20	20	20	20	20	20	20	20	20	20
Less stock gives NRS	–	20	20	20	20	20	20	20	20	20
Less WIP	–	–	10	20	20	30	–	30	20	20
Batch	–	–	30	30	30	30	–	30	30	20
GRS for assembly B1 (note 2 off)	60	–	60	60	–	60	60	–	60	60
Component Level										
GRS of A1 less stock gives NRS	–	–	13	–	20	–	20	–	20	–
Less WIP	–	–	–	–	18	–	20	–	20	–
Batch	–	–	–	–	30	–	30	–	–	–
GRS for part X due to product A	–	–	90	90	90	–	–	–	90	–
GRS of B1 less stock gives NRS	–	–	40	60	–	60	60	–	60	60
Less WIP	–	–	–	50	–	60	60	–	60	60
Batch	–	–	–	100	–	100	–	–	100	–
GRS for part X due to product B	300	–	300	–	–	300	–	–	300	300
Total GRS for part X	300	–	390	90	90	300	–	–	390	300
Less stock gives NRS for part X	100	–	390	90	90	300	–	–	390	300

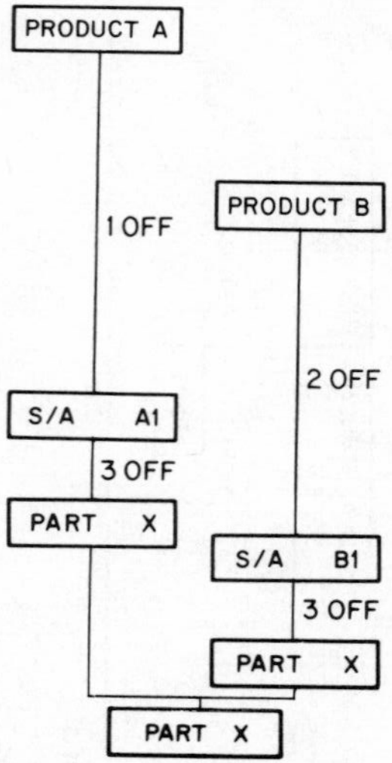

Figure 18   Generation of a net requirement schedule for component X (adapted from C. New, Requirements Planning, Gower Press, London 1973; reproduced with permission)

Independent or Dependent Stock Control Systems?

It seems logical always to make use of reliable information about future sales. This would make it incorrect to use a stock control system suitable for independent demand items for dependent demand items. However, it is important to consider the additional costs of using a modified system such as allocation stock control or a full requirements planning system. If the extra cost of such systems is greater than the potential benefits, then one should use independent demand stock control. Conditions which might favour the use of independent stock control systems for dependent demand items are:

(1) Standardized components with few design changes.
(2) Many items made from the item considered (so that demand is fairly continuous).
(3) Demand patterns with little variation.
(4) Low 'value added' items, which would be stocked as materials otherwise.

The only real approach to an integrated control system for dependent demand items is through material requirements planning (MRP) but the use of MRP techniques has implications for the total production inventory system which are far beyond the question of inventory control. Chapters 7 and 10 discuss this subject further.

Distribution

It would be impossible here to discuss in detail the operation of the distribution sub-system of the material flow system. What follows is a summary of the total scope of distribution.

Physical distribution is the range of activities concerned with the movement of finished products from the final production operation to the ultimate consumers. It may also include the movement of raw material from the supply source to the start of the production process; what is one company's supply line is another company's distribution network. Note that the company rarely has control over the whole distribution function and we are therefore normally concerned with distribution up to a certain point in the chain, for instance, the wholesalers. Distribution activities will therefore include:

(1) Freight,
(2) Warehousing,
(3) Materials handling,
(4) Protective packaging,
(5) Inventory control/operation,
(6) Distribution depot location,
(7) Customer order processing.

In addition, distribution will be involved with the achievement of satisfactory customer service and market forecasting.

The cost of the distribution system for a single company varies from 3% of sales up to 40% of sales depending on the product characteristics. Distribution costs are highest for food, chemicals etc. and lowest for high value per unit volume items like cameras. In addition, it is vital to ensure rapid distribution of perishable products, like dairy produce.

The Main Factors Affecting a Distribution System

(1) THE PRODUCT
    (a) The relationship between product value, volume and weight.
    (b) Fragility.
    (c) Special requirements, e.g. refrigeration.
    (d) Packaging.
(2) DEMAND CHARACTERISTICS
    (a) Seasonality.
    (b) Variability.
    (c) Geographical dispersion.
(3) SALES OUTLETS
    (a) Captive or non-captive.
    (b) Depot/branch structure.
    (c) Access times, e.g. shop hours only.
    (d) Service required, e.g. frequency, reliability.
(4) MARKET STRATEGY
    (a) Customer service objectives.
    (b) Promotional activities.
    (c) Competitive pressures.
(5) ECONOMICS
    (a) Economies of scale in production operations (Figure 19(a)).
    (b) The number of distribution depots (Figure 19(b)).
    (c) Is a company-owned distribution system justified?

All these factors are reflected in the managerial decisions necessary to design and operate an efficient distribution system.

(1) POLICY/STRATEGY DECISIONS
    (a) The role of distribution in meeting market objectives.
    (b) Own distribution network or contractor.
    (c) Depot (and possibly factory) location.
    (d) Warehousing and materials handling.
(2) TACTICAL DECISIONS
    (a) Coordination of sales forecasts, inventory and production plans.
    (b) Bulk transport and local delivery patterns.
    (c) Fleet size and configuration planning.
    (d) Warehouse organization.

The role of distribution in the total economy is undergoing enormous change as a

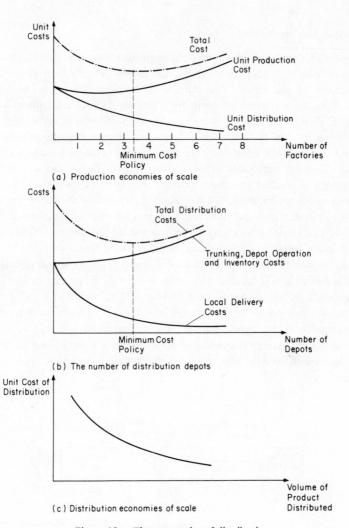

Figure 19   The economics of distribution

result of changing social, technological and environmental pressures. Some important trends are already established:

(1) Changing patterns of retailing — the growth of the multiple store, discounting, hypermarkets etc.
(2) Growth of specialist contract distribution services.
(3) New packaging/unitization methods, e.g. palletization.
(4) Rapid advances in warehousing techniques, e.g. on line computer control systems both for inventory control and warehouse handling.
(5) Possible new legislation restricting traffic access.
(6) Development of a coordinated EEC transport policy.

Distribution and Production

The impact of the distribution network on production plans is of major concern in companies which produce for stock to supply distribution depots, e.g. the manufacturer of ice cream. The effects of demand changes on such multilevel systems have been studied in depth by Forrester (1961) and others and can be illustrated through a simple example. Systems in which there is a chain of stock-holding points can experience large and exaggerated fluctuations in their stock and output levels when there are delays in the response to changes in demand. Suppose a factory warehouse supplies a distribution depot which in turn supplies retailers with a product at a sales rate of 100 units per week. Suppose that, as illustrated in Figure 20, there is a one week delay before the depot can adjust to a change in customer demand and that there is a two week delay before the factory warehouse can respond to a change in demand by the depot. 100 units are being supplied on a regular weekly basis between the depot and retail outlet and 200 units supplied on a fortnightly basis between factory and depot. If customer sales now rise to a new level of 110 units in week 2, the retailer cannot respond to this increase until week 3, and must deliver 120 to meet the backlog of 10. The factory warehouse cannot respond to the increase to 120 from the depot until week 5. Furthermore, if the depot manager assumes demand will stay at 120, he will order 240 for that time. This will give the depot excess stocks and the demand will later drop to only 190 in order to reduce these. Demand will then rise again until it stabilizes.

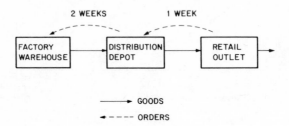

Figure 20   Interactions in the production—distribution system

Conclusions

We have reviewed the operation of the materials flow system in a company at three stages: purchasing, inventory planning and control and distribution. This has shown that the materials system affects the operation of the manufacturing system in fundamental ways. In the next chapter we examine some of the quantitative techniques developed to aid in the management of such systems and their relevance to practical operating problems.

References

Burbidge, J. L. (1968) *The Principles of Production Control*, Macdonald & Evans Ltd., London.
Corke, D. K. (1969) *Production Control is Management*, Arnold, London.
Forrester, J. (1961) *Industrial Dynamics*, Wiley, New York.
New, C. C. (1973) *Requirements Planning*, Gower Press, London.

Further Reading

The references above cover various aspects of inventory management, in addition:

Baily, P. and Farmer, D. (1968) *Purchasing Principles and Techniques*, Pitman, London.
Christopher, M. (1971) *Total Distribution*, Gower Press, London.
Wentworth, F. (Ed) (1970) *Physical Distribution Management*, Gower Press, London.

CHAPTER 5

Managing the Materials System (2)

Introduction

Chapter 4 reviewed the nature of inventory control systems and discussed their relevance to various demand patterns. It was concluded that:

(1) For *independent* demand, simple re-order point/re-order quantity stock control systems can be used.
(2) For *dependent* demand such systems are inappropriate and some form of parts explosion requirements planning system should be used.

Much has been written about the economic trade-offs involved in determining batch sizes and safety stocks for particular inventory control systems. This chapter considers the principles and limitations of the basic models.

Analysis of Use by Value

The first step in inventory control is to identify those stock items which are most important to operations, and which contribute most to the turnover of the company. The technique is known variously as ABC analysis, Pareto analysis and the 80-20 law. It is a method of classifying items by their relative importance.

The 80-20 law of inventory control states that 'for most inventory systems, approximately 80% of the total use by value (in money terms) is accounted for by about 20% of the items stocked'. An A–B–C classification usually takes the following form:

(1) The A class accounts for a large proportion, say 70%, of the use by value and includes about 10% of all items.
(2) The B class is intermediate, accounting for say 20% of the use by value and 20% of the items.
(3) The C class contains the remaining 70% of the items, which account for the remaining 10% of the total use by value.

Use by value for an item is defined as:

annual rate of use (units) x cost/unit

This gives the total amount of money 'turnover' for each part.

Use by value classification shows which parts of the total inventory account for most of the turnover. Tight and fairly sophisticated control over a small percentage of the items (the A class) can have tremendous impact on the cost of inventory and on production planning and control. It would not, however, be very sensible to apply the same control techniques to the relatively unimportant items in the C category. It should be noted, however, that in assembly situations where A, B and C items are combined, a C item out of stock causes just as much delay as an unavailable A item.

The analysis requires a list of all items, together with their unit cost and average rate of use. The calculations performed are then to:

(1) Calculate use by value.
(2) Sort the items into descending order of use by value.
(3) Compute the % of the total use by value attributable to each item.
(4) Show cumulative use by value % and the cumulative % of items covered against each item in the ordered list.

A typical use by value curve is shown in Figure 21.

An initial investigation to establish approximate breakpoints between the A, B and C classes can be carried out as follows:

(1) Take a representative sample of say 100 items.
(2) Make a use by value analysis of the sample.

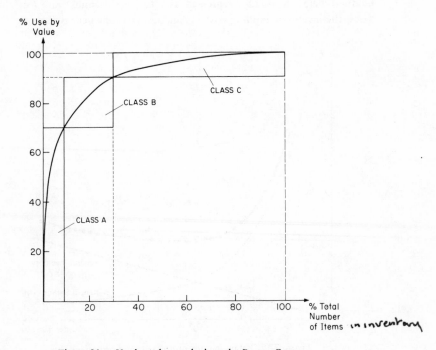

Figure 21   Use by value analysis — the Pareto Curve

(3) The breakpoints of the A, B and C classes in the total inventory should correspond with the sample breakpoints.

For example, if the rate of use for the lowest A class item in the sample is £5,000 p.a., then only items in the total inventory with rates of use above £5,000 p.a. should be included in the A class.

When the items have been classified into these groups, possible policies might be:

A items Special analysis (possibly based on MRP or allocation stock control), use of expediting staff, frequent stock reviews.
B items Routine re-order level control based on forecast demand.
C items Two bin system with no stock cards.

How Much to Order and How Frequently to Review Stock

Order sizes are first considered in the context of purchasing from outside suppliers. In deciding how much to order, the inventory holding costs must be balanced against ordering costs.

(1) INVENTORY HOLDING COST. Investment in inventory caused by purchasing parts ahead of requirement is costly. If an item worth £100 is kept unnecessarily in inventory for one month, the company will have to finance the extra working capital. In addition to financing costs, inventory involves storage costs, risk of obsolescence etc. If an item has a unit cost of £V, the inventory holding charge is usually expressed as a fractional annual rate I of the value. Thus, the inventory holding cost for one item for one year is £IV.

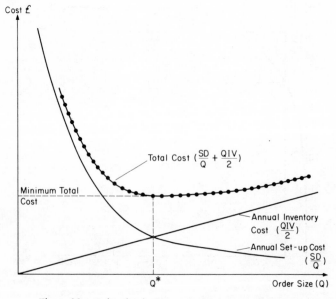

Figure 22   Balancing inventory costs and ordering costs

(2) ORDERING COSTS. These are costs incurred in procuring an order from a supplier. They include receiving and accounting costs. The order cost (S) is considered to be independent of the quantity ordered (Q) as it is incurred whatever the size of the purchase. (Quantity discounts require a modification to the basic approach.) Unit ordering costs can be expressed as S/Q. If total annual demand is D, the total annual ordering cost is SD/Q.

For a single item with a known demand, the relationship between order size and these costs is illustrated in Figure 22. Large order sizes require few orders per year but incur high inventory costs. Small order sizes incur low inventory costs but require many orders per year.

The economic order quantity is the quantity which should be ordered each time to give minimum total annual cost. Annual ordering costs are SD/Q. If throughout each stock cycle inventory is depleted at a uniform rate (from Q to zero), the average stock level is $Q/2$ and the inventory holding cost is $(Q/2) \times (IV)$. Thus, total cost $T(Q)$ is given by:

$$T(Q) = \frac{SD}{Q} + \frac{QIV}{2}$$

The minimum total cost occurs when the order quantity

$$Q = Q^* = \sqrt{\frac{2SD}{IV}}$$

where Q^* is the Economic Order Quantity (EOQ).

The use of the EOQ policy requires that each time an order is placed it should be for a quantity Q^*. Since the total demand is D, this means that D/Q^* orders are required per year. Thus, on a periodic review system, the item should be reviewed D/Q^* times per year, or every 52 Q^*/D weeks.

There are a number of limitations to this approach:

(1) Management are concerned with the aggregate inventory policy across all items. Straightforward application of the above formula could lead to a policy requiring far more orders than the purchasing department could cope with, or an unacceptable level of inventory investment.
(2) Many of the ordering costs are step functions and a policy can only be set for the whole inventory, for example, number of purchase officers required. This is also true for the storage cost component.
(3) It is difficult to estimate the opportunity cost of capital tied up. Strictly, it is the marginal cost of capital to the company.

It should, however, be noted that the total cost curve is relatively flat in the region of the minimum. Thus, it is possible to use 'rounded values' for the EOQ or the review period.

These limitations indicate that it is necessary to find a rational policy for the aggregate inventory which takes account of constraints such as the capacity of the purchase department or limited investment.

Aggregate Inventory Management

For a single item i in an inventory of M items the EOQ formula may be written in money terms as:

$$q_i = K \sqrt{A_i S_i}$$

where q_i is the money value of the order, A_i is the annual use by value and K is a constant which may be used to reflect management's trade off between inventory investment and the number of orders required.

The value of K used in this formula has a direct impact on the order sizes used and, therefore on the frequency of raising orders. A high value of K would give large order sizes and hence high inventories with few orders, whereas a small value of K would give low inventories and many orders. Figure 23 shows an 'exchange curve' for balancing inventory and ordering costs; every point on the curve corresponds to a different value of K and reflects a particular management trade-off choice.

The single 'optimal policy' of the EOQ is represented by the point on the exchange curve which has a corresponding value of K, for example point A in Figure 23. This defines both the number of orders necessary and the inventory investment required.

Every point on the exchange curve represents a rational ordering policy in the

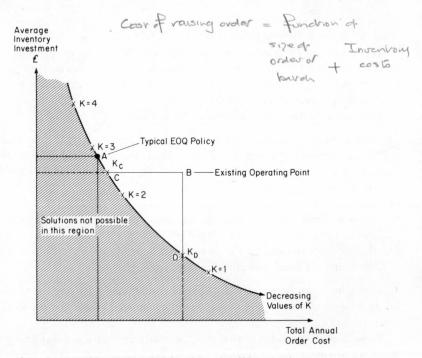

Figure 23   Exchange curve showing the trade-off between inventory investment and ordering costs

sense that ordering and inventory costs are balanced in the same way across all the inventory items. The policy represented by point B is economically irrational because it implies different trade-offs for different parts, a situation which cannot easily be justified.

Lower Inventory, Lower Ordering Costs or a Bit of Both?

If K is regarded as a policy variable, and the current operating point is B in the inventory system in Figure 23, we can choose to:

(1) Maintain inventory investment at its current level but reduce ordering costs by operating with $K = K_C$ at point C. This might make it possible to redeploy purchasing officers.
(2) Use the existing ordering cost to better advantage and lower inventory investment by operating with $K = K_D$ at point D.
(3) Reduce both inventory and ordering costs by operating with K between K_D and K_C.

The benefits of (1) and (2) above are far more concrete than a vague promise of 'optimality'; they offer something for nothing, always a worthwhile option. By contrast, the 'optimal policy' at point A would require an increase in inventory investment, though it would give large savings in ordering costs. To follow such a policy would require a great deal of faith in the cost estimates; though in theory the total cost would be the lowest possible. It is possible to change the value of K at any time to suit management restrictions on:

(1) Total average inventory investment.
(2) Total annual set-up cost.

It is relatively straightforward to compute the appropriate value of K to use in order to achieve a chosen operating point on the exchange curve; details may be found in Corke (1969) and Lock (1975).

Note, however, that even such 'rational' policies depend on getting the correct 'balance' between estimates of ordering costs and inventory values across items since under different policies the inventory investment is re-allocated in a more efficient way across items.

Quantity Discounts

The theory previously described can be modified to take account of reductions in unit purchase cost given for increased order sizes. This means that not only is the fixed 'order cost' spread over more items by buying larger batches, but the items are also cheaper. Both these gains must be balanced against the additional inventory costs incurred. This does not raise any particular problems but is too detailed to examine here. Corke (1969) examines the discount problem in a practical context. He provides a ready reckoner for deciding the level of discount at which it is worthwhile modifying the standard policy. It must be realized, however, that such modifications may nullify any apparent benefits from the exchange curve figures since the effects of discounts are not shown on the curve.

Production Batch Quantities

An economic model for production batch quantities (the EBQ model) can be derived in exactly the same way as the economic order quantity. In this case, the order cost S is treated as the set-up cost required to produce a batch. Set-up costs are those costs which arise through the issue of a batch of work to production and include the costs of initiating the order, of setting up the necessary machines and of controlling and keeping track of the order on its way through the manufacturing system.

The economic batch quantity rule has a number of limitations. These include:

(1) It tends to lead to large batch sizes which make multiproduct plants less flexible and extend customer lead time.
(2) When strictly applied, production planning and scheduling becomes complicated and load levelling almost impossible.
(3) It may be virtually impossible to specify an 'average' set up time, since this can depend on the order in which batches are processed, i.e. it is sequence dependent.

The batching of production orders has major effects on the production system in addition to the economic effects. Batching commits capacity now to items not yet required, possibly to the detriment of items which are required immediately. The application of the exchange curve principle may provide a rational economic policy but it cannot consider the other effects. In practice, what is required is a system which creates predictable batch sizes which can be fitted together to form a load plan for the existing facilities. This is usually best achieved, particularly in functional organizations, by setting batch sizes equivalent to the rate of use over a specified time period, e.g. 2, 4, 8 weeks.

It must also be noted that items produced on general purpose facilities are rarely subject to independent demand. Such items are usually produced in batches for stock and later assembled into finished products. Component demand is therefore dependent on final assembly schedules. It is wrong to use EBQ models to set such batch sizes because they assume uniform rates of use, a condition which rarely applies to dependent demand. While much of inventory control literature has been obsessed with determining quantities (the EBQ approach), the more important problem in dependent demand systems is determining timing. The batch size problem in a materials requirement planning (MRP) system is similar to the independent demand case, i.e. balancing set-up against inventory costs, but different methods have been suggested to take account of the variable demand patterns. The same short falls of the 'economic' approach to the independent demand case may also occur in a dependent demand case.

Setting Batch Sizes in MRP Systems

A number of 'economic' models have been suggested to batch up discrete quantity MRP schedules. These range from the 'optimum' dynamic programming approach to the 'economic time cycle' or 'periodic order quantity' based on EBQ calculations. It must, however, be repeated that although the use of such methods offers great economic advantages over the 'fixed batch size EBQ' policy, they are still based solely on economic criteria.

Safety Stocks to Cover Uncertainty

Where stock is used as a buffer between two stages, there will be uncertainty in supply from the first stage and in demand from the second. To allow continuity of operation for both stages, part of the stock between the two will be allocated as safety stocks. The level of safety stock is again a balancing decision between the cost of holding the safety stock and the service level required.

Safety Stocks for Independent Demand Items

In Chapter 4 we saw that for the simple re-order level system the ROL was given by:

$$\text{ROL} = \left\{ \begin{array}{l} \text{Forecast of demand} \\ \text{within production} \\ \text{lead time} \end{array} \right\} + (\text{Safety stock})$$

The safety stock must be sufficient to cover reasonable variations in demand during the lead time. If a standard service level (in terms of stockouts) is to be maintained, items with large demand variability will need more safety stock than items with little demand variability.

There are two methods of assessing safety stock requirements:

(1) Estimate *shortage costs*, i.e. cost of being out of stock of an item, and minimize the expected total cost of shortages and stockholding.
(2) Specify a *service level* and set the safety stock level from statistical theory.

In practice, method one is of little use because of the difficulty of making a prior estimate of shortage costs. The major problem with the second approach is determining the meaning of 'service level'. Possible measures are:

(1) Percentage of ordering cycles when no shortage occurs, e.g. 95% means that 19 times out of 20, a replenishment order arrives before a shortage occurs. This measure takes no account of the frequency of stock replenishment. A 90% service level for an item on monthly replenishment averages a stockout every 10 months, whereas an item on annual replenishment averages a stockout every 10 years!

(2) Percentage of demand satisfied immediately from stock

$$= \frac{\text{demand met from stock}}{\text{total demand in period}} \%$$

or in money terms for a total inventory:

$$\frac{\text{Money value of demand met from stock}}{\text{Total money value of demand in period}} \%$$

(3) Number of item-weeks of stock shortage per annum. This can be useful for captive demand e.g. specialist spares and internal component stocks, but it is difficult to set standards.

The variation in lead time usage

The usual statistical measure of demand variation is the standard deviation but for inventory control purpose the mean absolute deviation (MAD) is often used instead (see Appendix to this chapter). The MAD of use during a lead time (MAD_{LT}) is a measure of the uncertainty of demand during that lead time. When setting safety stocks, three options are available to management:

(1) *Base Safety Stocks on the Rate of Demand*   A rule such as 'hold three weeks use as safety stock' is easy to understand and to implement. However, such a rule would give very different cover for items with different order frequencies and also for items with different demand variability. Compared with this method, a reallocation of total safety stock could give substantial improvement in service for no increase in cost.

(2) *Base Safety Stock on the MAD of Forecast Error*   By use of a safety factor K, the safety stock can be related to an item's demand variability

$$\text{Safety stock} = K \times MAD_{LT}$$

While this is a more rational policy than (1), it results in varying levels of customer satisfaction because of the differences in cycle times for various items. It is equivalent to the first definition of service level.

(3) *Set Safety Stock to Give the Same Customer Service Level on all Items*   The use of different values of K for items with different cycle times can result in the same service level for all items. The computation of appropriate values of K is given in Brown (1967).

The effects of these policies in exchange curve terms are shown in Figure 24.

The use of warning limits on physical stock and of expediting systems can considerably raise the level of customer service for any given investment in safety stock. These will, however, add to the total cost of the system. In particular:

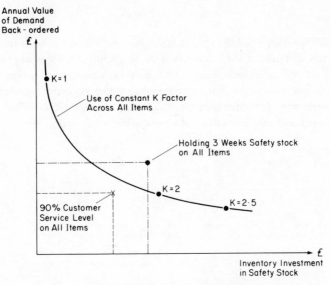

Figure 24   The safety-stock/back order exchange curve

(1) Accurate demand data for different conditions rarely exists.
(2) It is extremely difficult to establish statistical safety stock control procedures which are readily responsive to changing circumstances.

Safety Stocks for Dependent Demand Items

For dependent items the variation between schedule periods is not random. It is caused by changes in higher level batching and demand requirements. Also, stocks are usually withdrawn as large batches rather than at a steady uniform rate. It is, therefore, completely inappropriate to base safety stocks on the statistical calculations already described.

Three possible ways of catering for variations in materials requirement planning schedules have been suggested. Briefly these are:

(1) The use of safety time to bring parts into stock before the requirements plan indicates a need for them. This results in an uncertain level of safety cover and inflates lead times.
(2) Increases to the master schedule. This causes safety stocks at high levels which can be costly. Excessive stocks of common parts can occur.
(3) The use of a fixed quantity for safety stock. This can be done by showing a net requirement when stock fails to the safety stock level rather than to zero. This method raises the problem of determining the size of the safety stock and ensuring its replenishment without disrupting production.

Little real work has been done on setting safety stocks rationally for dependent demand items. It is still basically a process of trial and error.

Conclusions

This chapter has examined the role of economic analysis as the basis for controlling the materials systems. If such analysis is to be useful, it must relate to the whole inventory, not to individual items. The use of exchange curves which specify the trade-offs possible between conflicting management objectives provides a more rational approach for management decision making. Nevertheless the blind application of economic formulae will almost always end in disaster.

APPENDIX

Exponential Forecasting

Moving Averages

Notation:

Let x_t = actual demand in time period t

f_t = forecast of demand for month t

m_t = mean or average demand per time period based on actual data up to (and including) period t

n = no. of periods of data available

Also let $e_t = x_t - f_t$ = error in forecast for period t

If a forecast is made solely on the basis of past demand data, it is often useful to give more weight to the most recently recorded data and correspondingly less weight to older data.

For example, we might assess the current mean level of demand or 'moving average' (m_t) by:

$$m_t = 0.5x_t + 0.25x_{t-1} + 0.15x_{t-2} + 0.1x_{t-3}$$

(where the weights $0.5 + 0.25 + 0.15 + 0.1 = 1.0$)

One possible weighting method is to assign weights which decrease exponentially with time so that if $0 < a < 1$ the weights are:

$$a, a(1-a), a(1-a)^2, \ldots a(1-a)^n$$

so that

$$m_t = ax_t + a(1-a)x_{t-1} + a(1-a)^2 x_{t-2} \ldots$$

However, if this system is used we have also:

$$m_{t-1} = ax_{t-1} + a(1-a)x_{t-2} + a(1-a)x_{t-3} \ldots$$

and hence $m_t = ax_t + (1-a)m_{t-1}$

$$\text{or} \begin{Bmatrix} \text{New} \\ \text{Moving} \\ \text{average} \end{Bmatrix} = a \begin{Bmatrix} \text{Latest} \\ \text{Demand} \\ \text{Data Item} \end{Bmatrix} + (1-a) \begin{Bmatrix} \text{Old} \\ \text{Moving} \\ \text{Average} \end{Bmatrix}$$

This average is usually known as an *exponentially weighted moving average* (EWMA) and the estimate is said to be exponentially smoothed. The constant a is the smoothing constant and will usually have a value in the range 0.1 to 0.4.

The main advantage of this method of weighting is that it requires a minimum of data storage; only the previous average (m_{t-1}) and the latest data item (x_t) are required in order to determine m_t.

Forecast Errors

The forecast error is defined as the difference between the actual demand in a period and the forecast which was made for that period, i.e.

$$e_t = x_t - f_t$$

In general, we are interested in the standard deviation of the errors which occur over a number of periods. However, a more widely used measure (which is much easier to calculate than the standard deviation) is the mean absolute deviation (MAD). Over n periods the MAD would be given by:

$$MAD_n = \frac{1}{n} \sum_{t=1}^{n} |x_t - f_t|$$

If the moving average m_t is exponentially smoothed, it makes sense to do the same to the MAD every time a new demand figure is known and hence a new 'error' is calculated. Then the smoothed MAD is:

$$MAD_t = a|e_t| + (1 - a)MAD_{t-1}$$

This specifies the latest estimate of the inherent variability in *single period demand.*

Variation in Lead Time Use

It is reasonable to expect that the average percentage error for a single period forecast will be greater than that over a full replenishment lead time. The MAD for the lead time (l) would, therefore, be less than l times the single period MAD. This is important because any safety stock should be set in relation to the variation in *lead time use.*

Brown (1967) has suggested that the relationship is:

$$MAD_{LT} = MAD(0.66 + 0.34l)$$

This appendix has briefly outlined the nature of exponential forecasting in so far as it is relevant to the setting of safety stocks. The introduction of trends and seasonal variations considerably complicate the forecasting process itself. These factors are dealt with in depth in Brown (1959, 1967) and Lewis (1970).

References

Brown, R. G. (1959) *Statistical Forecasting for Inventory Control*, McGraw-Hill, New York.
Brown, R. G. (1967) *Decision Rules for Inventory Management*, Holt, Rinehart and Winston, New York.
Corke, D. K. (1969) *Production Control is Management*, Macdonald & Evans Ltd., London.
Lewis, C. D. (1970) *Scientific Inventory Control*, Butterworths, London. (Mathematical modelling)
Lock, D. (Ed.) (1975) *Financial Techniques in Production Management*, Gower Press, Epping.

Further Reading

The references above cover many topics in depth, in addition:

Baily, P. (1971) *Successful Stock Control by Manual Systems*, Gower Press, London. (A good guide to 'quick and dirty' methods)

Thomas, A. B. (1968) *Stock Control in Manufacturing Industries*, Gower Press, London. (General operation of stock control systems)

A particularly useful article covering a wide range of forecasting methods (not just statistical techniques) is:

Chambers, J. C. and coworkers (1971) 'How to choose the right forecasting technique', *Harvard Business Review*, pp 45–74, July–August 1971.

CHAPTER 6

Managing Quality and Reliability

Introduction

It is difficult to produce a precise definition of quality. For manufactured goods, quality will cover at least three aspects of the product. These are:

(1) PHYSICAL CHARACTERISTICS. This includes dimensions, tolerances, fits etc. and colour, opacity, feel, surface finish etc. Most of these characteristics are measurable although such items as colour and feel may be subjective.

(2) PERFORMANCE AND RELIABILITY. Manufactured goods are expected to have a given level of performance, for example a motor car usually has a stated maximum speed and petrol consumption. A refrigerator should only use a given quantity of electricity and be able to maintain the products contained at a specified temperature. Reliability implies that the product will perform at the stated specifications for a reasonable period of time. Reliability is usually less precisely specified for manufactured goods. Most items have an initial warranty period, commonly not more than twelve months, when the manufacturer will accept responsibility for failure during operation. However, the purchaser expects the item to operate trouble free for a far longer period than twelve months. Whether the life of the refrigerator should be ten or fifteen years, or of the motor car fifty, a hundred or two hundred thousand miles is not normally clearly stated.

(3) VALUE. Quality expressed as the value of an item is a far more subjective measure. A perfectly effective ball point pen can be purchased for 5p. A similar ball point pen, no more effective in terms of writing capability, can be bought for between £2 and £10 depending on the material used in the casing. Here it may be argued that the casing material itself, particularly if it is gold, has obvious and quantifiable value. The casing does not, however, improve the functioning of the item, but merely its visual appeal. This appeal will increase the quality of the item for some people but not for others. The concept of quality as expressed through value becomes even more subjective when works of art are considered. A painting may be priced at £100. For one art lover this may represent extremely good value for money. For another, it will be viewed as a complete waste of money. It is, in effect, a matter of taste.

It will be seen then that the quality of a manufactured article can be both objective and measurable and subjective and a function of the user's taste.

Generally speaking, the objective characteristic of quality can be improved during the design and manufacture of the product. This improvement will normally require greater expenditure.

The quality of a service is usually measured in somewhat different terms. Quality here can be defined as:

(1) AVAILABILITY. People using services expect them to be available as and when they need them. To arrive at an airport and discover that the last hire car has just been taken provides no consolation, no matter how good the motor car was. When the pipe bursts the plumber is required immediately, not in three days' time. Price can often be less important than availability, particularly under emergency conditions.

(2) REGULARITY AND RELIABILITY. If a service is offered on a specified schedule, the user expects the service to be available at the specified time. To arrive at the bus stop at the time stated on the schedule for a bus, only to find it has gone three minutes early does not impress the person left behind. Equally, having caught the bus, one expects to arrive at the destination at the time stated in the timetable and not minutes or even hours late.

(3) COST AND VALUE. Although the availability of a service can sometimes outweigh cost considerations, the user will normally have a cost value relationship in his mind. This may to a large extent be objective when, for example, comparing the cost quoted for an electrical repair by several electricians, (although the one chosen may in fact damage the decoration more than someone who would have done the job for a greater cost). On the other hand, the value of a meal in a restaurant is a function of objective and subjective factors. One expects the food to be well prepared and cooked. The waiters should be polite and attentive. Most customers would probably agree on these measures. But what of atmosphere? This is a largely subjective issue and an atmosphere that may be attractive and hence worth paying for to some people may be anathema to others.

Determining the quality of a product or service and then operating the system to achieve that quality on a consistent basis requires managerial decision and continuing attention. The remainder of this chapter considers various issues associated with managing quality and reliability. The role of statistical techniques in maintaining quality control is discussed but the details of the techniques themselves are not considered. Reference to these techniques is given in the bibliography at the end of this chapter.

The Responsibility for Quality

The quality of a product or service is defined by the needs of the market. Thus, the responsibility for the initial definition of quality must be that of the marketing organization. However, the marketing men may expect a level of quality at a price which in practice is unobtainable. The design and manufacturing functions in the organization must attempt to produce the product required at the specified quality and cost. If, however, this is not possible, then a compromise must be reached between design, manufacturing and marketing. Either quality must be reduced or price increased. The parameters of quality and cost are likely to be constrained within certain limits for a given organization. The quality and cost of the products produced by an organization are major factors in determining its image. To move either parameter outside the existing limits may be unacceptable. It could seriously damage the company reputation or result in the production of goods which the consumer does not associate with that company. This will increase the difficulty of the marketing task.

Quality constraints can also be imposed through statutory agencies. All food and drug items must conform to government standards. The safety standards of the automobile are constantly being affected by government legislation. Even where legislation does not exist, the company can be exposed to claims for damages as a result of accidents caused by the imperfect functioning of its products. The users of products are now far more organized. Consumer groups are effective in bringing pressure to bear on manufacturers to improve their products and in creating new statutory legislation to control the quality standards of manufactured goods. Even without the growth of these pressures, in the long run it is scarcely sound strategy for a manufacturer to produce substandard goods. The cost of regaining a reputation lost through the production of below standard quality goods, is far greater than any savings which may have accrued through reduced manufacturing costs and increased short term profits.

Quality can be achieved at three stages in the life of a product. These are:

(1) AT THE DESIGN STAGE. Design quality is a function of the specifications which the design engineer lays down for the manufacture of the product. This involves choosing materials, determining dimensions, tolerances etc. and specifying performance and reliability levels. Even at this stage, the designer is compromising between his desire to produce a perfect product and the materials and skills which are available to him and the cost of using these materials and skills.

(2) AT THE MANUFACTURING STAGE. The amount of quality built into the product is a function of how well the manufacturing activity achieves the design specifications. Here, less compromise should take place since every attempt should be made to meet the design specification. However, as discussed later, variability in manufactured components is inevitable and no matter how effective the quality control mechanisms, variation in product performance is unavoidable.

(3) AT THE SERVICE STAGE. A company can achieve quality for its products through the service offered when the products are in use. The user will perceive that he has a better quality product if he is able to obtain service easily. Service to the user will be a function of the availability of spare parts and of service engineers and the cost to him of the service activities. The user's view of the quality of a product is materially affected by its availability when it is required. Most manufacturing organizations incur far more quality cost in maintaining

the quality of their products at the service stage than building quality into the manufacture and design stages.

Value Engineering and Value Analysis

Greater value for a given cost or the same value at reduced cost can be achieved through value engineering and value analysis. Value engineering is carried out at the product design stage; value analysis is carried out on products which are already being manufactured. Both activities involve similar processes. Multifunctional teams usually involving design, purchasing, marketing, manufacturing and production engineering critically examine all components and aspects of the product. The purpose of the complete product is first established. The extent to which this purpose is achieved by the inclusion of individual components, the specification of particular dimensions, the use of given types and qualities of materials etc. is then examined. Elimination of components is the ideal outcome. However, cost can also be reduced by using cheaper materials, standard rather than unique components, simpler manufacturing methods etc. The advantage of value engineering over value analysis, is that it takes place before commitment has been made for material and component supplies and before any investment in a specific manufacturing process. Change is therefore easier to make.

The Concept of Reliability

No manmade machine has an infinite life span. Products are designed and manufactured to achieve an anticipated life expectancy if operated under appropriate environmental conditions. In practice, some products will fail after a relatively short operating period, while others will far outlast the anticipated life expectancy. By testing products to failure, a frequency distribution of life expectancy can be built up. Thus, a probability value can be placed on the likelihood of the product failing after a given operating period. This is illustrated in Figure 25.

Figure 25 shows that there is a relatively high rate of failure in the early stages of product use. This represents the items which contain defects not discovered by the quality control procedures. These early defects are often referred to as failures in the infant mortality period. When this period has passed, there is an extended time period in which a relatively small number of failures takes place. There is then a sudden increase in failure rate as the operating period approaches the designed life expectancy. The failure of the remaining products is usually normally distributed around the designed life.

Two measures are commonly used to express reliability. These are:

(1) The failure rate expressed as the number of failures divided by the total number of operating hours of the item under test in the evaluation period.
(2) The mean time between failure (MTBF) which is reciprocal of the failure rate.

It is important to recognize that the reliability of a total system containing many

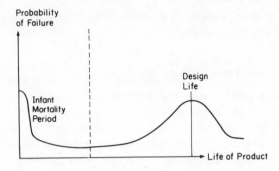

Figure 25   Frequency distribution of product life
expectancy

parts, the failure of any of which will cause the total system to fail, is no better
than the reliability of the most unreliable part. It should, therefore, be the objective
of the design and manufacturing process to produce components for a system with
equivalent levels of reliability. To make some components far more reliable than
others simply involves unnecessary expense.

Under these circumstances reliability of the total system is the product of the
individual reliabilities. This can be expressed as

$$R_s = R_{c1} \times R_{c2} \ldots \times R_{cn}$$

where R_s is the system reliability and R_{c1} is the reliability of component 1 etc. The
significance of this concept can be demonstrated by the following example. The
probability of failure over a 1,000 hour period for a system made up of 20
components, each of which has only a 1 in 50 probability of failing in a thousand
hours of operation, is 1 in 5. The multiplicity effect means that the total system is
not particularly reliable in spite of the high level of individual component
reliability. Fortunately component reliability in many complex systems, for
example electronic computers, is very high. The significance of system reliability
depends on the consequences of failure. If failure is likely to result in injury and
loss of life, far more effort will be put into avoiding failure than if it will merely
result in minor inconvenience. There are several ways in which the designer can
minimize the risk of failure. The system most commonly adopted with structures is
designing with an appropriate safety margin. In effect, this means the structure will
not fail even when subjected to loads several times those anticipated under normal
operating conditions. The fact that from time to time buildings and bridges do
collapse indicates that on occasions freak loadings take place or that design
concepts were misunderstood. Designing safety margins into structures does, of
course, cost money and the designer is therefore always seeking to compromise
between adequate safety margins and excessive costs. Safety margins can also be
obtained by derating the operating level of part of the system. For example, the
chances of failure of a motor will be considerably reduced if it is controlled in such
a way that it cannot exceed 3,000 r.p.m. even though it is designed to operate up to

speeds of 6,000 r.p.m. Finally, the designer can build redundancy into his system. This involves duplicating parts of the system. In the event of failure, a second identical component will immediately replace the one that has failed. An example of redundancy is an emergency power generator at a hospital which would provide power in the operating theatre in the event of failure in the main grid. Where failure is simply not acceptable, for example, in spacecraft, second, third and even fourth redundancy components can be provided in all parts of the system. Under such circumstances, cost is a very subordinate factor compared with system reliability.

Reliability and Maintenance

The reliability of plant to keep running for extended periods of planned production will often depend on the maintenance procedures adopted. This is particularly the case for the continuous systems discussed in Chapter 8. The function of the maintenance system is to provide facilities to cope with machine breakdown and to operate planned maintenance to prevent disruption of production. All machine parts, buildings, etc. deteriorate with age and this is reflected in the final quality of the product even if total breakdown does not occur. In outline the objectives of maintenance are:

(1) the prevention of breakdowns to production equipment;
(2) minimization of the disruption to production caused when breakdowns occur.

The first of these objectives must be met through planned preventive maintenance procedures and the second through rapid response breakdown maintenance.

Preventive Maintenance

This involves the inspection of critical parts to identify potential trouble before it occurs and the servicing of equipment so that regular cleaning, adjustment and lubrication can reduce wear and the risk of breakdown. Regular inspection by the machine operator is probably the most effective method of preventing unplanned breakdown. Regular servicing on a predetermined schedule is often the responsibility of the operator concerned.

The main problem of preventive maintenance is the establishment of a planned maintenance procedure. It is pointless and needlessly expensive to over-maintain equipment as this involves direct expenditure and may involve lost production. A balance must be struck between the cost of planned maintenance and the risks incurred by less frequent maintenance. This will usually require an accumulation of maintenance data on specific items of equipment in order to monitor the distribution of the time between breakdowns. This itself will be modified over time by any planned maintenance which is carried out.

In semicontinuous operations, e.g. the vehicle assembly line, it is often possible to schedule planned maintenance outside the normal production time though this usually involves a labour cost premium. In continuous process plants either a total shutdown is required or the use of inter-stage storage facilities and/or parallel equipment is necessary.

If a preventive maintenance programme for a single machine is operated in which the maintenance interval, i.e. the time between maintenance, is short compared with the average time between breakdown, then operating efficiency will be low because of the time spent on maintenance. As the interval is increased then more breakdowns will occur. However, if the time between breakdowns is very uncertain the overall efficiency will increase. It is, therefore, only worth using preventive maintenance if breakdown is relatively predictable. Morse (1958) discusses this issue in detail. In practice the problem of the maintenance department is often complicated. They must determine the total number of maintenance workers required and their assignment between planned maintenance and unscheduled repair for machines which have varying use patterns and breakdown behaviour. This is an area where quantitive analysis has been of little real value and where a good maintenance manager is invaluable.

Breakdown Maintenance

The sophistication of the repair procedures used will depend on the cost of a breakdown when it occurs. There is often criticism of a maintenance team who sit around playing cards all day. Yet in many palnts, particularly those which must shut down more or less totally even for planned maintenance, this is exactly what management really want. If the maintenance team are working the plant is not producing. It is true that in the past union demarcation disputes have been the cause of overmanning, e.g. a maintenance fitter may not be allowed to touch electrical installations even though he could easily be trained to repair them, and in many plants this may still be a prime area for productivity bargaining. However, such situations are becoming less prevalent. The typical maintenance team in continuous plants is now geared to short periods of intensive activity to rectify a breakdown interspersed with long periods of apparent inactivity.

In a more general purpose production facility, e.g. a machine shop, it is usually possible to transfer operators to other machines while repairs are carried out, so that loss of production is relatively minor. This is particularly the case when machines outnumber operators by a substantial margin. In such situations breakdowns are obviously less critical and machines may be left to wait the attention of a maintenance man for relatively long periods.

Controlling Quality in the Manufacturing Process

Quality control can be carried out at three separate stages. The first stage involves ensuring that raw materials and components purchased from other organizations are to the standard specified. The second stage involves checking the manufacture of components and assemblies as they are being made within the company's own manufacturing organization. Finally, completed products can be tested in the factory or in the operating environment to ensure that they are able to perform to specification. To inspect all raw materials, components, sub-assemblies and finished products exhaustively would be prohibitive in cost terms. Equally, to carry out no inspection and simply to rely on the inherent quality of the material and workmanship is likely to result in an unacceptable level of poor quality items.

It has already been stated that variation in products is inevitable. This is true no matter how good the workmanship employed on the product. The fundamental cause of variability lies in the fact that the machines and processes used to make the parts are themselves subject to wear and tear. This means that a constant dimension can never be produced. Unless machines are constantly readjusted, dimensions will gradually move outside accepted limits. Materials of all kinds are subject to imperfections. Human concentration can never be 100% throughout the working day. Thus, unacceptable quality in a small proportion of items produced is inevitable. The successful management of quality during manufacture involves devising procedures which identify the great majority of below quality items, but does not add excessively to the total cost of the manufacturing system. The application of statistical sampling to quality control has given rise to a subject area generally termed statistical quality control. Adequate references to this topic are given at the end of this chapter. The basic ideas underlying these schemes are as follows.

Acceptance Sampling

This is the technique used to ensure that components, sub-assemblies or finished products are not passed on to the next stage of manufacture or used if an unacceptably high proportion of the batch is outside the specified quality limit. A 100% sampling procedure should, theoretically, ensure that no defective unit is passed on to the next stage. In practice, even 100% sampling does not guarantee that no defective items are passed by the inspection procedure. Where inspection procedures involve human operators, their task is often very tedious and subject to inspector error. Other circumstances which make 100% inspection unacceptable include destructive testing, unacceptable time delays and deterioration through excessive handling.

In a sampling inspection process, a small sample is taken and on the basis of the number of faulty items found in the sample, the whole batch is either accepted or rejected. The design of the sampling scheme will involve:

(1) The definition of an acceptable quality level. This is the quality level which the user of the items requires and the sampling scheme must be such that any batch which is within this quality level has a high probability of passing the inspection test.
(2) The definition of an unacceptable quality level. This is the percentage defective level at which the user would wish to reject a batch. The sampling scheme must

give a low probability that such batches will be passed by the inspection process.

No sampling scheme is perfect. There will always be some risk that an acceptable batch will be rejected (generally referred to as the producers risk) and that an unacceptable batch will be accepted (generally referred to as the consumers risk). A sampling scheme can be devised based on a definition of the acceptable and unacceptable quality levels and the percentage chance of the producers' and consumers' risks. This will indicate the size of sample required and the acceptable number of defects in the sample for a given batch size.

This procedure is a single acceptance sampling plan which is essentially a go/no go procedure. Multiple sampling procedures can also be devised which provide a 'may-be' option as well as the go/no go options. In this type of scheme, a batch is accepted if the number of rejects in the first sample falls below a specified level or it is rejected if the number of rejects is above a higher limit. If the number of rejects falls between the two limits, a second sample is taken. Again, upper and lower limits are specified for the total sample size (i.e. the first and second sample) and again, a decision is taken. The inspector will continue to take samples until the number of rejects for the total sample taken either falls to an acceptable level or rises above the unacceptable level. This scheme is illustrated in Figure 26.

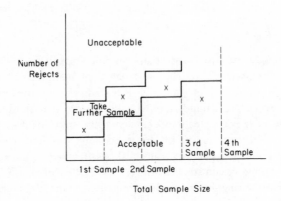

Figure 26   Sequential sampling procedure

Control Charts

Control charts are an inspection procedure designed to ensure that an acceptable quality is maintained during the production of items. Their purpose is to keep within acceptable limits the inevitable variations which occur during manufacture. Thus, the process itself is being kept under control during manufacture. The distinction should be recognized here between obtaining quality through maintaining ongoing control of the process and obtaining quality by inspection of components, assemblies etc. after the process is completed. Control charts can be used to control physical variables such as dimensions and attributes, e.g. surface finish. The use of control charts involves:

(1) Determining the characteristics to be controlled.
(2) Establishing a desired average value and the extent to which deviations above and below that value are acceptable.
(3) Ensuring that operating the process within these limits is economically viable.

When the desired average and upper and lower limits have been determined, a control chart and sampling procedure can be designed which will keep the process within the desired limits.

Where control charts are used to control dimensions, their use involves taking small samples of output at predetermined intervals, calculating the mean and range, i.e. the difference between the maximum and minimum value of the sample and plotting these on the appropriate control chart. Usually, both the mean and range of a dimension are controlled, since the movement of either may represent the production of unacceptable quality items.

Where attributes are being controlled, small samples are also taken and the number or percentage of defective items in the sample are established and the figure is plotted on the control chart.

When the points plotted on control charts fall outside the upper or lower acceptable limits, action must be taken to control the process. This may involve stopping and resetting the machine producing the items. The advantage of the technique is that it is usually possible to see that a process is gradually moving out of control as successive samples are plotted on the control chart. Thus corrective action can be taken before any items of unacceptable quality are produced.

The Successful Management of Quality

The management of any manufacturing organization will invariably declare that it is their intention to produce the highest possible quality of product commensurate with their resources and the cost of the product in the market place. Generally, considerable attention is paid to establishing programmes in the manufacturing process. Nonetheless, decisions are often taken without consideration of how they may eventually affect quality.

Typical actions which can result in reduced product quality are:

(1) Alteration of good, functional design for a visually more appealing design.
(2) Periodic design changes which do not allow adequate time for complete product evaluation before market exposure.
(3) Testing and inspection procedures which do not realistically reflect actual use situations.
(4) Arbitrary material substitution by the purchasing or manufacturing departments, without adequate engineering evaluation.
(5) Crash design revisions to incorporate new features in existing designs with minimum tooling changes.

(6) Errors in installation and service by personnel not in the manufacturer's employ.

(7) Reluctance on the part of production employees to reduce their incentive bonus by identifying below quality material.

(8) Failure to apply the same evaluation methods and safety criteria to purchased components as are applied to internally manufactured components.

(9) Incompatibility of the product with other materials with which the product will come in contact.

(10) Failure to anticipate misapplication of the product by the user.

(11) Too little consideration given to the wide variance in the physical and intellectual abilities of customers.

(12) Interpretation of the statistical quality control function as absolute quality assurance rather than a basis for action.

(13) Implementation of cost reduction methods and processes which require compromises in materials and manufacturing methods.

(14) Inadequate labelling advising the user of hazards or safety procedures related to the product.

(15) Inadequate packaging resulting in damaged, malfunctioning, or contaminated products.

(16) Failure of personnel to be aware of applicable codes, laws, and regulations.

Responsibility for Quality Control

The application of industrial engineering concepts which have led to job simplification have also resulted in the separation of the man doing a job and the man responsible for the quality of that job. In many organizations, quality is seen as the responsibility of a separate group of people, inspectors, who belong to a department which may not fall under the direct control of manufacturing line management. This system arises from the notion that the maintenance of adequate quality standards and the need to produce the required volume of output can lead to conflict. In such a conflict, pressures for output will override the maintenance of proper quality standards. By making quality control a separate, independent activity, these pressures can be resisted. The converse, however, is that if responsibility for quality is removed, the operator will lose interest in maintaining quality. This can result in a greater total cost for achieving a given quality level.

The advent of job enrichment has produced arguments for returning responsibility for quality to the operator carrying out the work. This, it is argued, both gives additional pride in performing the job properly and removes one element of control. Where inspection procedures involve straightforward tasks, like visual inspection or simple dimensional checks and they can easily be sequenced with work operations, returning inspection to the basic job is desirable. Where inspection procedures are more complex, perhaps requiring expensive equipment, it may not be possible to return inspection to each operator without additional expenditure. However, if the work is organized on a group basis, it may be possible to incorporate inspection within the work group's set of tasks.

It is appropriate at this point to discuss the issue of remuneration and quality. In traditional work systems where incentive payments operate, theoretically, payment is only made for work of acceptable quality. If an inspector discovers work of inadequate quality, it must be rectified by the operator responsible without payment, or, if it cannot be rectified, no credit is given for carrying out the job in the first instance. In theory this is sound, but in practice it rarely happens. There are several reasons for this. These are:

(1) It may be difficult to identify with certainty the operator responsible for the substandard work. This is often the case in a multistage process where poor work at one stage could result from slightly substandard work at a previous stage.

(2) The work flow procedure may not allow a particular operator to spend time rectifying work previously carried out. To take the operator responsible for the substandard work out of the line would cause major disruption to work flow. In such situations, work is usually rectified by a special operator paid on a day-wage system.

(3) The onus of proof that a particular operator carried out substandard work will rest with the inspector. By pointing out unsatisfactory work, the inspector is reducing the wages of the people he works with on a day by day basis. This is likely to cause conflict and resentment. Many inspectors will simply not be prepared to face such a situation. Thus, even though the operator responsible may rectify bad work, he is likely to be given further credit for the time spent so doing.

Management must therefore seek to minimize the conflict between the 'doing' activity and the inspection activity. To embrace both activities with the same person would appear to achieve this end. However, any payment system which is based on an incentive related purely to output can create conflict within the individual. Indeed, a major problem faced when seeking to place responsibility for inspection back with the operator, is devising a suitable payment system. The problem may be helped by changing to a measured day wage system.

Conclusion

The quality and reliability of an item must be defined as a basic part of the specification of the product. Many aspects of quality and reliability can be expressed in objective and measurable terms but certain aspects will always be subjective and based on users' opinions. While most organizations would prefer to make perfect products, in reality, the achievement of very high levels of quality and reliability are extremely expensive. Variation in the quality of manufactured items is inevitable and managerial decisions must therefore be made about the standards of quality and reliability which will be achieved and the cost which will be incurred in meeting these standards.

When quality and reliability standards have been defined, it is the task of operating management to achieve these levels within predetermined cost limits.

Complete inspection of all components, sub-assemblies and finished products is unlikely to be acceptable from a cost standpoint except where the consequences of failure are extreme or the product is very high priced. Management must therefore devise inspection procedures which are based on sampling theory. Fortunately, these concepts are now well developed and it is possible to maintain adequate levels of quality control by inspecting a relatively small proportion of the total items produced.

No matter how well quality control systems are devised, their ultimate effectiveness depends on the attitudes of the workforce towards maintaining desired quality standards. Although there are strong arguments for separating responsibility for quality from the line operating function, it must be recognized that doing so creates potential conflict on the shop floor. Responsibility for quality is one of the areas being affected by changing attitudes towards the role of the shop floor workforce. The trend appears to be that of placing responsibility for quality back with the workforce, particularly if this does not require large additional capital expenditure. It may be necessary, however, to accompany this change with changes in the wage payments system, moving from piecework-based to day wage-based systems.

Reference

Morse, P. M. (1958) *Queues, Inventories and Maintenance*, Wiley, London.

Further Reading

Brook, R. M. J. (1972) *Reliability Concepts in Engineering Manufacture*, Butter-worths, London.

Fetter, R. B. (1967) *The Quality Control System*, R. D. Irwin, Homewood, Ill.

Miles, L. O. (1972) *Techniques of Value Analysis and Engineering*, McGraw-Hill, New York. (2nd edition)

Nixon, F. (1971) *Managing to Achieve Quality and Reliability*, McGraw-Hill, London.

Oughton, F. (1969) *Value Analysis and Value Engineering*, Pitman, London.

Smith, C. S. (1969) *Quality and Reliability; An Integrated Approach*, Pitman, London.

CHAPTER 7

Production Planning and Control

Introduction

Production planning is setting the level of future manufacturing operations. The production plan must take account both of demand forecasts and the requirements for and availability of men, machines, materials and money. It will not specify precisely the products to be made, but it will state capacity requirements. The *Production programme* will specify detailed product requirements. This will be for a shorter period than the production plan; it will be the basis for short term planning and control.

Production control means directing items through the production process, from the requisitioning of raw materials to the delivery of the finished product. It should ensure satisfactory customer service, minimum inventory investment and maximum manufacturing efficiency. Production control necessarily includes inventory control.

Production Planning

The long term production plan will be based on forecasts of future requirements. In the short term, such plans may act as a constraint on the detailed planning necessary to achieve product output or customer delivery dates. It is necessary to ensure that high level planning, while providing guidelines for short term control, should not be too restrictive. Moreover, it is essential that feedback on actual performance should be used as a guide to the feasibility of long term production plans.

It is often assumed that because poor performance, like bad customer delivery, low labour utilization etc., is picked up at a low level, the fault is at a low level. However, it may well be that the real problem is in the long term production plan. Perhaps there is insufficient capacity of the right kind, inefficient production layout or an unrealistic inventory policy. These are all matters over which low level planners have little influence.

Policy planning means ensuring that the manufacturing system meets the company's marketing objectives. (See Chapter 14 for further discussions.) This will necessitate a *Production Stage Chart* showing corporate policy decisions concerning customer delivery periods and the location of stock holding points within the manufacturing process. Some companies will want to sell at least some products

92

'off the shelf', thus requiring a finished stock policy. On the other hand, a large one-off construction project will have a delivery period which includes not only the procurement time for all the materials required, but also any necessary design time. Often, a competitive delivery date can be offered only if some part of the total manufacturing cycle is already completed. This may mean stockpiling raw materials, components and bought-out items against possible future orders.

A production chart must be based on realistic estimates of the time taken to procure materials, purchase items, manufacture and assemble products and complete the necessary design work. Estimates must be based on current operations; possible improvements may be effected later. The various activities can then be represented diagrammatically as in Figure 27. If the total production time lies within an acceptable delivery time (rarely the case), then production orders only need to be initiated against firm customer orders (though there may be considerable pressure to increase efficiency by increasing batch size). More often, it

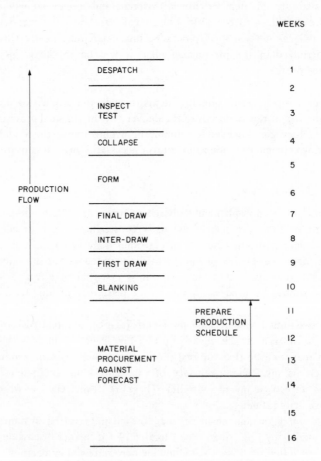

Figure 27   A production stage chart for the manufacture of metal bellows

will be necessary to operate policy stockholding points as described above, at stages in the chart.

Strategic planning. Within the framework of the delivery and stockholding policies specified by the production stage chart, it must be decided whether the given lead time is realistic. In a company where customer orders require some processing (rather than being issued from finished goods stock), there is clearly a limit to the volume of orders which can be accepted on a specified lead time. The lead times built into the chart are themselves dependent on assumptions about the load on the manufacturing facilities. If too many orders are accepted, there will be insufficient capacity and orders will be late. If the throughput time of the production facilities is to be controlled, it is usually necessary to hold such a backlog outside the physical production facilities as a paper 'order book', a point we raise again in Chapter 13. The use of commitment acceptance procedures does, however, assume that capacity planning has been carried out with the aim of matching forecast workload with available capacity. Strategic planning decisions are required which determine the available capacity. This requires a long term forecast which takes account of:

(1) Market growth/contraction.
(2) The sensitivity of the market to the economic climate (business cycles).
(3) The rate of technological change in the production process.
(4) The relative profitability of different product lines using similar facilities.
(5) The rate of product innovation.
(6) Capital availability and funding commitments.

The function of capacity planning is to ensure that the business can take advantage of expected sales opportunities.

The capacity plan must establish forecasts of future sales patterns and ensure that they can be converted into production capacity requirements. If 'capacity' and 'load' can be expressed in the same terms, e.g. tons of steel or number of electric motors produced, then this conversion involves few problems. In general, however, the load will be in terms of a number of very different products requiring varying amounts of capacity. A detailed specification of the load may only be possible at the 'standard hours' level. The comparison will then be more complex.

The time required for capacity changes must be carefully considered. While additional standard machine tools may be readily available at short notice, it will take time to procure specially built facilities. Moreover, it will not usually be possible or desirable to balance projected sales consistently against capacity and this will complicate the process. In highly seasonal businesses like garment manufacture, ice cream production etc., it will be necessary to agree a capacity level in conjunction with an inventory policy. This will level the production load and prevent long periods of underloading. In such industries, the production programme will not follow the sales forecast but will be buffered from it by anticipation inventories (stock built for future sales). Similarly, in a capital goods industry where business activity follows the trade cycle, the provision of sufficient capacity to meet 'peak cycle demand' without building up a backlog will involve considerable excess capacity during the slack part of the cycle.

The production budget and the capacity plan must obviously be compatible. In theory, the capacity plan should be the result of an analysis of budgetted sales and capital expenditure. However, the production plan would then take too long to prepare. It is usually necessary to make a broad production plan first and to modify the detailed budget as required.

Planning to Meet Seasonal Demand

Chapter 2 discussed the problem of balancing sales and capacity in the make-for-stock company. (A typical situation is illustrated in Figure 10.) Magee and Boodman (1967) distinguish two types of seasonal planning problem:

(1) Normal seasonal patterns which are reasonably predictable but which give wide variations.
(2) Short 'peak season' sales which are highly uncertain such as those which occur in the toy industry and in fashion wear. The uncertainty here is concentrated in a very short sales period when there is little freedom of action in the production programme.

The main decisions in case 1 concern the level of safety stock to be allowed at times of minimum inventory during the production/sales cycle and the setting of the production plan in order to achieve the desired stock building policy. The production plan must consider the demand for each item to be produced on a given set of facilities, the relative costs of stockholding and capacity variation and the possible effect of variations in demand levels. Continuous monitoring of the plan and adjustment will be necessary.

The more complex decisions in case 2 require an assessment of the business risk involved in alternative policies. If insufficient stocks are built, demand will not be met. The result will be either lost sales or costly special runs. On the other hand, if too much stock is built, obsolescence costs may be high or it will be necessary to store items until the next selling season; in fashion goods, they will usually have to be sold off cheaply.

It is often possible for the manufacturer to pass on some of this risk to his customers by offering attractive sales terms for advance orders, and indeed it is usually essential for large customers to order early to safeguard their supplies of, for instance, winter coats or summer dresses. There are, for example, some gramaphone record distributors who operate solely by taking such risks on items with uncertain demand. The best the manufacturer can do in these cases is to attempt to minimize the risk of loss.

Many service industries operate in markets with very similar characteristics to the 'peak sales' case. Most service products are 'unstorable' so that production smoothing does not apply. The system of reserving airline seats above capacity has received some attention recently as the result of court actions by passengers turned away. However, it is clear that if reservations are only accepted up to capacity and cancellations occur at the 'average' rate, then the aircraft will usually fly below capacity. This means lost profit for the airline and disappointed customers who would have been able to book. On the other hand, if bookings are accepted above capacity and few cancellations occur, some passengers holding firm reservations will be unable to fly.

Tactical Planning

Tactical planning has two main facets.

(1) There is a need for technical decisions related to process or operations planning, i.e. the specification of the production process and the order in which processing operations are to be carried out.
(2) There is a continuing need for low level scheduling of jobs and facilities, i.e. the planning of the actual flow of jobs in the manufacturing system.

In jobbing engineering production, formal process planning may not be necessary, such decisions being left to the workshop foremen. On the other hand, chemical processing plant will usually have process planning built into its design. In the batch component production system, formal process planning will usually be carried out by central production engineering staff.

Low level scheduling may involve the preparation of loading plans which specify the stop/start times of each job on each facility. This is intended to utilize the equipment fully, while achieving adequate progression of jobs. The preparation of such schedules requires a method for loading within capacity constraints. Relative priorities must also be specified. In practice, such detailed planning is rarely justified in functionally organized systems but will be a necessary requirement in line organization, since it amounts to a translation of the strategic plan into physical production rates.

Production Control

As we have defined it, production control is concerned with ensuring that production plans are achieved. There can be no question of control without such a plan. The initiation of production orders is necessarily a principal factor in such control which will therefore include the functions of materials management discussed in previous chapters. In particular it will include:

(1) Direct ordering procedures,
(2) Material requirements planning, and/or
(3) Inventory control procedures,

since these will be responsible for the generation of production orders.
    In addition, production control will include the following functions:

(1) The sequence of jobs — dispatching
(2) Monitoring of job progress — progress control.
(3) Ensuring adequate supplies of materials/components — shortage control.

These are discussed in relation to batch production in Chapter 10. Here we consider the role of production control in other types of production.

In continuous flow or line production systems, the sequencing of individual jobs is often unnecessary beyond the initial operation because of the unidirectional nature of the flow. In functionally organized systems it is not only necessary to have some means of deciding the order in which jobs should be processed at a facility, but it is also usually necessary to initiate the transfer of work from one facility to another. Although in flow production it may be unnecessary to control the sequencing of items between work facilities, the overall capacity of multiproduct lines is often affected by the sequence in which batches of different products are processed. For example, in the filling of tubes of artists' paints there are often preferred colour sequences in which batches should be run in order to minimize line cleaning time. Similar situations arise in paper making, steelrolling, textile cutting etc. In such cases, it is necessary to determine the 'best' sequence for the processing of batches either in terms of capacity utilization or material losses.

In mass production systems, the nature of the ordering procedure is usually something of a mixture of a requirements plan and a set of stock replenishment orders. Since the production plan is fixed (at least temporarily) some time in advance and demand is relatively continuous, the usual ordering procedure is to specify a 'call off' schedule covering long term future requirements. However, actual delivery requirements may be varied at short notice as a result of constraints on the final production line. For example, suppliers of components to car factories have to be prepared to switch their own production lines over to alternative models if the final assembly line plans are suddenly changed. Traditionally, stock control has played a key role in batch production systems. It is stock control which governs the load on production facilities, though as we have seen, material requirements planning techniques are usually far more relevant to such systems.

Progress control and shortage control are fairly straightforward procedures in flow production because of the relatively small variety of items produced. In batch production, as we shall see in Chapter 10, progress control is crucial to the achievement of delivery dates because it is usually impractical to produce detailed plans which have even a reasonable possibility of being met.

The Role of Computer Systems in Production Planning and Control

The vast amount of data involved in the day to day operation of the production system has made production planning and control a prime target for computerization, and initially, much was hoped for in this area. Data is available concerning:

(1) Product bills-of-material,
(2) Inventory records,
(3) Process (operations list) sequences,
(4) Work in process records,
(5) Standard cost data,
(6) Open orders.

In practice, while the computer has had considerable impact in data storage and in the areas in which decisions can be 'standardized' and programmed (primarily demand forecasting and inventory control) it has had relatively little impact on the production control problem faced by most job and batch manufacturing systems.

The main functions served by currently available computer production control systems are:

(1) Order analysis, including parts explosion and material requirements planning.
(2) Stock control, including stock recording and re-order point control.
(3) Work-in-process reporting, including job progress recording.
(4) Shop loading including loading with or without restrictions on capacity availability.
(5) Dispatching, including production of sequence lists for sets of facilities.
(6) Performance analysis, including recording of performance.

(1), (2) and (3) can be and have been successfully computerized. Indeed, it is not usually feasible to attempt parts explosion or material requirements planning without data processing facilities. However, (4) and (5) have benefitted little from the sophisticated scheduling packages which have been produced by most of the major computer companies and by many consulting organizations. Item (6), performance analysis, has apparently been successfully included as part of the management information generated by such packages but the performance measurements recorded, e.g. facility utilization, delivery performance etc. have tended to be too naive to be of use. It is certainly true that the computer offers the greatest hope for recording the data necessary to assess performance in such complex systems, but the actual data analysis may well be carried out quite independently of the operating system.

The greatest benefits in computerization will come from the automation of:

(1) Materials requirements planning/parts explosion, loading without capacity restrictions, and
(2) Stock control (if separate from MRP).

However, unless there are very special circumstances, loading within capacity constraints, stop/start time scheduling and the dispatching function are probably best left well alone.

There has been growing interest in recent years in the use of on-line systems, mainly for data recording. Although the ability to 'simulate' the effects of possible decisions has been improved by on-line and terminal facilities, the costs of using any but the simplest decision rules tend to be high. However, there is considerable benefit to be had from being able to prepare a number of possible load plans, unconstrained by capacity and based on different delivery schedules. In particular, these may be used at a high level to assess the impact of delivery quotations on potential orders, an area of great importance where real analysis is rarely done.

Conclusion

We have reviewed the role of production planning and control in a variety of organizational structures and market conditions. In succeeding chapters we shall be considering particular forms of production systems and will return to many of the points raised here in more depth. Production planning and control are necessary functions in all production systems but their relative importance and complexity will vary greatly from case to case. In plant dominated systems, particularly continuous flow processes, planning will be most important, the control function being largely automatic and governed by technological factors. In functionally organized systems detailed planning is almost impossible and the control function dominates. Computer systems have promised much, but achieved relatively little in applications involving complex decision making. Their main use is likely to remain in the processing of large amounts of data.

Reference

Magee, J. F. and Boodman, D. M. (1967) *Production Planning and Inventory Control*, McGraw-Hill, New York (2nd Edition).

Further Reading

Burbidge, J. L. (1971) *Production Planning*, Heinemann, London.

Greene, J. M. (Ed.) (1970) *Production and Inventory Control Handbook*, McGraw-Hill/APICS, New York.

NCC (1973) Factfinder 13, Production Control Packages and Computer Guide 9, Production Control, National Computing Centre Publications, Manchester.

Plossl, G. W. and Wight, O. W. (1967) *Production and Inventory Control*, Prentice-Hall, Englewood Cliffs, New Jersey, USA.

Wight, O. W. (1974) *Production and Inventory Management in the Computer Age*, Gower Press, Epping, Essex.

CHAPTER 8

Managing the Process — Continuous Systems

Introduction

The perfect continuous system is one which operates 24 hours a day, 7 days a week, 52 weeks a year, producing a steady flow of product to the required specification. Regrettably, no manmade plant is capable of this type of operation. The nearest approach to such a plant is the petrochemical plant which processes one or more crude oils on a continuous basis into a range of end products.

A wide variety of plants do, however, approach this type of operation. For example, electricity generation is a continuous operation although the load required from a given power station may vary considerably throughout the day. The production of paper, glass and cement involves continuous process operations, although, from time to time, the set up of the system may have to be changed to produce a different quality product. Continuous systems are also used more and more in the production of foods. The brewing industry is similar to certain types of chemical industry processes. Here, the plant is in continuous operation but a specific batch is processed for an extended period of time. The steel industry is a complex mixture of continuous operations which produce batches at intervals and continuous operations through which the product flows. Blast furnaces and basic oxygen furnaces operate continuously but produce batches at intervals rather than a steady output. The processing of semifinished and finished products is intermittent in that a slab, for example, might be rolled once every ten seconds although it may take a minute for the slab itself to go down the rolling mill. Thus, the rolling mill taken as a whole may be in a continuous operation but between slabs, the operation of a single stand is intermittent. Ideally, the processing of steel after casting should be entirely continuous since this would eliminate cooling and reheating, thus resulting in great savings. During the past ten years, a considerable amount of work has been undertaken throughout the world to develop the continuous casting and rolling of steel as one operation.

As this example from the steel industry implies, most of the so-called continuous industries constantly strive to achieve the ideal. These industries are, however, faced with a set of operating problems which are different from those associated with batch manufacturing industries. Such industries are highly capital intensive. They can normally only add to capacity in major incremental steps, each of which requires additional large capital investment. Profitable operation often demands that the plant be run at output levels relatively near total plant capacity on a three shift basis, seven days a week, fifty weeks a year. This can present major problems in the area of plant maintenance. Raw material costs are frequently very high and it is therefore important that the plant makes as efficient a conversion as possible from the raw material to the finished product. This requires extremely complex systems of control. The remainder of this chapter discusses these problems in further detail.

Plant Capacity

Manufacturing capacity in continuous process industries tends to be concentrated in a relatively small number of companies within a given industry. One of the major reasons for this concentration has been the economies of scale which have accompanied the introduction of ever larger plants. As the plants have grown larger, the capital investment required has grown accordingly, thus limiting the number of organizations capable of providing the necessary capital. However, this has also meant that the incremental increase in capacity has become greater and greater. This means that the risks associated with incorrect forecasts of demand have also increased. Equally, the cost penalties of running plants at outputs well below rated capacity have also risen.

Except where monopolies exist, a severe problem arises each time market demand outstrips the manufacturing capacity. All companies serving a given market are likely to interpret future demand in much the same way and conclude that additional capacity will be required. It is likely, however, that if each company serving the market builds a plant which is considered to be economic in size, there will immediately be an over-provision of capacity. Then, each company will strive to increase its market share in order to run the new plant at an efficient level. Generally speaking, the only mechanism available for increasing market share is reduction in price. Such price reductions will further contribute to the difficulties of running the new plant at a profitable level of output. Logic would argue that when new capacity is required, not all companies engaged in the market should build a new plant. However, short of collusion and agreement as to whose turn it will be to build (actions against the law in most Western economies), it is improbable that any one company will stand by and watch the others create new capacity which could give a permanent advantage in market share. There seems, therefore, an inevitability of a movement from under-provision to over-provision of capacity for many products which require large scale continuous plant for their manufacture.

Capital Expenditure for Continuous Processes

The requirement for high capital expenditures, and the risks associated with mistakes, imply that a company engaged in this type of manufacturing will develop sophisticated forecasting and capital expenditure appraisal techniques. The investment decision for a new plant is extremely complex. Such a decision will involve a collaborative effort between the financial, marketing and operations activities in the business. The following outline poses some of the questions which should be asked and answered.

Origin of Proposal

Is the proposal a complete new plant for an existing product? Is it required to remove a bottleneck in an existing process or is it a plant for a new product? If it is a new product, what is the basic reason for extending the business?

Sales Estimates

What is the forecast for the home market for the next few years? How do these estimates compare with experiences in other European countries and in the USA? What is the product used for? Which industries use it? Who will be the major customers and how will the market be broken down between these customers?

What share of the home and export market will be obtained? What are the strengths and weaknesses of existing competitive products? Who are the existing and potential competitors? How will they react to the introduction of increased capacity?

In the case of a new product, what are the advantages of it over the existing products and why can it expect to be substituted for them? What will be the technical/price advantages? What will be the impact of economic cycles on the operation of the plant?

Prices

What prices are forecast and on what basis? What is the price history of the product? How do the proposed prices compare with those in other major producing countries? What assumptions have been made regarding the impact of inflation on prices? What tariffs exist and how will these affect imports and exports? Are there possibilities of dumping by other countries?

Quality

Are sales sensitive to product quality to any significant extent? Will the product be better/worse in quality than competitors' products?

Process

Why has this particular process been selected? What are the competitive processes? Why have they been rejected? What are the relative capital and production costs for the chosen and rejected processes? What are the chances of technical obsolescence within the proposed plant life? Is the process a new one? Is there a significant risk that it will not be operational within the forecast time scale? Is the patent position secure?

Plant Size

Why has the proposed site been chosen? What are the variations in capital operating costs for different plant sizes and levels of output? How big are competitive plants? What problems of scale are anticipated? What will be the impact on operating costs and profitability of running the new plant at less than anticipated output levels?

Plant Location

Why has the proposed location been chosen? What alternatives were considered and what were their disadvantages?

Raw Materials, Utilities and By-products

What is the major source of raw materials? Is it protected? What is the position of competitors in relation to this and other sources of raw materials? What is the basis for the raw material price forecast? If raw materials are supplied from within the company, is sufficient capacity available or would further capital expenditure be required to support the new plant? What is the basis for the transfer price? Are there sufficient electricity/steam etc. facilities available within the existing complex for the new plant? Will additional capital be required to make them available? Will by-products be produced? If so, what are they, what are their uses and what sales revenue is forecast?

Research and Development Effort

Is the proposal dependent on continuing technology improvements? If so, how does the company research and development effort compare with that of major competitors?

Effluent

Will the new plant produce effluent problems? If so, how will these be dealt with? What additional capital expenditure will be required?

Manpower

Will the new plant require recruitment and training or will it create redundancies? What assumptions have been made in assessing future manpower costs?

Plant Life

What life has been assumed for the plant? Was this based on anticipated technological changes, improvements in engineering standards or product obsolescence? What is the effect of designing a plant with a shorter life?

Profitability

What is the return on capital, the DCF yield and the payback period? How does this compare with past performance for this product? What is the sensitivity of the financial calculations to changes in major assumption, e.g. capital cost, operating costs, start-up date, capacity level of operation? What is the total amount of money required and what is the timing of the requirement?

This type of analysis is obviously pertinent to all forms of capital expenditure on new plant. It is particularly emphasized here because the capital expenditure decision for continuous plant inevitably involves very large sums of money and is the most important operating decision taken.

The Role of Labour in the Continuous System

Continuous systems represent advanced levels of technology and automation. In most industries where continuous plants are in operation, there has been a long history of rundown in labour requirements. Capital investment and sales per employee are usually much higher than in other forms of manufacturing industry. Labour cost is, therefore, a relatively small item in the total cost stucture. Labour exists in the system to ensure that plant operation is maintained continuously and safely and at an appropriate quality level.

Generally speaking, labour falls into two main categories. The first group, often termed process workers, are those actually involved in the day to day operation of the plant. As a result of automation, particularly in the area of plant control (discussed below), process operators' jobs in many plants have been radically altered. While in the past they may have involved heavy physical work, often in adverse conditions, they now usually involve working in control rooms, the prime task being that of monitoring the overall performance of the system and taking action in the event of totally unexpected circumstances. Such jobs can be tedious and frequently do not require the skill formerly needed to operate the process manually. Under manual operation, control was often seen as an art which was only acquired over many years of experience. Operators would tend to work in gangs, progression through the gang taking many years. Leadership, however, bestowed considerable status

The second major group of operational personnel are those responsible for maintaining the plant in working order. This is a dual task. Firstly, the plant must be kept running throughout the fifty or so operational weeks of the year. This is usually accomplished by combining an emergency breakdown service with planned maintenance involving systematic overhaul of the plant by sections. Ideally, planned maintenance eliminates the need for breakdown maintenance, but in practice this is unlikely. The second major role of the maintenance group is carrying out the annual overhaul, usually completed in the weeks when the plant is closed for normal working. Generally, very careful planning of this annual maintenance is required to ensure that all the necessary tasks are carried out and plant start-up is not delayed. Managing this type of task is further discussed in Chapter 11. As plants become more complex, there is a tendency for the maintenance skills required to increase. This is particularly true in the area of electronics.

It can be seen therefore that there is a tendency for the skill requirements of one group of workers, the process workers, to decrease while that of the second group, the maintenance workers, increases. Both groups can experience periods of inactivity which result in boredom. Indeed, it can be argued that the more workers who are idle on a process plant the better. Their idleness indicates that the plant is operating properly without the need for human attention and intervention. Management is faced with a number of operational problems under these circumstances. Firstly, even though the size of the labour force is relatively small and represents a minor factor in overall costs, it is important to ensure that a correct balance of labour exists. Plant downtime must not be extended when emergencies occur through lack of labour, yet large numbers of men must not be constantly under-employed. Secondly, management is faced with the problem caused by the creation of jobs which basically involve dial watching and button pushing. These are unsatisfactory jobs and, where possible, should be eliminated through further extension of automatic control procedures. However, there is frequently a strong desire to keep some element of human control in the system. Process workers' loss of process knowledge can also present problems if the automatic control system breaks down and the skills do not exist to run the plant manually. Thus, there is the need to create flexibility amongst the members of the workforce. Traditionally, in many plants there have been clearly defined demarcations between tasks. This has been particularly true between the process workers and maintenance workers and between the various skilled trades amongst the maintenance group. Both for the sake of rapid action in the event of breakdown and to ensure reasonable manpower utilization, it is desirable to create flexibility between the various groups of the workforce.

Although numbers are often relatively small in continuous plants, the labour force can, nonetheless, exert considerable pressure. Because of the severe financial losses incurred in the advent of plant closure through the withdrawal of labour, labour demands are often readily acceded to. The desire, both to prevent disruption through labour disputes, and to obtain felexibility within the labour force, has resulted in a number of continuous operation industries negotiating productivity agreements. These have generally offered high levels of wages in return for collaboration across a wide range of manpower issues.

Safety, Environment and Continuous Plants

The issues of safety and the pollution of the environment must concern managers of all types of operations. However, continuous plants may well pose special problems in relation to these issues. The risk of explosion, no matter how remote, may in the future be a major factor in determining the location of certain types of chemical and petrochemical plants. There is likely to be increasing social pressure to ensure that they are not located near centres of population. The use of very high temperatures and large scale physical forces in such activities as glass and steel making demand cautious behaviour in the work situation. Water and air pollution and an unpleasant working environment are unfortunately all too common characteristics of many types of continuous process plants. There is now clear evidence that the control of water and airborne pollution will require increasing levels of capital expenditure which will show very little return when measured in conventional productivity terms. Management will constantly be faced with deciding between whether to provide minimum levels of pollution control as required by law or to exceed these levels in response to the demands of the local community. Legislation on pollution control tends to be limited and does not keep pace with requirements of the community. Yet, in exceeding these minimum requirements a company will be spending additional capital which its competitors may not see fit to spend. There is, therefore, some risk of creating a price disadvantage. Conversely, not exceeding the minimum requirements may result in the company being seen as socially irresponsible by the communities in which its plants are situated. This, in turn, may lead to difficulty in recruiting labour and poor relationships with the local community.

The Control of Continuous Processes

Complex control mechanisms have been built up in continuous process plants over several decades. Chemicals and petrochemicals are perhaps the outstanding examples. On the other hand, other processes, like paper making have continued to rely on the inherent skills of the operators, skills which have been acquired over many years of experience. In the past decade, major changes have taken place in control in all continuous industries through the introduction of the digital computer as a control device. The first applications took place in the later 1950s in the petrochemical, steel and power generation industries. By the mid 1960s, many other industries were experimenting with computer control. By 1970 there were approximately 5,000 installations on a worldwide basis. By 1975 this figure had probably passed 20,000. Two major factors have affected this rate of growth. Firstly, for individual companies and for particular types of application within an industry, computer control has moved from experimentation to a relatively well understood on-going exercise. Secondly, the advent of mini-computers greatly increased the range of situations which it was both feasible and economic to control by computer. The remainder of this chapter discusses aspects of, and problems associated with computer control systems.

The characteristics of a process which make it suitable for computer control are:

(1) Where a large volume of data must be recorded and analysed to maintain control of the process. Data volume may be large either because many variables must be scanned, or because some variables must be scanned very frequently.
(2) Where adequate instrumentation exists for measuring process variables. Computer control cannot be undertaken unless reliable instrumentation is available. This, on occasions, must be capable of withstanding extremely hostile environments.
(3) Where a process is well understood. The successful application of advanced control techniques requires understanding of the relationships between the process variables. Otherwise, computer models of the physical and chemical relationships of the process cannot be built. (However, the fact that a process is *not* fully understood can be a major positive reason for installing an on-line computer. This can record important process variables and explore interrelationships; ultimately, it may lead to the construction of a process model which makes computer process control possible.)
(4) Where the relationships between the process variables are complex. If the relationships between the variables are relatively straightforward, a human operator can carry out the necessary calculations to determine the appropriate control action. When the relationships are complex and speed of calculation is essential, the operator will require assistance in determining control action.
(5) Where accurate control is necessary. Control is fairly easy to maintain by conventional means when a process remains stable while variables move through a wide range. If, on the other hand, very small variations in certain variables cause the process to move out of control, extremely careful monitoring and quick corrective response is required.
(6) Where there will be high loss of sales revenue if a process moves out of control and starts producing off-specification material. If the resulting loss of sales revenue is small, then holding the manufacturing process under tight control may not be critical. However, if the production of off-specification material results in significant losses in sales revenue, it is desirable that the process be kept within the optimal zone, thus justifying computer control.
(7) Where the process is subject to frequent disturbance. A complex process which moves out of control slowly can probably be controlled by an off-line computer. However, if disturbances happen quickly and frequently, an on-line computer may be required to maintain control.
(8) Where computer control is economically viable. Normally, it is worth considering computer control only in plants with a large throughput, and several remaining years of operating life. Computer control is only justifiable if it represents a sound economic proposition for the plant as a whole.

The computer can be used to monitor different categories of equipment and process variables. These are:

(1) INSTRUMENT STATUS AND PROCESS VARIABLES. The computer is capable of detecting whether instruments are functioning properly by comparing readings from a series of instruments, measuring interconnected variables and checking for consistency.

Process variables are measured and checked against predetermined limits to ensure that the process is not moving out of control. Output data can be presented directly, or smoothed and presented as trends over time.

(2) EQUIPMENT STATUS. The computer can be used to measure variables such as bearing temperatures and pressure differences across pumps. This type of measurement permits identification of such problems as overheating, mechanical wear and leaks before they become serious. This helps reduce maintenance costs and loss of throughput from breakdowns.

(3) PRODUCT STATUS. In some processes, the use of a computer directly linked to such instruments as spectographs and chromatographs, permits on-line measurement of product quality. Variations in product quality can be rapidly discovered and control action taken.

Control Levels

Digital computers can be used to provide a range of control levels which are classified below:

(1) DATA LOGGING AND ANALYSIS. Data logging involves recording the value of variables. This is not strictly a control activity. Computer analysis of recorded data may take place either on-line or off-line. Data may be used for quality control purposes or to explore possible relationships between variables. This may lead to the construction of a model of the process.

(2) DATA DISPLAY, OPERATOR ALARM, AND OPEN LOOP CONTROL. Computer control systems can display process variable values to operating personnel. Values may be displayed at predetermined intervals or may only be available if specifically requested by the operator. The computer may also perform calculations on the data. At the simplest level, values may be compared with upper and lower acceptable limits to ensure that they fall within the required range. If a value is outside the range, or if the trend of the readings suggests it will shortly move out of the range, the computer can give a visible or audible alarm to the process operator.

At a more advanced level, the computer may carry out calculations based on a number of variable readings. It can then offer advice to the operator on action required to achieve a specific end product or to maintain control. The operator can decide whether to accept the advice. This system is known as open loop control.

(3) PREPLANNED SEQUENTIAL CONTROL. Sequential control can be carried out by computer. When a process has to go through a long series of steps to reach a required condition, the computer can guide it through each step,

measuring all the appropriate variables to ensure that control has been maintained. This application is commonly used for the start up and shut down of power generation plants.

(4) IMPROVED PLANT PERFORMANCE OR REGULATORY CONTROL This level of control uses techniques which yield improved plant performance by holding plant balance. The principal control techniques are:

(a) *Feedback control.* Here, variables associated with the output of a process, or part of a process, are measured. If they fall outside predetermined limits, input variables are corrected. The problem with this type of control is that the output moves out of specification before action is taken. Some poor quality output is therefore inevitable before the process is brought back under control.

(b) *Feed forward control.* Here, the control strategy is to anticipate and prevent deviations. When an upstream variable implies that off--specification material will be produced, settings for downstream variables are altered to counteract this. If feed forward control is successful, no off-specification material is produced.

(c) *Multivariable control.* The computer calculates control action on an integrated basis, taking account of a range of variables. For this to be done, the mathematical relationships between the variables must be understood.

(5) OPTIMIZING CONTROL. In the control methods so far described, the computer is concerned with achieving the desired variable values. In optimizing control, the computer is concerned with the economic implications of the control actions it formulates. The computer is given values of process and economic variables and optimises profit or minimizes cost. To achieve this, a model of the control process must be built within the computer.

(6) DIRECT DIGITAL CONTROL (DDC). This is a method of regulating process variables. It does not represent a specific level of control. In computer control, the principal process variables are usually regulated by independent feedback control systems employing continuous analog computing technology. With DDC, the digital computer communicates directly with the process through analog/digital and digital/analog converters, thus eliminating the analog control equipment. It is claimed that this provides greater flexibility in control system design, and permits more complex control strategies to be employed.

Benefits Attributable to Computer Process Control

The benefit of computer control may be affected by whether the process is production or market limited. In the former case, additional output obtained is immediately saleable and provides additional revenue. However, if production capacity exceeds market requirement, no benefit accrues from increasing output.

Benefits which may result from computer control and which can generally be expressed in monetary terms include:

(1) INCREASED THROUGHPUT. This may be obtained by operating the plant nearer its optimum level, or by better scheduling. If the process is production

limited, this will give greater revenue, reduce the fixed cost, and possibly the variable cost per unit of output.

(2) INCREASED YIELD. This may be obtained either from producing more saleable end products from the same material input, or the same output from a reduced input. Again, this is achieved by operating the process nearer its optimum level.

(3) REDUCTION IN SCRAP. This reduces reprocessing cost, and probably inventory carrying costs. In a production limited situation, the resulting increase in saleable output will increase revenue.

(4) IMPROVED QUALITY. This is seen by some as the most significant advantage of computer control. More accurate control results in a higher proportion of output either on specification or in higher specification categories. This may improve customer satisfaction and bring more revenue from increased sales of high quality products. There is the possibility of a price increase if a product is made to a tighter specification and there should also be savings through more efficient conversion of raw material. Manufacturing to a tighter specification is particularly valuable with a product like rolled steel plate with tolerances of −0.0 to +2.5 per cent.

On occasions, it may be both possible and advantageous to produce lower quality material under computer control. The impreciseness of conventional control methods may necessitate running the plant to produce an average quality level above that required to meet specification. This will increase costs. If computer control is more precise, the plant can be run nearer the marginal quality level thus reducing costs.

(5) REDUCTION IN OPERATING COSTS. This can be further subdivided:

(a) *Materials and services*. Better control may lead to a reduction in the use of catalysts and additives, and in maintenance supply materials, such as bricks for lining furnaces and oil for gear boxes. It may also lead to saving of electricity and steam, which are used in large quantities in many process industries.

(b) *Wages*. Computer control may reduce process manpower requirements. However, savings here may turn out to be as elusive as the manpower savings originally anticipated for EDP installations. Usually, savings do not materialize, and this is probably because computer process control is applied only to processes which have already advanced a long way through the spectrum of control techniques. Large manpower reductions have often been achieved during these previous control advances; by the time computer control is considered, the operating manpower is already extremely limited.

Automating the last man out of the system can also be prohibitively expensive; anyway, it is perhaps undesirable. Man is better than the computer at coping with unexpected emergencies. Reducing manpower may not, therefore, be an objective of the computer control system.

(6) REDUCTION IN INVENTORY COSTS. Where an on-line computer assists with the tracking of material through the processing and storage stage, both

finished goods and work in process inventories may be reduced. This, in turn, reduces working capital and hence financing charges.

Certain other benefits, not readily expressed in monetary terms, may arise from the introduction of computer process control. These may include:

(1) IMPROVEMENT IN INFORMATION AVAILABILITY. Computer control can make more information available more quickly and in more appropriate form. This information *should* result in better plant operation by facilitating post mortems when the plant goes out of control. A digital computer is probably the most economical means of providing continuous quality control data for a wide range of variables. In some circumstances, a product may not be saleable without such data, e.g. rolled tin plate.

(2) IMPROVED PROCESS KNOWLEDGE. As already stated, the accumulation of process information may enable a model to be built and tested which will increase understanding of the process. This may lead to better process operation, giving rise to quantifiable benefits.

(3) REDUCTION IN REQUIRED OPERATOR SKILL. Computer control may reduce the operating skills needed to run the plant. This is unlikely to reduce wage rates, but it may increase those able to undertake the various jobs. It may eventually reduce the cost of training, although the importance of maintaining manual operating skills has already been discussed.

(4) INCREASE IN PLANT SAFETY. The constant monitoring provided by computer control should ensure that any potentially dangerous situation in the plant is swiftly noted and corrective action taken. This capability may also permit a plant to be run nearer to safety limits than is possible under manual control.

Problems Associated with Computer Process Control

These can be considered under the three sub-headings: financial, managerial and technical.

Financial

The expenditure involved in a computer control installation can range from £10,000 to well over £1,000,000. Where new control applications are being tried for the first time, estimates of savings can be very uncertain and subject to a wide range of error. This is particularly true in terms of software development costs, personnel training costs (maintenance personnel and plant operators in particular) and start-up costs. Start up costs may be considerable if output is lost through full scale plant experimentation with the new control system.

Managerial

Managerial problems mostly arise from the failure of the technical and systems experts and plant management to understand each other's problems. Frequently, computer control is instigated by staff technical groups and there can be inadequate involvement of line management during the planning and implementation stages. This results in plant management having a limited understanding of the capability of the system when they take responsibility for it as an operational device. Plant management's lack of involvement during the implementation stage is often aggravated by this stage taking far longer than originally planned. Unfortunately, systems personnel tend to be optimistic over the time scales required. Extension of the implementation period is often caused by inadequate availability of system designers and programmers combined with frequent staff turnover.

Technical

Technical problems are most frequently encountered in faulty and inaccurate instrumentation. Instruments must record regularly and accurately. Imprecise and inaccurate data can result in the computer taking control action which actual circumstances do not require. Other areas of difficulty include poorly engineered plant, e.g. excessive play and backlash, and difficulty in the construction of computer models which accurately represent the operation of the system. Computer reliability is not now a serious problem. If 100% computer availability is required for the control system, a backup computer would be made available. This does not necessarily require idle computers. Where a plant has more than one control installation, each computer can act as a back up for another operating system. In the event of failure, one computer would carry out the critical control activities on two parts of the plant.

Computer control has now reached the stage where it is more appropriate to ask the question 'Is it economically feasible to computerize this system?' rather than the question 'Is it technically feasible to computerize this system?'. Often, the introduction of computer control has been on an *ad hoc* basis. This approach should be replaced by a specific operational policy covering the following issues:

(1) The long term level of investment to be made in computer process control systems.
(2) Determining computer control installation priorities. This will require detailed evaluation of existing systems.
(3) The level of systems manpower required to implement the planned rate of installations. This will need corresponding action for recruitment and training.
(4) The location of organizational responsibility for computer process control.
(5) Control of the interface between process control and EDP computer systems.
(6) The involvement of plant management in computer control systems.
(7) The long term effects of advanced computer control on the overall role of plant management.

Conclusion

The high capital investment involved in continuous processes and the large scale increments in which new capacity is added demand major focus on capital investment appraisal. Although the labour force represents a small proportion of total cost, its performance can nonetheless be critical. Through poor work performance or withdrawal of labour, millions of pounds worth of investment can be made idle, causing large scale revenue losses. Control of the plant is very important, both to maintain safety standards and to ensure that capacity is fully and effectively utilized. The introduction of the digital computer as a control mechanism in continuous plants is the most significant and far reaching innovation during the past fifteen years.

Further Reading

Constable, C. J. (1972) 'Managerial Problems Associated with Process Control Computer Installation', *International Journal of Production Research*, **10**, No. 2.

NEDO (1972) 'Process Industries Investment Forecasts', *The Seventh Report by the Process Plant Working Party*, NEDO, London.

Williams, W. D. (1974) 'Initiating a Computer Control Project', *Control Engineering*, **XXI**, September 1974.

CHAPTER 9

Managing the Process — Assembly Lines

Introduction

The assembly line is perhaps the ultimate achievement of classic industrial engineering. The pace of work can be controlled by the speed at which the line moves, individual work stations can be highly engineered, individual jobs highly simplified and virtually all discretion can be removed from the human element of the system. Although the past few years have seen much questioning and doubt about the assembly line process, its effectiveness in terms of reducing manufacturing direct cost during the past sixty or more years cannot be questioned.

The introduction of the modern assembly line is generally credited to the Ford organization. In 1913 an assembly line was introduced to assemble magnetos and the labour content was reduced from 20 minutes to 5 minutes per unit. Between 1913 and 1914 a number of experiments were carried out on vehicle assembly with the dramatic result of reducing vehicle assembly time from 12½ to 1½ man hours. Moving the product past many work stations, each containing the appropriate parts and stationary manpower, was shown to be a more effective method of assembling complex objects than bringing all parts to a single location where several people worked.

The moving assembly line was outstandingly successful because:

(1) It reduced the skill requirements. Because an individual operator only carried out a small proportion of the work, each job could be reduced to a semiskilled or even unskilled activity.
(2) It reduced manpower training time. Since the job was simpler it could be learnt in a much shorter time.
(3) It emphasized work methods. The very process of designing the assembly line requires a close analysis of the sequence of assembly. This is likely to result in a more efficient sequence of activities and to ensure that the product is designed in such a way that the assembly activity can be easily carried out.
(4) It encouraged workplace design. For simple short time cycle tasks it is possible to design extremely efficient work stations. Efficiency in this sense means that the components and hand tools required for the assembly task are properly located in relation both to the product and the operator.
(5) It reduced the work-in-process inventory. Compared with assembling in a static location, the assembly line can operate with a smaller volume of components

for a given output. Reduced throughput time further lowers the amount of work in process in the system.

As a result of these benefits, virtually all manufactured products made in high volume and assembled from separate components are now assembled on a flow type assembly line. Distinction can be made between two types of assembly line. In the first, the product under assembly is attached to a moving line. Work is carried out on the product while it moves. Thus, the time cycle at each work station is strictly controlled, and no provision is made for work in process buffers between work stations. In the second, the work is removed from the line and the task completed at a pace controlled by the operator. Work may be transported mechanically by a power driven conveyor belt or moved between work stations by simple gravity feed devices. This type of line permits small quantities of work in process to build up at any work station. This reduces the need for very accurate balance between stations. The purpose of this chapter is to examine the issues involved in assembly line design and to discuss why the assembly line is now being critically reappraised.

The Design of Assembly Lines

All assembly lines utilize a combination of machine and human capabilities. The machinery employed in the line may be used for transportation between jobs, to assist the operator to carry out a job or to perform a job without human aid. In the design of traditional assembly lines (where relatively little concern is given to the nature of the human task) the following factors influence the balance between machines and human operators:

(1) Anticipated product volume. Where a very high volume of similar products is made, higher levels of capital investment in automatic assembly machines will be economic. By and large, increasing the level of automation reduces the flexibility of the assembly line.

(2) Variety of models. This is related to the first factor. However, consumer demands currently result in a great proliferation of options and varieties around a basic model. This variety may modify initial conclusions reached when total volume only was considered.

(3) The nature of the product and the raw materials used. The first consideration is the inherent stability of the raw material used. Steel under normal environmental conditions is inherently stable; cloth, on the other hand, can be stretched. The amount of stretch can vary considerably with relatively small changes in physical force. The second consideration is the inevitable variability in the physical dimensions of manufactured components. Dimensional variations and material instabilities can create major problems when machines are handling components. The cost of designing a machine which can recognize variations in dimensions and then position and assemble components, taking account of these variations is likely to be great. Human skill in coordinating eye observations with hand movements is extremely high. This skill is, as yet, relatively cheap to employ compared with the cost of designing and building

machines with equivalent skills. This is the prime reason why there are as yet very few totally automated assembly lines.

(4) Availability and cost of capital and labour. The ready availability of semiskilled labour at modest wage rates, particularly if combined with a lack of skilled labour required to maintain complex machinery, is likely to reduce the extent to which machines rather than human operators will be used on the assembly line. Equally, the converse situation, where capital is readily available at low interest rates and semiskilled labour is lacking, is likely to lead to a high level of automation. Generally speaking, the decision to reduce labour utilization is viewed as a straight economic decision largely influenced by the prevailing wage rates. The higher the prevailing wage rates the greater the sum of money which can economically be spent eliminating the need for a human operator. This has, therefore, led to the greater automation of assembly processes in high wage economies like those of the United States and Western Germany.

The Balance of Assembly Lines

The most critical problem facing the designer of an assembly line is that of obtaining a balance between the various work stations. Balance is required to ensure that all work stations, be they machine manned or human manned, are kept fully occupied while the work in process between stations is kept constant and at a minimum level. The basic data required to design and balance assembly lines are a detailed method analysis and element times for each indivisible part of the job. The method analysis must describe the sequence in which the various elements should be carried out since this will place certain constraints on the assembly process; in practice, there is likely to be a very large number of possible sequences in which assembly could be carried out.

The first step is to establish the number of work stations in the assembly line. The theoretical approach to this would normally be as follows.

Suppose a given item is required at the rate of 1,000 units per 8 hours shift. It is planned to make the items on an assembly line with no duplication of work stations. The total assembly time required per item is 15 minutes. To produce 1,000 items in 8 hours, i.e. 480 minutes, requires the production of a complete unit approximately once every half minute. Thus, ideally, each work station should have a task cycle of half a minute resulting in 30 stations to complete the 15 minutes of assembly work.

Having adopted this approach, the assembly line designer would then examine the required work sequences and element times with a view to constructing jobs which take half a minute. The ideal design would result in jobs taking precisely .50 minutes rather than .49 or .51, and the line would be manned by machines and people that would work at a uniform pace throughout the 8 hour shift. In this perfect situation one assembled item would be produced every half minute throughout 8 hours.

In practice perfection is not achieved. Element times will be such that it is not possible to create jobs which have times of precisely .50 minutes. The sequence constraints and indivisibility of certain aspects of the job would probably lead to the various work stations having jobs of between .45 and .55 minutes with a mean of .50. Given this situation, the pace of the line is now theoretically controlled by the work station with the longest duration job, in our example .55 minutes. Thus, the actual time required to complete each unit will be 30 x .55 equals 16.5 minutes. Hence, 1.5 minutes of time is lost in the assembly of each unit through the lack of balance between the work station. This loss, known as the balance delay loss, is expressed as a percentage of the total time in the system, i.e. 1.5/16.5 = 9%. Assembly lines are rarely designed with a balance delay loss less than 5% and a 10% to 15% loss is quite common.

These theoretical calculations presume that the element times used for the calculations are precise. Since the design of the assembly line is taking place before the line actually exists, the element times being considered are based on estimates. Although many organizations may gather very detailed times for the various work activities involved in assembly, the fact is that planning assembly line balance is based on estimates which are subject to error. Thus, very precise calculations may turn out to be irrelevant since the base data is incorrect.

A further variable which is very difficult to assess when designing the balance of an assembly line is the variation in pace of different human operators. The pace of work at which humans are willing and able to work is as variable as the dimensions of the components they are assembling. The variation in pace can be viewed as an advantage or a disadvantage. Since these variations can be as much as 100% and are commonly as much as 50%, fine balance of the work between the stations of the assembly line can appear somewhat pointless. On the other hand, this variable can be used as a balancing mechanism in itself in that quicker workers can perform the task at the work stations with longer cycle times. To design a line with large variations in cycle time between work stations and to offset these variations by the differing work paces of the operators is to create a situation which is likely to lead to tension between members of the work group. It is probable that there will be a standard payment system for all members of the work group, be it a day wage or an incentive based system. Any members of the group who are clearly having to work harder for a standard reward are likely to resent this.

Problems in manning assembly lines are constantly created by absenteeism, variation in operator skill and lack of flexibility of movement between different stations on the line. Any assembly line with ten or more workers can anticipate an average of one person absent per day. Thus, each day the exact staffing of the line must be resolved. The problem can be handled in total personnel terms by manning up lines to take account of absenteeism, i.e. assigning say 22 workers to a 20 station line, or by using floating workers, who are able to work on a number of lines. However, this only resolves part of the problem. The person allocated to an unusual position in the line or floating worker, no matter how skilled, is unlikely to be able to work at the required pace to keep the line in balance. It is likely, therefore, that throughout any given day supervisors will be faced with a constant movement of personnel or variation in work load on the assembly line to resolve short term balance problems.

Solving the Assembly Line Balance Problem

The process of establishing a feasible solution to an assembly line problem is essentially a search or heuristic process. Since the number of possible solutions is very large, the time and cost involved in finding the optimal solution is also likely to be great. It is also probable that there will be a number of near optimal solutions and the advantage of finding the very best solution compared with one of the near optimal solutions is small. Also since, as already pointed out, the data is somewhat imprecise, the validity of seeking the optimal solution is doubtful.

The problem nonetheless is a complex one. The complexity can be further increased where the assembly line has to handle a variety of products which may require different processing times at the various work stations. The mix of the products fed into the line then becomes an additional variable which must be resolved when designing the line and the flow of work through the line. This situation can be handled either by batching together similar products and processing the batches independently or by allowing a free mix of products to flow down the line. The former may involve virtually rebalancing the line each time the batch is changed. In the latter case, the differing demands of the product at the various work stations can be used in the calculation of the line balance. In either situation, balance can be assisted by the ability to have work in process between the stations on the line. This creates more flexibility by uncoupling one station from another in the short term.

A problem of this complexity is obviously suitable for solution by modelling processes using a computer. This is a topic which has attracted considerable attention from operational researchers and a number of references are given at the end of the chapter

The Movement away from the Assembly Line

The assembly line has undoubtedly created a wide range of jobs throughout manufacturing industry which are repetitive and tedious. For several decades, this appeared to be a price which industrialized societies were prepared to pay to achieve reduction in the direct cost of manufactured goods. However, in the last 15 years there has been increasing uncertainty about the assembly line as a place for humans to spend their working lives. This questioning has led to the ideas of job rotation, job enlargement and job enrichment. Much of the research and experimentation of these topics has involved the assembly line process.

Job rotation, as the phrase implies, involves switching people between a variety of jobs rather than having them work at a single job throughout the day. This can be useful in relieving monotony where very short work cycles are involved and it also shares the less pleasant or more arduous tasks between different members of the work group.

Job enlargement means creating more variety in the work task. This has led a number of companies to reappraise their assembly lines, resulting in the creation of jobs with much longer time cycles and far fewer people on a given assembly line.

For example, a toy company engaged in assembling very high volumes of 75 different small scale model cars, switched from assembly lines, each manned by 12 to 15 female operators to a system of single person work stations. Each work station was equipped to permit assembly of all the model varieties. It was discovered that considerable savings resulted from this changeover. The greatest proportion of the saving came from the elimination of the handling time involved in picking up assemblies from the conveyor and replacing them on the conveyor after the work was completed. In the new work stations the use of jigs and fixtures, two handed working and combinations of hand and foot operations eliminated much of this handling requirement. Average job cycle times increased from 5 to 30 seconds. Further major advantages were seen in the elimination of the assembly line balancing problems caused by absenteeism and the greater flexibility that the total system provided. Previously there had been 20 assembly lines which would work on a single model with an average run length of 15,000. After the changeover there were 250 individual work stations. This permitted the assembly of all 75 models at the same time with daily output rates which could be varied with considerable ease.

Although the scheme was designed and installed to improve the working conditions, the major disadvantage that emerged from the scheme was an impoverishment of the working environment as seen by the operators themselves. In the assembly line system, girls sat on both sides of the conveyor belt and each was able to communicate easily with four or five people. Thus, the limited demand which the work placed upon the operator was, to some extent, compensated for by the opportunity for constant conversation. The new layout involved a work station design which included a semicircular banking of boxes to hold the components being assembled. This banking, together with the spacing between each work station effectively prevented each operator from talking to her neighbours. The increased mental demand of the job also required a greater level of concentration.

Job Enrichment

This involves the workforce in taking over some of the responsibilities previously held by someone at a higher level in the organization. The planning and control elements associated with the task are incorporated into it. Determination of job sequence, discretion over methods, setting the work pace, setting up machines and inspecting finished products are all aspects of work that can be incorporated into job enrichment. Job enrichment usually involves:

(1) Delegation of control to the individual worker.
(2) Increasing the accountability of the individual for his own job.
(3) Making jobs into complete units, thus permitting a clearer definition of work targets.
(4) Giving authority to the individual employee so that he can determine the tactics for achieving the set objectives.
(5) Increasing the amount of information divulged about the nature and purpose of the task to the individual. This involves constant and rapid feedback of results achieved.

(6) The gradual introduction of new and more difficult tasks, thus permitting the individual to develop and grow in the work context.

The disenchantment that is being expressed throughout the world with working on assembly lines suggests that the assembly line is a prime candidate for the application of job enrichment. However, as the definitions above indicate, it can only be applied by a complete restructuring of the job format. To date, most of the experiments in job enrichment have taken place in white collar, high technical content jobs rather than in shop floor blue collar jobs. This is not because the need of the former is greater than that of the latter, but simply because it is easier to design jobs which embody the principles of job enrichment in these areas. A limited number of experiments are being attempted on the shop floor in a number of European automobile manufacturers, notably Fiat, Saab and Volvo. To date, it is only possible to conclude that about 15% more capital is required to build plants in which job enriched activities can take place than was needed for previous conventional plants. To evaluate the long term operating advantages will require a number of years of working experience.

The major obstacles to applying job enrichment to assembly line type operations are generally seen to be:

(1) Where large numbers of interdependent people are carrying out routine tasks it is not possible to delegate planning and control of the task to them.

(2) Where any form of piece work payment system operates it is not possible to introduce planning and control of the task as part of the basic job. These activities cannot be sensibly incorporated into piece work rates. Where it has been tried, job enrichment has been seen as a rate cutting activity.

(3) Manual workers' trade unions are frequently not enamoured with job enrichment. They see its introduction blurring the distinction between workers and management. This is a distinction which British unions wish to maintain since it permits their own role to be clearly defined.

(4) The role of the first line supervisor becomes uncertain in the job enrichment process. What on the one hand may offer job enrichment to the shop floor worker, may on the other hand, offer job impoverishment to the first line supervisor.

Research to date on the overall value of job enrichment is perhaps inconclusive. Although the virtues of job enrichment have been extolled by a number of research workers (Paul, Robertson and Herzberg, 1969) others have concluded that:

(1) Many people carrying out routine tasks are simply not interested in having their jobs enriched. Some writers suggest that Herzberg's theories have more application to the educated middle-class workforce than to those who carry out manual tasks in industry. To them, it is argued, money is the motivating factor and satisfaction is not sought in the job itself, but in activities outside the job. There is certainly strong evidence to suggest that the variables of age, education and intelligence are very important when seeking to introduce job enrichment.

(2) Job enrichment frequently results in a reduction in the social interaction of the work place. This is a highly prized aspect of many people's work and they are not prepared to forgo it for someone else's idea of an enriched job.

(3) Job enrichment may produce feelings of inadequacy, a fear of failure and a concern for dependency on others in many workers. For such people, low level competence, security and relative independence are more important than the opportunity for greater responsibility and personal growth.

Conclusion

The assembly line has served industrial society well for the last 60 years. However, it is becoming increasingly difficult to persuade people, as they become better and better educated, to commit themselves to this type of work environment. The problems of the assembly line are most obvious in the automobile industry throughout the world. It is in this industry that the largest experiments are being carried out to find ways of working which do not increase the direct cost of assembling a complex product, but which do give greater satisfaction to the people carrying out the task. The long term implications of these experiments are, as yet, unknown. It seems probable that assembly lines will survive until the end of this century, but that greater and greater pressure will be placed on management either to automate the task entirely or radically to redesign the work.

Reference

Paul, W. J., Robertson, K. B. and Herzberg, F. (1969) 'Job Enrichment Pays Off', *Harvard Business Review*, March—April, 1969.

Further Reading

Benyon, H. (1973) *Working at Ford*, Penguin, Harmondsworth.
Kilbridge, M. and Wester, L. (1961) 'A Heuristic Method of Assembly Line Balancing', *Journal of Industrial Engineering*, XII, No. 4.
Paul, W. J. and Robertson, K. B. (1970) *Job Enrichment and Employee Motivation*, Gower Press, London.
Reif, W. E. and Luthans, F. (1972) 'Does Job Enrichment Really Pay Off', *Californian Management Review*, XV, No. 1.
Wild, R. (1972) *Mass Production Management*, Wiley, London.

CHAPTER 10

Managing the Process — Jobbing and Batch Production

Introduction

Chapters 2 and 9 have explained that the operations sequence is usually identical for all items in a line or flow production system. Lines may be modified to produce batches of similar items but the flow nature of the process remains. When the sequence of operations varies for each item, functional or group organization of the physical flow is required. This is often described as batch or jobbing production. It is important to note that the physical organization of this type of system has a major effect on its operating characteristics, regardless of the product. The distinction between mass production, which uses line organization and batch and jobbing production, which often use functional organization is clear. The distinction between batch production and jobbing is more one of degree. Standard products, possibly with minor customer modifications, are often made by batch production. Components are produced in batches, either in excess of current requirements on the basis of a product mix forecast or after consolidation of orders from different customers. Pure jobbing is producing items to customer specification on a one off basis. Design may be specified by the customer, as for example in tool making, or may be prepared by the supplier as part of the job. Batch sizes are usually very small; little opportunity exists for consolidating customer orders for common items and few repeat orders occur.

Flow or line organization exists in a wide variety of industries. Batch and jobbing production are mainly found in the engineering industry, although the garment and furniture industries have some batch production on a restricted scale.

Functional and Group Organization

Functional organization is very flexible. Any process route can be accommodated within the technological constraints of the production facilities. However, a high level of work in process is required in order to maintain facility utilization, and this extends the manufacturing time, possibly causing delivery delays. In mass manufacturing systems using line organization, the principal problem is one of planning a feasible production programme within capacity and demand constraints.

In batch and jobbing production, the critical problem is one of control, that is of ensuring that orders progress as planned. There are usually different customer relationships; batch production is often for a customer delivery promise whereas mass production systems generally make for stock. In mass production, detailed and realistic production plans can be made because there are few products and the equipment is specially designed; deviations from plan are usually caused by mechanical breakdown. In batch manufacture, the interaction between jobs is uncertain ? is the completion time of each operation. Deviations from plan in batch production occur for a multiplicity of reasons including:

(1) Operator performance,
(2) Tooling availability,
(3) Material movement,
(4) Machine breakdown,
(5) Variable queuing time prior to loading,
(6) Quality problems and reworking.

Planning and Controlling Batch Production

There are six main stages in the management of batch production systems:

(1) The provision of production capacity,
(2) Shop loading,
(3) The control of work output,
(4) The sequencing of jobs,
(5) Progress control,
(6) Shortage control.

Establishing objectives for a batch production system is a complex task. Objectives are not always compatible. For example, high labour and machine utilization requires high work-in-process inventories. Management must balance the various objectives to achieve an acceptable compromise, given current market conditions. The compromise however must not be rigid. Action which is appropriate at one time may well be inappropriate under different conditions.

The Provision of Production Capacity

Load is defined as the volume of work in the production system still to be processed by a facility, expressed, for example, in standard hours. Capacity is defined as the maximum rate at which the facility can reduce the total load. It might be, for example, 1,000 standard hours per day. However, the capacity of a production system is hard to pinpoint. If a machine can produce items at the rate of 1,000 per hour, then the capacity of the machine can be stated as 1,000 items per hour. On the other hand, a steel plant may have a nominal capacity of 5 million tons per year, but this output level is dependent on the size of orders. A large number of small orders with different specifications will reduce the plant capacity considerably. In an engineering machine shop, the capacity of each set of facilities is dependent on the number of available machines and operators. The actual output which can be achieved from a given set of facilities will, however, depend on the skill of the operators, the rate at which they work, the proportion of cycle times which are machine controlled and the mix of orders. Output is also dependent on a constant input which in turn requires a backlog of work. If a man or machine becomes idle because no job is available, then the output rate will drop even though the nominal capacity is unchanged.

To clarify both the definition and the measurement of capacity, it is useful to state what we understand by load, capacity and output rate.

Load is the volume of work in the production system still to be processed. This may be expressed for each type of facility or in total, e.g. as an outstanding load of 10,000 standard hours of milling, 5,000 standard hours of drilling etc. or as a total load of 50,000 standard hours.

Capacity is the maximum rate at which a facility (or set of facilities) is capable of working off the outstanding load with a given allocation of operators. Capacity is a function of both the facility, the nature of the outstanding load and the efficiency of the operators concerned.

Output Rate is the actual rate at which work is processed. Output rate depends on capacity and on the availability of work.

A simple analogy is the water tank shown in Figure 28. The existing load in the system is represented by the volume of water in the tank. The input and output rates

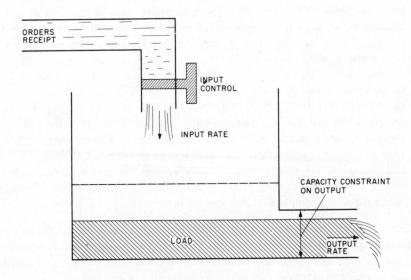

Figure 28   The water tank analogy to work flow in a production system

are the flows shown. Capacity is the maximum possible outflow controlled by the outlet pipe size. If the load is insufficient to provide a permanent backlog, output will be below capacity with consequent loss of efficiency.

The measurement of capacity is, from a practical viewpoint, impossible. However, output rate can readily be measured. For system control purposes, this is more useful, since it is the relationship between input and output which affects the load backlog. Measurement of the output rate and variations in the input backlog will indicate the potential capacity of a facility, provided the mix of work remains reasonably constant.

In the long term, capacity can be altered through additions to equipment and/or the labour force. In the short term, capacity is usually fixed, though reallocation of labour can substantially alter the capacity of a specific facility. However, labour may now be more inflexible than machine capacity, even though labour expense is traditionally regarded as a variable input in a cost-accounting system. The regulation of labour inputs is highly dependent on the skill levels required, Trade Union relations and the current condition of the labour market.

Shop Loading

The two principal shop loading techniques are illustrated in Figure 29. These are:

(1) CAPACITY REQUIREMENTS PLANNING. This involves determining the capacity which would be required during each time period to meet all desired delivery dates. A throughput time is assumed for each operation. Working back from the delivery date it is possible to calculate the time by which each operation must be completed. This will show the load on each separate facility by time period. This capacity requirement plan takes no account of actual capacity constraints. It is simple to add new orders or to make adjustments to the plan. Only addition and subtraction are required. This may be time consuming if done manually but can be computerized at low cost. The accuracy of the plan depends directly on the accuracy of the assumed lead times. These in turn are affected by the level of work in process.

(2) PLANNING WITHIN CAPACITY CONSTRAINTS. If the processing times of a set of orders and the available capacity of a set of facilities are known, a forward schedule can be constructed taking account of capacity limitations. This schedule will provide planned start and finish times for all operations on each order. If the time horizon is long enough, order completion will be calculated. The introduction of new orders or any change in priority of existing orders requires a complete rescheduling of the total load.

Because of its complexity, loading under capacity constraints is rarely used. Capacity requirements planning however, is cheap and simple to use. It allows the foreman on the spot to control work sequence and avoids the issue of detailed schedules which, in a dynamic situation, are inevitably inaccurate.

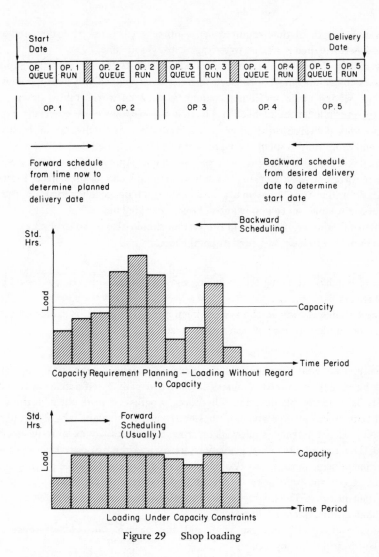

Figure 29   Shop loading

The Control of Work Input

Efficient operation of any system requires a minimum level of work-in-process to ensure that when a particular resource finishes a task, another job is available. This is generally well understood and failure to achieve this minimum is easily identified by rises in idle time attributed to 'waiting for work'. However, what is less well understood is that overfilling the system is just as damaging as underfilling it. This is not only because it increases work in process thereby raising the level of investment in working capital (although this is of course true) but also because each additional job in the shop beyond that which is necessary, further complicates the task of achieving efficient scheduling and facility utilization. It also automatically increases the average length of time required for a job to get through the shop, and average delivery performance is related to average throughput time.

Overfilling the system becomes a vicious circle. As the average throughput time increases, more and more jobs have to be specially expedited. This involves batch splitting, setting up in inefficient sequences or, even worse, taking down a set-up only to reset it after the rush job has been completed. Each job especially expedited and possibly delivered on time probably means two late deliveries in the future, as more and more time is spent trying to sort out revised schedules.

The extent of overfilling may be estimated quite quickly. Spot checks should be made in different work sections to see how many jobs are in the correct location on the day in question, how many are early (and hence cluttering up the place unnecessarily) and, more importantly, how many are late.

The total number of batches in the system should also be controlled. An increase in the number can have two fundamental causes:

(1) more batches are being fed in during a given time than can be processed in that time.
(2) The batches already in the system keep multiplying. This is caused by splitting batches under pressure of customer demand.

Finally, the level of activity of the progress chasing or expediting department should be closely examined. Progress chasing is usually a self-defeating activity. If capacity is properly planned and scheduled, progress of work through the system should require monitoring and not chasing. Expeditors create as many problems as they solve. If the activity is allowed to grow, it will destroy an orderly scheduling system. The rise of elaborate priority systems is often associated with growth in expediting. These, in turn, can also become self defeating. Multiple priority systems (the red, green and blue ticket syndrome) soon ensure that work only progresses if it has high priority. Thus, a higher than high priority has to be invented for 'special work' and so the system proliferates.

Many conflicts of interest arise and the person who suffers most is the bewildered shop floor supervisor.

The impact of increasing shop load is shown graphically in Figure 30. This shows the relationships between mean throughput time and the variance of the throughput time and the shop load. At higher work-in-process levels, the allowance for queuing time must be greater. Although this may give some additional output, it unfortunately also increases the uncertainty of the actual flow time as shown by the lead time variation curve.

Order can only be restored to an overloaded system by reducing the total volume of work in the system. If this is reduced from, say, ten weeks to five weeks, then average shop floor throughput time is halved. Carrying out this reduction requires a period of reduced input. This must be accompanied by a 'suction' process from the back end of the system. On the basis of planned priorities, work must be pulled out of the system at a rate faster than the input. This will create imbalance

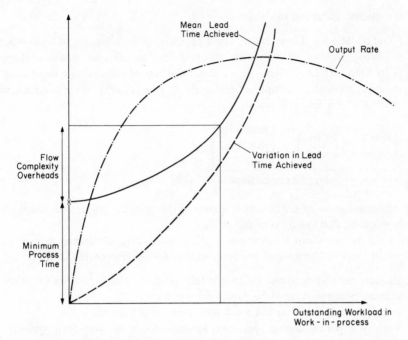

Figure 30   A conceptual view of the relationship between the work-in-process
level and the other performance criteria

between the parts of the system which can only be offset to the extent that the
labour force is flexible and can be moved from the early to the later operations.

Once the work-in-process level has been reduced, input should be restored to
match the system capacity. Reducing shop floor throughput time from 10 weeks to
5 weeks does not halve delivery time, since there is no substitute for insufficient
capacity. There will be a longer queue at the start of the system. However, this will
be a more self-evident queue and should prevent optimistic delivery promises. It
will replace the many smaller queues which can so easily be hidden in the system
and can hence conveniently be ignored. Altering priorities in this 'paper' queue will
be simpler than changing priorities of work already committed to the shop floor.

The Sequencing of Jobs

In a given work location, decision rules are required to determine which job should
be loaded when a machine becomes available. Usually this decision is left to the
foreman or, by default, to the operator. In a payment-by-results environment, the
most likely decision rule is 'load highest bonus job first'. Other arbitrary rules, such
as first-in-first-out or random selection may be used. A large number of more
rational rules have been proposed. Some, such as shortest-processing-time,
concentrate on reducing work-in-process inventories, while others concentrate on
raising machine utilization or meeting promised delivery dates.

Two distinct classes of rule exist:

(1) STATIC RULES. These enable fixed priorities to be allocated to a job when it is issued. The shortest processing time and due date rules fall into this category.
(2) DYNAMIC RULES. Here the relative priorities of jobs change depending on their progress. An example of this type of rule is 'slack time per remaining operation'. Priority is based on

$$\frac{\left\{\begin{array}{l}\text{Due}\\\text{Date}\end{array}\right\} - \left\{\begin{array}{l}\text{Time}\\\text{Now}\end{array}\right\} - \left\{\begin{array}{l}\text{remaining}\\\text{machine}\\\text{time}\end{array}\right\}}{\text{No. of operations to be done}}$$

The implementation of a dynamic dispatching rule requires continuous monitoring of job progress. This can be very expensive.

Dispatching rules can be evaluated against specified performance criteria using simulation models. The general characteristics of the rules suggested above are:

(1) Shortest processing time. Relatively few jobs late but very wide variation in lateness. Some jobs very late. Low work-in-process.
(2) Due date. More jobs late but much less variation in lateness.
(3) Slack time per remaining operation. Some jobs late but very little variation in lateness.

Dispatching rules are concerned with making local decisions, usually considering only a single work centre (more complex rules can consider succeeding work centres) to achieve global objectives such as due dates and facility utilization. In practice, rules such as 'shortest processing time' are almost never used because they make a few jobs very late. If lead times are not related either to the number of operations to be performed or the total work content of the job, then none of the rules perform significantly better than first come first served. Failure or inability to specify lead times on this basis probably explains why most jobbing and batch production systems make little use of sophisticated scheduling systems.

Progress Control

Progress reporting is the collection of data on work completed. Progress control should enable management action to be taken before jobs get behind schedule. One simple method of progress control often used is to 'target date' certain stages of the production process and to report on those orders which are running behind target. A major problem in progress control is the maintenance of correct relative priorities between jobs. In a production system governed by a material requirements planning system, the due dates on 'open orders' may change several times. Causes may include material shortages on other components, rejects and higher level demand schedule changes. In many progress control systems, it is relatively easy to raise the priority of an order but very difficult to lower it. Raising some priorities without reducing others inevitably destroys the balance of the production plan. It is therefore essential to have a dynamic system for ensuring that correct relative priorities are maintained. For component production to meet assembly requirements, the only practicable method of doing this is through the schedule priorities given in a material requirements planning system.

Shortage Control

The most common reason for failing to meet assembly schedules is a shortage of components or bought-out materials. Progress control on component and bought-out item deliveries is often termed shortage control. Ideally, it should act as a check on stock recording errors and be a final defence against stockouts. However, in practice, it is difficult to initiate two independent reports on stock transactions. Shortage control often takes the form of marshalling component stocks before the start of an assembly programme. This increases inventories and creates stock allocation problems. Such systems are often advocated in overload situations but they create problems rather than solve them. Component inventories are increased, more overloads are generated on the supply facilities and the assembly department builds whatever happens to be available. The result is misallocation of components, lower output and anarchy at the assembly stage.

Conclusions

Batch and jobbing production are frequently associated with functional organization of the production facilities. Such systems have very low throughput efficiency. Objectives such as meeting due dates and maintaining high facility utilization are not entirely compatible and a compromise must be reached between the various performance parameters.

In the make-to-order situation and in the production of components, the work input must be controlled before shop loading takes place. Capacity requirements planning involves preparing a statement of the capacity necessary to achieve particular output targets and takes no account of actual capacity available. Loading within capacity constraints requires detailed definition of both facility capacity and also the relative priorities of all the orders in the system.

Further Reading

Burbidge, J. L. (1968) *The Principles of Production Control*, Macdonald and Evans Ltd., London (2nd edition).

Burbidge, J. L. (1975) *The Introduction of Group Technology*, Heinemann, London.

Corke, D. K. (1969) *Production Control is Management*, Macdonald and Evans Ltd., London.

Edwards, G. A. B. (1971) *Readings in Group Technology*, Machinery Publishing Co. Ltd., London.

Gallagher, C. C. and Knight, W. A. (1973) *Group Technology*, Butterworths, London.

CHAPTER 11

Managing the Process — Large Scale Projects

Introduction

A wide range of operational activities fall into the general description of large scale projects. Obvious examples are civil engineering works (bridges, skyscrapers, dams), plant construction (refineries, steel works) and shipbuilding. This type of project involves producing a one-off end product. Large scale projects also include the design and development activities which may eventually lead to the manufacture of tens, hundreds or even occasionally thousands of the final product (Concorde, 1320 megawatt turbine generators). In non-manufacturing, managing the software design for a big computer system or performing a large scale scientific project has many common characteristics with large scale manufacturing projects.

This type of activity generally involves:

(1) A tendering process where estimates often have to be made with relatively limited information. If the contract is not obtained, the resources used in compiling the estimate are usually effectively lost.

(2) A commitment over an extended time period. Complex projects rarely last for less than a year and can extend for ten or more years (Concorde, nuclear power stations).

(3) The expenditure of large sums of money. Projects may not generate any positive cash flow until they are completed. This is likely to place a considerable cash flow strain on both the contractor and customer. This, in turn, may lead to financing difficulty.

(4) The marshalling of complex physical and human resources. Major contractors frequently subcontract parts of the project. This results in the involvement of many separate organizations at various stages of the project. The planning and coordination of the human and physical resources to ensure that the project is completed, both on time and at the original agreed cost, is an extremely complex task.

(5) Establishing a project management group for the duration of the project. The managerial characteristics and skills involved in managing an activity which by definition is temporary, are different in certain respects from those involved in managing a continuing situation.

This chapter considers the various operational management problems associated with managing large scale contracts.

Obtaining the Project

A major problem facing any organization whose work consists mainly of large scale projects is timing the flow of work to give an even work load. Work is obtained by submitting tenders in competition with other bidders. While the timing of the submission of tenders can be controlled, there is no guarantee that a given tender will produce work. There may also be a limit to the number of tenders which can be submitted, since each will require extensive estimating and preparation work by a skilled group of personnel.

The chances of success of a tender can be influenced by the size of the bid submitted. When work is short, profit margins may be cut, thus lowering the bid and increasing the probability of success. However, a shortage of work is often a reflection of the general state of the economy and may be common to all the organizations bidding for the contract. This can result in all round underbidding which can have disastrous consequences. The low bid which gets the contract may be unrealistically low. Although this may appear to be to the advantage of the client, even he may suffer. His main contractor may at best run into severe financial difficulties which may delay work on the project, or at worst go bankrupt leaving the client with a half-completed contract.

The vital skill at the estimation stage, is having a clear understanding of the amount and nature of costs involved in completing the project. This knowledge is necessary to take sensible decisions on the extent to which margins can safely be reduced without subjecting the organization to serious financial risk. It may be better to forego a contract that can only be obtained at a price which has a high chance of producing a loss, and temporarily contracting the overall size of the organization.

Project Planning

The first requirement of project planning is the definition of responsibility. This is particularly important where the contractor is working with client personnel and the boundary lines can be blurred. Failure to define responsibilities accurately can result in disputes over payment, delays in the project and perhaps most harmful of all, difficult human relationships between client and contractor.

The detailed planning of the large scale project is extremely complex. Basically, the planner must resolve what resources will be required, when they will be required, in what sequence they will be required, and how much they will cost. Because there are inevitably many interdependencies within a project, ensuring the correct sequence of activities can be vitally important. Failure to complete a particular activity by a given time may prevent the start of subsequent work which in turn may cause resources to stand idle.

During the past two decades, various techniques have been developed for the planning of complex projects. Initially, these techniques were graphical in nature and involved detailed manual calculations. Now computer packages are available, which, given appropriate input data, produce both diagramatic and numerical output. These techniques are generally termed Network Analysis but are also known by specific names such as Critical Path Analysis (CPA) and Project Evaluation and Review Techniques (PERT). The techniques of network analysis are relatively straightforward and several excellent basic texts are referred to at the end of this chapter.

The input data necessary for the construction of a network is:

(1) The total list of activities required to complete the project.
(2) The sequence and interdependency of these activities, i.e. those activities which must be completed before a given activity can commence must be defined.
(3) An estimate of the time required to carry out the activity.
(4) The type and costs of the resources required for a given activity.
(5) The extent to which it is physically possible to shorten the completion time of an activity below the estimated time, and the cost of implementing this reduction.

On the basis of the first three information categories, it is possible to construct a network diagram of all the activities involved in a project. The prime purpose of this network is to identify the sequence of activities which controls the minimum time in which the project can be completed. These activities are termed critical, hence the name Critical Path Analysis. Those activities which are not part of the critical sequence contain an element of flexibility. It is possible to start these later than the earliest possible time without delaying the final completion of the project. The network diagram can be used to identify the amount by which the start of these non-critical activities can be delayed (often termed the amount of float time). Understanding the amount of float time available can be valuable in the allocation of resources. When only a limited amount of each type of resource is available, it is desirable to minimize the demand at any given time for a particular resource. The analysis can identify activities for which the main contractor has insufficient resources. As a result, he may wish to acquire additional resource, or more probably, he will plan to subcontract the excess work.

The effectiveness of the network as a planning device is dependent on the accuracy of the time estimates for the activities involved. Techniques involving optimistic, probable and pessimistic time estimates have been developed. However, accuracy in the final count, is more likely to come from experienced personnel giving realistic estimates than from modifications of estimates produced by statistical techniques.

The greatest value obtained from constructing the network during the planning stage is that it imposes a discipline on the planners. It demands that the whole project be thought through in an orderly fashion. When the potential critical path has been identified, ways of shortening the activities on this path can be considered. The costs associated with shortening these activities can then be identified. This allows a comparison between these costs and the savings which would result from shortening the total project time. Naturally, as the critical path is reduced in time, other sequences of activities may become critical. Again, such sequences can be identified from the network diagram.

It has already been stated that it is necessary during the planning stage to identify which parts of the project are to be done in-house by the main contractor and which parts are to be subcontracted. Subcontracting may be necessary because the main contractor lacks required specialist skills, or peak loads occur which cannot be covered by the main contractor's normal manpower. The subcontracting process is to a lesser degree a repeat of the main contract. Again, it is important to identify clearly those parts of the job which are to be subcontracted and to ensure that all parties fully understand their precise responsibilities. Placing undue pressure on the subcontractor to reduce prices is not likely to be of benefit in the long run. The subcontractor has to make a profit to remain in business and must be allowed to do so. Care must be taken to monitor the progress of the subcontractors to ensure delays are not incurred which will cause the whole project to slip.

Project Management Teams

Each project undertaken by an organization requires a project manager. In the case of a complex project, he may be appointed before the contract has been obtained. He can then establish during the estimating stage the exact nature of the customer's requirement. For smaller projects, the project manager may not be appointed until a contract has been obtained. In general, the earlier in the life of a project that the project manager can be appointed the better. The project manager's principal responsibilities are likely to be:

(1) Finding and appointing the manpower to manage the project.
(2) Organizing liaison between his own organization and the client.
(3) Identifying the resources required and at what point they will be needed in order to complete the project on time. These are the activities described previously under *Planning the Project.*
(4) Preparing a budget for the project.
(5) Ensuring that the project is carried out to the planned time scale and budget.
(6) Liaising within his own company between line activities and his own project team which is a staff group within the total organization.
(7) Ensuring that any testing and validation procedures are carried out so that the customer will take complete acceptance of the item produced.

The role of both the project manager and his group is made more complex by its temporary nature and because both the manager and group must perform a mixture of line and staff activities. In that the project group has direct responsibility for ensuring the project is completed, its role is a line function. However, the group may not have direct control over many of the resources required for the project. In negotiating for resources from within their organization, perhaps in competition with the demands of other projects, they are acting in a staff role in relation to the heads of these activities. This may result in a matrix type organization being formed with functional activities as the columns and projects as the rows.

The temporary nature of project management poses problems with regard to continuity of employment and job progression and promotion within the organization. Considerable care may be required within a company to ensure that those involved in managing projects are not placed at a disadvantage with regard to career progression. Once a person is involved with a project, it may be very tempting for management not to consider him for promotion until the end of a project, since this would cause much disruption. Unfortunately, the appropriate promotional opportunities are unlikely to coincide with the ending of particular projects.

The main skills and attributes of the project manager and his group must be the capacity to work well together as a team, to communicate effectively with a wide range of personnel both inside and outside their organization and to coordinate a large number of complex activities. Pressure on the project management group is likely to be continuous and at times intense. During the life of the project, they are in a constant progressing role, often having to explain the failings of one group of people to a second group who are making unreasonable demands. Usually, they have no power to control the resources other than by persuasion, yet they often receive the blame if the project falls behind.

Controlling the On-going Project

Project control involves obtaining up to date data on the state of progress of the project and comparing this with the planned rate of progress. Having compared progress against plan, the project control system must then provide management with any information necessary to take appropriate corrective action.

Progress must be measured in terms of time scales, costs and the ability of each part of the system to perform to the required specification. Continued updating of the network to show which activities have been completed will enable time scales to be checked and controlled. Costs incurred to date for activities completed and begun must be compared with planned rates of expenditure. In controlling both time scales and costs, constant updating of the forecast time and expenditure to completion is usually made. This allows corrective action to be prepared and evaluated if the project is overspent and running behind time. If corrective action is not possible, it allows the contractor to inform the client of late completion and possibly to discuss whether the extra expenditure incurred should be reflected in any increased payments. The control of performance during the life of the project requires that specifications are predetermined for the separate parts of the system. As each part is completed, appropriate testing is required to ensure that performance is satisfactory.

Ideally, networks should be used for controlling project progress. In practice, the updating of a large scale network is a complex and time-consuming process. A decision must be made on the frequency of updating the network. This is unlikely to be more than once per week or less than once per month. Difficulty may be experienced in obtaining accurate and up to date information on the state of progress of activities and then processing the information rapidly enough to give output that is not already out of date. Even though a computer may be used for the updating process, the project site is often remote from the computer and considerable time can elapse in transmitting the data from site to computer and back to the site again. The provision of out of date data to site management can produce cynicism about the value of updating the network. This may diminish the effort put into obtaining accurate data for the updating process.

The Coordination of Many Projects

Some companies, for example civil engineering contractors and heavy plant construction engineers, are faced with managing a multi-project situation. Under these circumstances, balancing the inflow of work to the company's productive capacity can present considerable problems. Effective decisions at the policy and operating levels can reduce this balance problem.

At the policy level, a decision should be made on the proportion of capacity which should be committed to long term, to medium term and to short term contracts. It is also desirable to define carefully the markets in which the company will operate. By operating in several national markets, it may be possible to avoid extreme fluctuations caused by economic cycles within particular countries. Similarly, it will be advantageous to have a product range, all the items of which are not subject to the same capital expenditure cycles.

At the operating levels, various actions can be taken. These include:

(1) A careful loading of all the departments within the organization, smoothing out each contract load to the maximum extent permitted by promised delivery dates.
(2) The use of subcontractors for peak loads and taking on 'fill-in' work in under-load situations. This latter work can involve acting as a subcontractor for other organizations, or manufacturing proprietary items which are end products in themselves.
(3) Increasing and decreasing the selling effort according to future workloads. More or fewer contracts can be quoted for and margins can be raised or lowered depending on the state of the order book.
(4) Identifying potential bottle-necks in the manufacturing system and concentrating on accurate scheduling of these particular facilities.

Problems Associated with Managing Projects

The NEDC report on *Large Industrial Sites*, published in 1970, listed a number of factors which caused delay in the completion of contracts. The major reasons given were:

(1) Late design changes.
(2) Late delivery of materials or plant.
(3) Unexpectedly low labour productivity.

Other reasons included:

(1) Labour disputes.
(2) Poor subcontractor performance.
(3) Shortages of skilled labour.
(4) Faulty materials.
(5) Faulty workmanship.
(6) Late handover of work.
(7) Bad weather.
(8) Access problems.
(9) Inadequate management.

In more general terms these troubles are caused by:

(1) Inadequate project definition.
(2) Poor planning of the project, often resulting from a lack of, or inadequate use of, available techniques.
(3) Selection of poor and untrained project managers.
(4) Poor choice of subcontractors.
(5) Poor control of the on-going project.
(6) Labour problems on the site. These are often caused by the employment of several subcontractors, each with different conditions of employment, on the same site. The main contractor should establish standard conditions of employment on the site for each category of labour and make these required conditions when subcontracting work.
(7) Acts of God, usually involving the weather but sometimes associated with the physical conditions of the site which is not normally of the contractor's choosing.

Conclusions

Managing large scale projects imposes a particular set of operational management problems. These involve the marshalling of a complex range of physical and human resources in a manner that permits effective use of each resource during the life of the project. Planning and control techniques have been developed, largely based on network analysis. These techniques are designed to ensure that projects are carried out in the required time scale and at the forecast cost.

Project management is different from other forms of operations management in that it involves a constant cycle of selection, build up, run down, reselection etc. of the project management group. Those involved in project management must develop high skills in communication if they are to control and coordinate the many groups involved in the project. Top management must ensure that terms and conditions of employment are such that the project management job does not become unattractive through lack of opportunities for promotion and higher salary. Employment conditions must compensate for the constant disruptions to the project manager's personal life.

Reference

National Economic Development Office (1970) *Large Industrial Sites*, Report of the Working Party on Large Industrial Construction Sites, HMSO, London.

Further Reading

Battersnu, A. (1970) *Network Analysis for Planning and Scheduling*, Macmillan, London (3rd Edition).

Burman, P. J. (1972) *Precedence Networks for Project Planning and Control*, McGraw-Hill, London.

Hensen, J. H. (1968) 'The Case of the Precarious Program', *Harvard Business Review*, Jan-Feb 1968.

Jonason, P. (1971) 'Project Management, Swedish Style', *Harvard Business Review*, Nov–Dec 1971.

Lockyer, K. G. (1969) *An Introduction to Critical Path Analysis*, Pitman, London (3rd Edition).

Taylor, W. J. and Watling, T. F. (1973) *Practical Project Management*, Business Books, London.

Toffler, A. (1970) *Future Shock*, Bodley Head, London (see particularly the chapter 'The Coming Adhocracy').

CHAPTER 12

Managing the Process — Service Systems

Introduction

This book is concerned with operational systems in both manufacturing and non-manufacturing environments. This chapter considers in greater detail the differences between the two and the management problems peculiar to non-manufacturing systems.

Government national economic statistics draw clear distinctions between the output of different industrial sectors. Typically economic statistics are divided into such categories as agriculture, forestry and mining, the construction industry, manufacturing industry and a series of industries which can together be categorized as service activities. This final group includes transportation, communications, the provision of utilities (e.g. electricity, gas, water etc.), wholesaling and retailing, financial activities (e.g. banks, insurance, building societies etc.) and a final group, generally termed services, which includes hotels, entertainment etc.

A precise definition of a service industry is not readily available. One view is that a distinction between products and services can be made on the basis that the legal ownership of a product is possible whereas legal ownership of a service is not possible. Another view is that products are tangible items which can be purchased, stored and consumed at the purchaser's discretion at a time of his or her choosing. On the other hand, services are provided and consumed more or less simultaneously.

However, despite the lack of a precise definition, it is very clear that in developed economies the service sector is growing more rapidly than the product producing sector when measured in terms of contribution to gross national product. As Chapter 1 indicates, in many developed economies the output of the service sector has already surpassed that of the product producing sector. Given such statistics, it is clear that the study of operations management cannot ignore the rapid development of the service activity. It is necessary, therefore, for the student of operations management both to consider how techniques developed for and applied to managing manufacturing activities can be applied to service activities, and also to identify those problems peculiar to service activities and to seek solutions to them.

The Boundary Between Manufacturing and Service

Levitt (1972) argues that there is no such thing as a service industry. He suggests that there is a service component to all industries. It is simply greater in some than in others. He points out that approximately 50% of the employees of a major computer manufacturer and a major bank are engaged in giving service to the respective organizations' customers. The other 50% of the employees are engaged in the back-up systems required to give that service. In the case of the computer company, the back-up facility is the manufacture of computers. In the case of the bank, the back-up is the processing of paper. In spite of this more or less equal division between manufacturing 'activity' and service 'activity' in the two organizations, the computer company is categorized as a manufacturing company while the bank is classified as a service company. All manufacturers of products rely on a service type activity to sell their products, to ensure that they operate successfully and to obtain repeat business from satisfied customers. This applies equally if the product is sold as consumer goods or industrial goods. Unfortunately, far too many manufacturers of products view the service they give in the market place as an extra rather than as an essential part of the total operating system. Failure to recognize the totality of the system can result in poorly designed product lines, dissatisfied distributors, disgruntled customers and vulnerability to other organizations which do understand the complete requirements of the market place.

Levitt draws the following distinctions between the manufacturing and the service activity. He points out that manufacturing is seen to involve expensive machinery and the concentration of a workforce in a central place where the jobs are highly engineered and often dictated by the machine's requirements. In contrast, services are seen as being performed in many places, often on a one-to-one basis, resulting in people being loosely supervised and working under highly variable conditions. He argues that manufacturing has become so efficient because people have identified the job to be done and then conceived new, often radically different ways in which to do it. However, it is regarded as difficult, if not impossible, to make service activities more efficient because they are carried out in such loosely structured situations. Levitt suggests that when people start thinking about service activities in the way they have previously thought about manufacturing activities there will be dramatic improvements in the methods of providing customer service, and in the cost effectiveness of the service.

Even if one accepts such possibilities for great improvement in service activities, there are often fundamental problems associated with the provision of service which are different from those found in manufacturing activities. This chapter discusses these problems.

Establishing Objectives in a Service System

If a market exists for a manufactured product, that market will establish the price. The overall success of the company manufacturing for the market can be gauged by its ability to make a profit by efficient manufacturing and selling. The sub-systems within the total organization are usually measured in terms of labour efficiency, machine utilization, variations against budget etc. The overall measure of success in many service activities can, of course, be established by the level of profit and return on investment. However, there are a growing number of situations where such a measure is either impossible or inappropriate. Transportation systems in most developed countries can no longer make a profit in the conventional sense. Many bus systems have experienced the vicious circle of higher costs leading to higher fares, leading to fewer users, leading to reduced services and a smaller base to spread fixed overheads, resulting in higher costs etc. This demonstrates the inadequacy of the profit concept as a means of determining the system objective. In the United Kingdom, the whole medical system is, by definition, non-profit making. The British Broadcasting Corporation, seen by many countries as a model to emulate, is again, by definition, non-profit making. The objective in such circumstances then surely can be simply to balance expenditure with revenue. Unfortunately, the problem is not so simple. The amount of expenditure is determined by the level and quality of service offered. Revenue for many large scale service systems originates from the government. They, in their turn, have conflicting demands for the limited resources available. Thus, the basic objective of a service system may have to be defined in terms of the service given. This objective may be to provide transport to certain towns and villages with specified frequency or ensure that patients do not have to wait longer than a given number of days before obtaining treatment for certain ailments. Once these fundamental objectives are defined, it then becomes necessary to achieve them with minimum cost.

Objectives for operational units may also pose problems. Issues concerning the quality of the service to be given will almost inevitably arise. How long should a customer have to wait to be served at the bank during lunch hour when large numbers of other people also choose to use the facilities? How long should it take to check out at the supermarket? What should be the level of occupancy of the cafeteria in a motorway service station? Again, only when these types of objectives are defined, can labour and facility utilization percentages be fixed. Control by budget variances is often applicable but frequently, more direct and obvious control may be required in managing the operation.

Determination of service level is a fundamental requirement in all types of service activity. This may appear a self-evident statement yet the managers of many service systems fail to define this basic objective. Commonly, the level of service only becomes discussed in quantified terms when suggestions are made to cut manpower levels to reduce costs. This generally leads to the response 'but you will destroy the quality of service'. If the required quality of service has not been established, it is not possible to know whether reduction in the number of personnel will drop the service below the required level. We would argue therefore that it is vital to define the quality of service which the system has to provide and to incorporate this into the basic objectives set for the system.

Capacity Utilization

It has already been stated in Chapter 7 that one of the fundamental aspects of a service system is its inability to build up an inventory of its goods. The seats in a theatre, the rooms in a hotel, the seats on a train, the time of the television repair man cannot be stored. Seats are either full or empty when the play is performed or the train travels. Hotel rooms are occupied or empty. The television service man is either engaged on a job or idle. Yesterday's emptiness or idleness cannot be used to fill today's overload. The manager of a service system has a number of fundamental decisions to make about the capacity which he will provide. Capacity provided will naturally in some sense be related to demand. Demand, unfortunately, will vary throughout the day, throughout the week, throughout the month, throughout the year or even from year to year. Is the system planned, therefore, to provide capacity for the peak load which may be placed on it, for the average load, for some level between these two points, or even for a level below the average demand? Provision of capacity to meet peak load demands is most unlikely to prove economic. Therefore, it probably has to be accepted that some business will be lost since the excess demand will almost certainly move to a competitive operation. The traveller will use another airline, the theatregoer will go and see another play. In some systems, however, the peak load is not easily transferable. In a motorway service area, the peak load is unlikely to move on to the next service station, particularly if the load is caused by the arrival of several coaches within a short time interval. Management will have to accept that they give a less than adequate service under such conditions and hope that the customers will not be so delayed that on future occasions they avoid that particular service station. There may be no alternative available, as in the case of medical care. Queues will therefore simply have to grow or shrink according to demand.

The basic system employed to match demand to capacity and to reduce dissatisfied customers who cannot be served is the reservation system. The reservation plan for a theatre or an aeroplane is equivalent to the daily schedule in a machine shop. As demand is placed on the system, the facilities are utilized. Management does not, however, have to be entirely passive in this process of matching demand to capacity. The pricing mechanism can be used to fill capacity which might otherwise be left empty. Reduced rates for off-peak travel are now a well developed part of virtually all transportation systems. Urban transportation systems suffer from severe peak loads when people go to and from work. Unfortunately, it is not possible to employ staff only at these periods. They must be employed for a full working day. Thus, any additional revenue generated by off-peak travel is almost all gross contribution towards fixed running costs. The airlines have developed a system whereby people prepared to fill available vacant seats at the last minute may travel at a reduced price. There is, however, a risk of not being transported at all if no seats are available. This is yet another device for generating additional revenue.

Peak loads are, nonetheless, unavoidable in many types of service systems. Holiday resorts are only attractive at certain times of the year; football matches are still almost exclusively played on Saturday afternoons; theatre going, in spite of a few brave attempts at lunchtime theatre, is still basically an evening activity. Where peaks cannot be moved they must as far as possible be catered for. In labour intensive situations, this is usually done through the employment of temporary and part-time labour. The hotel industry is notorious for its migrant labour force.

Restaurants requiring evening labour may attract people who wish to carry out a second job (often termed 'moonlighters'). Married women may seek work for periods of fifteen to thirty hours per week. This makes them ideal for staffing peak load situations.

The labour force can, therefore, be to some extent flexible but, even so, this flexibility must be planned. This requires making a forecast of the demand that will' be placed on the service system and planning labour accordingly Unfortunately, demands on service systems, no matter how well forecast, can be extremely uncertain and extra labour may turn up only to remain idle, while the peak demand occurs at a time of low staffing.

Labour in the Service System

Virtually all service systems are labour intensive. Some, however, also involve high levels of capital, for example, vehicles in transportation systems or land and buildings in hotel and recreational systems. Whether the capital involved is high or low, the customer's satisfaction and his future custom will depend on his reaction to the people he meets within the service system. Efficient service will not be appreciated if it is accompanied by rudeness, untidiness or nonchalance. Thus, the ability to give service cheerfully and without subservience is of prime importance in a service organization.

Yet so many systems fail to achieve this very evident requirement. Often the tasks involved are simple and repetitive. Temporary labour is used in many systems and there is often a very high rate of labour turnover. Obvious steps can be taken to improve the ability of the labour force to perform the task adequately. These include the careful selection of labour, appropriate training and satisfactory working conditions, particularly with regard to pay. Pay should be high enough to ensure that proper remuneration is not dependent on receiving tips from the customers. However, personnel policies alone are not likely to engender the motivation that ensures the majority of the workforce will put the customer first and go to the necessary lengths to satisfy customer requirements.

Some organizations do, however, achieve this level of motivation. They create the belief that the organization exists to serve the customer and that they can do it better than any of their competitors. Such a highly motivated workforce, which takes pride in performing its job to the best of its ability, can only be created through prolonged management effort and example. However, it is the most valuable asset a service organization can acquire. It will receive repeat business which will make it the envy of its competitors.

To the customer, the particular employee who is serving him becomes, in his eyes, the company. It can therefore be argued that the individual employee's discretion should be minimized. Levitt argues that standardization of procedure ensures uniformity of service, thus ensuring a high proportion of contented customers. It also, he argues, makes it easier to train workforces which are often transient in nature. This argument is undoubtedly powerful but can be questioned.

Given that jobs often make limited demands on intellectual capability in many service systems, workforce satisfaction is derived from the human contact experienced in fulfilling a job. Further simplification of jobs and reduction, or even removal, of discretion in reacting to customer needs, could reduce motivation. Good procedures are certainly required but discretionary activity on the part of those giving service would seem to be a basic requirement for a system which will adapt to changing demands.

Organization of the Service System

Many types of service have to be taken to the customer, either to homes or to centres of population. Even when the customer goes to the service (hotels, restaurants, transportation etc.), each unit is usually limited in size to match the level of demand. Thus, managing a service organization involves managing many dispersed small units, each individually labour intensive. There are, therefore, likely to be a limited number of activities which can be carried out from the centre of the organization. These may be limited to:

(1) decisions for future new capacity,
(2) overall personnel policies,
(3) the purchase of major supplies,
(4) central control of operating results.

Successful operation of invididual facilities is likely to require a high level of delegation to the manager on the spot. A successful operation will, therefore, require initiative and motivation at local manager level. The demands, particularly on personal time, are likely to be severe since many service organizations operate on a round-the-clock, seven days a week basis. Therefore, the question of management motivation is just as significant as that of workforce motivation. Motivation generated by a sense of ownership can be very helpful. This has been achieved literally by some organizations which have adopted a franchising system. This involves the manager owning his own local operation although it provides a nationally known service. The back-up of a large organization can provide better promotion, cheaper purchasing, better staff training facilities and more readily available access to capital than the small unit can provide. The USA has adapted the franchising approach to service industries more extensively than the United Kingdom.

Organization of service activity is, therefore, likely to take the form of a line and staff system. The line is likely to be relatively short and very flat with large numbers of operating units, each with a manager who should be allowed considerable discretion in his day to day operational management. Staff functions are likely to be limited to those activities which can generate savings through central control and those which must be considered in a time perspective longer than that normally taken by operations managers.

Controlling Service Functions

Control of service activities represents a particularly difficult challenge. With objectives often difficult to define, operating units small and dispersed and the need to give greater discretion to local managers, a successful control system will need to be delicately balanced. Too tight a control from the centre is likely to destroy the motivation of local management. Cost cutting activities initiated from the centre may well damage the quality of the service at local level. On the other hand, inadequate control may result in over-diverse approaches to similar problems, thus causing unnecessarily high costs. Although it is often difficult to establish standards in service activities, such difficulties should not be made an excuse for not making the attempt. It has been argued in Chapter 3 that it is necessary to establish control in indirect labour areas as well as direct labour areas in manufacturing systems. It is also necessary to establish performance criteria for labour in service activities. Banks are a good example of organizations which have established explicit labour standards through the use of work measurement techniques. However, in all types of service system, standards are set when work loads are established. The decision on how many tables a waitress should service is a decision about work standards. Unfortunately, all too often such decisions are made using little factual data. The data can always be obtained, but it takes time and costs money to collect. The extent of the detail of such data must be determined in the context of the overall control system.

Conclusion

The service sector is growing in importance in all developed economies and, in many, has surpassed the product producing sector. No clear distinction exists between product producing and service producing activities. Indeed, it can be argued that all goods producing activities involve some element of service. Ignoring this aspect of the total activity can lead to failure to fulfil the requirements of the market.

Service systems are operations systems with particular characteristics. Probably the most important characteristic is the inability to build up an inventory of service. Service is consumed more or less as it is created. This problem is further compounded by the fact that most service systems face highly fluctuating demands. Peak loads may be several times the minimum demand load. It becomes imperative, therefore, to seek to utilize spare capacity and to devise systems to handle peak loads. The pricing mechanism has been used to fulfil this purpose.

Difficulties are often experienced in obtaining and maintaining motivated management and workforce. Management difficulties are compounded by the diversity of locations in which the service activity is carried out. Control of service activities must seek a balance between allowing discretion at the local management level and providing adequate guidance for the establishment of realistic targets.

Reference

Levitt, T. (1972) 'Production Line Approach to Service', *Harvard Business Review*, Sept–Oct 1972.

Further Reading

Reed, J. (1971) 'Sure it's a Bank but I think of it as a Factory', *Innovation*, 23.
Staib, W. C. and Suhm, R. T. (1974) 'The growth of Management Engineering in Hospitals', *Industrial Engineering*, Oct 1974, 44–48.

CHAPTER 13

The Measurement of Manufacturing Performance

Introduction

Systems Synthesis

In Chapter 1, we identified the operations manager's role as one of assessing the effects of interactions between sub-systems on overall system performance. In order to do this it will be necessary for the manager to have a set of objectives against which to judge system performance. This, in turn, requires a set of performance criteria. It is, therefore, necessary to consider the framework within which operations performance is to be measured.

Operating Systems Performance at the Company Level

The first step in determining the companywide effectiveness of an operations policy is a comprehensive analysis of performance over an extended time period. Company performance is traditionally expressed in financial terms; the analysis of performance that we suggest here is no exception to this rule. It should differ from the traditional performance review frequently given in company annual reports in two ways. Firstly, different ratios should be calculated and secondly, operations management should be deeply involved in both the calculation and interpretation of the data.

Figure 31 details the data to be collected and the ratios to be calculated. A minimum of five years' data should be collected, as the object of the exercise is to obtain and interpret trends. All financial data should be expressed in constant monetary terms, since current rates of inflation make meaningful comparison of actual figures impossible.

Most of the headings are self-explanatory but a brief discussion and commentary are included. The first set of figures show whether any movements are taking place in the proportion of raw material, direct labour, variable and fixed overhead costs. They also indicate the relative importance of each of these cost categories. It is important to understand these relationships. There is, for example, little point in establishing elaborate controls for direct labour while ignoring materials control, if

The following data and indices should be established ideally over a five year period. Where applicable, values should be adjusted to constant £ to remove the effect of inflation.

(1) *Movement of Costs and Profit £ and %*
  Sales
  Cost of Raw Materials
  Cost of Direct Labour
  Cost of Variable Overheads
  Contribution
  Cost of Fixed Overheads
  Profit before Interest and Tax

(2) *Significance of Own Manufacturing System £ and %*
  Share of Sales Made in House
  Share of Sales Bought out (Factored)

(3) *Structure and Cost of Employment*
  Number of Employees
  Number of Direct Employees
  Number of Indirect Employees
  Ratio Indirect: Direct
  Total Cost of Employment
  Total Wage Cost per Employee

(4) *Labour Productivity*
  Cost of Bought In Goods and Services
  Total Value Added (Sales — Bought In Goods & Services)
  Sales per Employee
  Value Added per Employee

(5) *Current Consumption of Value Added*
  Value Added per £ of Employment Cost

(6) *Utilization of Stocks*
  Total Value of Stocks
  Total Value of Raw Materials
  Total Value of Work-in-Process
  Total Value of Finished Goods
  Stock Turnover (Total Cost of Goods Sold: Total Value of Stocks)

(7) *Financial Resource per Employee*
  Total Capital Employed
  Total Capital per Employee

(8) *Physical Facilities per Employee*
  Investment in Fixed Assets
  Investment in Plant and Equipment
  Fixed Assets per Employee
  Plant and Equipment per Employee

Figure 31 A company-wide view of operating system performance

the former accounts for only 10% and the latter for 50% of the costs. The comparison of the proportion of finished products made in and bought out indicates whether the manufacturing facility is growing or declining in importance. If it is declining, this may indicate a reduction in competitiveness compared with similar manufacture.

The third set of data shows the cost of employing labour; the fourth shows output trends in terms of sales and value added per employee. Fifthly, the ratio between value added and total wage cost is shown. If this ratio were to fall to 1.0, then all value added would be used to reward labour. This would be an impossible situation since no funds would be available to replace capital equipment or to pay any form of interest or dividend on capital. Much of UK industry has exhibited a constant decline in this ratio during the past few years. Many companies are, in effect, using up more and more of what is produced in current payment.

The sixth set of data analyses the effective utilization of all forms of stocks in the system. Finally, the seventh and eighth sets of data consider the availability of capital per employee. Three figures are suggested: the total capital employed, the total fixed assets and the plant and machinery per employee. As already stated, these final two ratios show little growth in many organizations during the past few years.

It is important to re-emphasize that the purpose of the analysis is to determine current trends. Are costs moving relative to each other? Is the cost of employing labour growing much more rapidly than increases in sales and value added per employee? Is an ever greater proportion of the value added being consumed in wage costs? Are stocks being effectively utilized? Is sufficient hardware, in the form of plant and machinery, available to the employees in order to allow them to increase productivity? While trends within a given organization can be discerned and interpreted, the analysis will be even more useful if comparison can be made with other similar organizations. Such comparisons may be difficult to make where only published financial data is available. However, participation in interfirm comparisons may well provide much of the data suggested.

This form of performance analysis should identify any long term trends in the operating system, whether adverse or favourable. When a trend has been identified, it is likely that more detailed data collection and analysis will be required to determine its causes. It is likely that long rather than short term action will be needed to reverse adverse trends.

Internal Performance Measurement in Operating Systems

Most operating systems have performance measured on a weekly and monthly basis. Typically, weekly performance measures will cover:

(1) Direct operator efficiency measured against standard times. Information on payment for waiting time, unmeasured work etc. may also be included.
(2) Machine utilization (distinguishing idle time and breakdown time from utilization time). Utilization time, however, may not distinguish set-up time from effective operating time.

Monthly performance measures are usually expressed in monetary terms showing performance against budget. Variances are generally shown in terms of direct labour, indirect labour, material, volume and overheads.

Clearly, this type of weekly and monthly data provides a measure of manufacturing performance. However, it usually does little to help diagnose existing and impending problems in the system. There is just not enough data expressed in the right way to allow significant trends to be recognized and then to measure the effect of corrective action.

Other measures exist which would be far more useful for diagnostic and monitoring purposes. It must be stressed, however, that it is important to ascertain and understand trends in data. This means that 'snapshots' of the situation obtained by 'one off' exercises will do little to provide lasting control. Regular data is required if the nature and causes of fluctuations in system performance are to be understood.

Possible additional performance criteria are:

(1) ORDER PROCESSING
Delivery performance

$$\text{Throughout efficiency} = \frac{\text{(actual process time)}}{\text{(time in system)}}$$

Lost orders
Customer service (orders not satisfied from stock)
(2) QUALITY
Customer returns
Yield (scrap) losses
Reworking time
(3) FACILITIES
Manpower utilization
Machine utilization
Machine breakdown
(4) EMPLOYEES
Absenteeism
Turnover rates
Losses through disputes

We consider some of the more important of the above in more detail.

Delivery Performance

The ultimate effectiveness of the manufacturing system is its ability to attract a continuing flow of new orders. Two major factors are likely to influence the inflow of new orders: price and delivery. Measurement systems tend in a variety of ways to focus on cost, thus controlling prices. There is usually much less reporting on the ability of the system to meet planned and promised delivery dates. The simplest measure of this is to record the percentage of orders delivered by the promised date. A further dimension can be added by showing the average number of days late for those orders not delivered on time. The trend in these two simple measures readily shows the extent to which the manufacturing system is meeting the delivery demands placed on it.

While these overall measures are useful for observing the effectiveness of the total system, more detailed measures are required if action is to be taken to control decline in performance. This can be done by obtaining the same two performance measures for each section of the production system. This would require batches to have a planned departure from each section and would need to tie in closely with the progress control function.

These measures should not be recorded in isolation from changes in delivery promises. Average delivery promise time from receipt of order and actual delivery performance should be prominently displayed to everyone working in the operations system.

Volume of Work in the System

Several measures can be taken which highlight changes in the volume of work in the system. They include:

(1) The total number of batches in the system.
(2) The ratio of the time required to complete the work on a batch to the time the batch spends in the system (throughput efficiency). This ratio can be calculated as an average for all the batches produced in a given time period.
(3) A comparison over time, of the batches coming out of the system compared with the number going in. Two trends require monitoring here. The first is the balance between input and output. For this purpose, each batch number must only be counted when the first part of the batch emerges. The second trend is to measure the extent to which batch splitting is taking place. A measure of this can be shown by expressing the number of split batches leaving the system in a given time period as a percentage of the total batches leaving the system.
(4) The cost of the progress chasing or expediting activity expressed as a percentage of the direct labour cost.

Effective Working Time

It has already been stated that in functional organizations batches spend most of their time in the system in queues. Part of this queueing time, though often a relatively minor part, is caused because the processing system has to be set up before productive activity can begin. Set-up, although necessary, is not productive. However, it is easy to view it as useful work and therfore not to measure set-up time. The ratio of set-up time to running time should be monitored both by section and for the total system for each time period. It can be forecast that if the system is overloaded, the resulting batch splitting and poor sequencing will produce excessive setup time. Equally, in an underloaded system, set-up may be dragged out to give the appearance of full utilization.

Operator Performance

Most systems monitor direct operator performance. The effectiveness of weekly performance measures for discerning longer term trends may be doubtful. The basic trends which require monitoring are:

(1) The proportion of the direct labour wage bill which is paid for actual production work rather than set-up, waiting time, non productive unmeasured work, overtime premium etc.
(2) The actual total direct labour cost compared with the anticipated direct labour standard cost of the output achieved. This may be similar to the direct labour variance in the budget, if the budget has not been 'adjusted' to allow for anticipated levels of non-productive activity.
(3) The ratio of shop floor and other indirect labour costs to the direct wage cost for productive work, i.e. excluding waiting time etc.

These measures taken over time should indicate whether direct and indirect labour productivity are improving and the extent to which the payment system is manipulated to produce relatively constant wages, regardless of the level of productive activity.

This last issue is worth very careful examination. It is probable, whatever the wage payment system used, that wages will fluctuate far less than output. This is socially very desirable but must be recognized by management, who should not pretend that costs are variable if they are in fact fixed. Nonetheless, there may be ways in which the system is being unfairly manipulated by the labour force. Probably the most common manipulation is of overtime. Is this created to boost wage packets or necessary to obtain output? Circumstances will obviously differ but careful monitoring should indicate the real situation. The ratio of true productive hours (again excluding all extraneous items such as waiting, non-productive work etc.) to hours worked will probably show that the shorter the working week the higher the ratio and vice versa. Major revisions may be required in basic wage structures. However, the extent to which production could be increased within a standard working week, if the reward is high and overtime clearly not acceptable, might be surprising to many organizations.

We have presented a wide range of performance measures, though the list is by no means complete and many more detailed criteria may be used in individual areas such as purchasing and distribution. However, at the operations manager's level the detail will usually be summarized into the higher level criteria suggested, and in many cases only a small subset of the detailed measures will be readily available.

Although many 'quantifiable' performance measures have been suggested, there are many other important criteria which cannot be measured in quantitative terms. These include:

(1) Employee morale.
(2) The 'quality of working life'.
(3) Customer satisfaction.
(4) Flexibility of the system to react to market (and other) changes.

These criteria may have a considerable impact over time on the measurable criteria. Concentration only on quantifiable performance measures may, in the long run, have a detrimental effect. Typically, in manufacturing systems, engineering and technical staff are biased towards the achievement of short term objectives based on quantitative performance measures. For example, in terms of the long run profitability (and viability) of the company, it may be essential to retain considerable flexibility in the production system. The preservation of such flexibility will generally be expensive in terms of unit costs and capital utilization, and the manager must trade off such costs against the gains in flexibility. Thus, a problem of automation involves not only consideration of the effects on unit costs, materials usage etc., but also of the more intangible costs of flexibility and employee relations. The operations manager often finds it difficult to justify radical changes in the production system in order to achieve greater flexibility, if these changes involve higher costs in some of the more easily measured performance criteria.

The Volvo car assembly plant at Kalmar in Sweden has, for example, been designed to allow group working rather than straightforward flow-line (short cycle-time) work. The direct cost of making such work structuring possible is of the order of £1 million. The plant was initially estimated to cost about £9 million, roughly £1 million more than the cost of conventional plant. Labour turnover rates and absenteeism have been very high in the Swedish car industry (turnover of 50% or more per annum) and it is by no means certain that changes in work organization such as group working will necessarily have a favourable effect on either absenteeism or workers' attitudes to their jobs. Nevertheless, the management may expect considerable operating benefits in terms of quality improvement and flexibility from the new arrangements and these alone may justify the additional investment.

Similarly, the rearrangement of the assembly work for model cars described in Chapter 9 required extra capital investment at the individual work stations in order to give lower lost time due to handling. However, the benefits of increased production flexibility probably far outweigh the labour productivity gains, though they are very difficult to quantify. Similar arguments frequently arise with the introduction of group working. Many of the potential benefits are impossible to quantify while the direct costs are relatively easy to assess. Perhaps this goes some way towards explaining the relative infrequency of such changes in UK industry when compared with such countries as Sweden and Holland.

In summary, the measurement of manufacturing performance cannot be totally specified in a quantitative way and many of the important criteria are missing from traditional performance measurement systems. Judgement of the relative import-ance of the quantitative factors in a particular situation is a key skill of the successful operations manager. He must be able to assess the effects of changes in one set of performance criteria on other performance measures. It is particularly appropriate to consider here the time scale of the decision making processes with which we are concerned. Operations managers are often concerned primarily with short time horizon decisions and this can result in decision making on the basis of short-run costs/benefits (quantitative and qualitative) when they may not be the most important criteria. If any manager only expects to hold an appointment for a relatively limited period (say up to 2 years), there may be considerable pressure on him to obtain the best performance possible within that period, even if long term performance suffers. He may defend his action on the basis of future uncertainty. For example, in the short run it might seem advantageous to avoid an industrial dispute at any cost in order to maintain output. If such a policy continues for very long, the company may well be forced out of the market by high labour costs. Again, a production manager may often be pressed (by marketing or even by the managing director) into expediting a particular customer order. The effect of such action may create greater delay for other orders, resulting in more lost sales and a greater loss in profit than if no action had been taken. Operations managers in the make-to-order situation can rarely quantify the effects of such an action and therefore cannot justify a refusal. All they can do is try to minimize the effects.

Conclusions

Many criteria of production performance are criteria of efficiency, for example, stock turnover, quality reject rates etc. These may be improved through detailed analysis of the particular area of concern. Yet the operating system exists in order to achieve certain objectives such as acceptable, reliable delivery periods, the meeting of quality standards etc. and its performance should be measured in terms of the effectiveness with which it meets all these objectives. The relative effectiveness of the total system must be seen in terms of synthesis of all the interrelated sub-systems. Such synthesis has in the past been largely based on management judgement. However, the relative operational effectiveness of systems which have been carefully synthesized, such as automatic plants and, to some extent, assembly lines, has shown that there is a sound case for objective synthesis (Starr, 1972). Management judgement alone is no longer enough. We must be able to identify system interactions and trade-offs and to evaluate them rationally before we use judgement to reach a compromise between conflicting objectives. It is not simply a question of synergy, the whole system being greater than the sum of its parts, but also that the whole system is different in some fundamental ways from the sum of its parts. It has an organic character which is quite distinct from the sum of its inorganic constituents.

Reference

Starr, M. K. (1972) *Production Management, Systems and Synthesis*, Prentice-Hall Inc., New Jersey (Second Edition).

Further Reading

Ball, R. J. (1968) 'The Use of Value Added in Measuring Managerial Efficiency', *Business Ratios*, Summer 1968.

154

Craig, C. E. and Harris, R. C. (1973) 'Total Productivity Measurement at the Firm Level', *Sloan Management Review*, Spring 1973.

Moore, J. G. (1973) 'Added Value as an Index of Industrial Effectiveness', *Work Study and Management Services*, January 1973.

Norman, R. G. and Bahiri, S. (1972) *Productivity Measurement and Incentives*, Butterworths, London.

Williamson, D. T. N. (1970) *Trade Balance in the 1970's — The Role of Mechanical Engineering*, NEDO, London.

CHAPTER 14

Establishing an Operations Policy

Introduction

Operations are, almost invariably, the most complex part of both manufacturing and non-manufacturing systems. Running the operations incurs the greatest part of the organization's total expenditure. The need to establish clear objectives and strategy for operations has been recognized for at least the past decade (Skinner 1966, 1969). Unfortunately, many organizations do not understand the effect of conflicting demands on the operations system. Clear objectives and strategy are not established. The interaction between operations and the strategies of other parts of the business is not recognized.

To state that the objective of an operations system is to provide the highest quality product or service at the lowest cost is of little use to the operations manager. When determining strategies for his system, he has to consider many conflicting demands and pressures which will inevitably lead to the need for compromise. It is important, however, that operations policy is not formed by these conflicting pressures and demands. If it is, there will be no policy. Resources are likely to be poorly used and there will be confusion throughout the operations system. Operations policy must be formulated in a positive way. This can only be done by understanding the nature of the conflicting demands placed on the operations system, an understanding which can only be obtained by detailed analysis. This will determine the current state of a system and how it is performing. From the analysis, it is possible to establish an appropriate operations policy and to devise the necessary strategies for fulfilling the policy.

Conflicting Demands Placed on the System

Salesmen in the organization naturally feel their role is to provide the best service possible to the customer. Where stocks of finished goods are held, the sales department would like to be able to offer delivery of all items from stock. Items should never be discontinued from the product range but new items should be added constantly in order to increase the customer's choice. If the customer wants an item with a special modification, naturally the salesman wants to oblige while still maintaining delivery and with minimal increase in price. When a new product is introduced, it should be available for the market immediately in the necessary volume and without any teething troubles. Quality at all times should be perfect, but if there are warranty claims, spare parts should be available immediately to service the customer's requirements. Price should be beneath that of competitors and there should be plenty of scope for offering discounts to encourage the customer to buy.

Where products are not held in stock but made to customer order, the salesman naturally wishes to promise the minimum possible delivery time. Delivery promises are often offered which, given the state of the current order book, simply cannot be achieved by the manufacturing system. No salesman likes to turn away an order. Yet, the acceptance of additional orders within a given time period may simply mean that many customers will be dissatisfied with the delivery performance of the company and manufacturing costs will, in fact, be increased.

On the other hand, the accountants will wish to run the business with the minimum possible working capital. Inevitably, a major part of the working capital is the stock of raw materials, the work in process and the finished goods stock. Pressures to reduce stocks of all forms are a constant feature of most manufacturing organizations. The positive benefit of stock reduction is readily calculable on the basis of interest saved on the reduced working capital. What is not so readily calculable, however, is what effect the reduction of stock will have on the running of the manufacturing system. Nobody calculates the cost of delays when men and machinery are idle because of the lack of material; or the expense caused by later delivery to customers; or the cost of expediting orders through the manufacturing system for items out of stock; or for manufacturing items in uneconomical batch quantities. Clearly, stocks must be kept under reasonable control; but there is a dangerous illusion of achievement when the saving side of the equation can so readily be calculated but the potential loss side of the equation is so hard to calculate.

The operations manager should, of course, make sure that the latest process technology is used. This must, however, be done within limited capital availability and under the scrutiny of a capital appraisal system which implies a crystal ball ability in the forecasting of future events. When permission is given to spend capital on new process equipment, it is expected that it will be installed without causing any disruption to production. This is often a very unrealistic expectation.

The operations manager is expected to make constant reductions in his costs. This, in spite of rises in the price of materials which may be outstripping general rates of inflation and rises in wages, which in real terms far exceed any corresponding rise in productivity. Labour productivity should, of course, be increased but not at the expense of dissatisfaction among the workforce through redundancy, changes in manning levels or a demand for increased personal effort.

The operations manager will also face pressures both to improve the internal work environment and to limit damage to the external environment. In the former case, this will require warmer, lighter, quieter conditions, more interesting jobs, better training for the workforce and better social amenities. These improvements must not, however, disrupt the manufacturing system or at any stage add to the cost of the finished product. To satisfy environmental demands, noxious water and airborne pollution must be reduced and preferably eliminated, but with the minimum capital spending on what will be seen, in financial terms, as unproductive.

All these pressures will be exerted on the manufacturing system at one time or another. The precise nature of the pressure may vary. It may move from improving delivery, to reducing costs, to raising quality, to offering more product variety, to reducing stocks, to making the plant a more attractive place to work in. The operations manager must cope with all these changes in emphasis and in the long term, maintain a balance between what often seem to be conflicting demands. Ideally, he should educate those who present him with changing demands, about the consequences of shifts in emphasis. No system can remain rigid, but over-frequent change reduces operating effectiveness. The operations manager must establish the capabilities of his system, identify the long term trends and, on the basis of this knowledge, decide how to use the system most effectively.

Designing Operations Policy and Strategies

Given the nature of the many conflicting demands faced by the operating system, it is important that positive objectives and strategies are established. Without these, the operations system will be pushed first in one direction and then in another, depending on the latest demand and the loudest voices.

The derivation of any sets of objectives and strategies demands detailed analysis. Operations are no exception. We have already argued in the previous chapter for detailed measurement of operations performance on an on-going basis. This measurement of performance is only part of the analysis required to establish objectives and strategies.

Figure 32 shows a conceptual framework for the design and implementation of an operations policy. It can be seen from the diagram that the analysis stage involves two processes. Firstly, it is necessary to understand the operations in the context of the total industry. This analysis involves seeking the answers to many questions. Although the exact nature of the questions may vary from industry to industry, typically the questions which must be resolved are those listed in the appendix at the end of this chapter.

Analysis of the internal operations must establish information about operating performance, the product range, the availability of plant, equipment, capital, manpower and raw materials. Again, the necessary questions are given in detail in the appendix. The internal analysis should establish the strengths and weaknesses of the operating system given the currently available resources.

On the basis of these analyses, long term operating objectives should be established. Every effort should be made to quantify objectives. Objectives may be established in relation to the more obvious areas of costs, quality, delivery performance, stock levels and labour and equipment productivity. These are all areas where objectives can be quantified. Other areas which might have specific objectives established could include the introduction of job enrichment, the maximum number of employees in future (and even existing) plants or the change from functional to group working. Such objectives could be more difficult to quantify,

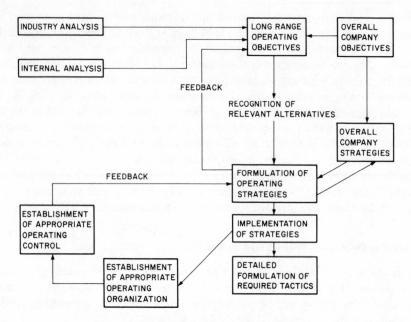

Figure 32   A framework for operations policy

particularly in relation to time. As Figure 32 implies, operations objectives must take account of the total company objectives. Equally, however, company objectives should not be set in isolation from operating objectives.

Once objectives have been established, it is necessary to design appropriate operating strategies to fulfil them. The process of strategy design must inevitably lead to the consideration of a wide range of alternative courses of action. Again, the nature of these alternatives will vary from industry to industry. Typical alternative courses of action are given below. These must be considered in relation to products, operating systems design, stocks, personnel and investment.

Examples of Alternative Courses of Action

Relating to Products

(1) Making products which demand design and prototype development skills.

v

Being a product follower demanding rapid changeovers and the ability to build up volume quickly.

(2) Many products creating complex shop floor scheduling problems and the need for a wide range of skills.

v

Few products requiring simple systems and few skills.

(3) Allowing constant product updating (i.e. many modifications) resulting in short runs and requiring manufacturing flexibility.

v

Rare product updating permitting long run and stable systems.

(4) Emphasis on 'after sales' service requiring lengthy active lives for components and high component stocks.

v

Limited life products with 'after sales' spares market given to other manufacturers.

(5) Wide quality range demanding separate manufacturing facilities and close control.

v

Narrow quality range demanding limited facilities and control.

Relating to the Operations System

(1) Single multipurpose facility making a wide range of products.

v

Several specialized lines each making a limited product range.

(2) Limited manufacture of components and products with high bought out volume giving low commitment to fixed facilities.

v

High level of in house manufacture with commitment to facility ownership.

(3) Limited automation, general purpose facilities permitting constant product changes.

v

Highly automated fixed facilities requiring long runs and infrequent change.

(4) Large scale plants for economy of scale.

v

Many small plants close to markets or raw material source.

(5) Manufacturing responding to short term demand fluctuations in order to minimize stocks, thus requiring constant change in labour and machinery utilization.

v

Constant output, giving steady use of people and facilities, but requiring stocks to uncouple manufacturing from demand.

Relating to the use of Stocks

(1) Make to order to minimize working capital but giving long lead times.

v

Hold semi-finished and finished goods stock to give short lead times and permit economic batches in manufacturing.

Relating to Personnel

(1) Direct incentive based wage systems which exert control on the system (see Chapter 3).

v

Non-direct incentive wage systems requiring closer first line supervision.

(2) Repetitive routine jobs requiring limited skills and training and giving limited responsibility.

v

Enlarged jobs requiring extended training and giving greater responsibility.

(3) In-house training and development to provide the full range of job skills required.

v

Little or no training and reliance on the labour market to provide required skills.

Relating to Investment

(1) Investment in plant and equipment to provide the latest process technology.

v

Investment in working capital to give customer service.

v

Investment in product development to give advanced products.

v

Investment in control systems to give increased output from existing facilities.

These are not mutually exclusive investment policies, but few organizations operate with unlimited capital availability. Therefore, in practice, a choice often has to be made between conflicting demands for capital.

Again, as Figure 32 shows, the establishment of operations strategies cannot take place in isolation. There must be a constant comparison between company and operations strategies to see how each will affect the other.

Once strategies have been established they must, of course, be implemented. Implementation will involve considerable tactical detail. Much of this text has been about issues which will have to be resolved at this tactical level.

Two specific issues, namely the operations organization and the nature of the operations control system, are highlighted in the conceptual framework under implementation. Both have already been raised as areas where specific objectives or strategies could be established. If they have not already been considered at one of these two levels, they should automatically be considered under implementation. As we have argued in various chapters, there is an urgent need in many companies to consider both the physical arrangement of facilities and the structure of the human organization. In the case of control, it is important to consider the effect of the control system on the motivation of those working in the operations system. Again, we have argued at various points that often the control used in operating systems does not motivate the work force towards the desired result.

Conclusion

Operations are too often the poor relation in the corporate planning process. In so many companies the process is left to the finance and marketing functions. Operations are left to achieve the aims of the corporate plan having little voice in their formulation. This chapter has argued that this must not be the case. A framework has been proposed for developing operating objectives and strategy. It is, however, vital to emphasize that designing a conceptual scheme is simple compared with the task of actually carrying it out in practice. As we have stated throughout this text, operations are the most complex part of any business and as such, require constant attention for the resolution of day to day problems. The operations manager has, therefore, the greatest difficulty in finding time to devote to long term planning. But if he does not devote some of his own time and some specific human resource to the planning process, inevitably, operations will fall into the state where they react to each pressure placed upon them, no matter how irrational. However, if the development of operations policy and strategies goes by default, only the operations manager can be blamed. It is up to him to take the necessary action which will ensure that the operations system makes the most effective possible contribution to the total system.

APPENDIX

Operations Policy

Questions to be asked during the analysis stage.

Industry Economics

What is the breakdown of manufacturing costs between materials, direct labour, overheads, depreciation?
What is the effect of changing volumes on costs?
What are the pricing practices of the industry?
How significant is working capital?
How often are capital and stocks turned over each year? What are the trends?
How do operating performance indices compare with competitive companies?
Are there economic barriers which prevent entry to the industry?

Industry Structure

How important is economy of scale?
Is the industry integrating backwards? Forwards?
Is plant location affected by source of raw materials? By markets for end products?
Is plant size in a given location limited by labour supply? Transportation problems? Pollution problems?
What is the minimum/maximum size of each incremental addition of plant capacity?
Are mergers/takeovers taking place? If so, in what way are these influenced by desire to rationalize manufacturing facilities?
Are there significant trends in the movement of imports/exports of the products? If so, how is manufacturing providing advantages/disadvantages relative to overseas manufacturers?
Are the purchasing habits of the customers changing? Longer/shorter contracts? More dual sourcing? Changing responsibility for stockholding?
What are the strengths and weaknesses of competitors operations? Are they significant? Can they be exploited?

Product Range

Is the product range wide, narrow, comparable with competitors?
If wider or narrower why? Are there operating disadvantages associated with the size of the range?
Is the basic product line growing? If yes why?
Is the customer demanding an ever increasing variety of options on basic products? What are the implications for operations?
Where are the innovative strengths/weaknesses of the organization?

Is the research and development manufacturing interface successful?

Are product specifications becoming more demanding? Do these demands originate from outside or within the company?

How is reliability built into the products? Through the design process, manufacturing process or through extensive after sales service? Is the balance between these correct?

Raw Material Input

What are the sources of raw material? How certain? Price movements?

What is happening to the technology of raw materials? Are substitutions taking place? At what rate? What is substitution dependent on? What is the impact of substitution on existing plant? On labour?

What is the cost of getting raw materials from source to plant? Does it fluctuate with trade cycles etc.?

Productivity/Labour

What are the trends in value added, sales and wages per employee?

What is the relationship of direct to indirect labour? Is this changing?

What changes are taking place in labour skill requirements? How will future requirements be met?

What demands will labour make on the organization? Does the company anticipate demands or react to them?

Are traditional payment systems still applicable? What are the implications of the payment systems used?

Are restrictive practices operated in the organization? Why? How can they be eliminated?

What is the impact of Trade Unionism on the industry? Will additional sectors of the labour force form or join unions in the future? What would be the impact?

Plant Operation

Are alternative ways of organizing the manufacturing facilities possible? If so what would be the advantages and disadvantages?

What purposes do stocks serve for the system as a whole? Are they held in the right place?

Are throughput times good, bad, satisfactory? Why?

Is delivery performance good, bad, satisfactory? Why?

Are the systems used for production planning and control the most effective possible? Does the company view investment in control procedures as equivalent to investment in plant and facilities?

How flexible is the operating system? Is the degree of flexibility too much? Too little?

What is the age of the plant and machinery? Would substantial advantage be obtained by acquiring modern facilities?

What are the trends in automation for the industry? What is the impact of automation on cost structure? Flexibility? Nature of labour skills required?

Is the cost of ensuring adequate quality increasing? What is the policy in relation to responsibility for quality?

Government Policy and Social Attitudes

Is the industry seen as vital to the national economy? Does it receive special support/aid from the Government? Is this fully exploited?

Is the industry dependent on the Government or Government-controlled industries as major customers? What would be the impact of changes in national economic policies on the industry?

What is the impact of regional and investment policies on plant location? Of taxation policies on investment levels, on the economics of employing labour?

Is the industry socially acceptable as a place to work? What attracts labour to the industry? Is it dependent on immigrant labour?

Does the industry attract critical social comment because of its manufacturing activities?

References

Skinner, W. (1966) 'Production Under Pressure', *Harvard Business Review*, Nov–Dec 1966.
Skinner, W. (1969) 'Manufacturing – Missing Link in Corporate Strategy', *Harvard Business Review*, May–June 1969.

Further Reading

Skinner, W. (1974) 'The Focused Factory', *Harvard Business Review*, May–June 1974.
Twiss, B. C. (1974) 'Developing and Implementing a Strategy for Production', *Long Range Planning*, April 1974.

Cases

Anglian Metal Protection Ltd (A.M.P.)

Origins

Anglian Metal Protection Ltd. was established in 1958, as a family concern, to nylon coat metal components. The owners had little success at first, but did succeed in establishing the feasibility of the process and gaining a few orders. In 1960 the owners engaged Mr. B. N. Jones as managing director. Mr. Jones was a practical engineer of considerable flair and wished to try running his own company.

Since Mr. Jones was interested in solving technical problems, he concentrated sales on the engineering industry. Plastic coating was presented as a means of meeting specific technical needs, rather than as a decorative finish. Mr. Jones' ability to talk to customers, who were often engineers, on their own terms resulted in increased sales. Margins in this sector were higher than in the consumer products field.

By 1962 the company was profitable with a steadily expanding turnover. Turnover continued to grow for the next five years (see Figure 1).

Year ending 31st March	Sales £000	Profit £000
1960	8	—
1961	14	0.7
1962	22	2.1
1963	25	2.5
1964	28	3.0
1965	38	4.1
1966	47	4.0
1967	58	7.5
1968	65	7.4
1969	66	6.0
1970	84	2.1
1971	122	(5.8)

Figure 1 (A.M.P. Ltd.)   Sales and profits 1960–1971

Expansion

By 1967 Mr. Jones had a staff of ten and he decided to move the company to a new 10,000 sq. ft. factory. It was from this point, Mr. Jones recalled, that everything began to go wrong. One of the problems was the new building; it was much larger than the previous premises, and the layout separated the offices from the production facilities much more than before. His style of management, in the absence of any formal controls, depended on keeping in close personal contact with all the activities of the company. There were now problems of communication, supervision and control in the larger space. To meet this he attempted to increase the company's production management strength, thus giving himself more time for administration. However, the Board still exercised tight financial control, and this limited his ability to pay attractive salaries. Over the next two years A.M.P. had a succession of unsatisfactory production managers.

Production problems were also increased by the introduction of electrostatic spray coating for epoxy resins. All previous work had been by the dip process. (See section on process problems.)

The business had grown to a size at which it could no longer be effectively controlled by one man. From 1967 to 1971, although turnover grew, profitability declined until the company was losing money. Mr. Jones stated that he was aware that his performance was declining. He was older, tired and under an increasing strain as a result of working excessive hours for a long period.

At a Board meeting in 1971, Mr. Jones said that he needed an administration manager or even a joint managing director. This would allow him to concentrate on the production control problems.

On the 6th August 1971, Mr. T. P. Henderson joined A.M.P. as chairman and managing director, Mr. Jones becoming technical director. Mr. Henderson had acquired a controlling interest in the business from the original owners. They had been discouraged by the recent loss and had decided to give their full attention to other business interests. A balance sheet for 1971 is given in Figure 2.

Mr. Henderson's Assessment of A.M.P.

Mr. Henderson felt that the control systems and staff were inadequate. He believed that low salary levels lowered the calibre of people that could be employed. In particular, Mr. Henderson felt that the production manager's job was a key one in view of the complexity of the work and the high level of customer contact involved in this jobbing service industry. The production manager at the time was the third to occupy the position.

Mr. Henderson's overall assessment was that the rapidly expanding market should make A.M.P. highly profitable. The company had a good workforce, but was short on discipline and control. In Mr. Jones the company had a fund of technical knowledge and engineering ability that was exceptional. Mr. Henderson saw himself as taking over the management and control of the company, freeing Mr. Jones to deal with the technical problems.

Current assets
Cash	1.2	
A/c Rec	38.4	
Inventories	35.1	
	74.7	

Current liabilities
A/c payable	25.3	
Bank loan	15.0	
	40.3	

Net current assets		34.4

Fixed assets
Building	25.0	
Plant and Machinery	18.6	
(less depreciation)	43.6	43.6

Total assets		78.0

Share capital	20.0	
Retained earnings	23.0	
Long Term Loan	35.0	78.0

Figure 2 (A.M.P. Ltd.)   Balance sheet 1971

As a first move Mr. Henderson decided to have a critical look at the nature of the present business and the organization, facilities and systems for dealing with this business.

Plastic Coatings

The application of a layer of plastic to a metal substrate, using dry powder as the raw material, was one of the most recent metal finishing processes. It was therefore in technological competition with other established methods, such as paint, stove enamel, vitreous enamel, electroplating and galvanizing. Plastic coating provided a decorative and very durable finish, resisting mechanical abrasion and general wear and tear. It also offered electrical insulation, and excellent resistance to chemical attack and general atmospheric corrosion. The choice of plastic depended on the particular properties required.

The range of end-users was very wide; domestic appliances, office furniture and equipment, wirework, marine fittings, instrument cases, lighting columns, window frames, pipework and storage vessels for chemical plant, and engineering components.

Large users had their own in-plant coating facilities. A.M.P. was concerned with the trade coating industry, offering a general coating service to industry.

Process Methods

The principal application methods were fluidized bed dipping and electrostatic spray coating. In the former, a stock of powder was held in a tank having a false, porous bottom. High volume low pressure air was fed in through the bottom. This separated the powder particles and held them in suspension, the resulting air/powder mixture having the free-flowing properties of a liquid. This method was used mainly with thermoplastics such as polyethylene, PVC and nylon. The article to be coated was preheated above the melting point of the plastic and dipped into the fluidized bed. Powder particles fused onto the metal surface to form a continuous coating. The thickness depended on the preheating temperature, the thermal capacity of the article, and the dip time.

In the electrostatic method, powder was fed by an air stream to the head of a dispensing spray gun, where it received an electrostatic charge of 80—90 KV. The charged powder adhered to earthed metal components. Any powder over-spray was recovered by extraction and filtration equipment linked to the spray booth. This method was used mostly with thermosetting plastics. Epoxy resins (eposides) were the most significant, though acrylics and polyesters were also used. After coating with the powder the articles were heated to cure the resin and form a continuous layer bonded to the substrate. Preheating could also be used if a thicker coating was required.

Dip coating thicknesses were normally $0.010''$ to $0.020''$ for most commercial work, though thicker coatings were possible. Spray coatings could be deposited in a controlled manner down to $0.002''$, a comparable thickness to paint.

With both methods, careful preparation of the articles to be coated was necessary to ensure good adhesion. As a minimum this meant degreasing. Shot-blasting was also used to clean the metal. Fettling was used when sharp edges had to be removed.

The quality of a coated product was determined by visual inspection to ensure that no breaks existed in the coating. In the long term quality was measured by the ability of the product or component to retain its coating under constant use. A major quality failure had been experienced in 1968 when coating had peeled off the outside of a batch of metal window frames after they had been exposed to the atmosphere for six months.

The Plastic Coating Industry

It was possible for dip coating operations to be commenced on very limited capital; less than £1000 would acquire a small fluidized bed tank, the initial powder stock, and a small oven. The industry started around 1950 as a number of one-man businesses, occupying small premises. As the industry developed, customers' demands became more complex. This meant further investment in larger tanks and preheating ovens. The cost of powder stocks also became significant. Current powder costs in 1972 were around £2000 per ton. A tank measuring 8ft x 3ft x 4ft required a base stock of over half a ton. The lack of capital had prevented the growth of many small firms.

The business also lost some of its simplicity as increasing life and performance were required from the coatings. Again, some firms were unable to move away from their early empiricism to a more technical approach. This excluded them from the high quality engineering market.

Managing growth was itself a problem, and companies failed because their founders were unable to cope with increased size and complexity. The most successful company in this respect was Plastic Coatings Ltd. with an estimated £2½ million turnover in trade coating in 1971.

Operations at A.M.P.

Organization

Figure 3 shows the formal relationships in A.M.P. after the arrival of Mr. Henderson.

In practice informal working relationships were important and there was a greater overlap of roles than might occur in a larger, more structured organization. For example, the production manager had considerable direct customer contact. Telephone queries concerning job progress and delivery usually went to him rather than to the sales office.

The technical estimator fulfilled a number of duties. He prepared quotations, priced orders received, initiated production control documentation and carried out process planning. Finally, he acted as invoice clerk. Those were his formal responsibilities. As he shared an office with the sales engineer, who was often away from the company, he also became involved in direct customer contact on sales and production matters. Thus his position was a very central one. He clearly enjoyed the somewhat freelance nature of his work and the wide range of tasks. He was one of the few original staff to remain after the arrival of Mr. Henderson and his knowledge and experience were extensive. There were, however, dangers in this situation. His absence from the company presented problems as it was difficult for anyone else to take over all or even part of his duties. Also, his involvement in commercial matters had been at the expense of contact with production, and his knowledge was becoming out of date.

Another organizational difficulty was the 'one to one' relationship between the production manager and the foreman. A formal relationship such as that could not work in practice, and the production manager had a good deal of direct contact with the chargehands. This meant that the foreman's responsibilities were ill-defined.

Works Facilities

These fell into five principal areas. The works layout is illustrated in Figure 4.

The toolroom carried out general engineering and maintenance, and made

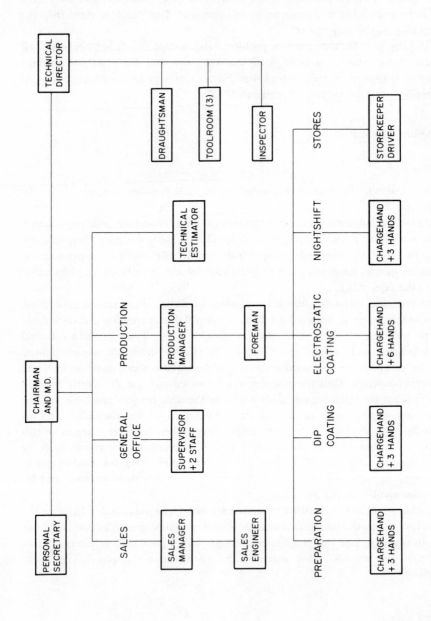

Figure 3 (A.M.P. Ltd.)   Organization chart

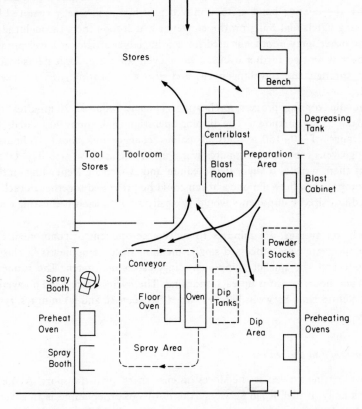

Figure 4 (A.M.P. Ltd.)   Sketch plan of works (not to scale)

production tools. The latter were jigs and handling equipment for supporting and manipulating articles during coating. The tool stores attached to the toolroom held both general purpose tools and special tools designed for particular jobs.

The stores area handled all goods inwards and outwards. The preparation area included a work bench with hand tools for fettling, a degreasing tank, facilities for stripping existing coatings (by burning or chemical action), and shot blasting. All goods for coating were degreased. The use of the other facilities depended on the nature of the job.

The dip coating area was equipped with three preheating ovens, water tanks for quenching, and six different sized fluidized bed tanks. Ideally, the smallest possible tank capable of taking the job was used, to minimize powder contamination. In practice the commonest nylon colours, white and black, were kept permanently set up in large tanks to minimize colour changes.

The electrostatic coating had a tunnel oven with a loop overhead conveyor track. Outside the oven the track ran past the two spraying booths. One of these was used for coating small particles, and was fitted with an umbrella-like rotating overhead frame. Articles to be coated were hung by two of the three man team on the frame, coated by the coating hand as they moved past him, and finally removed by the two backing hands and hung on the conveyor which took them through the curing oven. The other spray booth was used for coating larger articles at lower production rates. There were two further ovens; a floor oven for curing large items that could not pass through the travelling oven, and also a preheating oven for use when required.

In the dip coating process, preheating typically required 20 minutes, though 40 minutes was not unknown. The dipping operation took about 90 seconds, with a possible range of 30–150 seconds. A colour change took about 1½ hours. The preheating ovens required 30 minutes warm-up at the start of each day. Of the six dip tanks there were two large, two medium and two small. Depending on the size of the components, between one and ten could be processed together in each cycle. Four medium sized components would typically fit into each preheating oven at a time.

It took, on average, 1½ minutes to spray a component or component cluster. Large components were processed singly, medium sized components in clusters of up to four and the smaller components in clusters up to ten. The tunnel oven required one hour to warm up each morning. The curing stage took on average 15 minutes. Set-up time between batches varied between 30 and 90 minutes, typically being 60.

Office System and Procedure

Goods for coating arrived at the stores on customers' own transport, A.M.P.'s van or, occasionally, British Road Services. About 40% of orders came as an advice note attached to the goods, often with no prior warning. A similar proportion of orders came by post to the general office. About 20% of goods came without either an order or an advice note, and were given temporary documentation to identify them while the customer was asked for a formal order so that work could proceed.

Every morning the technical estimator would collect the order documents for goods which had been checked into the stores. He then wrote out a plan sheet (Figure 5) showing the process to be used for each item. The completed plan sheet was clipped to its order document. This bunch of papers, known as the 'plan-sheet set', formed the master controlling all other documents.

The plan-sheet set was returned to the general office, where two copies of a job card and a Stripdex programme strip were typed (Figure 6). These went to the works office as soon as possible. The plan-sheet set then returned to the technical estimator, who calculated a suggested price and passed the set to the Managing Director. He entered a firm price on the order in green ink. This was largely a formality where the price had been previously agreed. In the case of new work, he wished to ensure that the price covered the value the customer would place on the quality of work and service provided by the company. At this stage, a bad customer might be placed on the credit stop list. Otherwise, the set was sent back to the general office for an acknowledgement to be prepared. The set was held in the

PLAN SHEET

Item	Part No.	Description	Customers Advice Note In	Qty Advd	Qty Rcd	Std Time	Coating		Colour		Spec		Advice Note Out		
							Fettle	Braze	Degrease	Blast	Tool	Pigment		Qty	Date

CUSTOMER

Invoice to:

Route in:

DESPATCH TO:

Special Instructions

Route back:

JOB No.

CUSTOMER ORDER NO.

Date received:

Figure 5 (A.M.P. Ltd.) Plan sheet

176

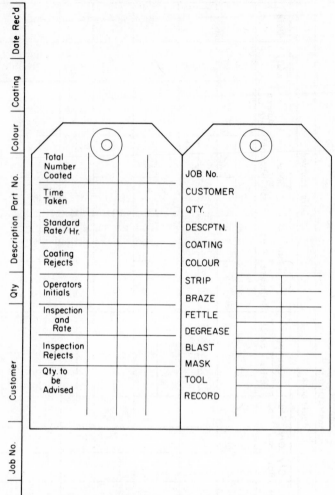

Figure 6 (A.M.P. Ltd.)   Job card and Stripdex

office, and the acknowledgement sent to the sales engineer (or the technical estimator in his absence) for signature and posting to the customer.

In the works office the production manager read the job cards to make a mental note of incoming work. He checked them against the credit-stop list. If any of the jobs were unfamiliar, he would discuss them with the foreman, technical estimator or technical director and might also inspect the workpieces in the stores. He slotted the Stripdex strips into holding boards by type and colour of coating and hung up the work tickets.

Every Thursday, he and the foreman would meet to prepare the production programme for the following week, so that each was fully aware of decisions taken. The strips were grouped onto daily plan boards in accordance with the decision rules (see below) and the dates on which coating was planned to start written on the corresponding job cards. One copy of the job cards went to the preparation chargehand, the other to the coating chargehand, a full week's work being handed out at a time.

After coating, the chargehand recorded the total number of articles and the number of articles and the number of rejects (on the back of the job card). The chargehand did most of the inspection, the foreman or the inspector only being involved on important or difficult jobs, or when there had been an unusual number of rejects from the customer. The job card then went to the works office, where the foreman or inspector signed the entry for quantity of finished goods. Next, the card went to the general office, where a 5-part invoice set was prepared. If the job was complete, the Stripdex was destroyed. If the job was part complete, the strip was altered accordingly, and the job card returned to the works office to be programmed again.

The production manager could specify the order of priority in which invoice sets were to be typed, to meet despatch plans. At this stage the invoice set carried only quantities for despatch, not prices. Two copies went to the customer, one as an advice note and one for him to sign and return as confirmation that he accepted the goods. When this was returned, the storekeeper noted the details of transport on it. Meanwhile, the technical estimator had priced the work on the two remaining copies, using the job card and the plan-sheet set. Two or three times a month, he would work out a final price, taking into account any rejections by the customer and delivery charges from the acceptance copy. One copy went to the customer as invoice. The other went to Mrs. Jones who did the book-keeping part time, visiting the company one day a week. If the job was complete, the plan-sheet set was then dismantled for its component documents to be filed separately. Otherwise it was held in the general office until the next portion of the order was complete.

The general flow of information is shown in Figure 7 and the decisions required in Figure 8. It must be appreciated that there was a good deal of ancillary paperwork, although not all of it, as Mr. Henderson observed (below) was kept conscientiously.

Decision Rules in Scheduling

Scheduling was a complex task. There were about 40 orders a week to consider, representing around 5000 items in a wide range of quantities, with a number of factors to take into account on each one. These factors were:

(1) Delivery date, which could either be 14 days from the receipt of the order and articles, or a firm promise of a particular day.
(2) Preparation process. The facilities required, estimated time and number of men required.
(3) Coating process. The type of plastic and colour, estimated time and number of men required, preheating temperature, and facilities to be used (e.g. any restriction on the oven that could be used).

A typical month's orders are given in Figure 9.

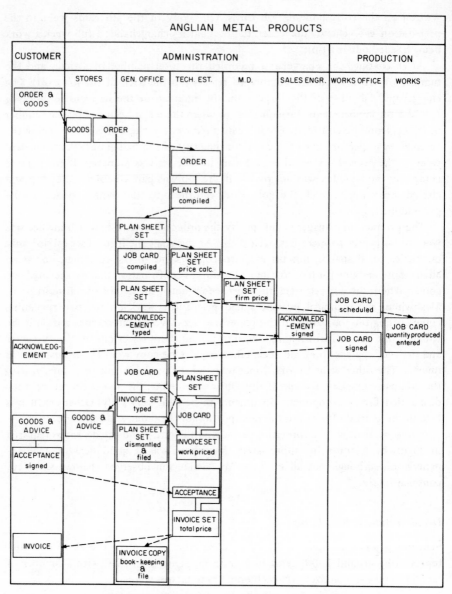

Figure 7 (A.M.P. Ltd.)   General information flow

The aim was to meet delivery dates and utilize labour fully while minimizing set-up times by avoiding changes of temperature and powder as far as possible. At the start of the programming session, the jobs were already broken down by colour on the holding boards. The production manager could then look through the delivery dates to see the number of colour changes that would be necessary. The jobs were thus broken down further into groups by colour and delivery date.

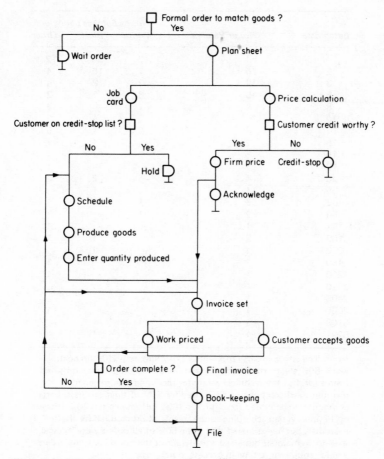

Figure 8 (A.M.P. Ltd.)   Logical tree of the office procedure, showing decisions required

The next consideration was the work load in the preparation area. The major facility, the blast room, had two grades of shot and changes had to be minimized. The coarse grade was used almost exclusively for dip coating jobs and the fine grade for both dip and spray coating. The pressure of work was usually on the epoxide spray area, so the production manager first loaded the work that had to be done in this area. He then worked out the load that this implied in the preparation area and then fitted in the dip coating work around it. This usually caused the dip area not to be worked to its full efficiency.

The other main problem in the epoxide area was to minimize colour changes and to minimize the time lost when changes were necessary. This was done by making the first job after a colour change one which required little preparation. This reduced the risk that coating in the new colour could not proceed because the preparation area had not completed its work.

Epoxide labour utilization was less of a problem. The total manning, including

Batch Size	No. of Batches	No. of Batches per colour		
		White	Black	Other
1	54	12	30	12
2	26	7	15	4
3	14	2	8	4
5	15	6	7	2
8	4	1	–	3
10	11	2	4	5
13	8	2	1	5
15	2	–	1	1
16	6	1	1	4
19	1	–	–	1
20	4	–	2	2
25	1	–	1	–
35	3	1	1	1
50	2	1	–	1
71	1	–	–	1
100	2	–	1	1
220	1	–	1	
480	1	–	–	1
1200	1	–	–	1
2120	1	–	1	–
2405	1	–	–	1
2600	1	–	–	1
5100	1	1	–	–
6221	1	–	1	–

Note: The above orders represented approximately 20% dip coating work, 80% electrostatic work by component volume. No records had been kept, but the technical estimator reckoned that in general medium sized components accounted for 70% of their business. Large components accounted for a further 10%, and small sized 20%. Process cycle times varied according to the specification required by the customer, but he estimated that some 60% of all orders were 'typical' with the remainder dispersed equally about the norm i.e. some orders would require more time in process, others less.

Figure 9 (A.M.P. Ltd.)   Orders received during May 1971 (4 weeks)

the chargehand, was four. Most jobs could be done by three men or less, though it could occasionally be necessary to take men from the dip coating side. Where less than four men were needed, the others did masking or preparation for later jobs. There was a problem with overtime on epoxide work. The production manager could not get all he needed from the standard crew. He had therefore decided to establish a night shift with six men and a chargehand.

Colour changes did not create major problems on the dip coating side. There were fewer colours in nylon than epoxide, and the standard colours (black and white) were permanently set up in large tanks. The main problem was the variety of preheating temperatures. It took longer to adjust the oven temperature than to change a colour. The colour/tank-size combinations were not a limiting factor more than a couple of times per month. As far as possible the job sequence was planned in order of increasing preheating temperature in order to minimize the time needed for temperature adjustments.

In practice the chargehands had a good deal of freedom to plan work for their own areas within the broad outline of the programme, in order to utilize their labour as effectively as possible. This was necessary because of the uncertain forward load at any time. The nature of the business was such that the company never had an order book of any length. As mentioned earlier, many orders arrived with the goods without prior warning, and there were three of four 'special delivery' jobs each week that had to be programmed at short notice. Thus the programme was subject to frequent alteration. To allow for additional work coming in, about 20% spare capacity was left in the initial programme for the week. This was usually full by the Tuesday. The production manager checked performance against the target each day and reallocated work as necessary.

Cost of the Coating Process

The cost of coating a given item obviously depended on the area of the item and the number in the batch. The range experienced by A.M.P. for both these variables was considerable. An approximate average breakdown of costs is given in Figure 10. In 1971 A.M.P. operated a minimum charge per order of £5. This had been introduced two years previously. Although there had been a few complaints there had been no decline in small orders. Mr. Henderson was considering raising the minimum charge per order to £10.

Item	Percentage of Total Cost
Direct labour	36
Coating powder	15
Other materials	5
Manufacturing overhead	26
General overhead	18
	100

Figure 10 (A.M.P. Ltd.)   Average cost breakdown

Problems Observed by Mr. Henderson

Mr. Henderson's main criticism of the office procedure was that the whole system was slow and cumbersome. Too many people were involved, and there was an opportunity for delay at each transfer of documents. For example it could take two days to issue a job card to the works office when in some instances a three day turnround was offered.

In some instances, work had to be done on temporary documents, or even with no paperwork at all. This led to errors being made. There were too many steps in the order acknowledgement procedure. It was possible if the pressure of work on the managing director was heavy, for the order acknowledgement to reach the sales engineer for signing after the quoted delivery date.

There was no simple system for reporting and recording delivery dates. Mr. Henderson had to make a separate approach to the production manager when acknowledging each order. The production manager had no record of routine dates that he had quoted, but only of firm promises of particular dates which he noted in his diary. There was virtually no regular collection and reporting of data, either as an aid to forecasting or for shorter-term operational control. Various systems had been tried in the past, but invariably they had been discontinued. Job times were no longer recorded on job cards, for example, although the card was designed to permit this. Process log cards used to be kept, but they were out of date and unreliable. The chargehands in the coating areas kept log books of process details, but this information was not available away from the shop floor as an aid to planning.

No formal system existed for ordering tooling for new jobs from the toolroom. Order had not been maintained in the tool stores, and time was wasted searching for existing tooling. This had led to friction between the toolroom and works personnel.

While the production programming method worked satisfactorily, too much information was carried in the memory of the production manager. Difficulties could quickly arise in the event of his absence for a few days.

The range of duties undertaken by the technical estimator restricted his contact with the works, and his knowledge of production methods was becoming out of date. The feedback of information to him needed to be improved.

Artcraft Limited (A) — Production Operations at the London Works

Company Background

Artcraft Limited is an old established firm engaged mainly in the manufacture of artists' materials such as powder, poster and oil paints, brushes, crayons and printing inks. The full product range offered to customers includes many items such as art papers which are bought in for resale and, for example, easels which are produced to Artcraft specifications by subcontractors specializing in woodworking.

The market for these items consists of three fairly distinct segments:

(1) Educational
(2) Trade
(3) Export

Educational sales come from art departments of schools, educational contractors (who resell to schools) or local authorities who buy for the schools in their areas. Trade sales come from direct retail outlets, wholesalers who resell to small retailers, multiple stores such as W. H. Smith & Sons and from mail order houses. Export sales include shipments to foreign subsidiaries.

The company has experienced some financial difficulties in recent years (see Figure 1 for financial statements) and towards the end of 1971 a new management group took over. After some initial changes to company policy the new management turned their attention to the production operations at the South London factory where UK production had been concentrated. Factory sales from London account for about 50% of company turnover and a record of past sales is shown in Figure 2 together with a forecast for 1972 operations. Figure 3 shows a breakdown of operating expenses for the London factory.

The Production Process

By the end of May 1972 the London factory operations were almost exclusively devoted to the production of paints (powder, water, oil, etc.) inks and varnishes, though crayons and some brushes were also being manufactured on the site.

| | £'000 | | |
	1971		1970
Goodwill			90
Fixed Assets	450		420
Investments	10		60
Current Assets			
Stocks	900		1,500
Debtors	600		800
Cash	20		30
		1,520	2,330
		1,980	2,900
Less:			
Current Liabilities			
Creditors	530		730
Current Taxation	80		120
Bank Loans	620		680
		1,230	1,530
		750	1,370
Capital Employed			
Share Capital	600		600
Reserves	100		740
Long term debt	50		30
		750	1,370

(a) Consolidated Balance Sheets (at 31st December)

| | £'000 | |
	1971	1970
Net Sales	4,100	4,800
Less Operating expenses:	4,180	4,980
Operating Loss	80	180
Net financing costs	70	40
Loss before Tax	150	220
Taxation	(20)	25
Loss after Tax	130	245

(b) Consolidated Profit and Loss Account (Year ending 31st December)

Figure 1 (Artcraft Ltd.)   Financial statements

The production of 'colour' items consists of two basic stages:

(1) The manufacture of the raw bulk coloured material.
(2) The packing of the items according to the finished product required.

The actual production process and facilities required depend on the final product (e.g. tins of powder paint, tubes of oil paint, etc.) but the basic stages are usually the same.

The overall production operation is shown diagrammatically in Figure 4.

	Education £			Trade £			Export £			Total £			1970–71 Change	1971–72 Change
	1970	1971	1972	1970	1971	1972	1970	1971	1972	1970	1971	1972		
JAN	38000	43000	48800	31800	37600	37200	27952	21064	23000	97752	101664	109000	4.0%	7.3%
FEB	50000	40200	45500	45200	39000	38400	31388	47559	52000	126588	126759	135900	0.1%	7.2%
MAR	54400	69400	78600	39300	55400	56400	42903	36284	39500	136603	161084	174500	18.0%	8.3%
APR	88220	107000	121000	36000	43600	44400	34214	36504	40000	158414	187104	205400	18.2%	9.8%
MAY	94500	124000	140000	30700	33900	34800	37154	43663	47500	162354	201563	222300	24.2%	10.3%
JUNE	96000	125000	141200	32100	36000	36600	40697	47915	52000	168797	208915	229800	23.8%	10.0%
JULY	104000	145000	164000	56600	45000	46200	42012	39915	43500	202612	229915	253700	13.5%	10.3%
AUG	81000	104000	117800	60000	49100	49800	47989	47353	51500	188989	200453	219100	6.0%	9.3%
SEP	71000	74500	84400	88000	74200	75500	35766	36820	40000	194766	185520	199900	(4.7%)	7.7%
OCT	54500	50500	57200	101000	119000	122000	37018	31874	34500	192518	201374	213700	4.6%	6.1%
NOV	82500	47500	53800	84600	112000	114800	59901	21874	23500	227001	181374	192100	(20.0%)	5.9%
DEC	47200	59400	67200	54600	64800	69500	39248	25230	27500	141048	149430	164200	5.9%	9.9%
YEAR	861300	989500	1119500	659900	709600	725600	476242	436091	474500	1997442	2135191	2319600	6.9%	8.6%

Note: Data has been adjusted for commercial reasons.

Figure 2 (Artcraft Ltd.)   Comparative sales analysis 1970–1971 actual and 1972 forecast

			£'000
Sales Less Discounts			2,135
Manufacturing Costs			
Materials		1,050	
Direct Labour:			
Colour	30		
Filling	50		
Other	30		
	—		
		110	
Departmental Overheads		200	
Factory Overheads		100	1,460
Gross Profit			675
Selling and Admin. Expenses			
Marketing		250	
Distribution		200	
Administration		160	
			610
Net Operating Profit			65

Figure 3 (Artcraft Ltd.)   Operating expenses in £'000s at the London factory (year ending 31st December 1971).

Bulk Colour Production

The colour manufacturing department contains equipment for grinding and mixing the raw materials to produce the appropriate colour and consistency for the product required. There are 13 mills of various types and capacities which grind the powder raw materials and do the 'dry' mixing. The mixing of liquids is usually carried out in one of the four vats.

The final product from the colour manufacturing department can be in the form of a dry powder (e.g. the powder colour range) or a bulk fluid (e.g. the poster colour range). In some cases, however, bulk powder is processed further using forming machines to produce, e.g. the powder block range (powder colour formed into cylindrical blocks, sizes 0, 1 or 2) and the powder disc range (water colours formed into small discs for insertion into paint boxes, etc.). The forming equipment consists of six machines of varying size. The bulk colour production department also operates an oil crayon plant consisting of one machine and a drying oven. The output from colour manufacturing may go back to the colour stores as part-finished materials to await packing (at this stage it is usually transported in 10-gallon drums or large paper sacks) or it may continue directly into the filling or wrapping departments. Because of deterioration 'bulk colour' cannot usually be stored for more than a few days.

Filling and Packing

Colour Filling

The largest of the packaging departments is colour filling where all the non-powder products are packaged. The tube filling department operates an ink line, an

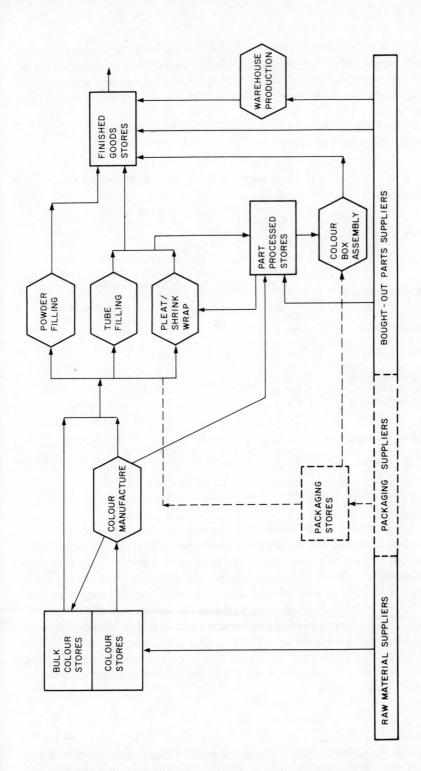

Figure 4 (Artcraft Ltd.)   Production operations

oil/varnish line and eleven tube/jar lines as well as three crayon labelling machines and two 'nipping' machines (for closing off tube ends). Three of the tube lines are largely semi-automatic and typically three operatives are required while a line is running though for some items only one operative is required and for others two operatives.

A total of eight different tube sizes are packed (seven ordinary lead tubes and the large 300 cc clear PVC tube):

Product	Sizes Packed	Price (£) (August 1972)
Artists Oils	37 cc	.27 to 2.90
	75 cc	.50 (white only)
	225 cc	1.25 (white only)
Oils	No. 3	.09
	37 cc	.22
	No. 20	.33 (white only)
	No. 40	.60 (white only)
	225 cc	.75 (not all colours)
Acrylic Polymer	37 cc	.22 to .40
	75 cc	.37 (Titanium white only)
	225 cc	.85 (Titanium white only)
Water Colours	No. 3	.09
	No. 8	.15
Poster Colour	No. 3 (new addition)	.10
	No. 8	.15
Powder Polymer	300 cc	.67
Powder Poster	300 cc	.42
Block Printing W. C.	No. 8	.17
	37 cc	.22 to .28
	300 cc	.70
Fabric Printing Colour	No. 8	.22
	No. 20	.35
Finger Print Ink	No. 3	.11

N.B. The non metric tube sizes are: No. 3 = 0.3 fl. oz.; No. 8 = 0.8 fl. oz.;
No. 20 = 2 fl. oz.; No. 40 = 4 fl. oz.   (1 fl. oz. = 28.4 cc)

In the past five years the production emphasis in colour filling has moved to some extent from tubes to the filling of plastic 'squeezy' bottles. This followed the introduction in 1967 of a range of ready mixed powder colours in liquid form. The special appeal of this line to the educational market had boosted sales to about 500,000 p.a. by 1971 (a sales value of about £150,000). The full range consists of fifteen colours in the 20 fl. oz. size and six fluorescent colours in the 125 cc size.

The normal colour range is sold to schools in packs of three of a single colour (at 99p net of educational discounts).

The production process for the readymixed range consists basically of mixing powder colour constituents with a liquid base and packing the resulting mix into transparent plastic bottles.

Powder Filling

The powder filling department is almost exclusively engaged in the production of a single product line – powder colour. This is transferred in bulk from colour manufacturing and is packed into 6 oz, 1 lb, or 5 lb tins. The high volume 1 lb tins are packed on an automatic line continuously. Another line packs the 5 lb and 6 oz tins as required by the production orders received.

Pleat and Shrink Wrapping

The wrapping department is mainly concerned with the wrapping of powder blocks (singly or in packs of six of the same colour) and powder discs. The equipment employed consists of five pleat wrappers for the powder blocks and one strip wrapper for the discs (which are sold in strips of six of the same colour).

The output from the filling/packing departments may go either to finished goods stores or the part processed stores for eventual assembly into colour sets consisting of, for example, one 37 cc tube of each of six colours of acrylic polymer paint.

Colour Box Assembly

Many of the product groups include 'colour sets' of various sizes which involve packaging a single container with a selection of the colours available in that product group. Some colour sets contain products in more than one product group.

For example, besides the 28 colours in the basic range (each usually available in four sizes: No. 8 tubes, ½, 1 and 8 fl. oz. pots), the poster colour product range includes the following sets:

Contents	Price
No. 0 palette Six ½ fl. oz. pots (assorted colours) 1 brush	0.95
No. 4 palette Twelve ½ fl. oz. pots (assorted colours) 1 brush	1.50
Six ½ fl. oz. pots (assorted colours) 1 brush	0.60

The largest colour box (CB12) contains ten No. 0 blocks in assorted colours, 14 ½fl. oz. pots of poster paints in assorted colours and 12 assorted oil crayons as well as two water pots, two mixing trays, one small and one large brush.

The assembly of these colour boxes and sets is carried out in the colour box assembly department. Materials are issed to the assembly area from a part processed store where the items required for the specification of the set are collected together and stored. Finished colour sets go directly into finished goods stores.

The assembly operations are all manual and little skill is required; however, it takes three to four weeks for a new employee to reach an output level comparable with the more experienced operatives.

Warehouse Production

In addition to the actual manufacturing operations carried out at the factory some 'repacking' is done in the warehouse itself. This consists mainly of splitting off small quantities of paper from bulk purchases and repacking them for sale. Coloured papers, for example, are purchased in bulk and sold in packets of assorted colours or in small quantities of a single colour.

The Production—Inventory System

Company policy is to supply all goods from finished stock on very short lead times (despatch time only), so that all production orders are orders for stock replenishment. Raw material stocks are maintained on the basis of forecast production plans and any work in process which is not actually being worked on would normally be in the bulk colour stores. The part-processed stocks are held so that all the items necessary for a set can be collected together (production would normally produce the various items at different times). The packaging stores contains all the boxes/labels etc. used in the production and assembly operations and for colour boxes this constitutes a considerable volume of 'stored air' since most boxes are non-collapsible.

Production operations are complicated considerably by the multiple uses for items and various packaging arrangements which are used. A No. 1 powder block in, say, lemon could after moulding be:

(1) individually pleat wrapped and sent to finished goods stores for sale as a separate item
(2) individually pleat wrapped and sent to part-processed stores for inclusion in a palette set
(3) left unwrapped in containers and sent to part-processed stores for inclusion in a colour set
(4) pleat wrapped in six of same colour and sent to finished goods stores.

Similarly a ½fl. oz. jar of green poster colour could, after filling, be:

(1) labelled, boxed and sent to finished goods stores
(2) sent straight to part-processed stores for inclusion in a colour box
(3) labelled and sent to part-processed stores for inclusion in a poster set.

Production Planning and Control

The Production Controller, Mr. J. Barnet, has a staff of nine clerks who carry out the task of generating production orders, preparing production plans and monitoring performance.

The basis for the generation of production orders is a pair of production 'programmes' which are the forecasts of the yearly requirements of each product week by week. The first 'programme' is for colour boxes (i.e. items which have more than one component) and the second 'programme' is for items sold individually or in standard quantities directly from finished goods store. A typical programme for a single product/colour range is shown in Figure 5 for the first 6 months of 1971. The programme shows the requirements for the three items which

Week No.	Bulk Colour 10 Galls.			No. 8 Tube			37cc Tube			300cc Tube		
	Programme	Issues	Rec'd	Programme	Issues	Rec'd	Programme	Issues	Rec'd	Programme	Issues	Rec'd
1	7	7								1008		
2	2	2										
3												
4												
5			2				2020					
6			7					2020	2190		1008	950
7												
8												
9	1	1	1	2000								
10	9	9			2000					1296	1296	
11			9									
12												1263
13	10	10								1440		
14						2040						
15	21	21	10							3024		
16								1010			1440	
17	7						1010	1010	945	1008		1404
18	1	1							1065		3024	6
19												1440
20												1623
21	20			4000			1010			2880		
22	1	1										
23	2											
24												
25												
26												

Note: 10 Galls ≃ 45,500cc
Standard Batch Sizes (From 10 Galls.)
   No. 8 — 2000
   37cc — 1010
   300cc — 144

Figure 5 (Artcraft Ltd.)   Six-month production programme for sienna block printing water colour (at end of week 22)

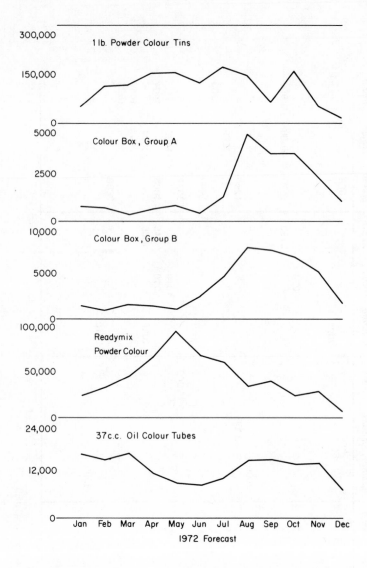

Figure 6 (Artcraft Ltd.)   Annual sales pattern by products

are sold in this product/colour (a No. 8 tube, a 37 cc tube and a 300 cc tube), and the colour manufacturing schedule for producing the raw bulk colour. Each item has three lines to record:

(1) The programme planned for the year's production.
(2) The issues of production orders made by the production control department.
(3) The actual receipts into stores.

The sales forecast and actual sales up to the end of week 22 for the 300 cc tube were:

(Opening inventory: 1000 tubes)

Weeks	Sales Forecast	Actual Sales (Units)
1–4	300	400
5–8	500	400
9–12	800	800
13–16	1,500	1,400
17–20	1,500	1,600
21–24	2,400	(1,000, 2 weeks only)
25–28	3,000	
29–32	3,600	
33–36	1,400	
37–40	1,000	
41–44	1,000	
45–48	600	
49–52	400	

The production plan for the rest of the year consisted of 3308 in week 27 and 3164 in week 34.

The colour box programmes are used as the basis for the generation of part of the requirements for each of the box constituents so that all the parts may be planned together for delivery into part-processed stores. The production 'programmes' have to be planned on the basis of the actual forecast of demand over the year. Many items have strongly seasonal sales patterns (e.g. educational products around mid-year and the colour boxes mainly pre-Christmas), as is clearly shown in Figure 2.

The 1972 forecasts for a number of different product groups are shown in Figure 6. The result of this is that individual programmes usually have to be based on producing for stock for a considerable period of the year on many items in order to utilize production capacity efficiently.

The basic procedure for planning an actual month's production is to use a planning horizon of three months for colour boxes and two months for other items. Each month, the next month beyond the existing planning horizon is brought into the 'firm' programme. Taking account of the existing stock condition and any outstanding orders, batch issue cards are produced by the production planning clerks for any items for which the inventory level would drop below the planned level of the total production programme. For the non-seasonal items this would normally be when stock-outs were forecast at the end of the new planning horizon. The colour box programme has to be ahead of the item programme to ensure that common parts can be produced together.

The normal stock policy for non-seasonal finished goods is to have five weeks usage at the end of each month. The many problems which can arise in production, sales variation and yield losses can cause considerable disruption to the original programmes.

The average number of production hours available in each department are:

Colour filling	700 hours per week
Powder filling	160 hours per week
Pleat/shrink wrap	170 hours per week
Colour box assembly	350 hours per week

	Raw Materials	Packaging Materials	Total Materials	Handling* Overheads	Direct Labour	Departmental† Overheads	Factory & Company Overheads‡	Total C.O.P. per 5 lb Tin
Brill Blue	.432	.100	.532	.053	.018	.036	.054	.693
Prussian Blue	.358	.100	.458	.046	.018	.036	.054	.612
Cobalt	.188	.100	.288	.029	.018	.036	.054	.425
Blue Ost	.345	.100	.445	.045	.018	.036	.054	.598
Turquoise	.182	.100	.282	.028	.018	.036	.054	.418
Purple	.345	.100	.445	.045	.018	.036	.054	.598
Brill Green	.188	.100	.288	.029	.018	.036	.054	.425
Viridian	.260	.100	.360	.036	.018	.036	.054	.504
Leaf Green	.163	.100	.263	.026	.018	.036	.054	.397
Emerald	.188	.100	.288	.029	.018	.036	.054	.425
Brill Red	.404	.100	.504	.050	.018	.036	.054	.662
Vermilion	.267	.100	.367	.037	.018	.036	.054	.512
Crimson	.390	.100	.490	.049	.018	.036	.054	.647
Red Ost	.228	.100	.328	.033	.018	.036	.054	.469
Orange	.286	.100	.386	.039	.018	.036	.054	.533
Gamboge	.130	.100	.230	.023	.018	.036	.054	.361
Brill Yellow	.143	.100	.243	.024	.018	.036	.054	.375
Lemon	.300	.100	.400	.040	.018	.036	.054	.548
Yellow Ochre	.143	.100	.243	.024	.018	.036	.054	.375
B. Sienna	.136	.100	.236	.024	.018	.036	.054	.368
B. Umber	.156	.100	.256	.026	.018	.036	.054	.390
Black	.188	.100	.288	.029	.021	.042	.063	.443
White	.156	.100	.256	.026	.017	.034	.051	.384

*Allocated at 10% on material cost.
†Allocated at 200% on direct labour.
‡Allocated at 100% on direct labour + O/H.
(This does not include head office allocated expenses)
Sales value per 5 lb tin is approximately £1.10 including normal discounts.
Data adjusted for commercial reasons.

Figure 7 (Artcraft Ltd.)   Breakdown of powder cost of production (1971).

(1) POWDER COLOURS

Bulk Powder Production

Materials input	1558.5 lb.	Mix	80 mins.
Expected yield	1512 lb.	Pulverize	140 mins.
(Store in 112 lbs paper sacks)			

Packaging

Tin Size	Lot Size (1512 lb) Input	Machine Type	Time per Gross (mins.)	Number of Operators	Total m/c time hrs.	Total Labour std. hrs.
6 oz	3732	Allen Transmatic Auto	14.9	3	6.4	19.4
1 lb	1440	Alite	7.8	2	1.3	2.6
5 lb	280	Allen Transmatic	26.0	3	0.87	2.6

(2) 37cc OIL COLOURS

Bulk Colour Production

Materials input	228.25 lb	Grind	80 mins.
Expected yield	221 lb	Mix	20 mins.

Packaging

Materials input 10 galls.
Expected yield 1010 x 37cc

Auto Line

(a) For Finished Goods Store
Fill
Label   5 operatives
Pack   75 minutes

(b) For Part Processed Store
Fill
Label   3 operatives
Pack in   50 mins.
Trays

Figure 8 (Artcraft Ltd.)   Manufacturing process data

A breakdown of the costs of production for a typical product (5 lb. powder tins) is given in Figure 7 and the manufacturing details for the oil range and the powder range are shown in Figure 8.

Annual sales figures of the 37 cc oil colour range are summarized below:

Number of colours with this demand level (1)	Average demand level (no. of tubes) (2)	Total 1971 sales (no. of tubes) (1) x (2)
1 colour	50,000	50,000*
2 colours	15,000	30,000†
5 colours	10,000	50,000
10 colours	5,000	50,000
12 colours	3,000	36,000
30 colours		216,000

*Approximately 40,000 used in sets   (Singles 136,000)
†Approximately 10,000 used in sets   (Sets   80,000)

It is expected that some 25% of the time one of the filling lines (which are manned for 40 hours per week) will be available for the production of the 37 cc oil colour range.

Batch Sizes

In colour making the 'batch size' must be a multiple of the machine 'lot size' which is either 10 galls. or 20 galls. for liquids depending on the mill used, or 1512 lbs. for powders. In colour filling the batch size is unconstrained but in practice is usually an integral multiple of the minimum 10 gallon 'lot size' from colour making. There is considerable advantage in scheduling multiple lots to run together in both departments. Wash down times between different products/colours in colour making are about one hour. In filling, where contamination is more important, the wash down time depends on the difference between the colours being filled. On average about 100 minutes are required to change one of the semi-automatic lines over to a different product or tube size including cleaning times, whereas the wash down time if adjacent colours in the same product range are run with no size change is about 40 minutes for water based products and 60 minutes for oil based products. (Note that the colour sequence has to be light to dark through the range.)

Besides the extra wash down time required for colour changes there is the question of the materials lost in the wash down process. Currently some 3% loss of material on the minimum batch size occurs in colour making due to wash down and wastage (it is estimated that the loss on cleaning is about 25 lb. in the powder mixers and 0.2 galls. in the 10 gallon mixers).

Yield losses in the filling department occur for two reasons:

(1) Wash down losses and wastage, and
(2) Losses due to 'overfill'.

For (1), the cleaning losses again amount to about 0.2 galls. for liquids and 25 lbs. for the bulk powders with other wastage of about 0.1 galls. and 20 lbs. respectively on the minimum batch of 10 galls. and 1512 lbs.

For (2), the loss rate is very dependent on the size of the finished product. An allowance of about 13% is made for overfill of 37 cc tubes while an allowance of 4% is used for the three powder colour tins. The actual losses due to overfill vary considerably from run to run.

Inventory and Service Levels

Management were becoming increasingly aware that high investment in inventories was not giving the required service level to the 10,000 or so customers who normally ordered Artcraft products regularly. An analysis of inventories was made and the results are summarized in Figure 9.

The normal practice is to reserve stock for an order on the computerized inventory records as soon as an order is received. There is, however, then generally some delay in the despatch of the order before the physical inventory is depleted.

Labour and Labour Relations

Labour relations at Artcraft have always been good and the management has always regarded itself as rather paternalistic in style in the tradition of the old 'family

MATERIALS AND WORK IN PROCESS   £

Part Processed stores	43,000	
Colour Stores (raw materials)	36,400	
Packaging Stores	80,600	
Labels	15,600	
Brush Stores (raw materials)	26,000	
Work in Process	35,000	
Other	42,400	
		279,000

FINISHED GOODS STOCK (at C.O.P.)

Made in	300,000	
Bought out items	91,000	
		391,000
		670,000

Figure 9A (Artcraft Ltd.)   Summary of stocks at 31st December 1971

TOTAL NUMBER OF FINISHED PRODUCTS = 2130
TOTAL SALES VALUE (APPROX)   = £2,200,000

39 MAJOR PRODUCT GROUPS (719 products)
Account for £1,700,000 of total sales £260,000 of finished goods inventory.

INDIVIDUAL PRODUCTS

Sales p.a.	No. of items	Total sales p.a.£	Average inventory value £
over £5000	63	900,000	95,000
£3000–£5000	54	270,000	45,000
	117	£1,170,000	140,000

BOUGHT OUT ITEMS ONLY
Sales value p.a.   = £230,000
Average stock value = £100,000
(including bulk orders for paper, shipments from abroad and brushes made out)

Figure 9B (Artcraft Ltd.)   Inventory analysis by product

firm'. Despite the necessity for a number of redundancies in the latter half of 1971 when the company was in a critical financial condition the labour force seemed to accept the situation.

The direct operatives are split into two major groups:

(1) A large number of full and part time female workers who operate the filling machines and carry out most of the packaging; and

(2) A smaller number of male workers in the colour manufacturing department. The work in this department is heavy, dirty and in many ways rather unpleasant. It has therefore proved difficult to get workers for this area and, in the main, few Europeans work there.

All the direct operatives are on piecework rates which usually give a 25% bonus above the 35p per hour 'standing rate'. This has caused some problems in the past when the semi-automatic filling lines are being cleaned down or reset by a 'service man' as the girls usually have to wait around while such changes are made. Sometimes odd packing jobs are available but usually by the time the girls have started them the line is ready to run again.

In addition to these major groups there are a number of craft and semi-skilled maintenance workers of various trades and a larger number of white collar workers in sales administration, production control, etc. A breakdown of non-management employees is given below:

Direct Production	*No. of Employees*
Packaging (including colour box assembly and filling)	79 (many part time only)
Colour Manufacture	17
Colour Stores	4
Brush Production	10 (part time, total 250 hrs per week)
TOTAL DIRECT	110

Indirects and Staff	
Sales Administration	15
Marketing and Export	14
Accounts	21
Production Control	10
Production Supervisory	10
Quality Control and Chemical Development	8
Secretarial Services	8
Despatch and Warehouse	5
Electricians	3
Labourers/Waste Disposal	3
Fitters and Other Maintenance	8
Cleaners	6 (part time only)
Others	30
TOTAL INDIRECTS	141
TOTAL	251

The Barwick Switch Company

Introduction

The Barwick Switch Company were one of two firms in the UK manufacturing precision switches, which had many uses in the automotive, industrial and domestic applicance fields. Between them these two firms held 80% of the UK market. Both divided their output between original equipment, i.e. switches sold to manufacturers who assembled them into their final product, and spares. Margins were low in the original equipment market, but considerably better in the spares sector. On the other hand, orders were much larger for original equipment. The competitive activity between the two companies, combined with additional competition from foreign manufacturers, had resulted in both companies making very limited profits. Barwick had in fact lost money in two of the previous five years.

Barwick had therefore built, and was about to commission a new, automated flow production line to manufacture a range of high-volume small switches. The line had a capacity of 60,000 switches/day and small switches accounted for some 20% of Barwick's annual sales of £15 million. The line was to be a profit centre, with the manager responsible for the mix and price of the product range, but not for purchasing or selling. The case describes the approach proposed for product mix and pricing structure.

Barwick's main factory was laid out as a traditional job shop with a functional organization. The theoretical throughput time was six weeks, but in practice batches frequently took much longer. The majority of the machines were fully depreciated. The new unit consisted of a number of flow lines, down which the switches travelled. Some parts were to be supplied from the main factory under a transfer pricing agreement, but in general the lines had been designed so that:

(1) Movement of parts between machining stations, as well as machining, was automatic.
(2) Changeover time between types of switch was minimal (15–30 minutes for the whole line).
(3) Much tedious inspection and adjustment at the assembly stage was eliminated by closer control of tolerances.

The unit, which would cater for 23 different switches, each offered with a choice of two electrical connection patterns and two types of cover, had been proportionately expensive to build.

The original policy had been to achieve better control of production and costs. The extremely narrow profit margins on the small switches meant that the primary targets of the new line had to be stability of production and minimization of production costs. The company felt they could no longer afford to sacrifice profit for the sake of flexibility. The intention was that marketing should sell the low cost output of the production line rather than production make what marketing had sold. This represented a change in policy aimed at reflecting the economic differences between mass and batch production. In the past all regular customers had been asked every year to give an indication of their next year's requirements month by month. These forecasts, together with an allowance for unforeseen orders, were used as a basis for planning production. The accuracy of these forecasts had always been poor. This had resulted in many changes to the main factory schedule causing lengthening delivery promises, and many late deliveries. In particular, this was cutting Barwick off from the spares market. Here it was often possible for a stockist to offer a repairer a switch of similar specification from another manufacturer. Barwick were therefore now doing their own forecasting, with the aim of providing an off-the-shelf-service. They had however discovered, as part of this exercise, that notwithstanding delivery shortcomings, stocks of finished switches were in total excessive.

Product Mix and Pricing Strategy for the New Line

The current product mix was the result of demand from specific customers and Barwick's pricing structure. For example, one switch accounted for 25% of current production and was supplied to a single major customer. To retain this customer in the face of strong competition, the price did not include a full contribution to overheads.

The problem to be solved was to select for the new line that mix of products which would give maximum contribution. The method had to:

(1) Be simple to use and understand.
(2) Produce a theoretical optimum product/price mix.
(3) Give results which could easily be made into a production plan.
(4) Allow for modification in the light of marketing and production constraints.

Method for Evaluating Product Mix — Summary

The main competitive determinant in the cheap switch market was price, although delivery performance and quality featured to a lesser extent. Barwick decided to make the assumption that it was, or shortly would be, matching its major competitors on quality and delivery. The company therefore decided to concentrate only on price as the determining factor of sales volume.

The method proposed for selecting the mix can be summarized as follows. An approximate price–volume relationship would be derived for each of the 23 switch types. The variable costs would be subtracted from the price to arrive at a contribution–volume relationship. The volume of each switch would then be selected so as to maximize the total contribution.

Details of the Method

Price–Volume Relationship

Barwick's marketing organization was evaluating the relationship between order size and price. Data was also being collected on quoted prices not accepted by the customer.

From this data, as illustrated in Figure 1, a price structure could be drawn which would give Barwick a high chance of capturing all enquiries, on the basis that a price of P1 could be expected to satisfy most enquiries up to an order size of S1 etc.

All enquiries could then be analysed to find the total potential business in each order-size band (i.e. 0 to S1, S1 to S2 etc.). This data would enable a forecast to be made of the number of switches which could be sold per day at a price P1, P2 etc. Figure 2 shows a suitable recording chart.

Variable Costs

The 'standard cost' used by Barwick was based on actual costs and not on a strict standard basis, though the company intended to introduce standard costs based on standard times in the near future. Its current standard costs consisted of:

(1) Raw material
(2) Components
(3) Direct Labour
(4) Scrap
(5) Variable overheads
(6) Fixed overheads

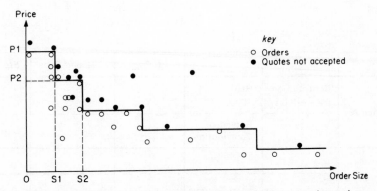

Figure 1 (Barwick Switch Co.)   Orders obtained and lost at various prices

		First Price	Second Price	Etc.
Switch A	Price			
	Order Size Band			
	Volume			
Switch B				

Figure 2 (Barwick Switch Co.)   Chart for daily volumes at different
price levels

Raw material and component costs could be considered fully variable. This was only valid because the components made in the main factory could be used elsewhere if not transferred to the new unit.

Direct labour was also variable because surplus labour could be absorbed elsewhere in the factory. Scrap was apportioned as a rate per unit volume and was therefore variable.

Barwick were interested in maximizing the contribution against both factory and company overheads so these four elements of cost (raw material, components, direct labour and scrap) would constitute the fully variable cost, which when subtracted from the selling price would yield the contribution.

The costs in use were the current standard, but Barwick's management considered them to be reasonably good estimates of the likely costs on the new production line.

Maximizing the Contribution of the Mix

By subtracting the variable cost from the prices in Figure 2 a contribution–volume relationship could be derived. The mix of switches to produce the highest overall contribution could then be calculated using the matrix illustrated in part in Figure 3.

			First Price	Second Price	Etc.
Switch A	Contribution per Switch	Rank			
	Volume	Extended Contribution			
Etc					

Figure 3 (Barwick Switch Co.)   Chart for contributions at different prices

Each element of the matrix would show for each switch and each step of the price structure (see Figure 1) the contribution per switch (price less variable cost), the daily volume saleable at that price, and the extended contribution (contribution per switch x volume). Once the matrix was completed, the elements could be ranked in order of decreasing contribution. The volumes of each element would then be summed in descending rank until production capacity was reached. Output for each switch above the cut-off point could then be summed both for volume, to give the mix of daily production and for extended contribution, to give the overall total contribution of the solution.

The solution could show that a particular switch or switches had insufficient contribution to justify manufacture. Such switches would not be produced on the new line, but in the main factory where factory overheads were lower.

In drawing up the matrix an important assumption was made; namely that switch capacity was homogeneous and producing 100 of switch A was equivalent to 100 of switch B etc. It was recognized that the matrix would be more accurate if standard times were used, but Barwick currently lacked the information.

Manipulating the Matrix

Using the matrix, it was possible to derive a theoretical optimum mix, but certain practical operating constraints might exist. These could be:

(1) Marketing constraints: where regardless of pricing strategy, there was not a sufficiently large market to sell the optimum number of switches.
(2) Production constraints: where earlier decisions had committed facilities to specific switches.

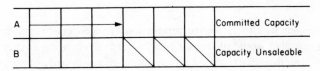

Figure 4 (Barwick Switch Co.)   Chart to show marketing and production constraints

The matrix could be easily adapted to cater for these constraints. In the first case, quantities of switches above the marketing 'ceiling' would be ignored regardless of contribution, and in the second all committed capacity would be allocated first and the remainder ranked and summed (see Figure 4).

The reduction in total extended contribution could be compared with the costs which might be incurred to achieve the optimum solution in terms of market penetration and production flexibility.

Use of Alternative Price Structures

It was felt that the price structure illustrated in Figure 1 might be difficult to establish with confidence. To overcome this, it was felt that two price structures

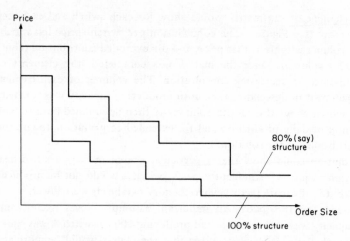

Figure 5 (Barwick Switch Co.)   Price structure to obtain 100% and
80% of possible orders

should be specified: a low one which could be reasonably certain of capturing all
orders in each price band and a higher one which could be expected to capture a
large proportion of orders. This proportion would be assessed on the sample data
available and, possibly, subjective marketing opinion (see Figure 5).

It was recognized that it would be too laborious to draw up matrices for all
combinations of high and low price structures for all switches, but the sensitivity of
the solution could be tested with certain switches.

Updating the Matrix

Although the aim was to minimize production changeovers by generating a firm
output plan, the plan would obviously need to adapt to changing circumstances.

The price structure charts would be continuously monitored. At regular intervals
enquiries would be sampled for changes in the proportion of orders obtained in
each order size band. Changes in variable costs would be analysed to determine
whether any change in mix was necessary.

As experience was gained, the price structure and variable costs would be
modified to take account of expected events which might invalidate historical data.
If the matrix was used in this way, it was felt that a fairly simple computer program
would be justified to do the collating, ranking and summation.

Sample Results

The Barwick Switch Company had not currently collected enough data to establish
price—volume relationships for all switches. However, data on the highest turnover
switch was available and is given as an example of the working method.

The first difficulty experienced was switch variants. The switches were offered

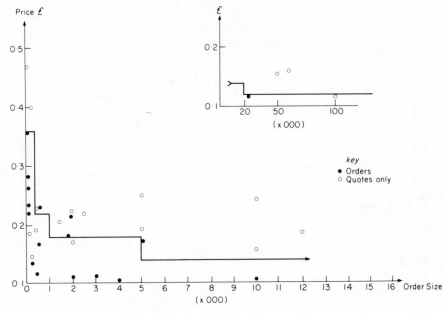

Figure 6 (Barwick Switch Co.)   Switch GIP

with a choice of two electrical connection patterns and two outer sealing covers. Each had different variable costs, requiring different pricing structures. Figures 6 and 7 show structures for two principal variants: a type G switch with spade connections and a type G switch with terminals and an outer sealing cover resistant to hot oil. The structures drawn were fairly arbitrary, particularly for larger orders but as experience and data accumulated, more accurate estimates were expected.

Figure 8 shows the price to daily volume relationship derived from the number of switches required in each order-size band from Figures 6 and 7.

The variable costs of each variant are £0.06 and £0.07 respectively. The contribution matrix is drawn up in Figure 9.

Figure 10 shows the summation of volumes in order of rank. If it is assumed that for the two switch types production capacity is 2,500 switches per day (for the 23 types it is 60,000 per day), then cut-off would be reached with 201 switches from the tenth element. The mix and contribution would therefore be:

	Volume	*Extended Contributions*
GIP	1436	130.9
G20	1064	113.4
	TOTAL	244.3

In order to achieve this mix, the marketing area would price G20 to the structure of Figure 7 for all order sizes between zero and 29,999. For orders of 30,000 and

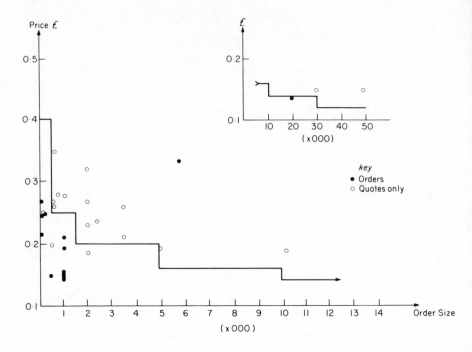

Figure 7 (Barwick Switch Co.)   Switch G20

above, enquiries would be quoted for at unattractive rates (say £0.16). If any such quotes were accepted, they would be referred to production for scheduled delivery at extended lead times.

Where only part of an element was required, as with the fifth element of GIP, the price would be raised for that element to a sufficient level to reduce the acceptance rate of quotes in that order-size band. In this case the price would be raised to reduce the quote acceptance by 55% so that only 200 instead of 422 switches were required per day. In fact in the full matrix it was probable that any part element would be insignificant within the accuracy of all the estimates made.

Where the capacity cut-off fell amongst equally ranked elements (see the eleventh in the example), then the matrix as it stood would not provide the solution. Reference back to the price structure might indicate that one switch could be priced slightly higher for that order-size range without significant loss of orders. It would then increase its contribution and rank within the matrix.

The tabulated summations in Figure 10 were not, of course, regarded as a production programme. Even keeping to the daily horizon, within the worked example two batches only would be made, not eight changes from type to type as indicated by the transitions in the matrix. In practice, the indicated daily rates of production, which might be quite small for the less popular switches, were to be aggregated to produce suitable production runs over some appropriate time scale.

	First Price	Second Price	Third Price	Fourth Price	Fifth Price	Sixth Price
Switch GIP						
Price	0.36	0.22	0.18	0.14	0.12	0.11
Band	0–399	400–999	1000–4999	5000–19999	20000–99999	100,000
Volume/Day	25	32	300	878	422	14,530
Switch G20						
Price	0.40	0.25	0.20	0.16	0.14	0.12
Band	0–499	500–1499	1500–4999	5000–9999	10000–29999	30,000
Volume/Day	12	131	327	84	510	1350

Figure 8 (Barwick Switch Co.)   Price to daily volume relationship

Switch	First Price		Second Price		Third Price		Fourth Price		Fifth Price		Sixth Price	
GIP	.3	2	.16	4	.12	6	.08	8	.06	10	.05	11
	25	7.5	32	5.1	300	36.0	878	70.2	422	25.3	14500	725
G20	.33	1	.18	3	.13	5	.09	7	.07	9	.05	11
	12	4	131	23.6	327	45.2	84	7.6	510	35.7	1350	67.5

Figure 9 (Barwick Switch Co.)   Contribution matrix

Rank	Element Volume	Cumulative Volume
1	12	12
2	25	37
3	131	168
4	32	200
5	327	527
6	300	827
7	84	911
8	878	1789
9	510	2299
10	422	2621
11	1350	3971
12	14500	18471

Figure 10 (Barwick Switch Co.)   Summation of volumes in order of rank

Conclusion

Although no full solution had been reached, Barwick thought that the data which was currently being collected would provide sufficient basis for deriving the full contribution matrix. The method satisfied the criteria of simplicity and flexibility, but it would be a laborious technique to use manually on an on-going basis. Barwick considered that once the method had been shown proved, the number-processing could be automated.

Bell Schönheitsprodukte GmbH

In January 1972 the management of Bell Schönheitsprodukte GmbH decided to give serious consideration to undertaking a major plant extension outside Germany. 1971 had seen the formal revaluation of the once floating German Mark to a parity of 0.3106 US Dollars. This revaluation represented an increase of 13.6% in the value of the deutschmark (DM) over the DM–Dollar rate of May 1971. 1971 had also seen an increase in the wage bill (including social benefits) at Bell GmbH of nearly 15%. As Bell exported over 60% of its rather labour intensive German production these events threatened a major reduction in the firm's profitability.

Internationalizing Bell's sources of production appeared to be the best way out of this predicament. A US-owned competitor which had previously been producing most of its output in Germany had just opened a plant in France and had started a price war. Wages in France were about 5 to 6 francs per hour. Wages in Germany were 6 DM per hour. (One franc equalled 0.627 DM in January 1972.) The problem facing Bell was the location of the new plant.

The Company and its Products

Bell Schönheitsprodukte GmbH was a German, family-owned company with a total European-wide turnover of 22 million DM in 1971. The product line consisted entirely of special opening, sliding and spring packagings for the cosmetic industry. Bell had over 200 customers including several very large multinational companies such as Unilever, Colgate–Palmolive and L'Oreal. The single largest customer purchased 10% of Bell's sales.

Bell's 'American' name arose from the fact that its product line was produced under an exclusive licence of an American Company, Bell Industries, Inc. The American licensor, however, had no ownership interest in Bell GmbH. Although Bell GmbH was a relatively small firm, it had already opened a plant in Great Britain in the mid 1960s. The UK plant had a capacity of 25 million units compared with the 200 million unit capacity of the main German plant located in Hannover. Both plants normally produced at 90–95% of capacity. About 18.8 million DM of sales came from the German plant's production; the remaining 2.3 million were accounted for by UK production. Because of the 9.6% EEC common tariff, UK production went only to the UK. All other European markets (including

Prepared by Dr. Lawrence G. Franko, Faculty Member, Centre d'Etudes Industrielles (CEI), Geneva, Switzerland. Copyright © 1972 by CEI, reproduced by permission.

other EFTA markets) were supplied by Germany. Indeed, the UK plant had only been set up because of the 9.6% *ad valorum* EFTA tariff facing German output. Thirty people were employed in the UK plant compared with 120 in Germany. Of the German personnel, 90 were women workers who assembled and decorated packages. The remainder consisted of administrative personnel and technicians. The latter designed and built much of Bell GmbH's machinery and handled the critically important quality control aspects of the business. None of Bell's enployees were union members. According to management, Bell was too small to have attracted the attention of the unions.

Sales were made throughout western Europe and also in Yugoslavia. Under the terms of its American licence, the company was restricted to selling in Europe and the socialist countries. The size of the total 1971 European and the US markets in units for the special cosmetic packaging products produced by Bell is shown below. Given normal economic conditions, that is 4—5% yearly growth in GNP, management expected 20% per year sales growth in the more developed areas of Europe and somewhat higher growth in countries such as Greece, Portugal and Spain.

Approximate Market Size (1971)
in Units (Millions)

UK	150
Germany	360
France	200
Benelux	90
Greece	5
Italy	150
Scandinavia	60
Spain	25
Portugal	5
Switzerland	40
Austria	10
Yugoslavia	5
TOTAL EUROPE	1,100
USA	2,400

Competition and Prices

Bell GmbH's competitors have the following characteristics:

Competitor	Ownership	Output of plants by Country 1971
A (large)	UK group	France 80% UK 15% Italy 5%
B (large)	US company	Germany 65% England 30% France 5%
C (small)	US (recently acquired)	Germany 100%
D (small)	Italian	Italy 100%
E (small)	Italian	Italy 100%

Bell's management suspected that the two small Italian firms were secretly backed by their government. This view was supported by the fact that the Italian price level was 10—15% lower than that elsewhere in the EEC. The two companies had tried to export a part of their production. However, their quality standards were apparently not as high as those of Bell and companies A and B. Moreover their plants were unionized and subject to occasional strikes. Thus, they had a poor reputation for meeting delivery dates outside Italy. However, they dominated the local market. Bell had once had 30% of the Italian market and was well known there, but with very low margins Bell found it increasingly difficult to compete in Italy. Nevertheless, in late 1971, just as the Italian situation began to look really hopeless, the President of Bell, Herr Kahler, had received a letter from two ex-managers of Italian company E suggesting that Bell start up a plant in Italy under their direction.

With the exception of Italy, prices elsewhere in Europe were relatively uniform. Bell's ex-factory price was 100 DM per thousand in the EEC. Company B, who had started the price war that had recently pushed prices down to 95 DM also billed in DM. Company A, who because of its dominant French position, billed in francs, by and large charged a similar price once value added tax adjustments were made. According to one Bell manager, 'we tend to react immediately to what A and B do, and vice versa. Everyone tries to differentiate their product other than by price, but finally, one packaging is like another'.

Estimates for the market share of Bell and its competitors in France, Germany, England and the whole of Europe are:

COMPARATIVE MARKET SHARES

(Rough estimates. No one in the industry publishes sales figures)

	BELL	COMPANY A	COMPANY B	OTHERS	TOTAL
Europe Total	19%	35%	25%	21%	100%
France	7%	70%	20%	3%	100%
UK	15%	30%	45%	10%	100%
Germany	22%	30%	30%	18%	100%

Alternative Courses of Action

In the face of competition, unfavourable exchange rate movements, wage increases in Germany and the Italian proposal, management felt that action would be needed soon. Her Kahler had received a phone call from company A suggesting that they try to counter company B's price cutting by 'an arrangement'. The virtues of such an arrangement from Bell's point of view, however, seemed questionable. Company A had 80% of its production in France where wages were favourable and devaluation more often than not the rule.

Putting up a new plant in France seemed a tempting possibility; all the more so since the French Government offered considerable investment incentives in certain parts of the country. In addition, some technical and design tasks could eventually be performed in France since indigenous skills were available. Ninety per cent of component needs would be supplied initially from Bell's usual suppliers in

Germany. However, by the second year of operations, perhaps 30% could be obtained locally, and, if necessary, all materials could be obtained locally after the third year. Last, but not least, in regions such as Alsace, French technicians and workers were generally fluent in German. Thus there would be few language difficulties during the plant start-up. However, management were concerned as to whether the French wage and exchange rate situations would continue favourable to exports. Moreover the investment incentives picture had recently been altered by the EEC agreement which limited incentive grants to 20% of project costs from January 1972. Management were also concerned by the possibility of labour disturbances similar to those of May 1968.

In some ways, adding 25 or 50 million units of capacity to the UK plant seemed the easiest thing to do. A plant and trained people were already in existence. Investment incentives might be available and the pound might be devalued again. It was possible that wages would not increase as fast as elsewhere in the now expanding EEC.

However, the UK was less attractive in the immediate future because it would probably take five years before tariff barriers finally disappeared between the UK and the EEC. As in France, local components could eventually be substituted for German made goods.

The request from the Italians reminded Bell management that a local plant might enable them to recapture its 30% market share. Technical skills and components would be as easily available as in the UK and France. Moreover, Italy could conceivably provide a relatively low wage base for exports. The lira had depreciated against the mark in recent times. But could any country that had taken 23 ballots to elect a president in 1971 be a stable place in which to invest?

One final option that appeared possible to Herr Kahler and other members of Bell's management was that of setting up a plant in Spain. Such a move might give the company a more lasting competitive advantage than some of the other possibilities. Whether or not components could be obtained locally was unknown.

	Alternative 1	Alternative 2
Annual Plant Capacity (Million Units)	25	50
Space Requirements	600 m²	1000 m²
Approximate yearly Rental Cost for Leased Plant*	28,800 DM	48,000 DM
Cost of Machinery (to be Purchased in Germany)	300,000 DM	500,000 DM**
Working Capital Requirements	100,000 DM	220,000 DM
Components Cost (per million units)	46,000 DM	46,000 DM
Direct Labour (per million units produced in Germany)	7,000 DM	7,000 DM
General Administration and Overhead (per year)	100,000 DM	150,000 DM**
Transport Costs	2% sales price	2% sales price

*Similar in all countries.
**For plants above 50 million units, machinery and overhead costs are roughly proportional to capacity.

Figure 1 (Bell GmbH)   Capacity and cost alternatives

	1965	1966	1967	1968 (Millions of US $)	1969	1970	1971 (Nov)
ITALY							
Official reserves	4800	4911	5463	5341	5045	5352	6431
(+) Balance on goods & services	1883	1779	1273	2336	2013	679	
Trade (goods) balance only	646	331	-21	1048	542	-340	
FRANCE							
Official reserves	6343	6733	6994	4201	3833	4960	7494
(+) Balance on goods & services			732	-238	-971	1148	
Trade (goods) balance only			356	-158	-1223	726	
UK							
Official reserves	3004	3099	2695	2422	2527	2827	5527
(+) Balance on goods & services	378	801	-115	-118	1613	1911	
Trade (goods) balance only	-664	-204	-1446	-1543	-338	7	
GERMANY							
Official reserves	7430	8029	8153	9948	7129	13,610	17,371
(+) Balance on goods & services	-86	1593	3970	4554	3780	3225	
Trade (goods) balance only	248	1878	4116	4485	3902	4024	
SPAIN							
Official reserves	1422	1253	1100	1150	1282	1817	3104
(+) Balance on goods & services	-846	-983	-907	-709	-959		
Trade (goods) balance only	-1759	-1992	-1781	-1574	-1871		

(+) Not including transfer payments.
Source: IMF, *International Financial Statistics*.

Figure 2 (Bell GmbH)   International financial data: Selected European countries

	1966*	1967*	1968*	1969*	1970*	1971*	1972(**) (Forecast)
ITALY							
Per cent increase in industrial output	11.3	8.5	6.3	2.9	4.0	-2.6	8.0
(++) Per cent increase in wages		5.2	3.6	7.5	21.4	14.5	15.0
Ratio of output to wage increases		(1.64)	(1.75)	(0.36)	(0.14)	(0.19)	(0.53)
FRANCE							
Per cent increase in industrial output	4.3	2.6	4.1	12.7	5.6	2.5	5.0
(++) Per cent increase in wages	5.9	6.0	12.4	11.3	10.5	11.1	10.0
Ratio of output to wage increases	(0.72)	(0.43)	(0.33)	(1.13)	(0.53)	(0.22)	(0.50)
UK							
Per cent increase in industrial output	1.8	-0.9	5.3	3.4	1.6	0.8	3.5
(++) Per cent increase in wages	6.7	4.0	6.8	9.2	9.6	12.1	12.0
Ratio of output to wage increases	(0.27)	(-0.22)	(0.78)	(0.37)	(0.17)	(0.07)	(0.29)
GERMANY							
Per cent increase in industrial output	1.8	-1.7	12.3	12.5	6.3	3.2	0
(+) Per cent increase in wages	7.3	3.9	4.3	9.1	12.8	13.3	6.5
Ratio of output to wage increases	(0.25)	(-0.44)	(2.9)	(1.4)	(0.49)	(0.24)	(0)
SPAIN							
Per cent increase in industrial output	15.0	6.2	6.5	14.5	7.9		6.6
(+) Per cent increase in wages	16.0	15.0	7.0	9.0	17.0		12.0
Ratio of output to wage increases	(0.94)	(0.42)	(0.93)	(1.61)	(0.47)		(0.55)

(+) Hourly earnings
(++) Hourly rates

Sources: (*) Calculated from OECD, Main Economic Indicators, various issues.
(**) Eurofinance-Vision Projections, Vision, January 1972, p. 38.

Figure 3 (Bell GmbH)   Wage increases related to output increases in industry: Selected European countries

Wage rates were thought to be low enough to compensate for the EEC common tariff. Although a 10% duty might have to be paid on components imported from Germany, it seemed probable that a rebate arrangement for re-exported components could be negotiated with the Spanish authorities.

The plant sizes that appeared most interesting for Italian, Spanish, UK or French operations were either 25 million or 50 million units per year. Factory buildings could be leased for very similar rentals throughout Europe. Details of the capacity and cost alternatives considered are given in Figure 1. The necessary machinery would either be made at Bell's main plant or purchased in Germany. Tentatively, it was thought best to finance a foreign plant by an equity stake equal to the cost of machinery. Working capital requirements could be met either by local borrowing or by the extension of account payable terms (for components) to the foreign plant.

As Bell management was preparing to draw up *pro-forma* economic forecasts and cash flow projections for the French, UK, Spanish and Italian alternatives, Herr Kahler reminded his colleagues of a letter he had received in November 1971. He suggested that this letter should stimulate Bell to examine the German economy a bit more carefully, too. The letter was from a Yugoslav company that was soliciting Bell's participation in a joint venture, the aim being to export back to Europe. Herr Kahler rejected serious consideration of such an alternative for the time being on the grounds that Bell was too small to enter into protracted negotiations with a prospective partner in a venture that might end up competing with already existing wholly owned facilities. Still, he felt it might be useful to look at the medium term outlook for Germany and the competitiveness of the headquarters plant. If a firm in a country like Yugoslavia were to enter into the packaging business, perhaps continued German revaluations and steep wage increases could make the position of the main 200 million unit capacity plant less and less tenable over the years. Up to this point, it had been assumed that German production would still account for most of Bell's sales, even after the new plant were added. It was quite true that the German stockholders might not want to shift a lot of Bell's current production to a foreign country, but efforts at automation

Year		Belgium	France	Germany	Italy	Netherlands	UK
1965		95.3	91.7	92.1	86.8	89.7	
1966		90.6	90.0	85.6	88.5	87.6	93.6
1967		90.2	87.0	86.7	89.4	86.7	
1968		90.6	96.8	93.0	90.0	91.2	96.9
1969		94.2	94.7	97.3	79.1	93.2	95.8
1970		92.8	95.6	94.0	87.3	94.0	94.5
1971	(1)	94.7	96.1	97.1	86.1	96.5	93.6
	(2)	92.2	93.2	95.4	82.1	94.8	94.2
	(3)	92.9	95.5	93.1	79.4	93.6	93.4

Source: 'Wharton Indices of Industrial Capacity Utilization in Europe', *Wharton Quarterly*, various issues (available from The Wharton School, University of Pennsylvania, Philadelphia, Penn., USA)

Figure 4 (Bell GmbH)   Indices of industrial capacity utilization (%) in selected European countries, year end, 1965—1970, and first three quarters 1971

	Austria	Belgium	Denmark	France	W. Germany	Italy	Spain	Switzerland	UK
	per month Schilling (+)	per day Male B. Franc (+)	per hour (M & F)* Ore (+)	per hour (wage rate) Francs (++)	per hour (M & F)* D. Mark (+)	per hour Lira (+)	per hour pesetas (+)	per hour Sw. Fr. (+)	per hour Male £ (+)
1965	3141	359.0	923	3.00	4.12	386	21.57	5.20	0.43
1966	3514	389.7	1040	3.18	4.42	401	25.13	5.58	0.46
1967	3781	414.2	1128	3.37	4.60	426	28.81	5.94	0.49
1968	4018	438.7	1283	3.79	4.79	445	31.16	6.24	0.52
1969	4263	474.1	1407	4.21	5.28	489	34.69	6.64	0.56
1970	5074	–	–	4.56	5.77	–	–	–	–

*Male & Female
(+) Earnings
(++) Rates
Source: ILO Yearbook of Labor Statistics (1970)

Figure 5 (Bell GmbH) Wages in manufacturing (all industries) in local currencies: Selected European countries

could only go so far. Bell had reduced the number of its women workers from 150 to 90 between 1970 and 1971 while increasing output. However, productivity increases could not be obtained at this rate in the future.

In considering their decision, Bell management drew up the economic data shown in Figures 2, 3, 4 and 5. The information prepared as a result of the original Italian proposal is shown below.

SAMPLE CASH FLOW PROJECTION FOR AN ITALIAN
INVESTMENT SHOWING RESULTS ASSUMING:
(1) No devaluation
(2) A 10% devaluation

Projected Cash Flows: Italian investment in 50 million unit plant Investment:

Machinery	DM 500,000
Working Capital	220,000
Total	720,000
less: 70% debt	(504,000)
Net investment	DM 216,000

Annual Cash Flows:

	Before Devaluation	After 10% Devaluation
Sales Revenue (DM 95 x 50,000)	DM 4,750,000	DM 4,750,000
Expenses: (−)		
Building rental	48,000	43,000
Components	2,300,000	1,970,000
Direct Labour	170,000	153,000
General Overhead	150,000	135,000
Transport costs	75,000	68,000
Interest (5%)	25,000	23,000
	DM 1,982,000	DM 2,358,000

Major Assumptions/
— All components supplied locally
— Income tax holiday provided by Italian government
— All production is for export
— Depreciation not included in 'overhead charges'

Berger Paints — Distribution

Introduction

This case deals with the reorganization and development of a paint distribution system. As paint is essentially a low cost item the costs of distribution are a vital factor in the profitability of the industry. The system described in this case has a budget in millions of pounds and handles tens of millions of litres of paint annually.

Company Background

Berger, Jenson and Nicholson Ltd. is a holding company for a number of subsidiaries and has several associated companies.

This case is primarily concerned with its major paint producing subsidiary in the UK, the second largest paint manufacturer in the UK in 1972.

In 1968 there were three main subsidiaries: Berger Jenson and Nicholson Paints Ltd., BJN Paints (Scotland) Ltd., and John Hall and Sons (Bristol and London) Ltd. In May 1969 British Paints Ltd. was acquired from the US company, Celanese Corporation Ltd.

BJN was taken over in January 1970, becoming a subsidiary of Hoechst UK Ltd., a wholly owned subsidiary of Farbwerke Hoechst A.G. of Frankfurt. Farbwerke Hoechst A.G. was a firm of similar size and character to ICI with a consolidated group turnover of approximately £1,525 million in 1971 and 142,110 employees.

During 1970 Berger Jenson and Nicholson Paints Ltd., John Hall and Sons (Bristol and London) Ltd., British Paints Ltd. and BJN Paints (Scotland) Ltd. were reorganized into two trading divisions on a marketing basis. These divisions were Berger—Hall Paints and British Paints and Chemicals. In 1971 these divisions were renamed as Berger Paints and Berger Chemicals respectively.

Products and Manufacturing Sites of the Paint-making Subsidiaries

In 1969 the main product categories were as follows:

(1) Paint for the retail trade.
(2) Paint for the decorative trade (professional decorators etc.).
(3) General industrial paints.
(4) Automotive finishes.
(5) Vehicle refinishing products.
(6) Can and coil coatings (for tinplate).
(7) 'Protection' finishes with special resistance for use on bridges etc.
(8) Marine and 'Little Ship' paints.
(9) Elastomers — special reactants for the aerospace industry etc.
(10) Resinous materials.

The five manufacturing plants were at Bristol, Stratford (London), Chadwell Heath (London), Newcastle and Glasgow. The Bristol, Chadwell Heath and Glasgow plants mainly produced paints for the retail and decorative trades plus vehicle finishes. Stratford specialized in the production of 'low flash' industrial paints, Newcastle produced retail decorative and marine paints, plus the elastomers and chemical specialities. Vehicle refinishes could also be blended to the correct colour from basic materials by some depots.

Typical trade names for the products were Magicote, Bergermaster, Robbialac, Luxol etc. There were several dozen product ranges and trade names, with up to 300 colours per range. The packaging also varied in size from small tins to large drums and bulk supplies to industry.

Competitive Background

An article in *The Financial Times* of July 1971 stated that the International Paint Company, ICI, BJN, Reed International and Donald MacPherson accounted for 60% of the paint market. Another six paint companies accounted for a further 15% of the market, leaving 500 small companies to share the remaining 25%.

Competition in the industry was based both on the technical performance of the paint and on delivery and service performance. Whilst technical innovation could substantially boost paint sales, paint was still a low cost item and an efficient distribution system was needed to control costs and take advantage of demand as it arose.

ICI, with its large market share, operated a well planned depot system with computer stock control, a good documentation system, modern mechanical handling and distribution via a paint merchant subsidiary. A typical claim for the ICI system in the conurbations was that an order placed by 4 p.m. today would have a 90% chance of delivery tomorrow.

At the other end of the market the small companies manufactured from materials supplied by the major companies and competed on the basis of fast distribution direct from the factory.

Due to the extreme rapidity of delivery, wholesalers, merchants and retailers tended to hold little stock whilst the manufacturers held high stocks and their delivery vehicles were poorly utilized.

Distribution System at the end of 1969

The distribution system was fragmented at the end of 1969 with each subsidiary operating its own transport system and marketing policies. John Hall operated a national policy of sales via merchants, but made local, direct, deliveries from Bristol and London. The long distance haulage was carried out by hired vehicles. Berger used both merchants and direct sales, with a local delivery system over a 20 mile radius from several depots. Freightliners were used between London and Glasgow manufacturing plants. Hired transport was used to supply the depots. British Paints, the smallest of the subsidiaries, had developed its own trunk haulage system to supply depots from its Newcastle factory. The depot system stretched from Aberdeen to Falmouth and made direct sales.

There was considerable duplication of effort through each subsidiary having its own depots. In London there were two distribution depots besides the two factories. Bristol had two depots and one factory. Similar situations existed in other major towns.

The Start of Rationalization

At the time of the takeover of British Paints Ltd. in 1969 a management consultancy organization was studying the organization of the paint subsidiaries of BJN. After the takeover the consultants recommended that a distribution division be formed to handle paint distribution. They also suggested that a headquarters staff should provide a service to a distribution structure based on seven regions, covering England, Wales and Scotland.

Bob Barrett joined BJN from Proctor and Gamble in mid-1969 to head the new division.

The initial moves to rationalize the situation were hampered by the small size and poor conditions of many of the depots, plus the problems associated with the wide product range.

By the end of December 1970 the group were still distributing from the 5 manufacturing units and 27 depots using 750 staff and 220 vehicles.

The main change that took place in 1970 was the division, on a marketing basis, into Berger—Hall Paints and British Paints and Chemicals. Berger—Hall Paints concentrated on the retail, decorative and automotive paints, while British Paints and Chemicals concentrated on marine paints, elastomers, protection and resinous materials. The nature of the split was further emphasized in the later (1971) name changes to Berger Paints and Berger Chemicals respectively.

In 1971 the first major steps were taken to rationalize operations by merging the paints more closely. Many brand names were dropped. Magicote became the brand name associated with retail operations, and Brolac the brand name for the decorative operations. This change produced some resistance within BJN and created problems associated with stock changeover and the rationalization of production. The problems of insufficient space, manufacturing programmes, and labour inflexibility in handling the unfamiliar brands combined to produce an unsatisfactory service position during these early days.

A New Distribution Structure

In 1971 it was decided to change the distribution structure from the seven regions recommended by the consultants to one based on four regions. The objectives of the change were 'to contain inflation' and 'stabilize distribution costs'. Also, every depot was to be made viable on a current market basis. The test for viability required that all depots should be compared on the same basis. Thus when the operating costs of both owned and leased sites were compared a (theoretical) current rental value was to be charged to the owned sites.

The design of the new system was developed by considering the factory sites to be major constraints. This led directly to the decision to build large adjacent warehouses at Bristol, Chadwell Heath, Newcastle and Glasgow. These warehouses were to carry a full range of stock and serve as the main bases for the system. The paint was to be stored in the base warehouses immediately after manufacture without factory storage. The staff organization for a typical base is shown in Figure 1.

The H.Q. staff in the new structure was to operate in two roles. One was as distribution consultants to BJN; the other was concerned with the planning, administration and operation of the distribution system. The consultancy role was required as distribution costs were passed on to the marketing organizations in BJN. Marketing was organized on a regional basis (unconnected with distribution) with separate selling forces for each product line. Before a major change could be made in the distribution system it was necessary to 'sell' the idea to marketing. Similarly ideas had to be 'sold' to the Board to obtain capital for the proposed changes.

'Selling' presentations to marketing were made by the distribution H.Q. staff at meetings with the sales director and his regional sales group. These meetings would produce compromise plans on delivery schedules, routes, costing formulae etc.

Apart from presentations, the H.Q. manager was directly concerned with business planning, property negotiations, distribution manpower planning and promotion, documentation, stock control systems and project work.

The customer service manager dealt with liaison and presentations to sales as well as monitoring service measures and complaints.

The group transport manager had direct control over the trunking operations and made the non-operational decisions, such as whether to lease or buy vehicles for the local delivery fleets. The transport inspector served as his deputy and maintained control over licences, insurance, maintenance standards etc.

The industrial engineer/national project manager was concerned with warehouse methods and equipment, as well as planning depot moves to new sites.

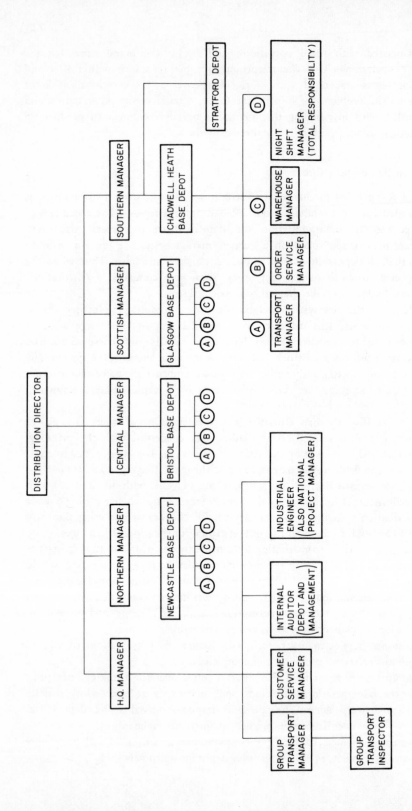

Figure 1 (Berger—Dist.)   The 1971 distribution scheme

The Depot System in 1971

Although it was planned to supply the distribution system from the four main base depots adjacent to the factories, there was also a need for other depots to supply all areas satisfactorily. Additional depots were required to reduce the length of some delivery runs and to meet a marketing requirement for emergency deliveries to be made within four hours. Depots were also temporarily needed to supplement warehouse capacity until the new base warehouses could be built.

To fill the major gap in the system it was planned to hold a full range of products at a main depot at Hindley (near Manchester). In keeping with the competition a main depot was also to be established at Birmingham, although the area had good communications with London, Bristol and Manchester. However, the Birmingham depot was not to stock marine or industrial paint.

Various other small depots were maintained in use to meet the demands of the marketing division. For example, marine paint was stocked at Southampton until the marketing personnel were convinced that sudden large demands could be met from the regional base warehouse or direct from the marine paint factory in Newcastle. Similarly a substantial stock of industrial paint was maintained in Newcastle until a major customer became convinced of the reliability of delivery from Stratford.

Some delivery problems were also met by using stockless depots. Vans were loaded overnight and driven to a stockless depot for a delivery driver to collect in the morning.

By December 1971 the number of distribution depots had been reduced by 9, to leave 5 factories and 18 distribution depots. Staff was reduced by 115, including about 50 drivers.

The locations of the main and base depots at the end of 1971 are shown in Figure 2.

Transport in 1971

The transport system operated at two levels. The first level was the local delivery fleets, which were operated by transport managers at each base warehouse. The second level comprised the trunking fleet, operated by the group transport manager through the regional transport managers.

This trunking operation was an essential requirement as none of the individual factories produced a complete range of products. Thus it was necessary to move products between base warehouses and between the depots and warehouses.

The group transport manager advised on the proper use of vehicles, the type required, maintenance needs etc. He also operated the group trunking service. He was accountable for meeting legal obligations, cost control, acquisition, replacement and for training the managers in operation and control.

The trunking service was organized on the basis of the British Paints trunking system, which had covered the country fairly effectively. This trunking system had

Key
————— Trunk haulage by BJN transport
– – – – – Trunk haulage by private haulier

Figure 2 (Berger–Dist.)   Base and main depots and proposed trunk haulage routes for 1973

taken paint out to the depots and back-hauled raw materials, but it had been underutilized at the time of the BJN takeover.

During 1971 the total number of delivery and trunking vehicles in use by BJN was reduced from 220 to 170.

The nature of the fleet also changed towards larger vehicles. In a typical depot reorganization in Birmingham, where two depots were merged to produce a main depot, the number of vehicles was reduced from 13 to 9. Whereas the 13 vehicles had been 5 ton, 3 ton, 30 cwt. and 15 cwt. vans, the new fleet was comprised of 7 x 7 ton vans and 2 x 15 cwt. vans for urgent deliveries.

Redundancy did not prove to be a major problem as some drivers did not wish to move to the new depots and some were approaching retiring age.

The Depot System in 1972

As the transport system proved itself, more depots were closed until the system was reduced to the four base warehouses, the two main depots (Birmingham and Manchester) and the Stratford factory by early 1973. Staff had been cut from 750 to 570 in 1973 while turnover had increased both in volume and value.

Construction had been started on a new main depot in the Manchester area, with the same floor area as the old depot, but twice the height. This depot was planned to be open by March 1973. The base warehouses at Bristol and Chadwell Heath are also being expanded.

To continue the depot closures during 1972 it was still necessary for the distribution H.Q. staff to 'sell' their ideas to the marketing divisions. To this end the distribution H.Q. staff made presentations to marketing, showing the relative delivery costs from base depots, main depots and sub-depots. These presentations showed the financial advantages to the group of using only a few major depots. An allowance was made for the loss of business from firms which had collected their own paint direct from the small distribution points. Figure 3 shows typical figures for the increase in delivery costs for 25 litres of paint sent by various routes.

The presentations were also used to influence marketing to offer discounts by quantity and to try generally to increase order sizes. The relationship between drop size and delivery costs is illustrated in Figure 4.

Distribution also sought to introduce a system by which their costs would be charged to the marketing divisions on a basis of average drop size. None of the major competitors used discounts based on order size, or minimum order size.

The variation in delivery costs with vehicle size was also presented. If the cost of delivering a litre of paint by a 1 ton van was taken to be 100%, then it was shown that the cost for a litre delivery by a 4 ton van would be 36%, and 21% from a 20 ton van. These costs assumed the then current figures for average vehicle loads.

Service Changes

During 1971 the quality of service had been under consideration by the distribution division, and management consultants were called in to do a detailed study early in 1972. The results of the consultants' study were presented in mid-1972, and as they confirmed the distribution divisions' own findings and opinions, most of the recommendations were implemented immediately.

A key feature of the recommended system was a change from the industry norm of very rapid delivery to a timetabled service. Market research by the consultants had revealed that most customers would be satisfied with a reliable service, which kept delivery dead-line times, as opposed to immediate delivery. Customers also expected high availability on high volume lines.

To implement this change a timetable was drawn up in agreement with marketing. This timetable showed the order day and the promised delivery day, if the order was received before 2 p.m. on the order day. The frequency of the

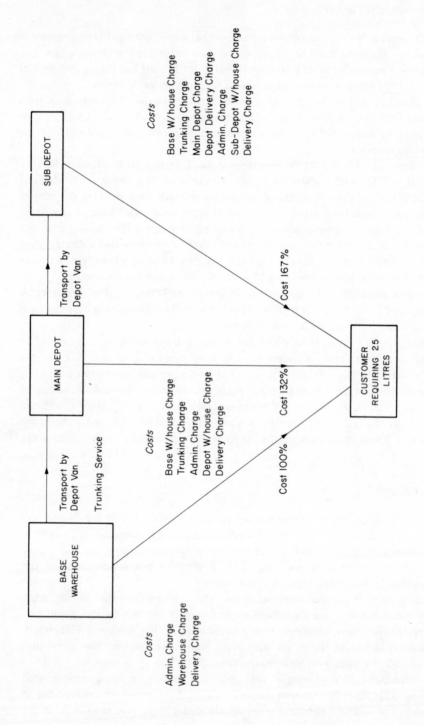

Figure 3 (Berger—Dist.)   The effect of indirect delivery on costs

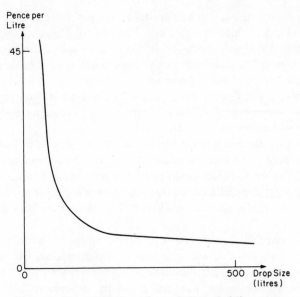

Figure 4 (Berger—Dist.)   The variation of delivery costs with drop size

delivery service ranged from daily in the conurbations to weekly and as needed in the rural areas.

A delivery monitoring scheme had already been drawn up and implemented in January 1972, before the timetable was produced. This monitoring system needed to be simple and not require extensive clerical effort, so a system of random sampling was evolved. A monthly sample of 100 orders per depot was required from the hundreds of orders handled per day. The system was designed purely to check the percentage of orders delivered on time and did not require any information on why deliveries did not run to time.

The opening and closing order numbers for each month were captured at the end of that month, and 100 order numbers were selected using random number tables. Orders involving second deliveries due to a stock-out, replacement orders and specially manufactured orders were rejected during the selection of the sample. From this sample a percentage showing the number of orders that were delivered on time could be directly produced. Confidence intervals were then placed on this percentage using binomial tables.

A short period after this measure had been introduced, it was presented as a league table to encourage further improvement. Finally it was incorporated into the regional managers' salary assessment. By this time the figures had improved considerably. Salary was paid under the Hay—M.S.L. system of job evaluation which rewarded for the performance of basic and key tasks, and it proved quite simple to incorporate a weighted relationship between a portion of salary and a service measure. Other performance factors relating to budget project work and management audits had already been incorporated in the payment system.

The next service measure to be introduced was a measure of the completeness of delivery of an order. This was highly important, as every time a second (back) order had to be raised due to a stock-out or non-delivery the administrative costs were more than doubled. This was due to the filing problem associated with identifying what had, or had not, been delivered. The measure for this was the 'complete delivery service reading', which consisted of the number of back orders per month expressed as a percentage of the total orders. This data could be easily captured due to the sequential numbering of orders and back-orders.

Although this measure quickly highlighted the presence of problems, analysis of the causes proved to be more difficult, as stock availability was recorded on a basis of percentage by item, neglecting the relative importance of items in the range.

As the greatest demand in any range was always for white paint it was obvious that a shortage of white paint would tend to produce more back-orders than any other product.

To obtain more data on the stock problems the operations research department were called in to produce a new, computer based measure of volume demand/ supply. However, performance measures for stock control remained to be devised as the manufacture of paint was scheduled by a separate materials planning department who worked to forecasts. Also, the base warehouses tended to have a worse stock position than the depots as they supplied both customers and main depots, taking the brunt of the large orders which were delivered direct from base. Some consideration was being given to splitting the stock into separate customer service and depot stocks, but this appeared to be an expensive way of obtaining a performance measure.

The next service measure to be developed was one to check for errors in delivery. As each product line had its own distinctly marked customer order set and separate stock area, the errors tended to be either in colour or size. Again a direct percentage measure was obtained as 'exchange and order forms' were filled in for each error. The number of these could be directly compared with the number of orders. As the errors tended to be picking errors, the pickers clock number was marked on each order and a minimal inspection of picked loads was continuously maintained. The local management decided the place of inspection, and a random number or random time basis was used for selecting loaded vehicles. If the total percentage level of error rose above a specified figure, then increasing levels of inspection were required.

To ensure that the checks were carried out the internal auditor (see Figure 5) demanded proof that the inspections had been made. The internal auditor carried out 2 to 3 checks per quarter on each depot. These covered service measures, overtime, routing, the physical state of the system and the storage of material. He also made a management audit using an index based on turnover per vehicle as a main guide. The results of the auditor's findings were used in a quarterly review of management performance and as a factor in the payment system.

As a further check on service, the customer service manager made personal visits to customers if he suspected problems or if an investigation was requested by a marketing division.

Typical of the customer service investigations were those into reports of damage and slipped loads. These problems were resolved by photographing randomly selected loads when they left the main base and on arrival at the customers premises. These photographs revealed that some can sizes travelled better than others, and that there was rope damage. This led to the introduction of purpose built, enclosed vehicles.

Customer service and group transport also used photographs and films to assist customers in overcoming the initial handling problems associated with the new vehicles and systems that were introduced. The visual aids showed the methods of operation, typical unloading problems and practical methods of solution.

A further aspect of service was the existence of a standard procedure which permitted the sales force to note complaints about distribution performance. A representative could take a complaint to his area sales manager who would fill in the form. Once the form reached the distribution manager involved, he was compelled to make a full reply. Copies of the documents were monitored by the distribution director. This procedure was felt to be very useful as it reduced personality conflicts and brought the issues out into the open. The number of complaints issued under this system steadily dropped throughout the year as liaison improved between distribution and marketing.

Several service issues still remained under development at the end of 1972. Two of the major issues were concerned with the differential treatment of both items of stock and customers.

Pareto analysis had been applied to each product line and it was considered possible that the stock situation could be improved by differentiating between colours and products. With this type of ABC analysis, white paint would be rated A, the five most popular colours B and the rest C. However, a suspicion remained that some of the small volume, slow selling, items in category C might be of vital importance.

An example of doubt over type C was with vehicle refinishes. Due to the vast range of vehicle colours they were blended and packed at depots, as required, from standard materials. Information was not available to indicate whether the high volume blends perhaps contained a vital, tiny, proportion of a C rated colour. If this proved to be the case then a stock-out of the C rated item could bring the blending system to a halt. Similar doubts existed over crated sundries and accessories such as thinners, primers and knotting.

Pareto analysis had also been applied to sales turnover. This led to the consideration of whether a differential service should be provided depending on customer importance. A typical application of differential service might be when the capacity of the transport system was exceeded. The arrangements then in use were F.I.F.O. or response to 'the loudest customer'. With a differential service policy the arrangements could be changed to supply the most important customers first as opposed to those who complained loudly.

Service variations were also being considered in relation to products, customer locations and promotions. Service anomalies were known to exist whereby high service was being obtained by placing urgent orders for small deliveries, often of low volume products. This required the diversion or hiring of vehicles and a policy had still to be developed regarding this issue.

Transport Developments during 1972

Several developments took place in 1972, including the introduction of purpose built vehicles, the introduction of a new livery and an extension to the delivery service. In the same period the vehicle fleet was reduced from 170 to 145.

To economize in the use of trunk haulage vehicles, efforts were made to get more back haulage to balance the pattern of freight movements. The system tended to be unbalanced as, for example, the Glasgow factory produced substantial quantities of paint for distribution by the other base warehouses but only had a limited demand for other paints.

Analysis of the system was performed by drawing up a standard matrix of the tonnage carried over the various routes. Destinations formed the top headings of the matrix and departure points the side headings. The system was then balanced by changing routes and obtaining more back haulage by carrying raw materials from suppliers to the factories and by obtaining loads from the Hoechst Group. This back haulage was facilitated by using day shift drivers to move the empty trailers from the depots to the suppliers and back, ready for the overnight trunk haulage runs.

Plans were also drawn up to reroute the trunker system when the new depot at Manchester was opened in early 1973. This new routing system would mean that vehicles bound from London to Newcastle would pass through Manchester as shown in Figure 6. The object of this exercise was to allow drivers to exchange trailers in Manchester and return to base overnight, thus eliminating the stopover at London or Newcastle. This had both social and recruitment benefits while also saving the lodging allowance. It fitted in with the load balancing plans as raw material back-loads could be assembled at the same point.

The haulage runs to Birmingham were to be handled by hired transport as the volume carried did not justify the use of company vehicles.

Distribution Performance to early 1973

By early 1973 the objectives of containing inflation had been more than met by the distribution system. There had been a reduction of 20 depots, 180 staff and 75 vehicles. Turnover had considerably increased in terms of cash and volume. Service measures indicated a much improved performance.

Efforts were still being maintained to achieve further economies by increasing drop sizes and by obtaining more freight from the Hoechst Group, which was still expanding by acquisition.

Hoechst and BJN both considered that the investment in the new system had been worthwhile at this point in time.

Berger Paints — Production Planning and Control

Introduction

Company Background

Berger Paints is part of the Berger, Jenson and Nicholson Group (BJN). It had grown via mergers and acquisitions over the past fifteen years. By 1974 it was the second largest British paint manufacturer. In 1970 BJN had become a wholly owned subsidiary of Hoechst Farbwerke AG of Frankfurt through that company's British subsidiary, Hoechst UK.

After the takeover there had been considerable rationalization in the paint company. Much of this early attention was directed at the paint distribution system. Increasing attention was then given to production and production planning and control facilities. A new Director of Manufacturing was hired in December 1971 to rationalize existing facilities. During the spring of 1974 changes in the production planning organization were being implemented.

Under the ownership of Hoechst, the company had improved financially and had also improved its position in the market-place. Hoechst was currently investing considerable sums of money in fixed assets for the company, while pursuing a policy of minimal interference in the daily management of it.

Company Products and Markets

BJN sought to promote the image of Berger Paints as an integrated, modern manufacturer with a long tradition of paint making. It was claimed that Berger had been making paint since 1760.

Nevertheless, it claimed to be in the forefront of technical development. Non-drip, brilliant white and vinyl emulsion paints were first introduced by Berger. At the present time its main competitors, ICI (Dulux), Reed (Crown) and MacPherson (Household) were equally innovative in the decorative market and Berger enjoyed no long-term product advantages.

In addition to its main competitors, Berger had several hundred smaller rivals. Many specialized in one particular type of paint. As a major producer, Berger promoted a full range of decorative paints, motor car finishes, general and special paints and coatings, both for the amateur and the professional customer.

Berger was particularly keen to improve its position in the decorative paint market, which was highly competitive but profitable. Paints for domestic use by the amateur were promoted under the brand names Magicote and Brolac. Trade decorative paints were promoted under Brolac, Robbialac and a number of 'own label' brands such as Topdec.

Product performance was an important selling point in the amateur market particularly with regard to ease of application. The trade was more concerned with price and availability. In practice, paint performance was similar, irrespective of manufacturer, because it was primarily a function of the raw materials used. These were commonly available to all manufacturers from the same suppliers.

In this situation Berger felt obliged to offer rapid delivery to its wholesale customers. This meant within 48 hours at most, frequently within 24 hours. To achieve this level of service the company was extremely reactive to short-term considerations. This was reflected in the distribution network that it operated and the service that the Manufacturing Division had to provide to the distribution network.

The Production Planning Environment

A sophisticated Operational Research approach to demand forecasting was employed. Nevertheless forecasting errors still occurred. A planning manager explained:

'In the first place we must recognize that we operate in a highly volatile business, particularly in the retail decorative market. I consider that if the company is able to forecast demand for a product brand range within ten percent we are doing quite well. By contrast, the demand for individual colours within any range fluctuates dramatically — plus or minus fifty percent is not unknown. Only the demand for whites and very pale shades is relatively stable. So in this situation although we can forecast total paint demand quite accurately, and brand range demand fairly accurately, we do have to be ready to take corrective short-term action where we fail to predict the right colour mix.'

To compensate for changes in short-term demand, finished goods inventory was held at 9—10 weeks of average sales. In addition, production had to respond to stock deficiencies created by unexpected demand as quickly as possible. This tended to upset pre-arranged production schedules, resulting in reduced efficiency. This was justified at board level by the need to maintain customer service. To a large degree the production facilities were required to act as 'backstops' to the distribution system, rather than the latter, through extensive stockholdings, acting as a buffer for the Manufacturing Division.

The production control problem was made complex because of the nature of the product offer. The site studied was expected to manufacture most of the company's products. Each type of paint consisted of a range of thirty to forty colours. Each colour was normally offered in three or four pack sizes. As a result the total product offer consisted of well over three thousand lines. In addition, sample quantities of new paints were frequently prepared for industrial customers and for test marketing purposes.

The site studied was at Chadwell Heath, Essex. Paint was produced in batches, with up to 4,500 litres in a batch. Annual production at this site was budgeted for 22 million litres in 1974 out of a total company plan of 62 million litres. In addition to Chadwell Heath the company had two other main production sites, one in Bristol concentrating on emulsion paints and the other, near London, producing mainly industrial and special purpose paints.

The distribution system incorporated several field depots which were serviced by the main finished goods stores or 'base warehouses', one of which was situated at Chadwell Heath.

All of the major paint companies were believed to participate in the Interfirm Comparison surveys. Berger strongly believed that it needed to stay competitive in all aspects of its business, particularly with regard to finished goods stockholding. In the spring of 1974 it was concerned that, relative to the average, its stock levels were high.

Organization Structure

The company was organized into functional operating divisions. These covered Manufacturing, Distribution, Industrial Marketing, Decorative Marketing, Sales and Research and Development. The Distribution Division was a recent amalgamation of the Distribution and Materials Planning Divisions. The latter had been subsumed within the Distribution Division under the title of Central Planning Department.

The Central Planning Department had responsibility for coordinating all sales forecasts from the various sales and marketing areas. In addition it participated in the statistical forecasting of demand in conjunction with the Operational Research Department. The outcome of this activity was a set of smoothed forecasts by product type and colour for the following twelve months.

The routine smoothed forecasts became the basis for the production site work loadings. Production planning and control was performed on a calendar monthly cycle. The Central Planning Department undertook to provide each production site with a Monthly Plant Loading at the end of the third week of each month to cover the production required for the following month.

Each plant manager was responsible for forecasting the expected productive capacity of his plant for the forward three months normally covered in each Monthly Loading Schedule. This forecast was usually accepted as given by Central Planning. Their attitude was that 'Each manufacturing site is a black box with an input and an output'. Nevertheless, capacity invariably depended on the product mix requested. For this reason there was an informal dialogue between each plant manager and Central Planning.

Prior to 1974 this situation would have totally described the production

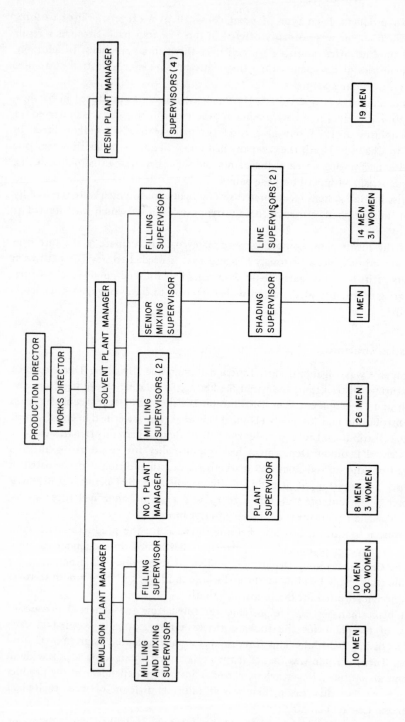

Figure 1 (Berger—PPC)   The organization structure

planning facilities, with the exception of the in-plant production control staff. At the time of the case study, a new Manufacturing Planning Department within the Manufacturing Division had been recently formed. This embryonic department was assigned the role of liaising with Central Planning and the production sites. The intention was for this new department to 'interpret' the Monthly Loading Schedules from Central Planning and to translate them into formal, workable production schedules for use at plant level. The reasons for this additional department will be examined later.

At the time of the study the new Manufacturing Planning Department consisted primarily of a manager and a skeleton staff. The Central Planning Department consisted of a manager, several planning managers who reported to him, and a number of schedulers, stock assessors and clerical staff. Much of the routine clerical work was handled by computer. A computerized stock planning system was in the process of being introduced. Each stock assessor was however still required to use a fair degree of judgement in his job.

The Manufacturing Division had four plants at Chadwell Heath. These consisted of an emulsion paint plant, two solvent paint plants and a resin plant. A works manager was responsible for the Chadwell Heath site. He reported to the production director. The organization structure is shown in Figure 1.

The resin plant produced a proportion of the basic resins, a major raw material of the paint. The No.1 plant produced thinners and allied products. This case is about the No. 2 plant which produced solvent-based gloss and undercoat paints for decorative use and industrial paints.

Of the nine supervisory staff who reported to the solvent plant manager, seven were more than 50 years of age. The youngest was 38. Most had been with the company for many years.

A Resume of the Paint-Making Process

The process consisted of the following stages:

(1) Marshalling of a set of bulky raw materials;
(2) Initial premixing of the powdered raw materials with the resins;
(3) Milling of the premixed constituents into a smooth viscous liquid or paste;
(4) Introduction of the paste into a large mixing tank preloaded with additional resins and solvents;
(5) Mixing stages in the tank. These consisted of adjustments to the viscosity and specific gravity of the paint followed by colour shading;
(6) Transfer of the paint from the mixing tank to conveniently sized tins for sale. The tins were filled on semi-automatic conveyor lines;
(7) Transportation of the filled tins to the warehouse using pallets.

In addition there were numerous quality control checks carried out during and after manufacture. Samples of each batch of paint were stored in case of future customer quality complaints.

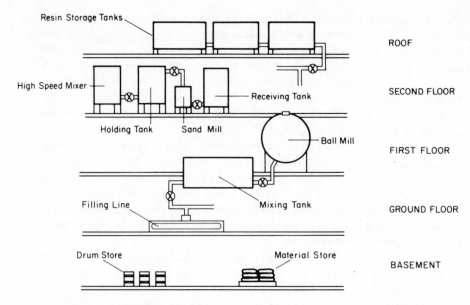

Figure 2 (Berger—PPC)   A diagrammatic version of the solvent plant in elevation

The solvent plant was designed and built around 1938. It consisted of three production floors, a storage basement and a rooftop storage area. Work flow was designed from top to bottom of the factory, as shown in Figure 2.

There was a great variety in the type, size and performance of the mills. The milling operation was itself unpredictable. Whereas a white paint could normally be ground in sixteen hours, most colours took two to three days and deep colours could take a week or more. The main reason for this was the difficulty of bringing out the desired depth of colour and of achieving a high gloss, which also depended on the resins used.

Because of this unpredictability, a great deal of 'fine-tuning' of each batch took place in the mixing tank. The original mixing formula was not followed exactly. For example, the final colour of a batch was obtained by adding small quantities of very concentrated liquid pigment to the batch in the mixing tank. These and similar operations were consequently very slow as they were all accomplished on a 'trial and error' basis. A typical solvent paint contained as many as thirty different ingredients, of which typically, six would be pigments.

The major contribution to cycle time came from the mixing tanks once again. The so-called tank turnaround time ranged from about one working week for whites to two or three weeks for colours. The average values were not routinely monitored but a survey on about 200 batches indicated that it was eight days on average. The survey covered a product mix of 40% whites, 60% colours, giving average times for these classes of product of 5 days and 10 days respectively.

The filling lines were laid out so as to minimize the distance from the line to the mixing tanks. This reduced the problems of pumping viscous liquids long distances, thereby minimizing paint loss. Small, holding tanks received the paint from the mixing tanks, filtering out solid congealed paint as it passed through. These tanks were connected directly to filling heads. The empty tins passed beneath a suitable filling head on a conveyor. Paint was dispensed accurately and automatically into each tin. Every filling line was adjustable to cope with different tin sizes.

The variability of process cycle times was a function of two factors, the indeterminacy of the process from a technical standpoint and the condition of the equipment, particularly the mills.

The first factor was aggravated by the difficulty of maintaining extremely consistent raw material standards, the second by the difficulty of extracting specific pieces of equipment from production for planned maintenance.

The Production Planning and Control Cycle

The Planning Cycle

The Central Planning forecasts spanned three months. Month one was documented with actual requisitions to manufacture and was a second revision of a prior forecast. Month two was a first revision of the prior month's forecast, while month three was always a first look in detail at that month.

Their strategy was based on holding an average of two weeks of stock of white paints and between 3 and 12 weeks of colours. The depots held their own stocks of each product at preset levels revised several times each year. Production requirements were based on the need to meet customer demand and to replenish stocks in the depots and the base warehouse.

The average stock level in the Chadwell Heath base warehouse was nominally 4—5 weeks, but was about 25% higher for accounting purposes since stocks in transit to the depots were not credited to them until the computer-based invoices had been processed.

Stock assessors were employed in Central Planning to determine stock requirements by product range and colour. They also made estimates of the pack-size distribution that would be required, but this was frequently amended at short notice.

At the end of each month a number of items required for immediate production would still be outstanding. This class of product was referred to as the carry forward for the next month.

The stock assessor produced a site loading requirement at least two weeks before the start of the month to which it applied. It followed that any specific item might not be actioned in production for six weeks after the start of the new month, that is, eight weeks after the schedule was devised. With ten weeks stock of finished paint, the stock assessor was therefore required to look up to 18 weeks into the future in detail. This is explained diagrammatically in Figure 3, assuming four week months, and a first-in, first-out inventory policy.

The drawback of this system was that in a changing demand situation it became

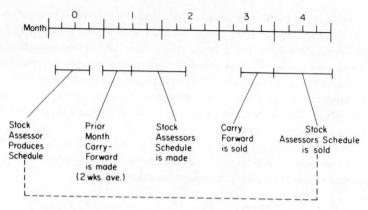

Figure 3 (Berger—PPC)   Time scale from scheduling to sales

necessary to revise schedules during the month of manufacture. This was done by the issue of supplementary requisitions, a practice described later.

The Work Schedule

The Monthly Loading document covered the first month in detail. Paint production was broken down into categories, namely, emulsion paint, gloss (solvent based) paint, undercoats, drum (industrial) paint, Electrocoat (industrial), thinners and miscellaneous.

The loading document stated a total manufacturing requirement for each category. Each category was further divided into product ranges. Each range was broken down into white and colours as one group. Individual colour requirements were stated only on the requisitions.

The loading document was substantiated by the issue of appropriate requisitions, one per batch. Batch sizes varied but the normal sizes were 4,500 litres, 2,250 litres, 1,125 litres etc. The requisition covered the product requirement in detail including volume, the distribution of tin sizes to be filled, colour, and delivery instructions (usually to the base warehouse). The paperwork was designed for easy computer processing.

Ideally all requisitions were received in the plants between the 18th and 20th of each month to cover the following month's production. In practice they were often later and arrived piecemeal. In addition supplementary requisitions were also received at various times during the current month for manufacture, if possible, during that month.

The principle by which the stock policy was controlled was simple in theory. When a requisition had been issued the paint to which it referred became inventory (even though it might not be produced for some weeks). As such it could be classified either as free stock, or stock committed to one specific customer. The intention was to maintain specified levels of free stock relative to demand, so as to hold an adequate stock backing against non-forecast demand. Decision rules were used to permit stock monitoring to be largely effected by computer. Nevertheless the assessment of these rules and the highlighting of stock problems remained a task requiring considerable judgement on the part of Central Planning staff.

The Monthly Loading document, part of which is shown in Figure 4, contained additional information. The lines 'Capacity' and 'Forecast Production' were estimates made by the plant managers. Budgetted production referred to the annual plan. The carry forward and actual production for each month were also recorded.

Assessment of Priority

Neither the Monthly Loading document, nor the requisitions indicated relative priority of manufacture.

During early 1974 carry forward at the end of each month represented about two weeks work. It consisted of requisitions placed on the Chadwell Heath site but not actioned. There was inevitably the problem of deciding which products merited the highest priority. This was resolved by an information system known as the 'Deficiency Report'.

This report, issued weekly by the Central Planning Department, listed those products for which there was a current stock deficiency in the base warehouse after allowing for stock corrections in the various depots. It told each plant manager which product range and colour he was required to produce most urgently, by informing him of the number of weeks stock that was currently available in each tin size.

A second means of assessing priorities was the 'Daily Whites Monitor'. Because white paint accounted for up to 50% of the volume of many product ranges it was felt desirable to monitor output of whites very closely.

The report indicated the actual daily stock level in the base warehouse of each white paint produced, together with the minimum and maximum predetermined stock levels for each tin size for each brand. The plant managers were expected to interpret this report and act accordingly. Their judgements were frequently supplemented by informal inquiries to the various storemen and salesmen involved with specific products.

The existence of the Daily Whites Monitor did not prevent white paint from appearing on the Deficiency Report. As a Planning Manager explained: 'If the system is working properly, then all items should have an equal probability of appearing on the Deficiency Report. If one item appears frequently, either the stock holding levels are wrong, or we have not requisitioned enough, or the wrong pack sizes have been filled.'

The plant managers were required to use their judgement in assessing these priority reports to decide whether any specific deficiency could be rectified with work currently in process or whether it would be necessary to start a fresh batch. Normally an appropriate requisition would be immediately available as part of the prior month carry forward or as part of the current month work order. If this was the case, it was necessary only to consult the inventory controller to ensure that suitable raw materials was available before production could begin.

240

PRODUCTION LOADING/CAPACITY PROGRAMME

BERGER PAINTS   MATERIALS PLANNING DEPT.

(000's Litres)   Date of Issue: _____

JAN.–JUNE		Emul.	Gloss	U/C	Misc.	Drums	Elec.	Thins.	TOTAL
END OF DEC. C/F									
JAN.	Monthly Req.								
	Total Loading								
	Capacity								
	Forecast Prod.								
	Budget Prod.								
	Actual Prod.								
	Surplus Cap.								
	C/F								
FEB.	Monthly Req.								
	Total Loading								
	Capacity								
	Forecast Prod.								
	Budget Prod.								
	Actual Prod.								
	Surplus Cap.								
	C/F								
MAR.	Monthly Req.								
	Total Loading								
	Capacity								
	Forecast Prod.								
	Budget Prod.								
	Actual Prod.								
	Surplus Cap.								
	C/F								
APR.	Monthly Req.								
	Total Loading								
	Capacity								
	Forecast Prod.								
	Budget Prod.								
	Actual Prod.								
	Surplus Cap.								
	C/F								
MAY	Monthly Req.								
	Total Loading								
	Capacity								
	Forecast Prod.								
	Budget Prod.								
	Actual Prod.								
	Surplus Cap.								
	C/F								
JUN.	Monthly Req.								
	Total Loading								
	Capacity								
	Forecast Prod.								
	Budget Prod.								
	Actual Prod.								
	Surplus Cap.								
	C/F								

Figure 4 (Berger–PPC)   Production loading/capacity programme

If no suitable requisition was available a supplementary requisition was required from Central Planning. This was a quite common practice although it was frequently anticipated by Central Planning. As the month progressed, additional stock deficiencies would be highlighted intermittently, resulting in Central Planning issuing additional supplementary requisitions to cover their manufacture.

When a supplementary requisition was issued, ideally a comparable, lower priority requisition was recalled, to maintain a constant site load. This did not always happen. As the inventory controller explained: 'Even where this is done, it may only disguise the fact that there have been gross changes in the product mix at short notice. This makes it very difficult to order raw materials accurately. In the past I attempted to monitor these changes in requirements to show the way our work load alters during the month, but no one seemed interested so I did not continue.'

The Central Planning Department was not responsible for the procurement of raw materials and supplies. This was coordinated at Head Office, but it was largely the responsibility of the inventory controller at each site to order the appropriate materials from each supplier and to negotiate delivery. He did not negotiate price or discuss delivery with new suppliers.

When asked about the impact of supplementary requisitions on material supply, a Central Planning manager stated: 'Even though the loading we place on the individual sites does fluctuate in response to changes in short-term demand, the individual production controllers are provided with a detailed three month forecast. If they have ordered sufficient materials to meet this requirement, including their own buffer stocks, then their problem really reduces to that of calling off some deliveries from their suppliers sooner than anticipated and some later. The key requirement is to be on good terms with each supplier.'

Monitoring of Performance

The expected lead time between the issue of a requisition and the availability of stock for sale would at worst be one month plus prior month carry forward, i.e. if made at the end of the month. However, the priority documents ensured that most higher priority paint was produced more quickly.

A key monitor from a planning standpoint was the carry forward. If this increased, customer service suffered. Paint sales exhibited large seasonal fluctuations. By maintaining plant output at a fairly constant level over the year, the carry forward was just kept under control, provided that each set of monthly requisitions reflected demand. That is, periods of high demand increased carry forward, but the subsequent periods of low demand produced less requisitions thereby enabling the carry forward to be reduced.

In practice Central Planning relied heavily on the plant inventory controllers for accurate statements of month-end carry forward. The situation was complicated by the issue of supplementary requisitions which made it difficult to monitor the performance of the production units. A hypothetical example is shown below.

Suppose that the initial requisitions for product X totalled 100,000 litres in month one, and that there was a carry forward of 12,000 litres of X from the prior month. Suppose also that supplementary requisitions were received at the end of the first and third weeks for 20,000 litres and 10,000 litres of X respectively. If there were four weeks in the month and the production of X was 25,000, 30,000, 35,000 and 25,000 litres per week respectively then the performance against outstanding requisitions would be:

			Week 1		Week 2		Week 3		Week 4	
Monthly Requisitions	Carry Forward	Total Accr. Work Load	Accr. Work Load	Bal.	Accr. Load	Bal.	Accr. Load	Bal.	Accr. Load	Bal.
100	12	112	132	107	132	77	142	52	142	27

(All figures in thousands)

In this example the production unit filled 115,000 litres of paint, 3,000 litres more than they were originally requested to. Nevertheless, because of supplementary requisitions they appeared to miss their target by 27,000 litres. The following month might also start off with requisitions for 100,000 litres, so that with a carry forward of 27,000 litres the total work load would be 127,000 litres. If there were cancellations of say 30,000 litres, it would be likely that the plant would overproduce, the converse of the previous month.

Production Control at the Chadwell Heath Site

Plant Scheduling and Progress Chasing

The responsibility for progress chasing lay with the plant manager and his supervisors.

The basic information needed to make each batch of paint was transferred to the production supervisors on mixing slips. These contained the type of paint required, the appropriate ingredients and any special instructions from the production chemist's department. The milling supervisor collected a wad of requisitions from the inventory control department and proceeded to sort them into compatible product types and colours.

He commented: 'I sort the mixing slips and put them into these folders. When a mill is dropped (emptied) we decide which batch to process next. I see the plant manager every day to decide priorities. The trouble is, he changes his mind frequently. I can charge a mill on Monday and by Tuesday we need to mill something quite different.'

In order to monitor events in the plant a visual display board was used which indicated the status of every batch and piece of equipment in the plant. This board was updated at least once per day by the supervisors. Every batch was represented by a card which was pegged to the board at the stage of the process it had reached.

In addition, different coloured pegs indicated whether a batch was actively being processed, whether it was waiting for test results from the laboratory or whether it was ready to proceed to the next stage.

Commenting on his scheduling problems the plant manager stated: 'Chadwell Heath is the largest mixed paint factory in Berger. Our problems tend to be much more complex because of this. This is inevitable when you consider our range of products and colours. Even the same colour may not always follow one another through the same equipment because the solvent bases are different and the colours will "bleed" one into another.'

The most severe scheduling problems seemed to occur in the mixing tank operation. Most mills were close to either two, four, or eight tanks, depending on their size. It was impracticable to transport milled paste very far although a number of mobile tanks existed for this purpose. Because the fixed mixing tanks were the only tanks in which batches in process could be held they tended to be always in use. This in turn created a restriction on the milling capacity and prevented the filling lines from accepting batches in an ideal sequence.

In practice it was not difficult to decide which batches to fill since this was determined by what was available in the tanks within range of each filling line and by the priority rankings. Neither was it difficult to decide what batches should be started. The problem was to maximize throughput of paint in the mixing tanks which represented the bottleneck.

Scheduling through the mixing tanks appeared to be extremely ad hoc. The plant manager responded to each and every urgent request as it was made. He was in a position where he could not 'win'. 'I consider that I am successful if I can keep the shouting to a minimum by responding to the various priority reports as I see fit and if at the same time I can maximize production by keeping schedule disruptions to a minimum. Obviously I cannot always do this. Sometimes I can look at the schedule and be confident that the company just does not need that much type X paint in stock. So I use my judgement and make some other type Y that I believe will be needed urgently next month. Quite often I can be asked to make 10,000 litres one month, nothing the next month and 15,000 litres the month after that, yet I know that the demand is relatively stable.'

The New Manufacturing Planning Department

This new department had not been in existence long enough to have established procedures, but the manager of the department summarized its objectives as follows:

'Our prime function is to interface between Central Planning and Production. This involves interpreting production requirements and translating them into smoothed site loadings across the company. We will also allocate products to each site.

We hope to establish suitable reorder levels and scheduling rules to reduce manufacturing costs. In addition, a policy of regional manufacture should reduce distribution costs and contribute to the company objective of reducing finished goods stocks.

We must ensure that production understands the need to provide good customer service in an aggressive market situation. Our task now is to work out the details of achieving these objectives.'

Bridge Electric Limited (A)

'Our aim was to review the whole manufacturing procedure in order to reduce costs and to create more stable jobs of a broader nature. I think we have gone a long way towards achieving this with many of the products at Bridge Electric, but the case of the Solar fire is a particularly good example of what can be done by the detailed study of a product.'

Graham Jackson, a member of the Baker Company's Central Industrial Engineering group, was describing his experiences at Bridge Limited in late 1971, approximately a year after the central group had first started working at Bridge.

Background of the Bridge Electric Company

Bridge Electric was a wholly owned subsidiary of the Baker Group, being acquired in the early 1960s. The Baker group had since 1967 been controlled by one of the major international electrical companies. However there had been little interference with the management of the Baker group. A number of new directors had been appointed, some from within the Baker group and some from the international company. One of these new directors had in 1970 been responsible for organizing a new Central Industrial Engineering group. Tom Simpson had been recruited in 1970 to head the group. He spent several months recruiting five members of staff for the newly-formed group and in identifying a suitable company in which the group could undertake its first major project. The basic criteria used by Simpson in selecting the company to be studied, was that there should be considerable potential for profit improvement.

Tom Simpson had resisted pressure to have his group focused on the loss making subsidiaries of the Baker group. He argued, and eventually convinced his director, that it was the incremental increase in profitability that was important and not turning loss making situations into marginal profit making ones.

As a result of this philosophy, the Bridge Electric Company was chosen for the first major exercise by the new central group. Bridge was founded prior to World War II and run as a family business until taken over the by Baker group. It had over the years developed a line of small electrical products almost all of which were used in the home. These included kettles, heaters, fans, tea-makers and hotplates.

The products had a strong element of seasonal demand since many of them were popular as Christmas presents. Heating appliances were also affected by higher demand during the winter months.

The Manufacturing Facilities

Manufacture took place in a modern single-storey factory. The floor space was divided up into five main areas of activity. These were:

(1) The power press department. This department made parts in batches of 500 to 10,000 from 18 gauge steel. The size of the parts varied from $6'' \times 6''$ to $2' \times 2'6''$. The energy for the pressing action was manually controlled. Up to 1,000 parts per hour were produced by a single machine.

(2) The fly press department. This produced smaller parts than the power press department. Average size was about $2'' \times 2''$ and average batch size about 5,000. For these machines the operator provided the energy source. Bending machines capable of bending sheet metal up to $2' \times 2'$ were also located in this department. A major storage of pressed parts was held after the power and fly press departments.

(3) Spot welding department. This department fabricated sub-assemblies from parts made in the power and fly press departments and from bought out items. The parts were issued according to final assembly requirements from sub-stores and main stores.

(4) Degreasing and spray shop. Items were taken from the welding area at the planned assembly rate. The first of the two final major activities was degreasing and paint spraying. After spraying, the parts and sub-assemblies moved on overhead conveyors through ovens which dried the paint. They then continued on these conveyors to the assembly area.

(5) Assembly. Prior to the work carried out by the Central Industrial Engineering group there were eleven assembly lines in the assembly area. (Figure 1 shows a sketch of the factory layout and the number of people employed in each section.)

The Investigation by the Central Industrial Engineering Group

In September 1970, Tom Simpson and Graham Jackson carried out a three week survey of Bridge's manufacturing facilities. They concluded that virtually every major area of manufacturing activity could be improved through a detailed industrial engineering study. They felt that sales forecasting was inadequate for producing a production plan which would permit effective use of the manufacturing facilities. Production planning was carried out on a six weekly basis, each six week plan being issued one week prior to the conclusion of the previous six weeks. Many alterations took place to the original six week plan during the course of its operation. They also believed that considerable savings could be obtained through the application of value analysis techniques and method study. To identify those

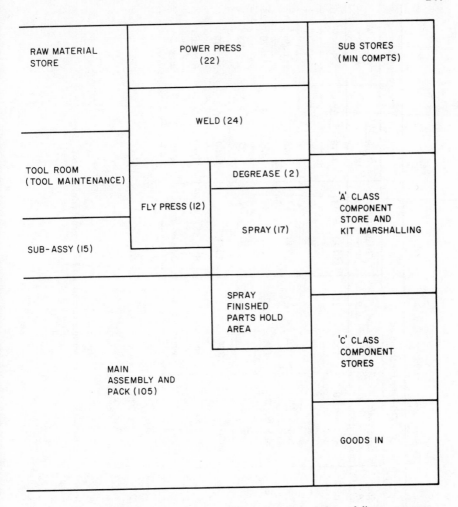

Figure 1 (Bridge Electric A)   Factory layout and original numbers of direct operators

products which should be given prior attention from a value analysis and method study standpoint, Tom Simpson carried out several Pareto analyses. He discovered that 25 per cent of the product line accounted for 78 per cent of the material cost and that 25 per cent of the products accounted for 74 per cent of the assembly labour cost. Six products were common to both these groups. It was apparent that the payment systems contained anomalies which had grown up over the years and that these created much dissatisfation throughout the workforce.

It seemed that most of the time standards used throughout the plant were derived from inaccurate work measurement. It was thought that the errors resulted mainly from inaccurate performance rating when the time studies were taken. Commented Graham Jackson: 'The industrial engineer who did the work had his

Department Sampled

	Press Shop A	B	Fly Press Shop A	B	Spot Weld A	B	Degrease A	B	Spray Shop A	B	Assembly A	B	Total A	B
Work	1007	72	566	85	827	56	131	37	770	46	3316	62	6617	60
Wait Work	22	2	13	2	8	1	14	4	36	2	30	1	123	1
Ineffective	99	7	35	5	183	12	98	27	283	17	588	11	1286	12
Away from Work	274	19	56	8	461	31	115	32	576	34	1394	26	2876	26
Other	4	–	3	–	6	–	2	–	16	1	32	1	63	1
Total	1406		673		1485		360		1681		5360		10,965	
Average Rating	88% BSI		88% BSI		80% BSI		84% BSI		81% BSI		79% BSI		80% BSI	
Effective	62%		74%		45%		30%		37%		49%		48%	

A = No. of observations
B = Percentage of Total Activity

Figure 2 (Bridge Electric A)   Results of activity sample carried out by external consultants

"bench mark" wrong. He was unfortunately "taken for a ride" on a good many occasions.'

Since the basis for several of the proposed changes would be accurate work measurement data, Tom Simpson decided at an early stage that a major work measurement programme would have to be mounted. His own group was not equipped to provide such an effort and Bridge had only one industrial engineer who had been responsible for much of the earlier work. He decided, therefore, to use outside consultants.

Initially he asked the consultants to carry out an activity sample survey of the various manufacturing facilities and to produce a proposal for compiling detailed work standards. The results of the activity sample are shown in Figure 2. The consultants reported that existing time standards were on average 30% loose. In spite of this, however, the time standards were not being met, particularly in the assembly areas. This, they considered, was due to high levels of personal time (time when operatives voluntarily removed themselves from their work places during working hours) and poor balance between the various operations on the assembly lines.

As a result of their internal survey, Tom Simpson and Graham Jackson drew up an action plan which they anticipated would take 15 to 18 months to implement. The plan covered three basic areas. These were:

(1) IMPROVED SYSTEMS. This included:
    (a) More accurate and detailed forecasting to permit better production planning.
    (b) Production planning and control to improve the flow of work on the shop floor.
    (c) Work measurement to provide accurate basic data.
(2) MATERIAL COSTS. This included:
    (a) Application of value analysis to reduce product material cost and to increase the value to cost ratio.
    (b) Materials management. This involved examining purchasing procedures to obtain better prices and improving stock control to reduce the level of working capital.
(3) LABOUR COSTS. This included:
    (a) Method study to reduce non-useful work.
    (b) Wage structure to ensure an equitable payment system which provided an appropriate incentive.

The remainder of this case describes the results of applying value analysis, method study and improved assembly procedures to a specific product. Changes made to the basic wage are described in Bridge Electric (B).

The Solar Fire

The Solar Fire was identified through the Pareto analysis as a product where considerable savings might be achieved, particularly in the assembly area. The fire

Month	Units
January	3,500
February	1,500
March	1,000
April	1,000
May	3,000*
June	3,000*
July	2,500
August	3,000
September	4,000
October	3,500
November	3,000
December	2,000

*Price of fire reduced during these two months to encourage retailers to build up stocks.

Figure 3 (Bridge Electric A)
Monthly demand for Solar fire
1970

consisted of a one kilowatt element and a reflector mounted in a case. It was sold at retail for £4.48. It represented one of the simpler, cheaper forms of domestic electrical heating appliance. Demand for the fire was running at approximately 35,000 per year, but this demand was highly seasonal. Demand in any one month ranged from 1,000 to 4,000. The 1970 pattern of demand is shown in Figure 3. The fire consisted of 101 separate parts. Of these, 93 could be classified as minor items and only eight as major items. Nearly all the minor items were bought out, but seven of the eight major items were produced in the press shop.

The Original Assembly Method for Solar Fires

Assembly of the fire involved a group of thirteen female operatives. Assembling the Solar Fire and a similar larger fire, occupied the majority of the line's time. However, overall demand, and fluctuations in demand, resulted in the line assembling two other products, usually for two or three weeks out of every three months.

The layout of the old assembly unit and a description of each of the jobs, together with the standard times for each job is given in Figures 4 and 5. Commenting on the original assembly line, Graham Jackson said:

'There really had been no work place design. Assembly was carried out without the use of any jigs or fixtures. This resulted in all work effectively being carried out in a one-handed fashion because one hand had to be used to hold the part being worked on. No power tools were employed and materials were badly located in respect to the line, resulting in much wasted time fetching and carrying. It was also apparent that the product had been designed with little thought for assembly method. Many parts were very difficult to put together. The total assembly time

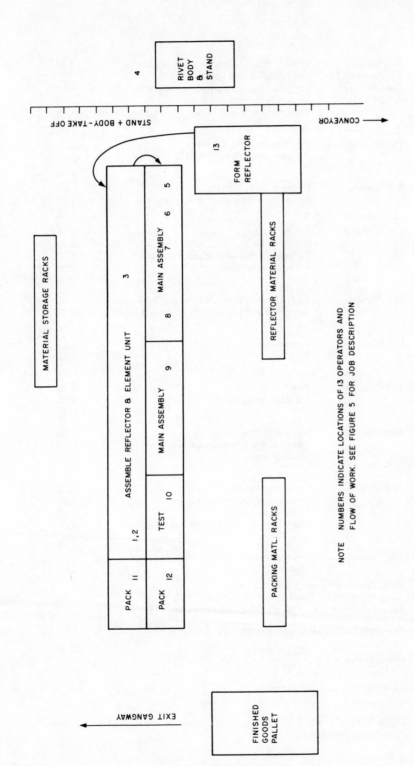

NOTE NUMBERS INDICATE LOCATIONS OF 13 OPERATORS AND
FLOW OF WORK. SEE FIGURE 5 FOR JOB DESCRIPTION

Figure 4 (Bridge Electric A)   Old layout for Solar fire

1st Operator ⎱	Inspect reflector and fit ele. terms	3.48
2nd Operator ⎰	and Ceramics and fit earth lead	
3rd Operator	Fit mains lead to element terminals	1.79
4th Operator	Inspect body and fit handle	0.78
	Fit foot Screws and nuts	1.08
		1.85
5th Operator	Fetch body from conveyor	0.19
	Fit back and side reflectors	1.64
		1.83
6th Operator	Connect earth lead to case	.70
	Connect mains lead earth to case	1.00
		1.70
7th Operator	Fit clips to back channel	0.95
	Fit rating label	0.37
	Thread mains lead thro' back channel	0.22
	Fit strain relief bush	0.26
		1.80
8th Operator	Fit back channel to case and coil lead	1.06
	Cut string and tie on earth warning label	0.72
		1.78
9th Operator	Fit element	1.19
	Fit guard	0.52
		1.71
10th Operator	Test	1.10
	Tie labels to guard	0.64
		1.74
11th Operator	Make up master carton	0.20
	Stamp and label master carton	0.20
	Make up insert	1.59
		1.99
12th Operator	Stamp and label small carton	0.22
	Make up carton and fit insert	0.63
	Pack fire and seal	0.85
	Seal master carton and remove pallet	0.20
		1.90
13th Operator	Clean and form reflectors and assist ops.	
	11 and 12	1.90

Total Standard Time = 23.47
Longest job is 11th operator = 1.99 minutes
Actual assembly time = 13 x 1.99 = 25.87 minutes

Therefore output per 8 hour day for 13 operators = $\dfrac{13 \times 8 \times 60}{25.87}$ = 241

Basic balance loss = $\dfrac{25.87 - 23.47}{25.87}$ = 9.4%

i.e. equivalent to 1.20 operators

Figure 5 (Bridge Electric A)   Solar fire — job descriptions and standard times for original layout

was approximately 25 minutes and this was split between thirteen operatives. Thus there were a large number of short, tedious jobs; a situation where time would inevitably be lost through lack of balance in the assembly line.

In redesigning the job we were interested in eliminating as many parts as possible through the use of elementary method study rather than very detailed value analysis. Eventually six man-weeks of method study resulted in the elimination of

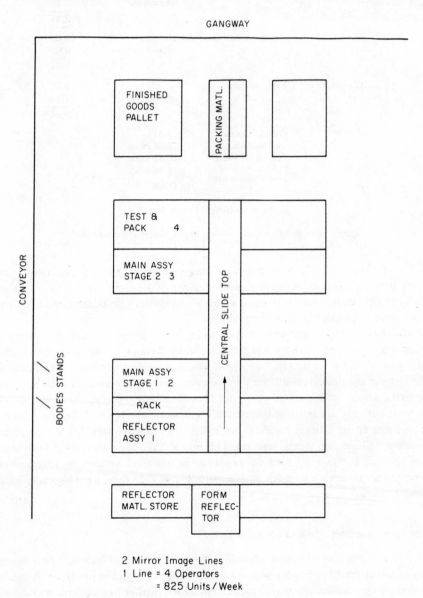

Figure 6 (Bridge Electric A)   New layout for Solar fire

STAGE 1	Form reflector, assemble element to reflector		2.08
		allowances	0.46
		STD Mins.	2.54

STAGE 2	Fit element and reflector to shell, fit handle, foot stand and guard		2.08
		allowances	0.39
			2.47

STAGE 3	Fit mains lead and back channel	2.41
		allowances	0.50
			2.91

STAGE 4	Test and pack		2.10
		allowances	0.44
			2.54

Control Stage 3 = 2.91
x 4 Operators = 11.64 mins.
Total STD Mins. = 10.46 mins.
Line Balance Loss $= \dfrac{1.18}{11.64} = 10.1\%$

i.e. equivalent to 0.4 operators

Figure 7 (Bridge Electric A)   Solar fire — new method standard

thirty of the smaller parts in the fire giving a saving of 8.0p per fire. Four other parts were modified resulting in a further saving of 1.0p per fire. We also finished up with a product which was much easier to assemble. I think these results justify our approach to this aspect of the problem.

We also wanted to redesign the assembly line to create a more interesting and worthwhile job, to reduce the lost time caused by the lack of balance in the original line, and to create an output rate which would permit us to make the fire steadily throughout the year. Again, I think we achieved this in the creation of the new four operator assembly lines. Obviously, we thought about complete assembly by one person, but this was not possible to achieve because the jigs and fixtures required would not fit in a single location. An individual operative would, therefore, have required at least two work locations. This would have been wasteful of both space and capital equipment. Also to produce the required volume in a year, four operatives would have to work on assembly. It did, therefore, seem logical to break the job down.'

The New Assembly Method for Solar Fires

The final design of the new assembly line is shown in Figure 6. The line was designed for four operators and an output of about 825 units per week. A second mirror image line was also built to accommodate a further four operatives. This was done to permit production of the larger more expensive fire, which had a relatively low volume of demand, at the same time as the Solar Fire. Alternatively, it allowed

	Old Cost	New Cost
	p	p
Raw Material	21.004	21.004
Miscellaneous Materials	47.526	38.526
Scrap Allowance	3.001	2.590
Direct Labour	37.920	27.920
Overheads	42.228	31.200
Material Handling	14.877	10.900
Reserves	2.864	2.864
	169.420	135.004

Old cost is normalized to the new cost to allow for inflation on material and labour.

The two standard cost figures are not truly comparable as the overhead is recovered as a % of direct labour. Excluding overhead, then true savings are:

	Old	New	Saving	
Materials and Scrap	50.527	41.116	9.411	pence
Labour	37.920	27.920	10.000	pence
TOTAL UNIT SAVING			19.411	pence

MATERIAL SAVINGS

Eliminated Parts		Saving	
2 off	1'' 2 B.A. Screws		
2 off	$\frac{5}{8}$ '' 2 B.A. Screws		
2 off	$\frac{1}{2}$ '' 2 B.A. Screws		
4 off	2 B.A. Nuts		
6 off	2 B.A. Serrated Washers	8.00	pence
4 off	Spire Clips		
4 off	2 B.A. Plain Washers		
2 off	2 B.A. Asbestos Washers		
2 off	Double Ceramic Insulators		
2 off	Single Ceramic Insulators		

Modified Parts			
1 off	Handle (Clip-on replaces screwed version)		
1 off	Reflector (Eliminated 2 pieced holes — no saving)	1.00	pence
2 off	Element brackets (Commoned up — no saving)		
		9.00	pence
	Scrap Allowance	(.411)	

Figure 8 (Bridge Electric A)   Standard cost — Solar fire

a doubling in the production of the Solar Fire when demand was particularly heavy. The line was designed on an all or nothing basis, i.e. it was either operated with four operatives, producing 825 units per week, or not operated at all.

The new job breakdowns, together with the standard times are shown in Figure 7. This shows that as a result of the methods changes and the redesign of the assembly, the basic standard time for assembling a Solar Fire had been reduced from 23.48 to 10.46 minutes. When the effect of lack of line balance was taken into account, the reduction was from 25.83 to 11.64 minutes. Figure 8 compares the cost of the fire before and after the investigation by the Central Industrial Engineering group. The combined material and labour savings reduced the cost by 19.41p per unit. At the forecast volume level for 1971, this represented an annual

256

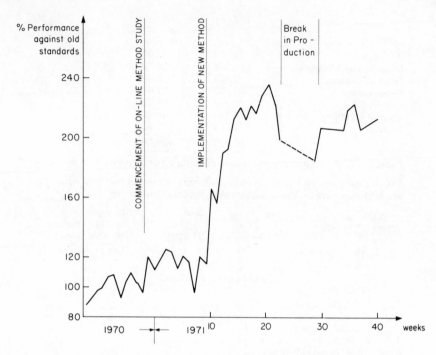

Figure 9 (Bridge Electric A)   Solar assembly – labour performance

saving of approximately £7,000. The previous assembly line had also required a separate full-time supervisor. The new Solar assembly line was now included with four other product assembly lines under a single supervisor. 'The actual cost of the exercise is difficult to define precisely,' said Graham Jackson. 'Approximately £500 was spent on new power tools, benches, jigs, fixtures and minor tooling for the two assembly lines. Obviously, the major cost was the time of the members of our group, together with a portion of the cost of the outside consultant doing the work measurement. I would estimate that a month of our time was spent on the project costing approximately £500. Really only a very small proportion of the consultant's cost could be allocated to the Solar fire, probably about £300. All in all, therefore, it does seem to have been a well worthwhile investment.'

The Results of the New Scheme

'Because we so completely redesigned the job there was relatively little resistance to a fundamental change in the level of output. When we arrived towards the end of 1970 and commenced our method study exercise, a certain amount of "Hawthorne effect" took place. However, this was very limited when compared with the results of introducing the new assembly line.' Figure 9 is a graph of the labour performance for the last quarter of 1970 and the first three quarters of 1971. Performance is calculated on the basis of the original standard for assembling the fire.

Bridge Electric Limited (B)

In late 1970 Tom Simpson took a team from the Central Industrial Engineering Group of Baker Limited to the Bridge Electric Company, a wholly owned subsidiary. Tom had undertaken to improve the profitability of Bridge by making a thorough revision of all aspects of the manufacturing operation.

Bridge made a wide range of small domestic electrical appliances. The company, its product range and various industrial engineering changes carried out by the Central Group are described in the A case. This case describes the new wage system proposed for the company.

The Bridge Wages System in 1970

'We arrived at Bridge and found that an incentive scheme had been introduced in June 1970, with a review promised by the end of the year. Given our role at Bridge we quickly became involved in the structure of the wage system. Local management seemed to expect us to provide the information required for the review.' Tom Simpson was discussing the work done by his group on the payment system at Bridge during 1970 and 1971. 'Our immediate reaction was to play for time. We quickly became convinced that the time standards used in the original incentive scheme were inaccurate and that a considerable amount of work measurement would be required to provide a sound basis for any scheme. It also seemed to us that the existing group incentive schemes were providing very little incentive. We discovered a number of anomalies within the system which needed careful examination.'

'Before we came to Bridge the basic rate for a female operative for a forty hour week was £12.25. They also automatically received a £1.00 'attendance' bonus and an output bonus if productivity exceeded 100%. This bonus was paid at the rate of 0.8% increase in wage for every 1% increase in output. Productivity bonus earnings rarely exceeded £1.00 per week and generally speaking no bonus was earned during 50% of the weeks. You can see this quite clearly for the Solar assembly line on the graph of labour performance (see Figure 9 in Bridge Electric Limited (A)) during the 10 weeks before we commenced the method study exercise. The attention created by the method study exercise resulted in output increasing by about 15%

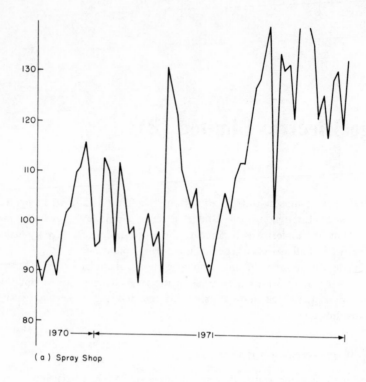

(a) Spray Shop

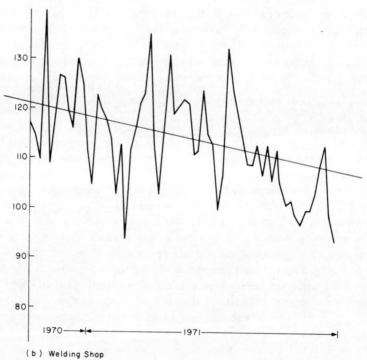

(b) Welding Shop

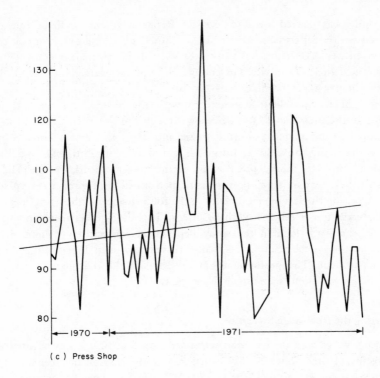

(c) Press Shop

Figure 1 (Bridge Electric B)   Labour performance in (a) spray shop
(b) welding shop (c) press shop

and the average bonus earned went up to between £2.00 and £2.50 per week. When we were ready to change over to the new assembly method in February 1971, we froze the wage level at the average earnings over the previous month plus £0.50. This was equivalent to approximately £16.50 per week and this rate is still being paid pending the introduction of the new bonus system.'

The major anomaly in the existing pay rates was seen as the four grades in the degrease and spray department. These ranged between £15.00 and £22.00 per week. There was little variation in the work and it was questionable whether four rates were justified. The variety of rates, and the differential between the highest rate in the spray shop and those in other departments for male operatives, caused a constant series of minor disputes.

As well as the attendance bonus, previously mentioned there was a 'star' system whereby any operative could gain up to four stars. Each was worth an additional £0.25 per week on the basic rate. No formal system existed for allocating these 'stars', the awards being made on the basis of supervisors' recommendations. Bonuses were paid on a group basis. A bonus was earned in a given week when the productivity performance exceeded seventy on a sixty to eighty rating scale. A separate bonus was therefore calculated each week for the power press, fly press, welding and spray departments and for each of the ten final assembly lines. No upper limit was placed on the level of bonus payment. Indirect operatives associated with a department were paid two-thirds of the bonus rate for that group in any given week. Overtime was worked by virtually all the male operatives but by none of the female operatives. On average eight hours overtime was worked per week, this being paid at 1½ times the basic rate.

Typical of the problems encountered with the existing scheme was work recording in the press shops. Work passing through the two press departments was not credited to the operatives until it passed into the intermediate stores between the press shops and the weld, and degrease and spray operations. The large volume of work in progress in the press shops meant that the work credited did not necessarily bear any relation to the work performed in a given week. Also by holding work on the last operation over to the following week, the operatives could manipulate the bonus scheme. With no intermediate storage between spraying and assembly, the work load in the spray department was entirely dictated by the demands of the assembly lines. This frequently resulted in an ill-planned load in the spray department. The performance in the press, weld and spray departments during the last six months are shown in Figure 1.

Negotiating the New Wage Structure

'The incentive scheme in operation when we arrived at Bridge was negotiated by Mr. Greenway, the former factory manager, and Mr. Hobson the accountant. Mr. Greenway left the company at the end of 1970. He had joined the company when it was a family business and his qualification was more one of being a friend of the family than any particular expertise in factory management. Perhaps, in a way, he was a bit of a scapegoat, but it was generally felt he had to go and he was asked to leave at the end of the year. Bob Green joined the company as the new factory manager coming to Bridge with a background of factory management in the motor and machine tool industries.' Tom Simpson was describing the background to the negotiating procedures which took place during 1971.

'The meeting to review the incentive scheme did not, in fact, take place until the middle of February, 1971. Bridge's representatives at this meeting were Mr. Green, Mr. Hobson and myself. As previously stated our main concern was to gain more time to permit a thorough review of the whole wage structure. We wanted to get agreement at that meeting to remeasure all the work and to start job evaluation. We were prepared to concede a rise in the minimum bonus level in return for a concession to delay the review of the system and to permit us to carry out the work we felt necessary. The outcome of the meeting was that we agreed to fix the minimum male weekly bonus at £2.00 and the female at £1.50. Consensus on the structure of a job evaluation committee was also reached. It was accepted that there should be three permanent members, namely the chief shop steward, the production manager and an 'independent' person from within the company. It was settled that this should be the female supervisor in charge of training. Finally it was decided that there should be two temporary coopted members of the committee when each section was considered. There were to be a workers' representative and the supervisor of the section. We felt after this meeting that we were in a good position to make a major improvement in the wage payment structure at Bridge.'

Following this meeting job evaluation and work measurement proceeded and were complete by the end of July 1971. A number of meetings took place in June and July with Mr. Coker, the Union's area representative, and shop stewards of Bridge. These meetings were held to discuss the progress being made with work measurement and job evaluation, and to discuss such items as:

(1) the rate which would be paid for the basic job evaluated work level,
(2) the rate of bonus which would be paid for performance above the basic level,
(3) equal pay between men and women,
(4) the age at which male and female operatives would qualify for the full adult pay rate, and
(5) the level of bonus to be paid for indirects.'

These meetings were generally conducted in a cooperative and friendly attitude. Mr. Green conducted most of the bargaining for the company and Mr. Coker for the Union. There was, however, an undercurrent of feeling particularly between Mr. Hobson and Mr. Coker.

Talking of these meetings Tom Simpson said: 'Mr. Hobson always seemed to feel that the Union were not to be trusted. He felt that inevitably we had to disagree with them. He did not seem to realize that the basic objective of coming together was to reach an agreement. This culminated in the "coffee incident" at the last meeting in July. Mr. Coker was present for the Union with three male and three female shop stewards and the three of us represented the company. Coffee was brought in by Mr. Green's secretary and placed on a table at the side. At the previous meeting one of the female shop stewards poured the coffee out. However, on this occasion no-one made any move to pour the coffee out and it simply stood at the side for some ten minutes or more. At this stage M. Hobson said to Mr. Coker "Would one of your women please pour the coffee out". Mr. Coker replied rather sharply, "You pour the coffee out". Mr. Hobson lost his temper and after being somewhat abusive left the room. We had prior to this incident had the initiative at the meetings but we completely lost it to Mr. Coker as a result of the outburst. I can't help feeling that Mr. Coker had specifically told his people not to pour the coffee out realizing that some incident might well take place. As a result of this Mr. Hobson did not attend any of the further bargaining meetings and this probably turned out to be advantageous to both sides.'

The final negotiating took place in September 1971 and at the end of this meeting an agreement was signed. A copy of the agreement is detailed in Appendix 1 to this case. It was agreed that the new wage structure would be introduced starting in November 1971 over a six-week period. Each week a new department would be introduced to the revised wage structure. It was accepted that the initial department would be the press shop where the basic job evaluated rate was higher than the old rate by the greatest margin.

APPENDIX 1

Wage Agreement

1. INTRODUCTION

    The following clauses shall form a basis of agreement between Bridge Electric Limited and the Amalgamated Union of Engineering Workers, hereafter referred to as the Company and the Union respectively.

2. SCOPE AND OBJECTIVE OF AGREEMENT

    This agreement will cover the rates of pay and conditions of employment of the Company's hourly paid operatives.

    The object of the agreement is to provide an improved and simplified pay structure.

3. LEGAL ASPECTS

    This agreement is not legally binding on either the Company or the Union.

4. FUTURE NATIONAL PAY AWARDS

    The Company will discuss any future pay awards with the Union and continue to give earnest consideration to terms of national agreements covering the engineering industry.

5. HOURS OF WORK

    The standard week shall be a five day week, totalling forty hours.

6. ANNUAL HOLIDAY

    There will be an annual two weeks shut-down, the third week will be taken separately, as arranged between the Company and the individual.

    Holiday entitlement is *pro rata* for periods of employment of less than one year.

7. STATUTORY PUBLIC HOLIDAYS

Easter Holiday	2 days
Spring Holiday	1 day
Later Summer Holiday	1 day
Christmas Holiday	2 days

8. BASIS OF PAYMENT

    The pay structure is in two parts.

8.1 Part I — Job Evaluated Rate

    The job evaluated rate which has been determined by means of a joint job evaluation exercise.

    This exercise resulted in six basic pay grades providing six basic pay rates for male and three basic rates for female operatives, and proportional rates for junior operatives, male and female.

8.2 Part II — Incentive Payment

    The incentive payment will start at 75 BSI rating which is coincident with the job evaluated rate of pay.

    20% of the job evaluated rate will be paid for the 100 BSI level (step 6).

The scheme is a stepped incentive scheme with steps from 75 to 110 BSI (eight steps).

For each of the 5% steps from 75 BSI to 110 BSI 4% of the job evaluated rate will be paid.

The ceiling for the incentive payment will be at 110 BSI which is equivalent to 28% of the job evaluated rate.

To provide stability of earnings, operatives will contract their incentive pay performance for each six week period in advance.

9. ADULT RATE

9.1 Will be paid to females at 18 years of age.

9.2 Will be paid to males at 20 years of age.

9.3 Will be paid to males at 19 years of age from 31 December 1972.

9.4 Will be paid to males at 18 years of age from 31 December 1974.

10. EQUAL PAY

The female adult, 17 years, 16 years and 15 years of age rates are fixed at 80% of the respective male rate.

10.1 85% of the respective male rate will be paid from 31 December 1972.

10.2 90% of the respective male rate will be paid from 31 December 1973.

10.3 100% of the respective male rate will be paid from 31 December 1974.

11. OVERTIME PAYMENT

Overtime payment will be made as follows:

The first two hours, job evaluated rate plus one third.

Over two hours, job evaluated rate plus one half.

Midnight Friday to Midnight Saturday, job evaluated rate plus one half.

Midnight Saturday to Midnight Sunday, twice job evaluated hourly rate.

Statutory public holidays, twice job evaluated hourly rate.

Notice of overtime will be given before noon on any respective week day, and before the normal finishing time of a Friday for weekend working.

12. HOLIDAY PAY

Holiday pay will be paid at (National Minimum Time Rate + One-Third).

13. PAYMENT DURING TRAINING

The training period referred to is that specified in the job description of the job evaluation scheme. Job evaluated rate will be paid for the training period.

14. PAYMENT FOR WAITING TIME AND NON-PRODUCTIVE WORK

Non-productive work and waiting time due to organizational short-comings, will paid at the job evaluated rate, plus the contracted level of incentive payment.

15. PAYMENT FOR UNMEASURED WORK

Payment for unmeasured work will be paid at the job evaluated rate plus the agreed contracted level of incentive payment.

16. PAYMENT FOR DEFECTIVE WORK

Operatives will be expected to maintain defined acceptable quality levels of workmanship.

Defective work will be returned to the operative for rework, for which no excess time will be allowed.

Excess time will be allowed for rework caused by:

(a)　Previous operation
(b)　Faulty materials
(c)　Materials handling

17.　PAYMENT BY EXCEPTION

Where a differential exists for certain grades above the JER rate, this difference will be retained in respect of the person or persons concerned for the duration of their employ.

New operatives will be started at the job evaluated rate for the job.

The incentive payment rate for the job will be calculated relative to the job evaluated rate for the job in all cases.

18.　TRANSFER BETWEEN JOBS

The Company reserves the right to transfer employees from job to job as the work in the factory requires.

Requests for transfers by operatives will be considered dependent on:

(a)　Suitable vacancies
(b)　Operator performance

An employee transferred to a job with a different grade shall retain the job evaluated rate of the grade from which he was transferred, for a further twenty working days. Thereafter the operative will be paid the job evaluated rate for the new job.

19.　METHODS

The Company reserves the right to review methods and implement changes, where and when considered necessary.

20.　TIME STANDARDS

The Company reserves the right to review and implement time standards, where and when considered necessary. Union representatives will be consulted before any change of time standards is effected.

Job Evaluation

1.　INTRODUCTION

1.1　The first part of the two part pay system is the basic rate. This rate has been established for all jobs by means of a joint job evaluation exercise.

1.2　The various basic rates established by job evaluation are called the job evaluated rates (JER).

The job evaluated rate for a job is used to determine:

(a)　The incentive rate for the job
(b)　Overtime payment
(c)　Holiday payment
(d)　Payment during training
(e)　Payment for waiting time
(f)　Payment for unmeasured work
(g)　Payment for defective work

2.   OBJECTIVES

The purpose of job evaluation is to rank jobs as a basis for a pay structure.

It is a method of comparing all jobs under review using common criteria to determine the relationship of one job with another.

3.   DEFINITION OF THE JOB

A job is a complete occupation, such as:

(a)   Assembler

(b)   Press operator

(c)   Paint sprayer

It is not an occupation or task performed as part of an occupation.

4.   SUMMARY OF JOB EVALUATION SCHEME

4.1   The Company has adopted a factor points evaluation scheme. Five main factors were used as the criteria for the evaluation. Each factor was broken down into sub-factors, and to each was allocated a certain number of points. All jobs were then assessed by sub-factor and the points totalled.

The total points for a job thus gave the relationship of that job to any other evaluated job.

4.2   Each job was evaluated by a joint management, union and worker's representative committee. Coopted members from each section provided detailed knowledge of the job under review.

4.3   Evaluation was carried out by reference to a job description in each case.

4.4   Six pay grades were established covering all hourly paid operative jobs, male and female.

4.5   An appeals procedure allows for a review over a disputed grade.

4.6   The Company will maintain the scheme for all existing and new jobs until further notice.

5.   JOB EVALUATION COMMITTEE

The function of the committee was to examine all shop floor jobs in relationship to one another and to assess these jobs in terms of points in an unbiased and consistent way.

The committee was made up of permanent members, to ensure consistency of rating, and temporary members, coopted from the department being evaluated, to provide information regarding the job.

5.1   Permanent Members

1 Chairman (Management)

1 Senior Union representative

1 Mutually acceptable member

5.2   Coopted Members

1 Supervisor   } from the shop being evaluated
1 Shop representative

5.3   The committee will reconvene to consider appeals and evaluate new jobs as required.

6.   JOB EVALUATION PROCEDURE

6.1   Before evaluation of a job, the Foreman or Supervisor will prepare a job description and this will be given to the committee when it meets (see Figure 2).

6.2 The committee then examines the job on site, if required. Advice would be sought from the operator where necessary. The committee would then discuss the job description and make amendments as necessary.

6.3 The job is analysed by each sub-factor. Following the discussion of a sub-factor, each member should independently assess the number of points to be awarded to that sub-factor. This is done with reference to the summary sheet of jobs which have already been evaluated.

6.4 The allocated points from each member are collected on to an assessment form by the Chairman and examined for variation. Those members whose points vary widely from the average are' asked to re-examine that sub-factor and amend it if necessary.

6.5 After *complete* agreement by the committee, the assessment form should be completed. This procedure is then repeated for each sub-factor. The Chairman is responsible for completing the assessment form, which is then signed as correct by both Union and Management.

MAIN FACTORS	SUB-FACTORS	POINTS RANGE	
Skill	Dexterity	0—151	
	Education	0—59	
	Previous Experience	0—74	39%
	Time to Learn Job	0—106	
Responsibility	Plant and Equipment	0—44	
	Safety for Others	0—34	
	Teamwork for Others	0—40	22%
	Quality (Material)	0—52	
	Supervisory	0—50	
Mental effort	Concentration	0—70	
	Monotony	0—47	15%
	Documentation	0—33	
Physical Effort	Operating Heavy Machines	0—40	
	Lifting Heavy Weights	0—44	13%
	Working Position	0—46	
Working Conditions	Hazard	0—24	
	Fumes	0—26	
	Temperature	0—19	11%
	Dirt	0—21	
	Noise	0—20	

Note: Additional detail of two sub-factors, dexterity and concentration are given in Appendix 2.

Figure 2 (Bridge Electric B)   Job evaluation scheme — factors, sub-factors and points

7. EVALUATED GRADES

Six basic grades have been determined by the job evaluation procedure. These base rates form the payment structure for the Company. All new jobs introduced to the Company will be evaluated to determine the requisite pay grade (see Figure 3).

Male Grades Sept. 1971	Hourly Rate £					
	20 & above	19	18	17	16	15
GRADE 1 Up to 225 points	.385	.330	.290	.250	.210	.190
GRADE 2 226 to 315	.425	.360	.320	.275	.235	.215
GRADE 3 316 to 405	.465	.395	.350	.305	.255	.235
GRADE 4 406 to 495	.505	.430	.380	.330	.280	.255
GRADE 5 496 to 585	.545	.465	.410	.355	.300	.275
GRADE 6 Above 586	.585	.500	.490	.380	.320	.295

Female Grades Sept. 1971	Hourly Rate £			
	18 & above	17	16	15
GRADE 1 Up to 225 points	.335	.220	.185	.165
GRADE 2 226 to 315	.345	.225	.190	.170
GRADE 3 316 to 405	.375	.245	.205	.190
GRADE 4 406 to 495	.410	.265	.225	.205
GRADE 5 496 to 585	.440	.285	.240	.220
GRADE 6 Above 586	.475	.310	.260	.240

Figure 3 (Bridge Electric B)   Proposed basic rates (job evaluation rates)

8.   APPEALS PROCEDURE

8.1 Supervisors, shop stewards and workers' representatives will be informed of the result of job evaluation in their section by the job evaluation committee.

8.2 If the operator is not satisfied that the evaluation committee has taken full consideration of all the factors in his job, he has the right to appeal, He should submit, in writing, to the evaluation committee, via his foreman, his grounds for appeal.

8.3 The committee will consider one appeal, after which the decision of the job evaluation committee is final.

9.   MAINTENANCE OF THE SCHEME

9.1 One person, designated by Management, is responsible for filing and updating all records of the committee's proceedings and for bringing new jobs in the factory to the notice of the committee for evaluation. The Chairman is responsible for ensuring that each assessment form is signed by the Management and Union and that the job is added to those on the summary form.

9.2 The Management will review the scheme at such intervals considered necessary to ensure the equity of the basic pay rates.

Any matter arising as a result of such an investigation shall be communicated to the District Organizer for Union membership. No action shall be implemented until uniform agreement has been reached.

This agreement will remain in force until either party gives six months notice of intent to discontinue the agreement.

The Incentive Scheme

1.   INTRODUCTION

1.1 The first part of the two part pay system is the basic rate. This has been established by job evaluation and is known as the job evaluated rate (JER).

1.2 The second part of the two part pay system is the incentive rate which is a variable rate dependent on the performance of the operator.

1.3 The gross pay rate is the basic rate plus the appropriate incentive rate.

2.   THE INCENTIVE SCHEME

2.1 The incentive scheme is a stepped scheme with eight performance steps between 75 BSI and 110 BSI.

2.2 For each performance step a different incentive rate will be paid.

2.3 The performance steps advance in 5% intervals. The incentive rate advances in intervals of 4% of the job evaluated rate for the job (JER) as follows.

2.4

Step	Performance % BSI scale	Incentive rate % of (JER)
1	75	—
2	80	4
3	85	8
4	90	12
5	95	16
6	100	20
7	105	24
8	110	28

2.5 The minimum acceptable level of operator performance is the 75 BSI Level for for which the job evaluated rate is paid and no incentive rate is paid.

2.6 The expected average performance level is 100 BSI for which the job evaluated rate is paid plus an incentive rate equal to 20% of the job evaluated rate.

Standard performance is the rate of output which qualified workers will naturally achieve without over exertion as an average over the working day or shift provided they know and adhere to the specified method and provided they are motivated to apply themselves to their work.

This performance is denoted as 100 on the BSI standard rating and performance scales.

2.7 The ceiling performance will be 110 BSI for which the job evaluated rate is paid plus an incentive rate equal to 28% of the job evaluated rate. This is the maximum incentive rate payable in this scheme.

3. CONTRACTED PERFORMANCE LEVEL

3.1 A special feature of the scheme is the contracted performance level. A performance step is negotiated with each operator. The operator is paid at the negotiated rate for a period of six weeks irrespective of the actual performance returned in any particular week or averaged over the six week period. The contract is renewed each six weeks. The operator's actual performance is considered when negotiating the rate for the next six week period.

3.2 Following the training period specified in the job description, each operator will undergo a four week qualifying period. During this period the operator will be paid the job evaluated rate plus the incentive rate actually earned (to the nearest performance step) in each of the four qualifying weeks.

3.3 The average performance over the four weeks will act as a guide in negotiating the contracted incentive rate for the first six week period.

3.4 To advance to a higher performance step, it is necessary to exceed the contracted level of performance. A minimum of 4% improvement must be averaged over the contracted six week period to advance one step.

Two steps is the maximum advance allowed in one review period. This will require a minimum of 10% improved average over the previous review period.

3.5 Shortfall of more than 5% average over six weeks will require an operator to drop one performance step.

3.6 Shortfall of 4% or more averaged over two consecutive six week periods will require an operator to drop one performance step.

3.7 Shortfall of more than 10% average in one six week period will require an operator to drop two performance steps.

4. SCOPE OF THE SCHEME

4.1 The contracted scheme is open to all direct operatives. It will apply to individuals or small groups of operators working as a team.

4.2 Indirect operatives (hourly paid) will not be covered by the scheme.

Payment to indirect personnel will be at the job evaluated rate for the job plus 75% of the expected average incentive rate.

The expected average incentive rate is at the 100 BSI performance step.

This percentage will be paid as a fixed rate irrespective of the performance of direct operatives.

5.   TIME AND OUTPUT RECORDING

5.1   Each batch of work will be accompanied by a job ticket.

On completion of the operation the operator will record the time taken on:

(a)   the job ticket

(b)   and, or a time sheet

At the completion of the batch the job ticket will be returned by the operator to the line supervisor.

5.2   Waiting time will be recorded by means of non-productive cards. The operator will obtain a card from the supervisor at commencement of waiting time and return the card at the end of the waiting time period.

The operator may additionally be required to record the period of waiting time on a time sheet.

5.3   All cards productive and non-productive and time sheets must be returned to the line supervisor at the end of each shift.

5.4   Clock cards will be passed to the line supervisor each morning after first clocking. After checking the previous day's bookings the line supervisor will return the clock card to the card rack.

6. GROSS PAY RATES

Figures 4 and 5 give the hourly rates for adult male and female workers for each of the job evaluated grades and for each incentive step.

GRADE	STEP 1 Hourly Rate £ JER	STEP 2 Hourly Rate £	STEP 3 Hourly Rate £	STEP 4 Hourly Rate £	STEP 5 Hourly Rate £	STEP 6 Hourly Rate £	STEP 7 Hourly Rate £	STEP 8 Hourly Rate £
1	0.385	0.401	0.416	0.431	0.447	0.462	0.478	0.493
2	0.425	0.442	0.459	0.476	0.493	0.510	0.527	0.544
3	0.465	0.483	0.502	0.521	0.539	0.558	0.576	0.595
4	0.505	0.525	0.546	0.565	0.586	0.606	0.626	0.646
5	0.545	0.567	0.588	0.610	0.632	0.654	0.676	0.697
6	0.585	0.608	0.632	0.655	0.678	0.702	0.726	0.749

Figure 4 (Bridge Electric B)   Adult male, September 1971

GRADE	STEP 1 Pay Per 40 Hrs. £ JER	STEP 2 Pay Per 40 Hrs. £	STEP 3 Pay Per 40 Hrs. £	STEP 4 Pay Per 40 Hrs. £	STEP 5 Pay Per 40 Hrs. £	STEP 6 Pay Per 40 Hrs. £	STEP 7 Pay Per 40 Hrs. £	STEP 8 Pay Per 40 Hrs. £
1	0.335	0.348	0.362	0.375	0.388	0.402	0.415	0.429
2	0.345	0.359	0.372	0.387	0.400	0.414	0.428	0.442
3	0.375	0.390	0.405	0.420	0.435	0.450	0.465	0.480

Figure 5 (Bridge Electric B)   Adult female, September 1971

APPENDIX 2

FACTOR:	Skill
SUB-FACTOR:	Dexterity
POINTS TO BE ALLOCATED:	151
DEFINITION OF FACTOR:	Assess (a) The degree of complexity of hand movement.
	(b) The degree of coordination of hands, eyes and feet.
	(c) The accuracy of positioning of components, jigs and tools that the job requires.

Points Range	Description
0—12	(a) Simple hand movements.
13—25	Few components to manipulate at any one time.
26—38	Several components to manipulate at one time.
39—50	Difficult positioning of components with awkward hand movements.
0—12	(b) A degree of coordination for both hands for small part of cycle.
13—25	Some coordinateon of both hands for all the cycle.
26—38	Considerable coordination of both hands for the majority of the cycle.
39—50	Considerable coordination of hands, eyes and feet.
0—12	(c) Simple placing of materials on racks or packing cases.
13—25	Visual alignment or use of jigs to position components.
26—38	Positioning and aligning to moderate degree of precision.
39—51	Precision positioning and aligning required.

FACTOR:	Mental requirements
SUB-FACTOR:	Concentration
POINTS TO BE ALLOCATED:	70
DEFINITION OF FACTOR:	Assess the effort required to ensure the correct positioning and finish of components within tolerance specified, with consideration to the complexity of the work.

Points Range	Description
0—15	No close attention required at any time. Simple controls to be adjusted without precision; no need to consider finish or tolerance.
16—35	Periodic concentration required for close adjustments, setting up or infrequent inspection.
36—55	Close attention required during part of repetitive operation of cycle time less than about 30 seconds. Concentration needed to follow involved or intricate drawings or instructions.
56—70	High degree of concentration needed for large percentage of short cycle operation.

Great Northern Fluids Limited

On October 15, 1970, Mr. W. Adams, the Spares and Service Manager of the West Works of Great Northern Fluids was completing a report which examined the spare parts manufacturing efficiency and the potential for expansion at each of Northern's three pump manufacturing centres. His report was written in reply to a set of guidelines for spare parts expansion, prepared by Mr. R. Bright, Northern's Manufacturing Director.

The Company

Great Northern Fluids was the major company in the Engineering Division of the Mornex Group of companies. In 1969, the group's sales totalled approximately £60 million, with profits of £4.4 million. The engineering division contributed £33 million sales and £1.7 million profit to these totals. Northern manufactured a wide range of custom and standard pumps in three major categories: Power, Marine and Industrial. The Power Division supplied boiler feed pumps, circulating water pumps, condensors, feed heaters and deaerators to thermal power stations around the world. Northern's Marine Division provided packaged boiler feed systems, sea water distillation plants and a complete range of auxiliary pumps to the vessels of many nations. Marine and Power Division pumps were manufactured at West and in the nearby smaller works at Hutton. The Industrial Division was based at Attersley, a small community within 50 miles of the parent West Works. This division produced special pumps, turbines and motors for use in a wide variety of industries and public water supply and sewerage operations. In both the Power and Industrial Divisions a lot of system design work and on site installation was done by Northern engineers.

Spares and Service

Great Northern had three spare parts centres, one in each plant. Each centre consisted of manufacturing facilities and staff, as well as complete administrative support and a spares manager. Each centre manufactured spares for original equipment made in its own plant, but could also make spares for the others. The spare parts manufacturing facilities were set up as completely separate plants, within their parent plant. A complete range of machinery was available for spares manufacture. Scheduling, inspection, machine loading, and so on, were carried out completely independently of the main plants. Field service orders, which were requests for engineering help, were centralized at West. Sales volume for spares and new equipment for each plant are given in Figure 1.

Spares inventory policy was dictated by the board of the Mornex Group. In 1970, spares inventory was not to exceed £625,000. Reorder points and lot sizes were based on historical usage rates. It was estimated that there were approximately 60,000 different spare parts which could be demanded by Northern's customers. The Company's policy was to make spare parts for any pump, no matter how old. The majority of the spares orders were for custom parts, but Northern advertised that stock spares were available on one week delivery, for standard pump models.

Mr. Adams indicated that the spares and service part of Northern's business was very important. All major customers would only buy pumps for which they knew spares and fast service would be available. Mr. Adams stated that service was more important than price to many customers, since downtime of a vessel, or a power generation station was very expensive. Three major oil companies collectively purchased over £0.5 million of Northern spares yearly for ships and refineries. Northern had invested approximately £20,000 in establishing spare parts depots on the worldwide trading routes of these companies, so that if spares were needed they would be available quickly. Another service which Mr. Adams intended to implement was that of selling a spares contract to major customers under which Northern would advise on the interchangeability of parts within different pumps owned by the firm, give technical advice on new pumps, a regular overhaul service and so on. It was Mr. Adam's belief that the sale of spare parts could be considerably increased with marketing efforts such as these.

Mr. Adams stated that his department at the West Works received an average of 490 orders per week, 70 of which were for field service, 195 for stock spares and the remainder for custom spares. On October 15, 1970, Mr. Adams indicated that his department had 5,619 orders in hand, of which 974 were for field service, 588 were overhauls, 414 were for stock spares and the remainder were for custom spares. A total of 1901 orders were overdue, anywhere from 1 day to 18 months late. He estimated that probably 50% of these orders were less than 6 months overdue. Of the overdue orders, 351 were overhauls and 1600 were spares.

Mr. Adams had analysed this overdue overhaul problem in the following way: 38.5% of the overhauls were 'within control' i.e. that material was available to do the job; 31.5% were held up because of slow delivery on finished parts from outside suppliers; 19% were held up because of outside castings which had not been delivered; 10% were waiting for stock pump parts. He further estimated that of those overhauls which were currently 'within control', two-thirds had earlier been held up because of missing parts. Mr. Adams stated that in spite of the heavy overdue situation Northern did not lose many spare parts customers. He indicated

	1959	1960	1961	1962	1963	1964	1965	1966	1967	1968	1969
New Work											
West	7,621	6,221	4,851	5,814	4,445	5,224	4,804	5,367	6,264	9,675	9,476
Hutton	3,984	3,330	2,508	2,474	2,342	2,621	2,630	2,828	2,813	2,719	2,496
Attersley	2,565	2,076	2,465	2,932	2,500	1,881	2,546	3,502	3,956	3,232	3,077
	14,170	11,627	9,824	11,220	9,287	9,726	9,980	11,697	13,033	15,626	15,049
Spares											
West	1,433	1,311	1,359	1,874	2,311	2,286	2,552	2,831	3,695	3,911	4,047
Hutton	546	554	663	797	742	805	872	1,116	1,314	1,367	1,413
Attersley	300	298	348	450	455	445	466	569	716	812	677
Southern	175	175	215	228	240	264	309	347	353	322	345
	2,454	2,338	2,585	3,349	3,748	3,800	4,199	4,863	6,078	6,412	6,482
Total											
West	9,054	7,532	6,210	7,688	6,756	7,510	7,356	8,198	9,959	13,586	13,523
Hutton	4,530	3,884	3,171	3,271	3,084	3,426	3,502	3,944	4,127	4,086	3,909
Attersley	2,865	2,374	2,813	3,382	2,955	2,326	3,012	4,071	4,672	4,044	3,754
Southern	175	175	215	228	240	264	309	347	353	322	345
	16,724	13,965	12,409	14,569	13,035	13,526	14,179	16,560	19,111	22,038	21,531

Notes:
(1) The West figures exclude Fluid Handling Ltd.
(2) The Attersley figures include Central but exclude overseas companies and Motor Division.
(3) Southern figures represent Northern Service (Southern) Ltd.

Figure 1 (Great Northern Fluids Ltd.) Invoiced sales (£'000s), 1959–1969

that spare parts fell into three categories:

(1) spare parts for which Northern had the patterns and it would be difficult for the customer to go elsewhere;

(2) spare parts for stock Northern pumps which Northern made in large volumes and could sell at a lower price than most manufacturers;

(3) simple spare parts, such as a simple shaft which could be made by any machine shop; these orders could be lost

Twenty percent of Northern's customers in the first category requested a statement of price and delivery when they placed their orders.

Mr. Adams was given a great deal of freedom to run his department. The prices were set by him and costs calculated separately for his department. On average his works cost was 60% of sales, to which had to be added an eleven percent of sales general works overhead charge, which in theory was the charge to his department for technical assistance granted by the rest of the firm during the year. Prices were standard on most parts, the given percentage being added to the standard works cost. However, on exceptional jobs Mr. Adams often set the price himself, occasionally making 100% profit.

Increased Spares Capacity

In September 1970, Mr. Bright prepared a set of guidelines to govern the expansion of Northern's spare parts manufacturing capacity. He suggested that owing to a severe labour shortage Attersley should not be expanded. As to whether to expand West or Hutton, Mr. Bright favoured Hutton since labour and floor space were more available than at West, and the present plant utilization at Hutton was only 60%. He suggested that West was past optimal size. Mr. Adams felt strongly that if any shift were to take place in spare parts manufacturing, it should be toward centralization at West. His report which explained his reasoning is shown in the Appendix to this case.

APPENDIX
GREAT NORTHERN FLUIDS LTD.

INCREASED MACHINING CAPACITY FOR SPARES MANUFACTURE

Introduction

The purpose of this note is to briefly examine the possibilities for an increased spares manufacturing capacity by possible expansion or rationalization of the existing spares manufacturing centres at Hutton, Attersley and West. An attempt will be made to identify the current relative performance of the three areas (as a guide to expansion potential) and the guide lines for expansion laid down by Mr. R. Bright will be discussed and where possible their effects quantified in more detail. Finally, an attempt will be made to describe various possible frameworks suitable for both the long and short term expansion of the Spares and Service activity for Great Northern Fluids Ltd.

Current Performance

Since the function of any business organization is to maximize the return to the Shareholders, it has been decided to identify the performance in terms of only the return for money invested and to this end the comparison of performance at the three spares organizations is made on the basis of extrapolating the performance at Period 6 (4 week periods) to the end of the years.

Real Growth

Figure 2 shows the real and actual growth percentages for both Sales and Profit, taking into account the various spares price increases. Only West shows any real growth in terms of sales, i.e. expansion, the reduction in Attersley is the most dramatic and indicates that the problems in transferring from Central were probably underestimated. No satisfactory reason for the decline in Hutton's sales performance can be offered without a much fuller investigation. It should be noted that of the West extrapolated sales of £5.5 million, approximately only £600,000 is attributable to Field Service. Unfortunately, the available statistics do not enable a comparison with 1969 and thus the real growth in the service activity cannot be identified separately.

It is worthy of note that at both West and Hutton, the real growth in profits exceeds the real growth in sales, i.e. neither unit is doing more to get less, whether or not this derives from increased efficiency or a more highly developed sense of commercial acumen could only be established after more detailed investigation. The fact that Hutton increased profit with a reduced turnover is significant, since it could indicate that the Hutton establishment has almost reached the optimum size in relation to the existing management systems and procedures in operation there.

			SALES (£000s)			PROFIT (£000s)	
		Actual Output	Actual Growth	Real Growth**	Actual Profit*	Actual Growth	Real Growth
West	1969	4,660	+18%	+6.6%	1,641	+23%	+10%
	1970	5,505			2,086		
Attersley	1969	800	−7½%	−16%	325	−1.5%	−10%
	1970	740			316		
Hutton	1969	1,410	+5%	−6%	486	+17%	+5%
	1970	1,480			566		

*Before works overhead allocated at 11% of sales.
**Real Growth derived by considering the following price increases since the beginning of 1969:

    West   — 5% September, 1969: 10% January, 1970.
    Attersley — 5% April, 1969: 10% December, 1969.
    Hutton   — 10% January, 1970.

Figure 2 (Great Northern Fluids Ltd.)   Real and actual growth percentages for sales and profits

Investment in Overheads

A review of the ratio of overheads to direct labour indicates that West benefits from the economies of scale since the ratio for West is 22% lower than Attersley and 48% lower than Hutton, these figures being shown in Figure 3. Care must be exercised in the interpretation of these figures and it is the trend rather than the absolute value which must be considered since the apportionment of general works accounts to the overhead accounts associated with the three Spares and Service centres is dictated by accounting practices which are reviewed only once per year. These figures apply only to the Works cost and a further examination of investment in indirect labour at the three plants is necessary. Perhaps the easiest method of doing this is to refer to the report produced by the West Spares and Service Management earlier this year in which the ratio of direct labour to the administrative indirect costs was considered for the three plants. Figure 4 restates the situation and a recent check reveals no significant alteration. This again shows the economy of scale as far as West is concerned. The ratio A to B does indicate that the intrinsic profit levels at Hutton and Attersley are reduced in relation to that at West by the

	Direct Labour	Overheads	Ratio
West	372	775	2.08
Attersley	28	64	2.29
Hutton	44	137	3.09
TOTAL	444	976	2.55

Figure 3 (Great Northern Fluids Ltd.)   Works on cost rate (£000) (to Period 6, 1970)

	A Administration Bill	B Direct Labour Cost	A/B
Attersley	£30,100	£50,540	60%
Hutton	28,100	72,610	39%
West*	73,200	301,900	24%
TOTAL	£131,400	£425,050	31%

If the West Administration percentage is applied to total direct labour costs, it gives an administration cost of £102,000 which represents a saving of £30,000 at 1969 wage and salary levels.
*The West figure includes £229,400 direct costs in the works and £72,500 as one third of Field Service direct labour costs representing the level of Administrative effort chanelled to Field Service.

Figure 4 (Great Northern Fluids Ltd.)   Relation of total administration bill to total labour costs*

increased investment in indirect overheads associated with the administration. As indicated in Figure 4 an additional saving of some £30,000 per annum could be effected by centralization of the administration.

Relation Between Sales Recovery and Cost of Labour

An accurate reflection of the relative performance of the manufacturing capacity at the three plants can only be obtained by considering the material and labour content of the cost of sales separately. Figure 5 shows the net sales associated with the labour content of the total cost of sales, this having been derived by considering the material cost of sales, 'marking it up' by 60% and subtracting it from the total sales. The ratio of net sales to direct labour is then shown for each Plant. It should be noted that the £600,000 sales associated with the Field Service has been removed from the West figures.

	Net Sales*	Direct Labour	Ratio
West	1195**	131***	8.75
Attersley	183	28	6.5
Hutton	276	44	6.3

*i.e. total sales − (material x 1.6)
**corrected to exclude Field Service and Power Division Erection
***corrected to exclude Field Service Sales

Figure 5 (Great Northern Fluids Ltd.)   Relation between sales (£000) and cost of labour (to Period 6, 1971)

Comparison of the ratio for the three manufacturing centres shows that Hutton and Attersley are very similar while West shows a significantly greater ratio of productivity. This is surprising and further detailed investigation of this would be necessary to identify the root causes, it is, of course, a partial explanation for the real growth at West.

Summary

Attersley, although showing no growth this year to date in either sales or profit does not reflect unfavourably in relation to Hutton from the standpoint of the ratio of net sales to direct labour. The fact that Hutton shows an increase in real growth for profit against a reduction in sales is encouraging and if it can be proved that this is not the direct result of commercial enterprise, i.e. writing down of stock, etc., then the harnessing of this greater efficiency to increased sales should show a good return. The fact that no real growth is shown, however, could be serious, since nothing has basically changed at Hutton and all dynamic organizations should show steady growth. If major expansion is to be considered at Hutton, then a serious review of the causes leading to the lack of growth should be undertaken, before any significant capital investment is undertaken at that location.

West shows real growth in both sales recovery and profit, and in fact this represents expansion at present without the benefits of any significant capital investment. It would thus appear that the optimum size has not yet been reached at West in relation to the Management systems and procedures operated there and the possibilities of further expansion at that centre cannot be ignored.

Expansion Possibilities

Two possible routes to expansion have been considered, the first involves the use of all three spares manufacture centres, while the second considers the possibility of concentrating spares manufacturing at only two, perhaps even one, manufacturing unit.

Expansion Using Three Manufacturing Units

Perhaps the best method of examining this possibility is to comment on the guide lines laid down by Mr. Bright and to this end consideration is given to each manufacturing centre in turn.

Attersley　　The proposal to defer any expansion at the Attersley centre meantime seems sound, no counter argument is offered.

Hutton　　The statement that Hutton has the greatest potential for expansion with regard to manufacturing floor area, skilled personnel and office accommodation cannot be questioned, there are, however, other factors which must be taken into consideration. If the Hutton spares output is to be increased by almost 250% as suggested, then a radical re-organization of the systems and procedures, which are at present providing a stagnant sales recovery situation there, would have to be undertaken. This would cost both time and money. Even allowing for an increase in productivity associated with the introduction of more sophisticated machine tools, an increase in the direct labour of at least 100% to around £145,000 per annum would be required. The associated increase in Works and Indirect overhead expenditure would be at least a total of £125,000 per annum. This figure being arrived at by the optimistic assumption that the full West economies scale, i.e. 2.08 (Figure 3) and .24 (Figure 4) could be achieved. A more realistic figure is probably between £145,000 and £210,000.

West   The real growth and value added figures shown in Current Performance, indicate that contrary to the suggestion made in Mr. Bright's guide lines that West has passed the optimum size, there does, in fact, seem scope for further expansion at that centre. The problems faced at Hutton are reversed at West, i.e. the systems and procedures at West seem adequate while the floor space shortage is acute unless expansion into the new work manufacturing area is to be accepted. Consideration of other current changes in the manufacturing set up at West gives rise to the hope that further expansion is possible by the methods outlined below.

At present, the West Spares and Service Machine Shop has a capacity of 92 machines with a 78% utilization; of these machines, 15 are involved in the manufacture of Department of Defense (DoD) spares contract components. An additional 12 are used for Product Support emergencies, mainly related to Field Service work, while 12 are used for Product Support Shop overhauls. Only 52 machines are therefore confined solely to the manufacture of commercial spares, with the additional 13 being used for the machining associated with the overhaul and repair work in the West shops.

It is a fact, therefore, that only 65 machines in the Spares and Service Machine Shop are associated with the manufacture of commercial spares and repairs and Figure 6 which identifies the various elements in the total make up of the Spares and Service output, indicates that these 65 machines are associated with a total Commercial Spares and Repairs sales recovery of £2,880,000 that being 95% of the total Commercial Spares and Repairs output (the remaining 5% being produced by Main Production).

DoD Spares	£1,604,350
Field Service	601,600
Stock Components	448,200
Commercial Spares* and Repairs	£3,031,200
TOTAL	£5,685,350

*95% of this produced in Spares and Service Machine Shop, i.e., £2,880,000.

Figure 6 (Great Northern Fluids Ltd.)   West spares and service sales recovery (estimate for 1970)

Turning now to the various possible methods of increasing turnover:

(1) An increase in the utilization to 90% will *pro rata* provide a 15% increase in output by the recruitment of 21 additional operatives.

(2) When the 15 machines used for DoD manufacture are transferred to Q Shop (not part of the Spares Manufacturing Workshop), these could be replaced during 1971/72 by more modern machines to be used for the production of commercial spares, i.e. an increase from 65 to 77 machines, or a potential 19% increase in output.

(3) As Field Service becomes more autonomous with respect to machining capacity, then the 12 Product Support machines could, over a two year period, be used to form a Product Support Workshop at West entirely separate from the Spares Manufacturing Workshop. The 12 machines used for this purpose could be replaced by newer machines which would be utilized only for spares manufacture, i.e. an increase in machine capacity from 65 to 89 over two to three years showing an increase in spares manufacturing capacity of 37%.

Superimposing the 15% to be derived from increased utilization, on the increases available from the larger number of machine tools, shows the growth potential to be significant, amounting to over £1.5 million, this being detailed in Figure 7.

The move described above would help to introduce a more effective control of spares manufacture in general, since one of the main problems currently experienced is the maintenance of an adequate production rate for DoD spares in the situation which demands that the spares are manufactured over a wide area both in Main Production and Spares and Service. Manufacture of the bulk spares orders for DoD in Main Production has not been a success and centralization of the manufacture of these spares in Q Shop will undoubtedly lead to better control and must result in higher productivity. Coupling the higher productivity for DoD work to the Commercial growth shown in Figure 7 will undoubtedly lead to an overall growth in West spares and repairs of between £1.7 and £2.0 million over the two to three years considered. It must also be pointed out that the expansion of turnover at West as described above can be achieved with virtually no increase in indirect labour. Indeed, it is hoped that over the next three years with the introduction of EDP systems in the production and commercial areas that a net reduction in indirects will be effected.

The creation of a Product Support workshop while being desirable from a Customer Services standpoint is not particularly urgent and, in fact, from the point of view of machine utilization is not desirable at present since the allocation of 12 machines to Product Support only would undoubtedly reduce their utilization and this is not compatible with our present thirst for growth. It should be noted that the growth in spares production described above can be accommodated by finding the space for only 12 additional machines and it is likely that with the integration of all DoD work in Q Shop that the Naval Pump

	1970	1971	1972/73
Machine shifts per 24 hours	101	130	160
Annual Sales (£000)	2,888	3,720	4,572
% Increase relative to 1970	–	29%	58%
Actual Increase in Sales			
Recovery (no allowance			
for expansion) (£000)	–	832	1,684

Figure 7 (Great Northern Fluids Ltd.)   Potential spares and repairs
capacity growth at West

Section area in Spares and Service will be vacated and most of the 12 machines
can be located therein.

The capital expenditure required for implementation of the above proposals
would be that, associated with the purchase of 24 machine tools, i.e.
approximately £150,000.

Expansion Using Less Than Three Manufacturing Units

When considering the best route to take with regard to consolidating the spares
manufacture organization for Great Northern which will provide the required
growth over the next five or even ten years, consideration must be given to the
relative size of the three different units. Of the total spares output for 1970, it
would appear at this stage that 70% will be provided by West, 20% by Hutton and
10% by Attersley. Focusing on Attersley, it is now a fact that the Boiler Feed Pump
overhauls previously carried out there have been done by West and as from the end
of this year, feed pump spares for all utilities will be being produced at West. In
addition to this, the repair proportion of the Attersley spares and repairs output is
likely to decline as customers become aware of the facility for site overhauls or
even local workshop overhauls now being made available by the Field Service
Department. Considering these facts it is difficult to envisage where the increased
input is to come from for any expansion at Attersley, and the case for the
continuance of Attersley as a spares manufacture centre, with an associated
continuing investment in overheads seems hardly justifiable, especially in the light
of the critical manpower recruitment problem now existing in that area. Transfer of
the spares manufacturing manpower to new work would help to ameliorate the
conditions there and the absorption of the 10% sales could very easily be
accommodated by either Hutton or West or by a combination of the two.

It is suggested therefore, that any expansion of the spares capacity for Great
Northern Fluids Ltd. should be preceded by a move towards centralization in order
to maximize the benefits accruing from the economies of scale. The exact form
which this centralization should take must be the subject of a much more detailed
study and this short note will conclude with a seed planting exercise by identifying

a number of alternative routes towards centralization. These are as follows:

(1) A first phase involving centralization of the administrative function at either West or Hutton (as in the report of May this year) together with the continuance of Hutton and West as separate spares manufacturing centres.

(2) The creation of a separate Spares and Service Division at Hutton with all spares manufacturing capacity being centered there together with the appropriate administrative back up for both Spares and Field Service. The increased spares capacity to be provided by the transfer of the Hutton new work to West.

(3) The creation of a Spares and Service Division for Great Northern within West. The space for the increased spares manufacturing capacity to absorb Hutton and Attersely spares output to be created by the transfer of all Fluid Handling* new work and spares to Hutton with the subsequent creation of a Fluid Handling manufacturing centre for new work and spares there. It should be noted that the Fluid Handling spares output for 1970 will be approximately 60% of the total Hutton output.

Conclusions

The evidence available indicates that both West and Hutton have equal potential for expansion of the spares manufacturing capacity, the required attendant increase in overhead expenditure being much greater at Hutton than at West. Before any plans are finalized for the rapid expansion of Northern spares turnover, a thorough and detailed investigation of all the possibilities available must be made in order to ensure that the return on the not inconsiderable capital investment is maximized over the next three to five years. It is further recommended that this investigation is started immediately.

*Fluid Handling pumps were a specific line of Northern Pumps.

Lemont (B)

Introduction

The Lemont hot strip steel mill was commissioned in 1957. In 1967 it was still manually controlled, although its owners were aware of competitive developments in computer control of steel rolling mills in America, Japan and Europe. The Lemont mill was a medium width mill capable of producing strip up to 18 inches wide. Existing computerized mills in 1967 were all wide strip mills.

Studies of the benefits of automatic control of the Lemont mill indicated that full automation could produce benefits of £100,000 a year for an estimated capital expenditure of about £650,000. The benefits would accrue through increased output, improved yields (i.e. lower scrap rates), improved quality and better customer service. Improving the average quality of the steel strip was considered a competitive advantage likely to be of increasing importance in the future, thereby extending the useful life of the mill. A further benefit of future significance was that computer control would permit the mill to operate profitably with much smaller batch sizes, a feature in line with market trends.

The conversion to automatic control would be in two stages. Stage one was the implementation of automatic set-ups. On the basis of the required specification the computer calculated the optimum mill settings using programs based on a combination of theory and best practice. The positions of the many rolls, side guides, speed controls used in producing finished strip could be adjusted prior to the rolling of every slab, by the central computer and its associated servo systems.

Stage two, an extension of stage one, was called automatic gauge control (AGC). A system based on stage one alone could not monitor and correct the mill settings if necessary during the rolling cycle. Stage two would permit the computer to monitor the thickness (gauge) of the strip as it was being rolled. Off gauge tendencies could therefore be corrected during the rolling cycle.

It was decided that stages one and two should be implemented sequentially. After stage one was operational the expected marginal benefits of stage two were to be reassessed and compared with the marginal expenditure required. This decision reduced the initial capital expenditure by approximately £118,000.

In August 1968 the contract for the scheme was awarded to SED. Technical discussions had been held for about 18 months and the contract contained many detailed clauses related to the performance of the computer control system.

The Project Timescale

Lemont were keen to avoid mill downtime at each stage of the project. In consequence the time scale was extended to take account of this constraint. At the time, both parties were confident that it was a realistic, though tight schedule, designed to get the earliest possible benefits from the capital expenditure. Lemont's project manager, Paul Muller, stated: 'We produced a comprehensive network analysis of the whole programme. We were confident that we had covered all foreseen contingencies quite adequately.'

The time scale for the project was as follows:

August 1968	Contract placed.
August 1968—July 1969	Lemont and SED engineers to complete detailed studies of the mill; finalization of procurement plans.
July—August 1969	Final discussions to settle matters of detail.
August 1969—August 1970	Procurement and installation of mill hardware.
April 1970	Installation of the compter.
August 1969—September	1970 Production and debugging of the software.
September 1970	Commission of computer software.
September 1970—April 1971	Completion of the cold acceptance mill trials.
April 1971—December 1971	Completion of the hot acceptance mill trials.
December 1971	Commission of the automatic plant.

The acceptance trials were to be of two kinds. The cold acceptance trials were formal checks that the computer could correctly calculate the appropriate mill settings for each type of slab to be rolled. They also established that the computer could successfully command the various slave systems to conform to the required set-up configuration. The hot trials were fully operational checks that the mill could function correctly under automatic control. It was a contractual obligation that hot trials should be performed on every type of slab produced by the mill. Each trial would be deemed successful if the first twelve slabs of a new rolling size were rolled correctly. This proved the validity of the set-up algorithm. This had to be followed by the correct rolling of twelve subsequent slabs to ensure that the dynamic updating procedures were correct.

The Project Management

Lemont and SED agreed to set-up a joint project team. The two halves were responsible to a Lemont and SED project manager respectively. The team members were drawn from the various parts of each organization according to their skills. The Lemont members maintained functional responsibilities outside the project, in addition to their project responsibilities. The structure of the two halves of the project team mirrored one another. The composition of the team changed according to the current work load and to accommodate the individual strengths and weaknesses of client and contractor. The SED project manager was Mr. Charles Martin. His opposite number resigned early in the project and was replaced by Mr. Muller.

Both men missed a great deal of the contractual negotiations prior to the signing of the contract. Both recognized that it had hindered later communications to some degree.

Mr. Muller: 'Although major organizational changes did not adversely affect the project, there is no doubt that managerial continuity was not good in the 1969—70 period within Lemont. SED were more fortunate in this respect, but we experienced continuity problems when negotiating with them subsequently.'

Mr. Martin:'The written contract was pushed through rapidly in 1968. The resulting specifications were therefore not as satisfactory as either party might later have wished. Paul and I, however, had no opportunity to influence what was already decided — we just had to make it happen.'

The SED team consisted of Charles Martin, three systems engineers and 4—5 software designers and programmers. The Lemont team consisted of Paul Muller, 3—4 systems and software personnel and 3—5 site engineers. Lemont were responsible for the physical refurbishing of the mill hardware, including the installation of new hardware and of the computer. The software was to be a shared responsibility.

About half of the proposed expenditure was to refurbish the existing mill equipment. Paul Muller: 'Our philosophy was to extract maximum performance from the mill. When this had been achieved we could then implement the automation proposals. Automation would be acceptable only if it achieved consistently what our earlier experimental mill pacing project had demonstrated was possible. That is, slab to slab times of ten seconds or less, while maintaining the desired target tolerances on output gauge.'

Lemont personnel had gained much experience from this prior project. They hoped to use this expertise to produce slab software for the new computer. Lemont were to handle the data interfacing and message handling aspects of the new software, while SED concentrated on the basic program routines (data input and output via the visual displays, analogue to digital conversions, commands, and the overall system organization). SED was also required to devise the basic control engineering relationships necessary to permit automatic on-line control. These relationships, called alorithms, had been under development for 18 months prior to the contract date. Indeed SED's theoretical understanding of the mill was a prime reason for their selection as main contractors.

A Lemont senior Systems Engineer stated: 'In retrospect Lemont could probably have handled the entire software, but we needed SED's expertise in producing the algorithms.'

Mr. Martin replied: 'In general SED now insists on full responsibility for the software production on a new project. Of course we have a lot more experience than we did then.' Mr. Muller: 'We experienced problems when we tried to put together the various parts of the software. It was difficult to achieve common specifications; I suppose the moral should be not to split the responsibility for software.'

Project progress was monitored at monthly progress review meetings attended by both project managers, senior Lemont management and by individual team members as appropriate. These meetings were supplemented by weekly meetings as necessary and by meetings of a Steering Committee chaired by the mill Works Manager at 2–3 month intervals. Project personnel were of course in daily contact.

Mr. Martin:, 'My team practically lived at Lemont for long periods. From the start I intended to do everything I could to maintain enthusiasm and morale during sometimes difficult circumstances. I put in comfortable site offices where they could even cook simple meals, bearing in mind the long hours often needed. I also obtained two project cars to facilitate transport between Lemont and our headquarters, eight miles away. At the time that was an unusual benefit, but a very worthwhile one.'

The Steering Committee was authorized to consider broad issues such as control of capital expenditure, additional capital requests and commissioning costs on the mill.

Mr. Muller: 'As time went by, costs escalated due to inflation. In fact contract escalation alone accounted for an additional £40,000 as SED's costs were indexed in accordance with the contract. About £110,000 of additional expenditure was sanctioned, including escalation on SED's and Lemont's bought out equipment, although not all of this was spent. Our management took a firm line over the projected expediture on AGC. They said in effect that we had used the additional money allocated for AGC in the stage one project and that further expenditure would be justified only on an incremental basis. AGC was not subsequently justified, rightly so, in my opinion.'

Early Progress

The progress review meetings started during the first quarter of 1969. Early discussions centred on aspects of engineering detail, particularly the final specifications required to meet the terms of the contract. The main drive speed controls were of particular concern. An outside contractor, Crick, was asked to provide and install this important equipment as a subcontractor to SED. Discussions with them started in July 1969.

Meanwhile the formal work programmes were agreed. The fundamental importance of the software to the overall success of the project necessitated separate software progress meetings. To establish users' operational requirements, SED circulated a questionnaire on system design. Disagreement over the control philosophy emerged, particularly over the degree of manual control that was required. SED persuaded Lemont that two VDU consoles were needed, not one as originally planned. One was to handle mill set-up details, the other was to handle batch production control inputs. The concept of the automatic mill was to remove operators from the floor of the mill and to locate them in an elevated 'pulpit' from which they could easily monitor and direct mill operations. The pulpit was similar to a railway signal box except that in place of levers and switches there would be visual displays (VDUs) and teletype terminals. There was a considerable discussion over the nature and quantity of the information to be displayed on these terminals. Ultimately a solution was reached, but not until March 1970.

Engineering and system design considerations were explored during the rest of 1969. Meanwhile the refurbishing of the mill had started. A minor setback was experienced in January 1970 because the characteristics of the mill drives required unanticipated use of mill time for testing.

By March 1970, Lemont was aware of potential delivery delays to items of hardware. It was important that the mill shutdown fortnight in August 1970 should be used to install all equipment that could not be installed under normal operations, or during weekends. Delivery delays could not be allowed to disrupt this part of the plan. In the event hardware installation was well managed. In spite of frequent but sometimes unpredictable deliveries necessitating on-the-spot decision making, installation proceeded on schedule. The computer hardware arrived late in March, as planned, and was installed in a specially constructed clean room by the end of April. Paul Muller commented:

'The potential early benefits of having the computer installed were not realized because the software was not ready. With the benefit of hindsight one can say that Lemont had an expensive computer sitting idle for the best part of two years. If we had opted for a two level hierarchy we could have phased in the computer installation. We could have commissioned those parts associated with mill setting and used the manual input facility to speed up existing setting times long before we had to use the algorithms which then required the more complex software and the main computing facilities.'

However in March 1970, SED was still confident that the project would continue on schedule. The installation of the computer meant that data-logging exercises began, as planned, at the start of June. These exercises were an important procedure prior to producing the final algorithms. A misunderstanding over who should first do the data-logging exercise led to a formal redefinition of task responsibilities.

The first unavoidable slippage from the project schedule was caused by late deliveries from Crick. Commissioning was scheduled back three months as a result. Also, some transducer cables were accidentally damaged, hindering the data logging exercise. Other equipment gave trouble during this period.

By now programming had become a major activity of the total system build up. Lemont completed the software for information transfer from disc to core store. They had also agreed to assist SED in producing an instruction manual to document the systems procedures, although this was, strictly, a task for the contractor. During this period Lemont lost several programming staff. Mr. Muller explained:

'Programmers were much in demand in 1969 and 1970. By 1970 several people had left, taking with them much of the accumulated background knowledge and experience. Continuity inevitably suffered. It began to seem as if we had to re-invent the wheel.'

SED apparently did not suffer in the same way and progress during the summer of 1970 appeared satisfactory. In September, Crick was on site to install the speed control equipment. Subsequently, delays in manufacturing spare parts caused Lemont to insist on the maintenance of mill output at the cost of further delaying completion of the installation.

September 1970–December 1971

Cold acceptance tests could not be started in September 1970, because of the delays already incurred. SED were concerned because delays put back stage payments. Software deficiencies were identified and the computer supplier was asked to help. Lemont were also unhappy at the rate of progress and stipulated a very tight work schedule for the remainder of the project. This led SED to criticize Lemont's own software progress. Further delays resulted from a failure of the air conditioning in the computer room and then from a crane accident in which signal cables to the computer were severed.

Further software delays during October were attributable to the VDUs. SED accepted responsibility but criticized Lemont for the lack of mill availability for cold testing. The original data exercise had yielded poor results which, SED argued, made it all the more important to gain access to the mill. The completion schedule was officially deferred by a further three months.

From November 1970 the main drive speed controllers functioned unreliably. Nevertheless the hardware cold testing continued and was largely completed by April 1971, including the troublesome speed controllers.

Software developments were less satisfactory. A system called the 'Small Executive Program', supplied by the computer manufacturer, but modified by SED, was constantly delayed up to August 1971. Meanwhile hot acceptance testing had been discussed in detail. Originally the specification called for twelve strips of steel to be produced under automatic control before each test could be considered successful. However Lemont agreed to reduce this to six to eight strips if results were within target tolerances. Some other concessions were also made. SED stressed the importance of first class mill maintenance to ensure test repeatability.

Mr. Muller commented: 'Lemont and SED were still working on linking modules for the total software package. A major problem was the interfacing of modules. We were both under considerable time pressures and Lemont was suffering from loss of personnel. Naturally the delays created a degree of friction between us in the formal contractual relationship.'

Much of the detailed work was intensely time consuming. For example, to begin operator involvement and training sessions, it was necessary to write instruction manuals for mill operating procedures. This type of activity suffered during periods of crisis in the software development.

System build up was not advanced enough to allow on-line testing before the shutdown fortnight during late July, 1971. The first runs were scheduled for 9th August, but VDU faults hindered progress. The computer supplier was called in and reported that the VDUs, which were a new design, would require extensive modification. When they were reinstalled in October they continued to malfunction. In addition there were several analogue failures in September. The costs of rectification of these failures (which were attributed to vibration) were shared.

By now everyone was working under extreme pressure. The remaining cold tests continued whenever possible. This was assisted by Lemont's decision to run the mill on a two shift basis for six weeks from October. No further progress was made that month. Then, quite catastrophically, a major software fault was uncovered. It was demonstrated that under certain conditions the computer core store was inadequate to handle SEDs combination of programs.

Mr. Martin explained: 'From the very early days we realized that core store might be a constraint. Lemont set us a limit, which we accepted at the time, of 16,000 words of store in order to economize on capital expenditure. Of these 16,000 words, 4,000 were allocated to the small systems organizer and VDU handling. 4,000 words were used for programs normally held on tape, leaving 8,000 words for 'core-resident' programs. 7,800 of these were always in use. When certain programs were run together the spare 200 words became inadequate to complete the system and overload resulted.'

A Lemont programmer commented: 'Since 1968 the cost of core store has reduced by a factor of four. Today we would not limit core store as we did then. However in fairness, in 1968 16,000 words represented a big computer. We had already achieved a fantastic amount with 12,000 words in a different installation, so with a large backing store and 16,000 words we were then confident of success.'

In any event economies had to be achieved in the use of core store. During October and November programmers worked seven days per week redesigning the total system structure. About 1,000 words were released by transferring library routines onto disc and a further 500 were made potentially available by identifying rearrangements of the program modules.

'Economies in hardware certainly resulted in software diseconomies,' suggested Mr. Martin. 'Not only that, but the revised programs were inevitably more sophisticated and difficult to understand. Therefore the system as a whole became more difficult to "service" and potentially less reliable.'

A disc failure on 29th October resulted in further lost time as there was a total loss of data from that file. Cold software testing was deferred to November 20th and in the event this was achieved only one week later. The first hot trial was successfully run on December 13th, 1971, although some software problems remained. Future tests were scheduled for January 1972, but the project still seemed a long way from completion.

The Conclusion of the Project 1972—74

The second hot trial took place on January 28th, 1972. Further core store problems had caused additional delayed events with system 'debugging' taking most of January. Of the three trials on January 28th, only one was successful. A third hot trial on January 31st had three successful runs out of five. Power cuts interrupted both sets of trials and there was disagreement over when to abort a trial. Lemont wanted to abort quickly so as to utilize the mill time thus saved, SED wanted as much test time as possible.

There was a successful trial on March 3rd and several 'qualified successes' later that month. In April an analysis of completed trials indicated that the use of incorrect grades of steel could have contributed to the failures. SED admitted that it was still learning by experience.

Mr. Martin: 'We found certain anomalies in our results. For example, under some conditions we found that rolling loads decreased as the temperature of the steel slabs was reduced, whereas we had predicted the reverse.'

This learning process created scepticism among the Lemont mill management and operators. 'In fact there were times when many Lemont mill people doubted that the computer system could function properly,' commented Mr. Muller, 'but fortunately we never lost the support of senior Lemont management.'

It seemed that mill management and operators underestimated the problems facing the project team. In consequence they were unsympathetic to the delays in implementing automatic control. SED hinted that the mill personnel did not make it easy to obtain adequate test time. Certainly no one denied that the mill personnel saw maintenance of output as their top priority.

Mr. Martin: 'The delays we experienced prevented us from obtaining as much operator involvement as we wanted because the operators remained unconvinced that the computer could do as good a job as they could. Every time we upgraded our rolling theory with actual results it seemed to the operators that we were merely copying their skills. Our prime objective was consistently to achieve results as good or better than best manual rolling practice. The emphasis was on consistency allied to rapid sequence changing.'

'Because the early tests were disappointing we lost the commitment of the operators. During later tests SED had to operate the mill virtually on its own. Certainly we did not achieve the progressive hand-over of the mill controls to the operators as we had planned. Even now I doubt if the mill personnel consider themselves the "experts" at running the system, even though they are now fully conversant with it.'—

Testing ran through the summer of 1972 until October when a breakthrough occurred. During a four week period in October and November more good slabs were rolled than the cumulative total up to that time. On 18th November more than 60 slabs were rolled automatically. The end of the project seemed in sight.

Contract testing was arranged for a three week period beginning 8th January, 1973. An input error resulting in a damaged roll stand and a hardware failure in the computer involving both the disc store and the VDU, prevented the tests from starting on schedule. SED was very frustrated and commented on the unavailability of suitable product during normal operating hours and last minute changes in the production schedule. The latter, it was claimed, made it difficult to update the computer quickly enough to permit automatic rolling. In March 1973 four hot tests were successful but an unfavourable order book prevented further contract tests. After a test failure on stainless steel in May, Lemont insisted that subsequent stainless steel tests be deferred so as to avoid unnecessary waste of expensive material. SED argued without success that stainless and high carbon steels were made to tighter specifications than cheaper steel and were therefore normally more predictable to roll. The stainless tests were deferred, increasing the testing period. In fact tests continued intermittently for over a year.

By March 1974 most of the contract tests had been attempted with a success rate of about 83%. If the contract was adhered to strictly, this was not acceptable. There were mitigating circumstances, however, and most of the 'failures' were marginal and therefore were saleable. After further extended runs it was finally agreed that the contractors had fulfilled their obligations as realistically as was possible and the project team was wound up. It was undoubtedly a relief for both parties to conclude the project, but SED remained in contact with Lemont during 1974 and gave further advice periodically. The final contract payment was made in January 1975.

The Lessons of the Lemont Project

Mr. Muller: 'Although we calculated the benefits in 1968 which gave the required rate of return, we recognize now that it is difficult to quantify the precise benefits of automation because we have no way of knowing how we would cope with our present situation if the mill was still entirely manual. Also about half of the total project cost was for refurbishing mill hardware. This would have produced benefits even without the computer.'

A mill shift manager commented: 'Today our order book contains a large number of 5-ton orders whereas five years ago 50 tons was typical. Computerization has made it economic to handle small batches because we can maintain mill productivity by eliminating delays between orders. I would say that mill management is very satisfied with the new system's capability.'

A major feature of the project was its duration. Mr. Muller stated: 'We consider that although the delays were regrettable, the lack of interruption of mill production was a major achievement. Obviously if we repeated the project now, with the benefit of experience we could probably avoid many of the problems we encountered, particularly in respect to the division of responsibility for software.'

Mr. Martin: 'With all due respect, I think we should recognize that the highest level of management in Lemont underestimated the cost implications of the project. In a number of instances SED reluctantly agreed to use less expensive hardware than we would have wished, for example, the computer itself proved too small and the VDUs were of a new and much cheaper type. They were also unproven in prior use. The cost reductions on hardware were subsequently swamped by the excess software development costs.'

Mr. Muller: 'We must also remember that the SED algorithms required considerable updating as time went by, although the programming itself was unquestionably the major problem. Not only did the programmers consistently underestimate the time they required to complete assignments, but they also had difficulty in interlinking the various modules in building up the system. Progressing and managing software development was a constant problem. We have learnt useful lessons for the future from this project. Certainly it should be possible to estimate a project's requirements in terms of man years, but I admit that begs the question of which men. Our turnover of programming staff did not assist our progress. Three men left us in 1970. We also used a machine code level of programming. Today we would use a high level language.'

'Today, it is unlikely that we would specify a single large computer,' said Mr. Martin. 'We would go for a hierarchy of small computers, one to handle the mill settings and one for the message handling. We would not fall into the trap of letting core store constrain us. From an engineering standpoint we would require more flexibility. That means less sophistication in the style of the software, perhaps at the expense of extra modules. Too much sophisticated software is difficult to service, and if an engineer cannot readily comprehend it, on-line trouble-shooting is difficult.'

Mr. Martin' 'At the time SED was very keen to obtain the reference implicit in handling a project of this nature. Today, of course, we have the experience and the skills. Then we were prepared to agree with Lemont to pare costs thereby reaching mutual objectives. Now I hope we would be strong enough to persuade a client against unadvisable cost reductions. For example the VDUs are a critical factor in the performance of this kind of system. They are the main interface between programmer, engineer and operator. To economize here is asking for trouble.

'The contract specifications were tied down vey much in Lemont's favour. I feel that more informal terms might have worked better. A contractor who is bound by a written agreement naturally avoids doing more than is necessary. Personally I would have preferred a "gentleman's agreement" over performance testing and I believe the results would have been achieved much faster.

'We at SED certainly grew frustrated at the protraction of the testing time on the mill. We suspected that Lemont never had complete confidence in us even though we became steeped in the mill operation. The mill management would not always accept our statements. Working so closely with the operators meant that sometimes they would give us ideas for improvements. Some of these, though potentially worthwhile, we rejected as being outside the terms of our contract. We had to monitor our work carefully to avoid costing Lemont extra money.'

Mr. Muller: 'In the planning phase we constructed a comprehensive PERT network. Unfortunately it did not take account of the competitive demands for time on Lemont personnel through their functional organization. We tried to budget for the cost of lost production during commissioning, but this was difficult because we did not know what the order book would be like at this stage of the project.'

Current Mill Practice

Figure 1 is a diagram of the mill layout. Mr. Martin commented: 'I think we all recognized from the start that both the mill layout and the operators' attitudes to working in a modified existing mill would not be the same as if we had been able to design a completely new mill. Indeed a number of modifications to the control

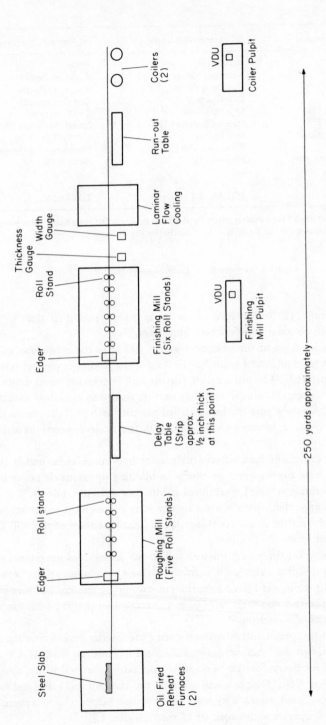

Figure 1 (Lemont B)   Schematic elevation of the strip mill

Steel Slab

Oil Fired Reheat Furnaces (2)

Edger

Roll stand

Roughing Mill (Five Roll Stands)

Delay Table (Strip approx. ½ inch thick at this point)

Edger

Thickness Gauge   Width Gauge

Roll Stand

Finishing Mill (Six Roll Stands)

VDU

Finishing Mill Pulpit

Laminar Flow Cooling

Run-out Table

Coilers (2)

VDU

Coiler Pulpit

250 yards approximately

(a) Prior to Conversion	(b) Interim Structure	(c) Present Structure
Roller	Roller	Roller
Assistant Roller	Assistant Roller	Assistant Roller
Roughing Roller	Roughing Roller	Roughing Roller
Coil Gaugers (2)	Coil Gaugers (2)	Coil Gaugers (2)
Coiler Operators (2)	Coil Operator	Coil Operator
Speed Operators (3)	Speed Operators (2)	Speed Operators (2)
Flying Shear Operator	Mill Feeder	Mill Feeder
Mill Feeder	Roughing Mill Operator	Roughing Mill Operator
Roughing Mill Operator	Helpers (4)	Helpers (5)
Helpers (4)		
TOTAL: 17	TOTAL: 14	TOTAL: 15

Note: Meal breaks were taken during shifts by the crew covering for the absent men. Breaks were therefore staggered throughout the shift. Normally the mill ran continuously throughout the shift.

Figure 2 (Lemont B)   Lemont mill operators

layout, for example, the coiler desks, were made after a period of time in use. Industrial relations considerations are very important.'

Figure 2 provides a list of the operators before and after the conversion of the mill to automatic control, and Figure 3 an outline of the computer control system. Mr. Muller commented: 'The justification for the mill conversion never depended on major labour savings. We expected that two or three less operators would be required but that was not part of the identified benefits. Indeed if the justification had hinged on reduced labour costs, I doubt if the project would have been sanctioned.

'A greenfield site might have offered us greater opportunities, although there would probably have been greater problems in building up to maximum output. Naturally the operators retained established habits. For example, I doubt if any of them would exchange their overalls for a lounge suit, although the environment in the pulpit should be that clean. As things are it is an extension of the mill shop floor, not an office area.

'Prior to automation there were thirteen skilled and semi-skilled operators in the mill plus four non-skilled helpers on each shift. During the negotiations between management and men it was agreed that the crew would be reduced by three men. The remaining operators had their rates of pay increased so that the total earnings of the crew was virtually unchanged.

'We continued to operate in this manner during the interim period after the mill had been refurbished but before automatic control came on line. When that happened it was necessary for the most senior operator, the mill roller, to take charge of the set-up VDU. His place was taken by the assistant mill roller and so on right down the line. That meant they were short of one helper who was therefore reinstated. We now operate with a total of 15 men. (Figure 2,)

'At the beginning of each shift the management must decide whether the mill is

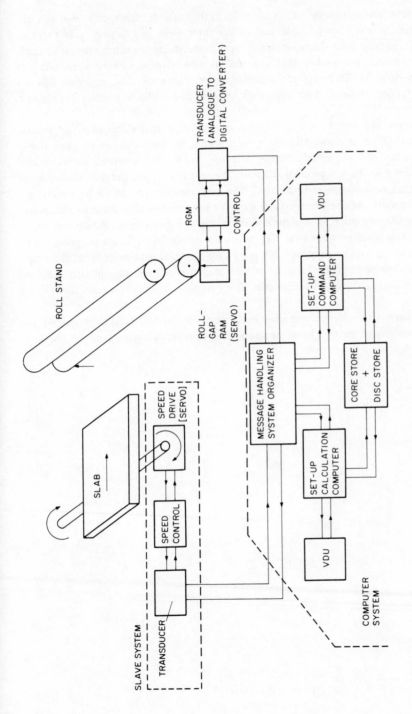

Figure 3 (Lemont B)   Schematic of the computer control system

to operate automatically or under manual control. Obviously we operate automatically whenever possible, but in our three week production cycle I reckon there are usually four shifts on which special products requiring manual control, must be rolled. Remember that the mill is now around twenty years old and operates close to the limits of its performance. There are some products which I believe cannot be handled by computer because of the risk of overloading the mill stands.

'However, the men have decided that every shift must be designated automatic or manual. If it is automatic then each man steps up to the next level of job responsibility and is paid the higher rate for that job. If, however, the computer breaks down we have a problem. Lemont has elected to pay the men at the higher rate for the next complete hour only. The men have insisted on the higher rate for the whole shift. At the present time we have not reached agreement on this point.

'Using the computer is straightforward when you know how. We do not get all the information that we would like, but we can ask for different programs to be installed for particular purposes. We get an up-to-the-minute printout of the actual and predicted settings of the mill for each slab. We can compare predicted rolling loads with actual loads, for example. The computer is usually within one or two percent.

'I believe that the project has been very successful. It should extend the operational life of the mill in an internationally competitive situation.'

The Midwich Hospital Outpatients Department

The successful application of medical knowledge depends on what patients think, and feel, about doctors, nurses and hospitals. A patient's decision to become one, his willingness to be examined, his acceptance of treatment, depend on his confidence in the skill and humanity of doctors and nurses and on his feelings about the institution where he may be treated.

In recent years there has been a growing opinion within the hospital service that more attention should be paid to the views of the patient. A Ministry of Health report of 1963 refers to the 'need for more "Customer" research, and the importance of paying increasing attention to the patients' point of view',

This case study describes an attempt to provide data on the level of service given in the outpatients department of a general hospital.

The Midwich Hospital

The Midwich Hospital is situated at the periphery of one of the Metropolitan Regional Hospital Board areas. It is located in a town of about 80,000 population and serves a large rural area with a total population of approximately 215,000. The hospital is split into two wings located at opposite ends of the town and provides approximately 700 beds. Development was taking place to increase the number of beds to 850.

Outpatients Service

In 1970 a total of 48 million attendances were made at outpatients departments in England and Wales. Of this total 15.8 million were 'new' patients. The term new is used to indicate the first of perhaps several attendances at a particular clinic for a course of treatment. If a patient attends more than one clinic during the year or the same clinic for two unrelated ailments they would be recorded as new patients on each occasion.

A patient normally attends an outpatient clinic when his G.P. refers the case to the hospital for specialist opinion, or investigation or treatment which is not within the resources of the G.P. On receipt of the G.P.s 'referral letter' the hospital makes an appointment for the patient to be seen by the appropriate consultant. There may be a delay of several weeks before non-urgent cases can be offered an appointment. As a result of the consultant's examination the patient may be admitted to hospital for treatment or further investigation, begin a course of treatment as an outpatient, or be referred back to his G.P. for treatment.

No objective standard exists to guide the G.P. in his referral of a patient to a hospital outpatient department. Consequently there is a wide variation in the number and seriousness of cases referred by G.P.s. Some G.P.s may refer only a dozen or so cases a year whilst others may refer as many as 25 per week. Practices can obviously vary in terms of patient numbers, age and general health. Also the ability of G.P.s is not standard. However, the wide variation of numbers referred suggests that other factors contribute to the level of variation. The view has been expressed that patients tend to place more pressure upon the G.P. for referral to hospital. This trend may be associated with the impression given by newspapers and television programmes that the quality of medical care is related to advanced technology rather than the relationship between doctor and patient. It is also considered that some G.P.s simply pass on their work to the hospital thus enabling them to handle more easily their case load.

Resistance by consultants to unnecessary referrals may well be limited since consultants normally depend for their private patients on the recommendations of G.P.s. Hence the consultants are anxious to maintain goodwill with the G.P.s.

The Midwich outpatients department was situated in the west wing of the hospital. In 1971 there were 64,500 outpatient attendances of which 18,800 were 'new' patients. All told 3,100 clinic sessions were operated in 19 specialities. Over the five year period 1966–1971 outpatient attendances had increased by 29 per cent. The population in the catchment area had only increased by 10 per cent during the same period.

The Outpatient Department Study

In the summer of 1972 the Midwich hospital decided to study outpatient's views on the level of service they felt they received.

Very little guidance exists on the subject of adequate outpatient service. The Department of Health has suggested that 'Outpatient procedures should be designed to cause the patients the minimum of waiting, inconvenience and embarrassment'. Waiting has received greatest study both by hospital authorities and independent researchers. As long ago as 1958 the Ministry of Health suggested that 75 per cent of patients should be seen by a doctor within 30 minutes of their appointment time and no more than 3 per cent of patients should have to wait for more than one hour.

To study aspects of service other than waiting time it was decided to construct a simple questionnaire which would be completed by a selection of outpatient users.

Questionnaire Design

Initially the researcher undertook a series of informal interviews with a small sample of patients. This was done to gain some indication of the aspects of service which they considered to be of importance. Difficulties were encountered in carrying out the preliminary interviews. To determine a patient's attitude to service it was obviously necessary to wait until service had been received. However, when patients had completed their visit to the hospital many were anxious to catch buses or ambulances and were reluctant to delay their homeward journey to be interviewed. Also there was a tendency to be preoccupied and anxious about their medical condition. Inviting objective comment at such a time was rather similar to asking someone to criticize the fire brigade when their house was on fire.

As a result of the preliminary interviews and discussions with hospital staff the questionnaire shown in Figure 1 was designed.

Application of the Questionnaire

The questionnaire together with a letter and a prepaid reply envelope (see Figure 1) was issued to all patients who were prepared to take one during a two week period in August 1972.

An overall response rate of 27.5 per cent was obtained. The response rate for 'new' patients was significantly lower at 20.6 per cent than for the 'old' patients at 30.7 per cent.

Results of the Questionnaire

The appendix summarizes the result of the questionnaire.

Survey of Waiting Time

Various methods were considered for recording the timing of outpatient arrivals and movements through the hospital. Eventually practicality and economics dictated that nurses and receptionists should be used to record arrival and departure times of outpatients in the various clinics.

During the two week period when the questionnaire was administered, each clinic was provided with an additional copy of the appointments list and the times of arrival, consultation and departure for each patient were recorded. Also recorded during the period was the starting time of each of the clinics. Figures 2 to 8 provide the results from this part of the survey.

MIDWICH GENERAL HOSPITAL
Out-patients Department

QUESTIONNAIRE

1. About how long did your journey
   to the hospital take?
   (please tick)

less than ¼ hour	between ¼ and ¾ hour	more than ¾ hour

2. Did you have any difficulty in finding
   your way to the departments you had
   to attend?
   (please tick)

Yes		No

3. Do you think the amenities at Out-patients are good or poor?
   Please tick for each of the following:

	Poor	Fair	Good	Very good	Don't know
a) Comfort of waiting rooms					
b) Magazines in waiting rooms					
c) Toilets					
d) Refreshment bar					
e) Direction signs					
f) Public telephones					
g) Changing cubicles					
h) Ambulance service					

4. Are there any additional facilities, that you think should be provided. If so, please enter
   your suggestions here:

   _____
   _____
   _____
   _____

5. What do you think is a reasonable time to wait, from the time of your appointment, until
   you are seen by the doctor?

   Please enter here . . . .

6. What was the attitude of hospital
   staff towards you?
   (please tick)

Very considerate	Fairly considerate	Not very considerate

Figure 1 (Midwich Hospital)   Out-patients questionnaire

7. What is your sex?   Man [   ]   Woman [   ]

8. What is your age group?
   (please tick)

Under 20	20–40	41–64	65 or over

If there are any other comments or suggestions you would like to make about the service provided at Outpatients we shall be pleased to have them. Please use the space below:

_____

_____

_____

_____

_____

Thank you for your help. Your answers will be a great help to us in our efforts to provide an efficient and considerate service. May we ask you to post your replies back to us as soon as you can. Thank you.

LETTER

August, 1972.

Dear Outpatient,

    We would be very grateful for your help.

    We are trying to find out what you, and other patients think about the service provided at the Outpatients Department. We want to know what you think is good about the service, and what you think could be improved.

    May we therefore ask you to complete the enclosed questionnaire, and post it to us in the reply-paid envelope provided.

    Your answers, together with those of other patients, will help the hospital to improve its service, so please complete the questionnaire as fully and frankly as you can.

    You will find space on the form for any additional comments or suggestions you might like to make. We look forward to hearing your comments, but there is no need to sign your name, because all answers will be considered anonymously.

    It is important that we should have answers from everyone, so please send us the form even if you have few, or no additional comments to make.

    Once again, we would like to say how grateful we shall be for your help.

Yours sincerely,

A. N. Other
Survey Organizer.

Figure 1 (Midwich Hospital) *(continued)*

Conclusions from the Survey

In presenting his report to the hospital the researcher drew the following conclusions:

(1)   WAITING TIME. Waiting time at Midwich compares favourably with that at other hospitals, as the figures below show.

Waiting (Minutes)	Up to 30	31–60	More than 60	Mean
Midwich	83.7%	13.5%	3.8%	19 mins.
Nuffield Survey of 60 hospitals, 1964	66.2%	22.9%	11.5%	25 mins.
'What' Survey of 6 hospitals, 1970	61.0%	30.0%	9.0%	22 mins
Recommended Standards	75.0%	20.0%	3–5%	–

However, the number of people waiting more than an hour is above the 3% figure originally suggested by the Ministry of Health as reasonable.

It should also be remembered that the waiting times referred to are from the time of appointment, and not from the time of patients' arrival at the Outpatients Department (O.P.D.). 13% of ambulance patients arrive more than 30 minutes early, and thus face considerable additional waiting over which they have no control.

The primary causes of waiting are considered to be:

(a) Delay in starting clinics.
(b) Booking patients at a somewhat greater rate than that at which they are seen by the doctor. By comparison, lateness and non-arrival of patients has only a minor effect on waiting time.

Recommendations

(a) Greater effort be made to start clinics on time. If a clinic starts late, the delay tends to be perpetuated throughout the course of the clinic, increasing the waiting time of most patients as a result.

   If doctors arrive consistently late, for whatever cause, there seems to be no reason why appointments should not begin correspondingly later.

(b) Patients should be booked to within about 15 minutes of the time at which the clinic usually finishes; *not* to the time which appointments are *traditionally* closed.

   Consultation time, during the survey, averaged 15 minutes, whereas the last patient left the clinic on average, 35 minutes after the appointed time.

(c) In those clinics where appointment intervals are still 30 minutes, consideration should be given to reducing this interval to 15 minutes. This will reduce the number of patients who are given the same appointment time, and wait unnecessarily as a result.

(d) Special attention should be given to the booking of appointments for ambulance patients in an attempt to improve punctuality and reduce waiting time.

The recommendations made above will have negligible effect on the amount of time a consultant is without a patient. Indeed, by booking patients at a rate which corresponds to the doctor's mean consultation time, as suggested, a very considerable premium is placed upon the value of the doctor's time, compared with that of the patient.

One final discerning comment upon waiting was made by a patient during the survey, when she pointed out that if waiting time was reduced, the provision of waiting room amenities such as magazines, refreshments etc. would be largely unneccessary and that the size of the waiting rooms themselves could be considerably reduced.

(2) WAITING FOR AN APPOINTMENT. Little mention has been made so far, of this aspect of service, mainly because the hospital is aware of the problems in this area. Data on the delay between receipt of a doctor's referal letter and the patients first non-urgent appointment, is recorded in the Hospital quarterly returns.

In only 6 out of 18 clinic specialities included in the Hospital's quarterly return dated 30th June, 1972 were appointments being given within two weeks; beyond which, the Department of Health suggests, it is undesirable to wait. Delays of 6 weeks or more were quoted with respect to five specialities in the June 1972 returns. These delays are not untypical of those quoted throughout the period 1969–1972, and although improvements have been made in some areas, no significant overall improvement is apparent.

Recommendations

Whilst primarily a problem of available material and human resources, it is perhaps possible that some improvement could be achieved by closer liaison between hospital and general practitioner with regard to the type of case referred, and by the hospital returning patients to the care of their G.P.s as soon as possible after diagnosis and commencement of treatment.

(3) ANTI-COAGULANT AND DIABETIC CLINICS. It is considered that the appointment system used in these clinics is an appointment system in name only. Patients are given appointment times which are quite meaningless, since they are usually seen in arrival order regardless of the time of their appointment.

Appointments begin at 9.0 a.m. although patients are seldom seen by the doctor until 10.0 a.m., after blood/sugar tests have been made. A delay of one hour between test and consultation, activities of only a few minutes duration each, is considered unnecessary. The first batch of test results can be made available by the Pathology Department within 15–20 minutes.

Recommendations

(a) Open appointments be instituted whereby patients attend at any time between say, 9.0 a.m. and 11.30 a.m. on a stated morning.

(b) A numbered disc, or similar system, be used to call patients in arrival order.

(c) Consideration be given to advising patients by post of any change in treatment, which blood/sugar test shows to be necessary, and calling only those patients for consultation whom the doctor considers it necessary to see in person.

(4) AMBULANCE SERVICE

Recommendations

(a) That a new attempt be made to establish better coordination between Hospital and Ambulance Service requirements with regard to patient appointment times.

(b) That implementation of the above recommendation be made the specific responsibility of a member of the hospital staff.

(c) That a further survey of ambulance patient punctuality, and time spent waiting for transport home, be made in, say, 6 months time to evaluate any improvements made, preferably against a pre-agreed target for improvement.

(5) HOSPITAL AMENITIES. As the results of the patient questionnaire show, with certain exceptions, patients are happy with the amenities provided, and in comparison with other hospitals, Midwich General appears in a generally favourable light.

Considerable variation does exist, however, in the standard of provision in different waiting areas, and some consideration might be given to bringing the standard up to a common level in all areas.

Of considerable urgency is the need for better provision for the accommodation of waiting children. Ideally, a creche or similar accommodation should be provided, and some priority should be given to the allocation of funds for this purpose.

Recommendations (a) and (b) below are short-term suggestions aimed at relieving, to a limited extent only, problems which require considerable financial outlay for their proper solution.

Recommendations

(a) Mobile high chairs be provided for young children, similar to those available in the Midwich Public Library. These would relieve mothers of the burden of carrying small children, both in waiting areas and consultation rooms, and reduce inconvenience caused to other patients by small children.

(b) O.P.D. and Accident Department staff be requested to park in the main car park. This would increase the space available for patients in the car park adjacent to the Accident Department.

(c) Two additional telephones be provided, one on the first floor of O.P.D., and the other on the ground floor near the main reception desk.

(d) Assistance of voluntary bodies be sought in providing additional reading material. It is thought that a ready supply of magazines is available if the hospital makes its requirements in this respect known to such organizations as W.V.S., etc. In this way improvements could be achieved at no cost to the hospital.

(e) Some provision be made for refreshments on the first floor of O.P.D., preferably by means of a trolley service, which would also be helpful to less mobile patients in ground floor clinics.

(6) COMMUNICATION BETWEEN PATIENT AND HOSPITAL. It is felt that some improvement could be made in this area which would reduce patient anxiety and, at the same time, reduce pressure on hospital staff.

Recommendations

(a) A simple brochure be produced and sent to each new patient when an appointment is given. The brochure should serve as an introduction for the patient, to the hospital, its layout and procedures. It should include a plan of the hospital on which entrances and departments are clearly shown, together with locations of telephones, toilets and refreshment facilities.

In addition, the appointment system should be described together with the procedure to be followed by patients in making subsequent appointments.

The fact that some waiting may be involved, and that several doctors may see the patient, should be explained and reasons given. Consideration should be given to producing the brochure in a variety of languages or, alternatively, in a single multi-lingual form.

(b) New direction signs be provided, both inside the hospital and in the approach roads, of uniform style, and properly sited. The external signs should be illuminated at night. It is recommended that outside advice be sought on the design and sighting of these signs.

Application of Survey Results

A number of suggestions for improving service, in the light of the survey results, have been made above.

However, the value of the survey lies not so much in what it reveals of present needs, useful though this might be. More importantly, perhaps, the results can be used as a bench mark against which standards of service can be compared in the future.

In business, a single set of accounts provide no great insight into a firm's progress. It is only when several successive sets of accounts are examined together that trends become apparent, progress can be assessed, and if necessary corrective action can be taken to ensure that desired objectives are attained.

It is suggested that a similar approach could be adopted with respect to outpatient service and that surveys of this kind, though not necessarily as extensive, might be carried out annually. In this way progress towards agreed objectives in terms of service could be assessed on a continuing basis.

A futher reference to the business environment may also be appropriate here. Few successful companies simply respond to their customers' demands — they anticipate them!

Similarly in the hospital service, a progressive and imaginative management team will not be content merely to keep up with patients' ideas of service but will aim for standards in advance of those considered satisfactory by contemporary opinion.

APPENDIX

Response to Patient Questionnaire

Survey period 15th–29th August, 1972.

No. of questionnaires distributed to 'new' patients	360
No. of questionnaires distributed to 'old' patients	800
Total questionnaires distributed	1,160
No. of questionnaires returned by 'new' patients	74
No. of questionnaires returned by 'old' patients	245
Total questionnaires returned	319
Response rate, 'new' patients	20.6%
Response rate, 'old' patients	30.7%
Response rate, overall	27.5%

Results of Patient Questionnaire

Question 1

About how long did your journey to the hospital take?

Less than ¼ hour	84	(27%)
Between ¼ and ¾ hour	193	(61.5%)
More than ¾ hour	36	(11.5%)
Total responses	313	

Question 2

Did you have any difficulty finding your way to the departments you had to visit?

Yes	16	(5.2%)
No	293	(91.5%)
Total responses	309	

Question 3

Do you think the amenities at Outpatients are good or poor?

(a)	Comfort of waiting rooms:	Poor	2	(0.6%)
		Fair	42	(13.5%)
		Good	164	(51.8%)
		Very good	108	(34.1%)
		responses	316	
(b)	Magazines in waiting rooms:	Poor	51	(18.2%)
		Fair	99	(35%)
		Good	98	(35%)
		Very good	33	(11.6%)
		responses	281	
(c)	Toilets:	Poor	3	(1.1%)
		Fair	19	(7.2%)
		Good	130	(49.2%)
		Very good	111	(42.5%)
		responses	263	

(d)	Refreshment bar:	Poor	7	(2.7%)
		Fair	32	(12.4%)
		Good	122	(47.5%)
		Very good	97	(37.4%)
		responses	258	

(e)	Direction signs:	Poor	15	(5%)
		Fair	31	(10%)
		Good	162	(54%)
		Very good	91	(31%)
		responses	289	

(f)	Public telephones:	Poor	29	(15.6%)
		Fair	45	(24%)
		Good	76	(41%)
		Very good	36	(19.4%)
		responses	186	

(g)	Changing cubicles:	Poor	12	(5.3%)
		Fair	56	(24.5%)
		Good	105	(45.6%)
		Very good	57	(24.6%)
		responses	230	

(h)	Ambulance service:	Poor	10	(7.2%)
		Fair	17	(12%)
		Good	50	(35.4%)
		Very good	64	(45.4%)
		responses	141	

Question 4

Are there any additional facilities that you think should be provided?

Patients' Comments and Suggestions   178 (56%) of respondents made suggestions and/or comments on service. The following aspects of service accounted for most frequent criticism, and/or requests for improvement.

Criticisms		*No. of references*
(1)	Excessive waiting time (inc. waiting for ambulance − 7 references)	31
(2)	Lack of provision for children	30
(3)	Inadequate parking space	13
(4)	Reading material	11
(5)	Direction signs	8
(6)	Refreshments	7
(7)	Decoration/general appearance	7

Favourable comments by patients		*No. of references*
(1)	On hospital staff	52
(2)	O.P.D. service/facilities	20
(3)	Comparison with other hospitals	8
(4)	Ambulance staff	5
(5)	Waiting time	3
(6)	Refreshment bar	1

Question 5

What do you think is a reasonable time to wait, from the time of your appointment, until you are seen by the doctor?

Up to 15 mins.	109	(36.4%)
16 to 30 mins.	153	(51%)
31 to 60 mins.	35	(11%)
more than 60 mins.	3	(1%)
responses	300	

Range of waiting time considered to be reasonable was from zero (woman, aged 41–64) to 2 hours (man, over 65).

Question 6

What was the attitude of hospital staff towards you?

Very considerate	278	(90%)
Fairly considerate	26	(8.5%)
Not very considerate	4	(1.5%)
responses	308	

Question 7

What is your sex?

Man	130
Woman	187
responses	317

(two respondents did not state sex)

Question 8

What is your age group?

Under 20	14
20–40	98
41–64	129
65 or over	78
responses	319

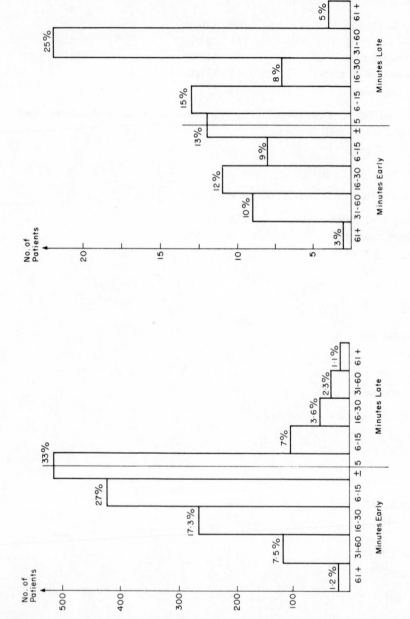

Figure 3 (Midwich Hospital) Punctuality of ambulance patients

Figure 2 (Midwich Hospital) Punctuality of patients

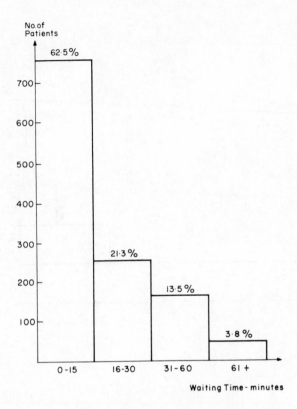

Figure 4 (Midwich Hospital)   Patient waiting time from time of appointment until seen by doctor

Clinic	No. of sessions	No. of patients	% seen within 30 mins	% waiting more than 1 hour
General Medical	11	79	80	6.3
Traumatic and Orthopaedic	18	247	72	6.5
Oral surgery and orthodontic	5	33	91	0
Geriatric	4	20	70	15
Rheumatology and Physical Medicine	2	32	97	0
Radio therapy	2	45	93	0
E.N.T.	8	76	65	1.3
General surgery	17	388	91	3.4
Paediatric	8	57	67	7
Opthalmology	4	100	96	0
Neurology	.2	23	78	0
Dermatology	6	106	68	3.8
Plastic surgery	2	14	100	0

Figure 5 (Midwich Hospital)   Waiting time in various clinics

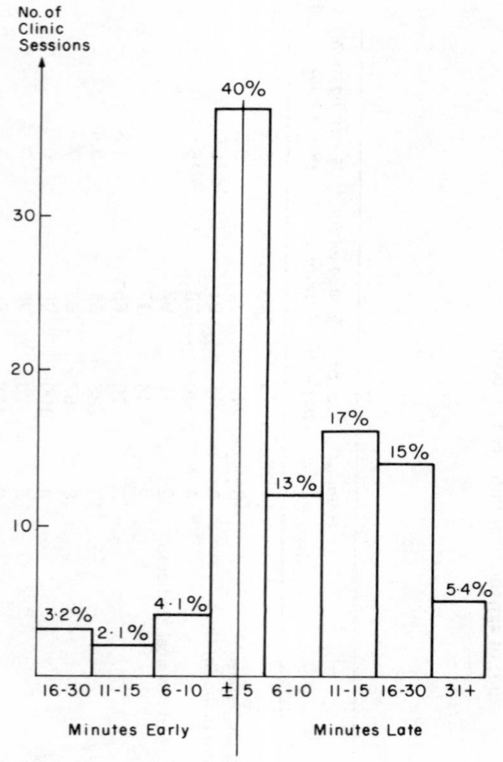

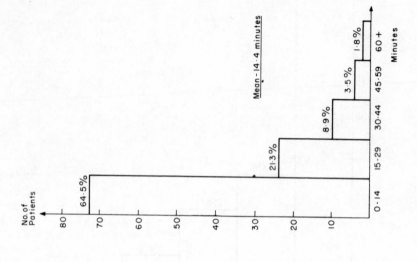

Figure 7 (Midwich Hospital)   Consultation times

Figure 6 (Midwich Hospital)   Clinic starting times

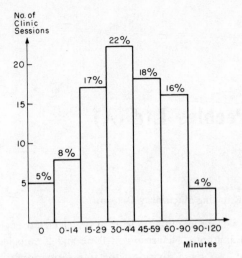

Figure 8 (Midwich Hospital)   Time between
last appointment time and last patient leaving
clinic

Parsons Peebles Ltd (A)

Parsons Peebles — Rotating Machinery Division

Parsons Peebles is a large manufacturer of heavy electrical engineering equipment with factories at Edinburgh, Newcastle-on-Tyne and Birmingham. The Edinburgh Factory consists of two main divisions: the transformer division and the rotating machinery division. The manufacture of transformers has many of the characteristics of flow line production, and, although dealing with large items, the control problems in the transformer division and relatively straightforward in principle and the two divisions are quite separate. The rotating machinery division, however, manufactures in relatively small batches producing electric motors and machines for individual customer requirements. It has a turnover of approximately £3 million annually and an establishment of about 600 staff.

Most orders come from past customers although the customers are not necessarily ordering the same product. The customers include consultants acting for companies, equipment manufacturers, and exporters. There are about 250 customers in total with 30 key accounts. The electric motors and machines produced by Parsons Peebles may be destined for a pump with flame proofing for the oil industry, for ventilation equipment, for installation in a rolling mill, or for stand-by power supplies.

The major competitors of the company are GEC in the UK who manufacture rotating machinery more on a production line standard product basis, and Siemens (Germany) and ASEA (Sweden). Parsons Peebles focus on custom built features and operate on a make to order basis. Only one customer, the National Coal Board, sometimes place a contract for a fixed series of orders. The company considers that they lead the field in price setting and that other competitors have usually followed the pattern Parsons Peebles set. Prices are raised by about 15% every several years.

The total demand pattern tends to follow the business cycle although the Edinburgh order book does not seem to have fallen off too badly in recent recessions. The sales staff expressed some doubt about the best method for managing demand levels. Traditionally, as an order book builds up, longer delivery times are quoted and extra overtime is introduced raising prices only later on in the boom. But the alternative policy of raising prices to manage demand levels might offer a better alternative to keep delivery and capacity under control.

The electrical products are divided into three classes dependent on their kilowatt and speed range. The standards for delivery together with the price range and the maximum and minimum monthly sales values are shown below:

Class	Size	Delivery Time	Price Range	Monthly Sales Value 1968 (£'s) Min	Max
1	Small	16 to 20 weeks	£1,000–£6,000	15,000	100,000
2	Medium	26 to 35 weeks	£3,000–£10,000	65,000	240,000
3	Large	25 to 45 weeks	£10,000 and above		

(Class 3 motors were planned to be transferred to Birmingham towards the end of 1969.)

The delivery time is a critical factor in the market. Orders increased significantly in April 1967 when there was no backlog and all deliveries were being met on time. Sales staff also judge that prices could be increased if the delivery time could be reduced. Frequently a penalty of 0.5% per week on price is imposed for late deliveries and a bonus can be obtained for early delivery. This can make significant inroads into the targeted 20% net profit on orders.

Management Structure and Facilities

The management structure of the Rotating Machinery Division is shown in Figure 1.

Of the total of 600 staff employed in the division, about 450 are direct production staff. The Electrical Trades Union and Amalgamated Engineering Union are represented in the works. Labour relations have generally been good. Within the last year there have been two one-day stoppages in connection with national strikes on Government Industrial Relations Policy. A strike of one day also occurred as a protest against the bonus system. The absence of labour relations problems may be partly attributable to the lack of alternative employment in the Edinburgh area for the same types of skills as are needed in Parsons Peebles.

The division is split up into nine major sections, each of which contains its own producing and testing facilities. The sections correspond to the various stages involved in the manufacture of motors and generators. They are indicated in the layout of Figure 2.

For costing purposes the sections are divided into 11 cost centres broadly corresponding to the major processing stages. These are listed in Figure 3, together with the labour hours worked per week. Parsons Peebles reckon to achieve about a 75% actual utilization of labour on production work. All sections work a 40 hour basic week, together with, in alternate weeks, two three-hour evenings, and eight hours on Sundays, giving 46/48 hour alternative regular weeks as a standard pattern in April 1968. Operators are paid a weekly wage, earnings varying from £20 to £30 dependent on skill. Direct overheads are allocated to the cost centres at 40% to 70% of labour costs.

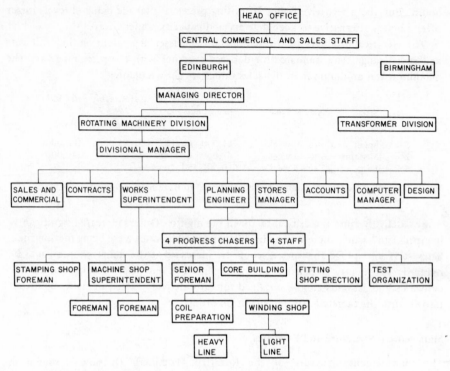

Figure 1 (Parsons Peebles Ltd. A)   Organizational structure in early 1968

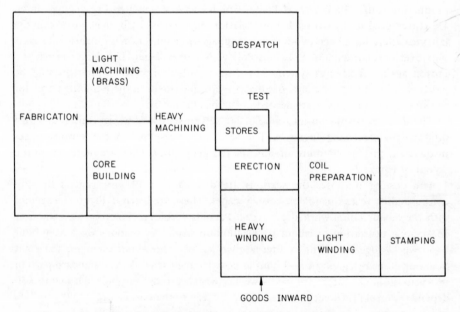

Figure 2 (Parsons Peebles Ltd. A)   Factory layout

Cost Centre Number	Processing Functions	Hours per Week
202	Machining Frames	3,650
203	Stamping	966
204	Core Building	1,150
206	Coil Preparation	3,000
269	Light Winding	1,200
209	Heavy Winding	2,100
211	Erection	1,650
213	Brass (light machinery)	900
503	Fabrication, tank making	500
504	Fabrication, preparation	450
508	Fabrication, general	1,800

Figure 3 (Parsons Peebles Ltd. A)   Departmental capacities *max*

The capacity figures may be altered from time to time by moving selected operators from one department to a neighbouring department within their skill limitations. Supervisors and foremen plan these manipulations as appropriate when the workload is out of balance in the different sections.

Orders Planning System

Between 15 and 20 orders are received each week although this figure had fallen to 13 by the end of 1968. When an incoming order has been agreed between the commercial staff and the customer, the design and planning engineers prepare documentation for manufacture. This is the first of three stages in the production of an order:

(1) Preparation of drawings and specification.
(2) Procurement of outside parts and materials.
(3) Manufacture.

The first stage takes from one week on a repeat product to twelve weeks on a new product and is a full time task of 40 design office staff. For each order an 'R Shop Specification' is prepared which shows all the parts required to be purchased, stocked and to be manufactured. There are approximately 300 different component types in the manufacture of a single motor. One sheet of a typical specification is shown in Figure 4.

About 90% of these parts will be standard designs and well known for an order, with the other 10% requiring special design office work. Besides giving the description of all the items required for the manufacture of the product, the Shop Specification shows in the last two columns the Stores Classification and the number of operations for items to be manufactured. The planning engineer enters the date of requirement of materials on requisitions for outside purchased material and these are obtained by the buyer within the stores organization. Excepting some very specialized parts the materials can usually be obtained within 4 to 6 weeks. Many of

R. SHOP SPECIFICATION

PARSONS PEEBLES LTD.,

ORDINARY MATERIAL TO BE ORDERED BY **400** MAIN & SPECIAL MATERIAL REQUIRED BY **460** SPECIAL MATERIAL TO BE ORDERED BY **370** WRITTEN BY

DELIVERY DATE **26-1-71** DATE OF ISSUE **16-10-70** WINDING SHEET No. CHECKED BY

DESCRIPTION **T.E.F.C. FLP. Sq. C. IND. MOTOR** APPROVED BY

ORDER TYPE **GOH** FOR COMPLETE ORDER MULTIPLY QUANTITIES BY :- **1** PERIOD :- **500**

3. 1970

ORDER No. **252864** ON COST NUMBER OF MACHINES **1** FRAME SIZE **VBS 9354** SHEET No. **1**

SPEC ITEM N	QUANTITY PER MACHINE	DESCRIPTION of MATL. COMPONENT or ASSEMBLY	DRG. PART No.	DRAWING No./REVISION	MATERIAL REFERENCE NUMBER	weight lbs	Stores Class	No of ops
		PACKING COSTS		(01)				
				AA1				
		CARRIAGE CHARGES		(02)				
				AA2				
		JIGS & TOOLS		(03)				
				AA3				
		OUTSIDE ERECTION		(04)				
				AA4				
		FINAL ERECTION		(0)				
	1	MOTOR OUTLINE		RE 2249				
		S.G.						
		NAMEPLATES						
1	1	C. BRS NAMEPLATE S# 3624		95561	38511-1016		SF	
		FLP No 4642 GROUP II						
		HP 60 RPM 2975 VOLTS 420 AMPS 74.5						
		PHASES 3 CYCLES 50 INSUL 'A' RATING CMR						
		TEMP. RISE 55°C STARTING TORQUE 75%						
		STARTING AMPS 223.5 SPEC 2613/1957						
		TYPE VBS 9354. CONN-DELTA SERIA No 252864/1						

Figure 4 (Parsons Peebles Ltd. A)   A Shop specification

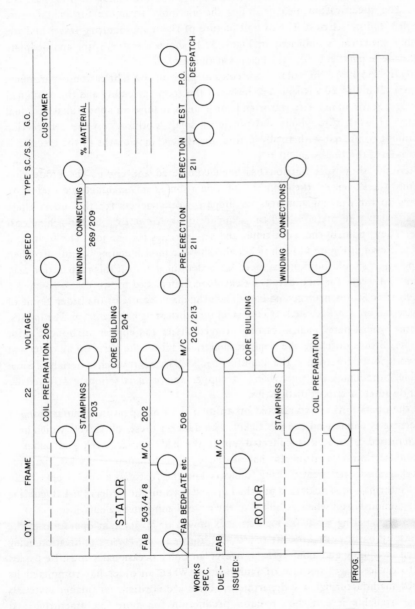

Figure 5 (Parsons Peebles Ltd. A) Manufacturing Stages

the smaller items are bought by stores in bulk and issued to orders as required, but these will constitute only abour 5% of the value of the order. A few of these components require processing at Parsons Peebles and these may be processed as a batch. The specification also describes the assembly structure for manufacture through a coding scheme. The overall picture of the manufacturing stages and the assembly structure is indicated in Figure 5. It shows a stator, rotor and bedplate being made in parallel before final erection and test.

Broadly speaking, the total work content given in the fabrication departments 503, 504, 508 and 202 is split 1:2 between the frame assembly and the combined stator and rotor units. The stator and rotor units require an approximately equal quantity of work throughout and provide a small workload on the pre-erection department compared with final erection; on average nine-tenths of the erection is undertaken at the final stage.

When the shop specification has been completed and copied the Production Planning Clerks enter the number of operations for manufactured items by referring to the drawing number and prepare works tickets for the order. These tickets specify the material and the sequence of operations on each machine cost centre. They indicate the work times and set-up times for the job. The form of a ticket is shown in Figure 6. Each ticket also shows a month ending to indicate when the operation should be done to meet the order due date. All this preparation may take up to 4 weeks for an order. The tickets are then passed to Stores.

Thereafter Stores manage and coordinate the manufacture of the order. Some of the materials are stocked, such as core steel for fabricating the frames and bedplates, but some special parts such as castings, forged shafts and copper are bought in for the order. Stores purchase the required materials, kit-up the parts for an order and issue work to the foremen in the manufacturing departments when materials become available. Sometimes the purchasing of copper and steel is seriously affected by labour disputes or import difficulties.

As the operations are completed on an item the time spent in manufacturing at each centre is entered on the job ticket. The data on these job tickets which have been returned to stores is collected up at the end of each week and taken to Accounts section. Operators also have to notify their foremen of any lost time due to breakages or time spent waiting for work and the foreman keeps a weekly tally of this information. The data is punched up and used on the Orders Cost Recording weekly computer run which is linked to the payroll computer calculations.

After completing work on an item it is moved on to its next operation in the sequence by barrows or fork lift trucks, the allowed time for transportation being between two days and one week. However an order occasionally must be passed back to earlier stages because of faulty work. When an order has completed its required manufacturing in a department, stores are notified. As further materials become available it can then re-enter production for more manufacturing and assembly work. If all is going smoothly, the work on a motor can progress roughly on a parallel working basis in departments i.e. if 100 hours of work is involved in a particular department the work can be completed in about a 50 hour time span. The total work content of an order varies between a few hundred and more than

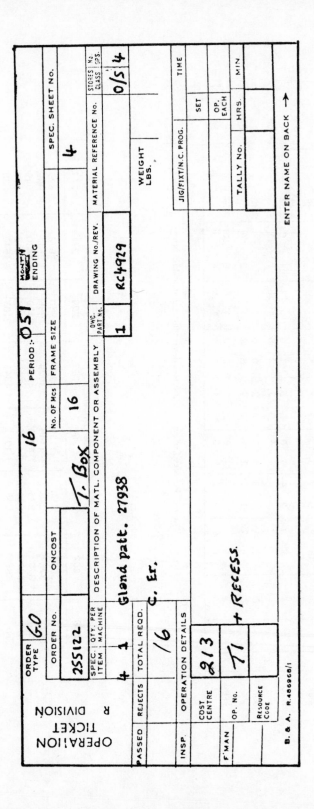

Figure 6 (Parsons Peebles Ltd. A)   A job sheet

Figure 7 (Parsons Peebles Ltd. A) — Lateness despatches against due dates

Date 1968	Class of Motor	Early	Weeks Late															Cl. 1	Cl. 2	Total Orders Late
			0	1	2	3	4	5	6	7	8	9	10	11	12	>12			
Jan.	I		2	0	2	2	0	0	5	1	9	7	4	1			31	22	53
	II				1	1	0	1	7	4	4	4							
Mar.	I	3	35	9	9	7	5	13	1	1	1						46	21	67
	II	1	2	7	13	1													
May	I		1	0	2	4	5	6	3	3	1	0	0	1	1	6	32	36	68
	II	1					1	1	3	3	2	6	4	3	2	11			
Jul.	I	22	2	1	1	13	4	3	4	2	0	0	2	5	2	4	30	34	64
	II	2	1	2	1	1	2	1	2	4	6	3	1		0	4			
Sep.	I		1		0	2	1	4	5	2	12	13	4	8	0	0	58	28	86
	II						5	5	3	4	1	4	4	0	4	0			

[Handwritten circled annotations in right margin, top to bottom: (33), (108), (69), (11), (87)]

Figure 7 (Parsons Peebles Ltd. A)   Lateness despatches against due dates

1968	Department						
	202	203	204	206	209	211	213
Jan	3000	831	1135	3249	1980	1673	876
Mar	3267	1243	1146	3529	1985	2511	982
May	3700	1825	1090	4519	2419	1430	949
Jul	3996	1089	1439	4445	1934	1813	1017
Sep	3861	946	1321	4345	2103	1540	880

Figure 8 (Parsons Peebles Ltd. A)   Capacity levels: Times clocked for one week

1400 hours. The proportion of work on each department also varies between orders irrespective of the size of the order owing to individual design characteristics. Two orders with the same total work content may vary by as much as a factor of 3 in their demands on individual departments. Recent records of four orders show the following labour content in hours at the various cost centres:

		Departments										
KW/Speed	Stator/Rotor	202	203	204	206	209	211	213	269	503	504	508
123/8	WIRE/S.C.	169	51	58	–	2	30	32	130	12	20	69
276/4	DZA/S.C.	186	93	91	346	100	65	42	–	7	32	119
147/6	WIRE/C.C.	133	6	18	–	5	29	20	116	4	14	25
201/4	VA/B	160	27	34	205	69	117	32	–	8	53	112

The Delivery Problem in 1968

Towards the end of 1968 Parsons Peebles were facing a serious production control problem in their Rotating Machinery Division in Edinburgh. The order book for electric motors and rotating machines had fallen by 20% over the last six months despite a continued growth in the industry generally. Continual criticism was coming from customers about late deliveries of their orders which were running on average four weeks late with some orders eight weeks late. Yet the more that was done about it the less effective were the results. The Managing Director, the Divisional Manager of Motor and Generator Division, Sales and Contracts Staff had all been attempting to help with the task of meeting deliveries. Whenever they were contacted about an order they would personally check with the works superintendent, progress chaser, foreman and even operators to see how the work was getting along and if necessary persuade the operator to switch priorities.

By September 1968 the Divisional Manager was beginning to recognize that this sort of system was not really achieving results as the pushing of one order probably meant the postponement of another. The records were showing that despite this frenzied activity, work in progress had been steadily building up, output was going down and the operators were completely confused about their objectives. At one time he found that 112 out of a total of 370 orders were 'crisis' orders. He decided, therefore, that to bring some sort of order to the chaos he would have to appoint a new production controller with clearly defined responsibilities. He also considered that some form of computer assisted scheme could prove helpful. As a first step in the analysis of the problem he checked on the distribution of lateness of actual orders despatched during 1968 and also checked on the hours worked. These figures are shown in Figures 7 and 8.

Peterborough Motor Components Ltd

Peterborough Motor Components (PMC) is a major subsidiary of an international manufacturing company. Its main factory is located in the East Midlands though a small plant is also operated in the Southwest. The East Midlands factory is solely concerned with the manufacture of a range of fairly complex components mainly for use in the motor industry.

The manufacturing facilities consist of a large machine shop of some 400 general purpose machines manned by about 320 operatives on the day shift and 160 on the night shift.

Many of the operatives do not set their own machines but work at machines set up for them by 'setters', though some operatives are capable of setting a limited range of machines. Figure 1 shows a breakdown of employees.

Shop Organization

The shop is organized on a functional layout with foremen in charge of one or more departments and chargehands, who report to the foremen, for groups of about 15 operators. There are three turning departments and departments for milling, drilling, grinding, broaching, gear-cutting, the press shop and heat treatment.

Industrial relations in the company was generally considered to be 'better than average', though the newly-appointed Production Manager, Mr. Jim Burgess, was of the impression that this was mainly because the old management had usually avoided confrontation by conceding claims. Mr. Burgess had joined the company in January 1973, previously he had been a works manager for a much smaller engineering firm in the Southeast.

The Payment System

The firm is non-federated and as a result the management has had little contact with the district officers of the various unions represented (see Figure 2). Basic rates of pay are negotiated centrally with trade unions and follow those in federated engineering firms. However, these are supplemented by an average of

PRODUCTION	*Days*		*Nights*
Foremen	8		3
Chargehands	24		9
Setters	50		15
Semiskilled machinists	300		150
Indirects	60		15
	442		192
		634	
INSPECTION			
Foremen	2		
Chargehands	3		1
Skilled Inspectors	14		6
Semiskilled inspectors	40		12
Indirects	10		2
	69		21
		90	
MAINTENANCE			
Craftsmen and mates	20		6
		26	
TOTAL		750	
STAFF		80	
TOTAL WORKFORCE		830	

Figure 1 (P.M.C. Ltd.)   Workforce structure

three hours overtime per week and a loose bonus system superimposed on job evaluated differentials.

In April 1973 the average basic rate was £.80 per hour in the machine shop and a 12½% premium was paid above this for shift allowance on nights. Participation in the bonus scheme started at 80% performance on the BS scale (standard performance is 100%) and bonus earnings on time saved over standard were split between management and the worker on an equal basis so that:

$$(\text{Earnings}) = (\text{base rate} \times \text{hrs. worked}) + (0.5)\left\{ \begin{matrix} \text{base} \\ \text{rate} \end{matrix} \right\} \left\{ \frac{100}{80} \left\{ \begin{matrix} \text{standard} \\ \text{hours} \\ \text{produced} \end{matrix} \right\} - \left\{ \begin{matrix} \text{hours} \\ \text{worked} \end{matrix} \right\} \right\}$$

GUARANTEED MINIMUM PAY   INCENTIVE PAY

	AUEW	*TGWU*	*Other*
Chargehand	37	—	—
Setters	60	—	—
Inspectors (skilled)	16	—	—
Inspectors (semiskilled)	25	18	—
Semiskilled Machinists	200	100	—
Maintenance	14	—	12
Indirects	—	52	6
	352	170	18
Shop Stewards	10	4	2

Figure 2 (P.M.C. Ltd.)   Union membership

The standard working week is 40 hours and 4 weeks p.a. are allowed for to cover holiday allowances, etc. so that about 48 weeks p.a. are available in terms of attendance time. The average weekly earnings for machinists during the first quarter of 1973 was £40.20/wk excluding shift payments.

Multi-machine Manning

Because of the relative complexity of the parts produced in the machine shop and the materials used, machining operations often took a considerable time on automatic cycles. That is, once a component was loaded in a machine by hand the operator was idle until the machine finished its preset cycle. This situation was most acute on gear-cutting where it was not unusual for an operator to run four machines at once (in fact the layout of the gear cutters had been arranged with this in mind). However, there were occasions when some of the operators ran two

PART NO.	BX 164921		
Description	Coupling Shaft		
Operation No.	6	OF	10
Machine	Fischer S.I. Copy Lathe	Standard Timed By	*T. A. Som*
Operation Description	Turn External surface contour from template using follower		
Tools Required	Fixture No: BXF 8091 Template: TBX 207		

Set-up Time Allowed :   45.0 mins

Operation Time Element	Time (mins)
(1) Set tooling for start of cycle	0.10
(2) Pick up job from pallet	0.15
(3) Locate job in fixture	0.10
(4) Secure location pin and clamp	0.40
(5) Start m/c cycle	0.20
(6) TURN CONTOUR (auto)	9.40
(7) Disengage tooling, open fixture	0.45
(8) Remove job and transfer to pallet	0.20
TOTAL	11.00
Multi-operation allowance 5%	.55
Personal time 5%	.55
Fatigue allowance 2%	.22
Contingencies 4%	.44
STANDARD TIME	12.76

Figure 3 (P.M.C. Ltd.)   Standards card for the copy lathe operation

Part No.	BX 164921		
Description	Coupling Shaft		
Operation No.	7	OF	10
Machine	CIN—H2Q Horizontal Mill	Standard Timed By	*T. R. Jones*
Operation Description	Mill Flat on 8.40″ O/D		
Tools Required	Fixture No: BXF 8092		

Set-up Time Allowed	22.0 mins.

Operation Time	
Element	Time (mins)
(1) Walk to mill	0.06
(2) Pick up job from pallet	0.15
(3) Locate job in fixture and clamp	0.30
(4) Start cutter, engage feed	0.20
(5) MILL 1 flat (auto)	3.60
(6) Remove job and transfer to pallet	.20
(7) Reset worktable for next job	.20
(8) Walk to lathe	.06
	4.77
Personal time (5%)	.24
Fatigue allowance (2%)	.10
Contingencies (3%)	.14
STANDARD TIME	5.25

N.B.: Operation done during auto cycle on Op 6. Operator paid on Op 6 standard hours produced.

Figure 4 (P.M.C. Ltd.)   Standards card for the milling operation

dissimilar machines at the same time. This was only possible where close proximity of the machine departments allowed since in general the shop layout was by groups of similar machines.

For example, the finish turning and milling operations of the BX 164921 Coupling Shaft were often done by the same operator simultaneously using a copy lathe and a milling machine (see work-study times in Figures 3 and 4). The element times were arrived at by studying a number of cycles of the operations concerned. The work study engineer who timed the jobs rated the operator's performance and took account of all the conditions under which the operations were carried out in order to arrive at an 'objective' time. This time was then offered to the operator and usually after a certain amount of wrangling (possibly involving the foreman and the shop steward) a time was agreed. The usual areas of disagreement focused on the more subjective elements — allowances for contingencies which included such things as tool changes, etc., and also on the setting-up time for which there was usually only one set of time study data available.

Coupling Shaft Machining Requirements

PMC manufactured mainly to call off schedules for the large motor vehicle companies and the BX 164921 coupling shaft had been produced for about 18 months for a tractor contract. The production level in April 1973 was running at about 1600 units per week though requirements had varied from 600 to 1800. However, in early April Mr. Burgess had negotiated a new delivery schedule starting in June which ran at a level of about 2400 units per week, varying from 1600 to 2800.

Since this new contract was only part of a fairly rapid increase in demand for a whole range of items Mr. Burgess anticipated that the company's manufacturing capacity could be under considerable pressure within 2—3 months and with tight delivery schedules this was bound to create problems. He therefore asked Mr. Peter Atkins, the chief work-study engineer to have a close look at the efficiency with which the men and machines currently available were being used and, in particular, at jobs where multi-machine manning was used. Mr. Burgess called a meeting on April 16th 1973 to discuss proposals for improved efficiency.

A Meeting in Mr. Burgess' Office, April 16th 1973

Present: Jim Burgess — Production Manager
        Peter Atkins — Chief Work-study Engineer
        Brian Thompson — Workshop Superintendent
        Terry Gordon — Production Controller
        Andrew James — Factory Personnel Officer

Burgess: 'Well you all know that within the next two months our production capacity is going to be stretched. We don't really have any more space available out on the floor and anyway extra machinists are pretty hard to come by. It looks as if we have to get the most we can out of what we already have.'

Atkins: 'That's about it but I have been looking into our utilization of current labour and it looks as if there is a lot to spare. Take the BX 164921 shaft, we have eight operators on that job right now but we could get the same output from four operators if we used a 4-machine basis using one mill and three lathes together.'

Thomas: 'Now wait a minute, Pete, I don't have that many copy lathes to spare, you know.'

Atkins: 'Well we use four of them almost all the time now, if we allocated six to this job and used them night and day shift we would only need two operators on each shift.'

James: 'But surely that means the operators have to work three times as hard. How long do you think we'll keep the labour we have if you try that on? Anyway the Unions would never stand for it.'

Burgess: 'Well, that may be true but a replacement copy lathe could cost us £10,000 whereas a new mill could only be around £4,000. If we need extra capacity and can find room for it we would be better off underutilizing the mills than the copy lathes.'

James: 'I still don't think the machine utilization matters a jot, you'll never get the men to accept it.'

Burgess: 'It might be well worth our while to pay them to accept it if we think it is a good idea. Let's leave this point for the time being and get on with the agenda. Peter, could you look into the details of the BX 164921 shaft operations for me and let me have them? I will arrange a meeting with the day shift operators involved and their shop stewards and we will discuss your proposals with them together.'

The meeting then proceeded with other business. Figure 5 shows the details put together by Peter Atkins. Mr. Burgess set up the proposed meeting for April 23rd, 1973 to which he invited:

(1) Two of the four day operators currently working on the BX 164921 shaft.
(2) The foreman of the milling department.
(3) The foreman of the copy lathe section.
(4) The senior AUEW and TGWU stewards.

For the management, he and Peter Atkins attended.

From P. Atkins, Chief Work-study engineer
To J. Burgess, Production Manager

1. *Critical Operations*

Operations 6/7 on this item are done concurrently by a single operator. All other operations are done individually on widely separated facilities.

2. *Time summaries of operations 6/7*

Op. 6 Copy Lathe		Op. 7 Mill	
	Mins		
Load/Start	0.95	Load/Start	0.71
Run	9.40	Run	3.60
Unload	0.65	Unload	0.46
	11.00		4.77
Unload/Load/Start	1.60	Unload/Load/Start	1.17

3. Since the copy-lathe has a relatively long automatic element we may consider combinations of a mill with one, two, or even three copy lathes. With one lathe and one mill (the current situation) the mill has to be operated once during each lathe cycle. If another lathe is added the mill must be operated twice within the total cycle. Similarly it must be operated three times in the cycle if three lathes are run in parallel. Per unit produced the capacity required is:

Copy lathe	-11.00 mins	(9.40 mins. run)
Milling M/C	4.77 mins	(3.60 mins. run)
Operator	2.77 mins	(loading/unloading)

For the alternatives considered we have:

one operator + one mill with:

No. of lathes	No. of pieces per cycle	Capacity required (mins)		
		Operator	Lathe/	Mill
1	1	2.77	11.00*	4.77
2	2	5.54	11.00*	9.54
3	3	8.31	11.00	14.31*

* = overall cycle time required.

The man/machine activity charts for these alternatives are shown in the Figure attached.

4. Currently we have 4 machine pairs in operation manned by operators on both day and night shift. Average output over the last 3 months has been 190 units per operator per week, though there is considerable variation between operators and between weeks.

Man / Machine Chart for 1 Lathe and 1 Mill

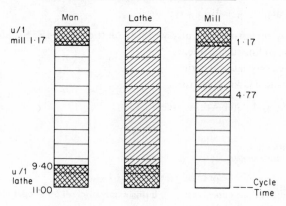

Man / Machine Chart for 2 Lathes and 1 Mill

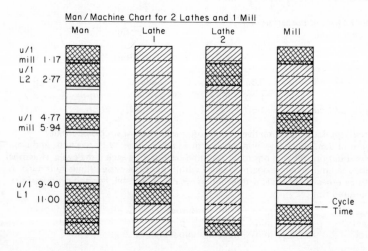

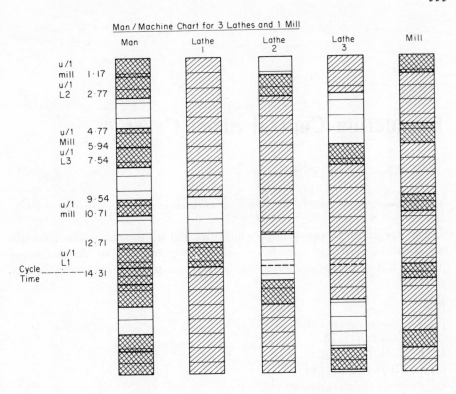

Figure 5 (P.M.C. Ltd.)   Man−machine utilization on the BX 164921 coupling shaft

Production Control Short Cases

The following cases describe the operating environments of a number of different companies.

You are asked to consider the similarities and differences of the situations described. In particular, consider the relative sophistication of the production planning and control systems required for adequate planning and control in each situation.

Case:

(1) Aero Components Ltd.
(2) Copylak Paints Ltd.
(3) Precision Tools Ltd.
(4) Lost Wax Castings Ltd.
(5) Coventry Heat Treatments Ltd.
(6) Domestic Appliances Ltd.
(7) Murray Construction Co. Ltd.

Case 1: Aero Components Ltd.

Aero Components Ltd. operate as a subcontractor to a number of large companies in the turbine engineering field (gas/steam/water). Most of their work consists of large components such as turbine shafts which have many intricate machining operations. A typical shaft would have about 15 hours machining time consisting of 30–40 operations on 15 different machine groups. Typically, it would be rough-turned and bored, faced, finish turned and bored, spline cut, heat treated (out of shop) and finish ground to size.

Orders come from customers as a schedule of demands for delivery by the end of each month for about 12 months in the future, however only those quantities required with the allowed lead time (usually between 3 and 7 months) were regarded as firm orders. The customers reserve the right to change the design on parts for periods more than one-lead time in the future.

Material supplies consist of specially made forgings which are ordered by the customers from the forging contractor concerned but are delivered directly to

Aero Components. Although the orders within lead time are nominally fixed, in practice the purchasing agents for customers often renegotiate schedule changes within lead time, with regard to due dates and/or quantities. Aero Components management regard this as an essential feature of this high technical content market. They do not think there is enough work of an adequate skill level available outside this market. The management are particularly worried about skilled labour because almost all of their machinists have to be of a very high skill level, both setting and operating their own machines. A few 'dilutees' are employed to operate machines (usually copy lathes) set up by full-time setters.

Over the past year, the company has had contracts for the supply of about 500 different items, the finished factory cost ranging from £100 to £300 per unit depending on the item. About 50% of this cost is material value which is usually the customer's responsibility. The average requirement is for about five orders per year per item, each order being for about ten items.

Case 2: Copylak Paints Ltd.

The industrial paints plant of Copylak make about 300—400 different products for industrial and motor applications, accounting for some 30% of the company orders (by volume).

A customer order will specify the volume required, the 'package' in which the paint is to be delivered and the detailed manufacturing specification.

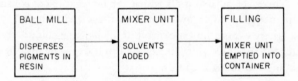

Figure 1 (P.C. Short Cases)   Materials flow in the Copy-lak Paints Co.

Specifications are usually agreed between Copylak specialists and the customer in the light of the conditions of use of the paint. They are often changed.

Although customers usually order the same product several times per year, they do so on separate orders for each delivery. The normal lead time for processing an order is about four weeks, although occasionally 5—6 weeks are available.

The production process for a batch of paint consists of three basic stages as shown in Figure 1. In the ball mill resin intermediates and pigments are mixed to obtain good dispersion. This process takes about 48 hours per load and usually several ball mills are in use for the same order.

The mixing process is carried out in an appropriately sized mixer unit where solvents, extra resins and about ten additives are combined and thoroughly mixed to obtain consistency. The mixing process is highly quality dependent and can take anything from one day to 2—3 weeks (even for the same specification). The mix is sampled regularly during the mixing period and not until the correct consistency, colour and technical qualities are obtained, is the process finished. If the tests are negative, further additives are put in according to the change in characteristics desired. For the exact colour matching sometimes demanded by customers, tests can only usually be made on a single shift, as the test operator who judges the colours must be the same for each test.

Filling is a relatively straightforward process, which consists of draining the mixer unit into drums or cans or directly to a tanker depending on the order and the customer. The time taken does depend on the method used, and occasionally shortages of large drums have caused problems. However, the process does not usually take more than one day.

The major cost of production is for materials. Most raw materials are stocked, including the 150 resin intermediates used (which are produced in a separate plant) and several thousand additives and pigments. Some 300–400 materials are on short notice delivery from outside whenever an order calls for them.

There are usually about 150 batches in the course of manufacture, with another 300 waiting to be scheduled. Often customers have more than one order for the same specification in the system at the same time. Since customers usually have a working buffer stock themselves, due dates are not usually crucial, except in special cases, though all orders are allocated due dates according to the expected lead time. The loss rates on batches are unimportant except when quality difficulties cause the whole batch to be scrapped (about 1% of throughput).

Plant capacity depends on machine availability and manpower limits on various labour groups. There are 50 ball mills which can be regarded as consisting of about 30 types, a type being specified by size, colour usage and technical type (types can be changed but there is a set-up time involved in changing colours etc.). Three men operate on each of the three shifts in the ball mill department. They are engaged solely on emptying and filling the mills.

The mixer units are classified mainly by size, though colour changes are minimized. The mixers available are:

No.	Size (galls)
30	600
13	1200
5	1300
2	1500
8	2500

The main labour requirement at mixing is for operators to sample the mixture and control the additives necessary.

Case 3: Precision Tools Ltd.

Precision Tools Ltd. manufacture specialist machine tools to customer orders. They are a small independent firm and have been relatively very profitable in their market.

There is some standardization on simple parts e.g. rollers, bolts, etc. but almost all the major components of each order are specials to that order. About 80% of parts are manufactured internally in the part machining shop, but all the bearings and some components are bought out from manufacturers standard ranges or are subcontracted.

Most of the detailed design work is undertaken by the Company's own engineering staff and it is thought that this is where the major company strengths lie.

The production departments are split between parts machining and assembly. Parts machining consists of very general purpose machine tools manned by highly skilled machinists (jigs and fixtures are rarely economical). The assembly department consists of skilled fitters who build up sub-assemblies (which are often returned to the parts shop for final machining) from components and final assemblies from sub-assemblies. In many cases the linking together of 'final assemblies' into a finished product is done in the customer's own plant by the company's installation engineers.

Some orders have been undertaken for electronically controlled machines for which the control systems are supplied by a nearby electronics company, but these have so far been regarded as 'research projects' and have been unprofitable in cash terms.

Each order can be broken down into 1000–5000 parts, lead times are about 6–8 months and there are usually about 100 orders in work-in-process at any one time. Raw materials consist of a few standard lines (sheet, bar, etc.) which are stocked and special forgings/castings which are ordered specially from outside suppliers.

Case 4: Lost Wax Castings Ltd.

Lost Wax Castings Ltd. (LWC) is not yet in operation, but a plant is being built by a parent company to replace a number of ageing facilities scattered all over the country. LWC will be an operating subsidiary of the parent company and will have complete responsibility for supplying the group's requirements for precision castings from its single plant (it may do this by making or by arranging subcontractors).

The Lost Wax process for precision casting is very old in principle (the Romans used it) but LWC will have a considerable amount of expertise not generally available. The process consists of four major stages as shown in Figure 2.

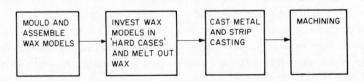

Figure 2 (P.C. Short Cases)   Materials flow in Lost Wax Castings Ltd.

The Process

(1) Wax models of the required part are made by injection molding.
(2) Individual models are joined together by wax runners to form a 'tree' of from four to ten models.
(3) The 'trees' are left to harden (deterioration takes place after about three days).
(4) Each tree is 'dipped' several times in a slurry of minute particles (like weak cement). Between each dip the coating is allowed to dry and harden (1 to 2 hours), often about 20 dips are required to give the required wall thickness (known as 'investment').
(5) The coated trees are heated until the wax melts and it is then drained off leaving a hollowed out shape the exact copy of the wax tree.
(6) Molten metal (often vacuum melted) is poured into the moulds so produced to form a metal 'tree'.
(7) The coating is cracked off and removed.
(8) The 'tree' is cut into individual components and each of these is rough machined at the joints.

The process is expensive and is only used for complex shapes which cannot be easily machined (e.g. aerofoil sections for turbines). Losses can occur at any stage. Typical losses are: wax models 30%, trees 4%, metal trees 20%, machining 2%.

The factory will be required to produce to production schedules supplied by other companies in the group on a continuing basis. Normally about 6—8 weeks lead time is available on each part, though orders may be changed within this lead time. Outside of this lead time there is considerable risk of obsolescence through design changes.

Some of the operations are highly labour intensive (wax 'tree' assembly, stripping and investment) while the vacuum furnaces are very expensive and must therefore be carefully scheduled.

Case 5: Coventry Heat Treatments Ltd.

Coventry Heat Treatments Ltd. is a small company set up some years ago by two former heat-treatment supervisors from a nearby factory. Their aim was to give a specialized service for heat treatments (annealing, tempering, case hardening etc.) to act as a buffer capacity for the numerous local engineering firms. In this, they have been very successful, although they recognize that as subcontractors of 'short-term' capacity, they are operating in a high risk situation. To off-set some of this risk, they have recently accepted a long term contract from their former employer for the heat treatment of crankshafts to supplement their own capacity. This contract, however, represents only about 10% of Coventry's capacity.

The equipment consists of four large furnaces and six small ones, plus a continuous flow furnace for small jobs. The normal procedure is to load as many as possible of the parts into a furnace and keep them there for the desired time, then unload and reload until the whole order is completed. For crankshaft work, the parts usually have to be supported at special points in order to limit distortion, so that usually only 4–5 can be put into even a large furnace in a single load. The temperatures and times for 'soaking' in the furnace are all specified on the order and are completely controlled by the customer.

The shop is run by the two founders who negotiate orders and schedule them. They employ three operators on each of the three shifts (6–2, 2–10, 10–6) to keep the furnaces warm and loaded for as long as possible. The shop closes over Saturday and Sunday, but in order to have the furnaces hot for the 6.00 a.m. shift on Monday, one of the owners usually goes in late on Sunday evening to switch them all on (or whichever of them he knows will be required).

With their experience of operations in the large company they worked for before starting this enterprise, the owners set up a very complex pricing system for their work, whereby orders which were multiples of single furnace loads were much cheaper than part loads.

This system was however occasionally relaxed for large regular customers with a small rush order. Also the cost for each cycle was progressively less down to a minimum charge, for example:

PART:	XV128 SHAFT
CUSTOMER:	24
CYCLE:	2 hrs. 35 mins. at 240°C
QTY/LOAD:	10 (Large furnace)

COST/CYCLE:

1st	2nd	3rd	4th	5th and after
£5.0	£4.6	£4.2	£3.8	£3.6

COST/PART CYCLE:

QTY	9	8	7	6	5 and below
	£4.8	£4.6	£4.4	£4.2	£4.0

The idea behind this system was to maximize the effective utilization of the furnaces by minimizing change rounds and to encourage larger orders. Customers were also allowed a percentage reduction of their total monthly account which depended on the total amount of the account. The main factor in getting any individual order was however delivery performance since given time the customers could usually do the job themselves.

The main factors which determine furnace utilization are thought to be change-round time and loading/unloading time. Change-round time is the time required between orders for the furnace temperature to be adjusted. This depends on the temperature change involved and can be quite considerable (about 1 minute per centigrade degree depending on the temperature level).

Case 6: Domestic Appliances Ltd.

Domestic Appliances Ltd. makes an almost complete range of the larger electric domestic appliances (washing machines, refrigerators, spin dryers, tumble dryers, dishwashers, food mixers, cookers) in four widely separated plants. The largest plant which is situated in Scotland manufactures washing machines, spin dryers and dishwashers. A full list of products is given below:

Appliance	Model	Production Line Usually Used
WASHING MACHINES	DAD TWIN TUB DAD TWIN TUB DE LUXE DAD 707B (SINGLE TUB)	LINE 1
	DADOMATIC DADOMATIC DE LUXE DAD PROGOMATIC	LINE 2
SPIN DRYERS	DADOSPIN B526 DADOSPIN B526 DE LUXE SPINMATIC	LINE 3
DISH WASHERS	WASHORINSE WASHORINSE 714 WASHUP (PORTABLE)	LINE 4

Many of these products have a large number of common parts, for example the heating units on the Twin Tub de Luxe, the Dadomatics and the Washorinses are identical. Most of the components are manufactured internally in the part machining and fabrication shops except for a few standard items such as the bearings which are purchased from specialist suppliers.

Final assembly is done on four lines as indicated above, changeovers are scheduled for the items on a given line in order to obtain the desired product mix, usually at least three shifts are worked on each item before a changeover.

Before final assembly, however, many sub-assemblies are built up (e.g. the heating unit). In general, individual components are manufactured and put into part stores and these are issued against 'kitting lists' to make a batch of sub-assemblies which are again returned to stores and may be issued against a further kitting list to form a 'higher level' assembly which is returned to stores to await final assembly. As many as six levels may be identified for some assemblies and four including raw material is common (see Figure 3).

Although the sub-assemblies which go into the final assembly of an item may not be identical, many of the *components* of the sub-assemblies are common. For example, the heater unit for the Progomatic has identical components (8) to that of the Dadomatic except for the heating coil, the insulator and a switching unit which are all slightly larger and the addition of two other components not used elsewhere.

The component and sub-assembly stores, besides supplying the needs of the assembly lines, also supply spares stores but the requirement is usually for sub-assemblies such as the complete heater unit. However, two service centres operate rebuild lines, and these usually place orders for components rather than assemblies.

Orders for components and sub-assemblies are based on a periodic review system with a critical level and re-order quantity rule based on past usage of the particular item.

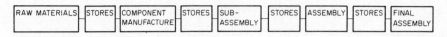

Figure 3 (P.C. Short Cases)   Materials flow in Domestic Appliances Ltd.

The management of the company have been very concerned about the amount of capital tied up in inventory and have recently installed a large computer system (run on the company computer adjacent to the washer plant) which records movements, locations and levels of all inventories.

Case 7: Murray Construction Co. Ltd.

The Murray Construction Co. Ltd. is a major world contractor for the erection of large, complex flow-production facilities. Its operations range from the design and erection of large oil refineries to the construction of small fertilizer plants for underdeveloped countries.

The multi-national operations of the company require considerable mobility amongst the design and erection engineers (civil mechanical and chemical) who form the basis of the company's skill and expertise. Local labour is usually used for unskilled work, but the location of the sites often means that workers must be housed temporarily on site. In some cases labour has to be brought in from other countries when sufficient suitable local labour is not available.

The field staff are backed up by a head office team based in London who are mainly responsible for initial design and tendering for contracts and for the large purchasing and expediting function which is required to procure and ensure delivery of the many components which go into the construction of a plant.

Murray do not actually manufacture any items themselves though they do hold their own stocks of some items which are 'normal' requirements for contracts (e.g. pipes, valves, motors and control instruments).

The central office also has a large planning team whose function is to plan the work stages of a contract and to monitor the performance of the construction teams. The projects planned may range from large contracts requiring about 100 field engineers over up to five years down to small 'maintenance' items requiring two or three engineers for about two weeks.

The Sonimage Company

Description of the Firm

The Sonimage Company situated in Orleans, France, produces colour and black and white television sets. At the end of 1972 the company employed some 800 people, of whom about 600 were production workers (mostly women).

Sonimage was formed in 1967 to produce televisions based on a new technology. At that time, television used a large number of valves connected by hand-wiring. Such a design required a complex manufacturing process (owing to the risk of bad connections) and the finished sets were somewhat unreliable.

While employed at the Atomic Energy Commission, Mr. Manier had the idea of producing televisions that would be almost fully transistorized, utilizing printed circuit boards. He successfully convinced a financial group of the potential of such an innovation and formed the Sonimage Company with himself as Managing Director.

It quickly became evident that the firm's results were not meeting the original high expectations. While the product had been fine as a laboratory prototype, mass production was another thing. The components supplied by subcontractors were not identical from one shipment to the next, resulting in the need for considerable adjustments. In addition there had been difficulty in establishing a sales network and retailers had not been particularly well selected. Because of the newness of the product the average television engineer was not capable of repairing the Sonimage sets and this did not encourage sales.

Mr. Manier was a remarkable technician and had constructed the best product possible. However, he had assumed that it would simply sell itself. By the end of 1970 the cumulative losses had consumed 75% of the firm's capital. Because of the rapid growth of the colour television market the financial backers still believed in the viability of Sonimage and replaced Mr. Manier with a new Managing Director, Mr. Bernard Causse. Mr. Manier became Technical Director. On appointment Mr. Causse took the following action:

(1) Established close control of the product line.
(2) Technical stabilization of the product, i.e. a reduction in design modifications.
(3) Sales training and instruction for retailers.

(4) A network of factory trained repair people across France.

(5) Sales force motivation through contests and prizes.

SONIMAGE profited along with the general growth of the colour television market (200,000 units in 1970, 300,000 units in 1971) and 1971/72 activities were relatively successful:

Year	Turnover (francs)	No. of Sets Sold Black and White	Colour
1970	19 millions	9,500	6,700
1971	40 millions	25,000	12,800
1972	80 millions	53,000	25,000

By the end of 1972 the company ranked as the third largest French producer of television sets.

The factory was enlarged in 1972, new storage space was built and an automatic conveyor belt was installed. For 1973 the production target was approximately 50,000 colour and 50,000 black and white sets.

Sales Organization

The customers are divided into two quite distinct segments: on the one hand the sales distribution network and on the other the specialist outlets.

The sales distribution network is organized so that thousands of ordinary retailers are in contact with Sonimage through regional agents who control stocks for supply to the retailers. These stocks still belong to Sonimage. The distributive trademarks are 'Images de France' and 'Ruper Electronic'.

The existence of this network does not exclude sales to large outlets but in this case individual trademarks and external cabinets are used in order to avoid competition with sales through established channels.

Part of the specialist market is concerned with sales to particular customers. Some SECAM sets are produced for large foreign manufacturers who cannot obtain this type of set from their own factories and some PAL sets are produced for foreign wholesalers. (N.B. The SECAM system for colour sets is used in France and the PAL system in Germany.) Export orders created particular problems because delivery against shipping schedules was very important and profit margins were often very low on high volume orders.

PAL–SECAM sets capable of receiving either type of transmission are produced for sale in areas which can receive both types. These may be sold directly or through the specialist markets.

Overall the forecast for 1973 included 32 different models, 9 black and white and 23 colour.

The Production Process

Production is carried out in two stages:

(1) Assembly of components to form printed circuits and the assembly of these circuits into a metal base called a chassis.

(2) Final assembly in which the chassis and tube are fitted into the cabinet. Then comes the final adjustment necessary to obtain a picture.

We examine each stage in detail.

Component Assembly

Component assembly is carried out on a non-mechanical assembly line. At various stations along a conveyor, trained workers fit electronic components onto a printed circuit (diodes, resistors, etc.).

A foot-operated machine automatically cuts and forms the component leads; the circuits pass from station to station until they reach an inspector who checks for

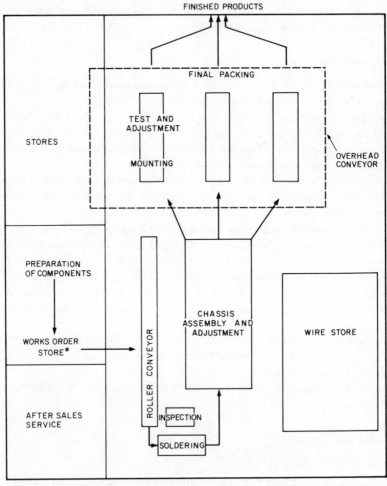

* The components for manufacturing orders are collected here

Figure 1 (Sonimage)   Factory plan

the presence of all components. The components are then soldered to the printed circuit by an automatic machine (solder wave technique). The printed circuits with their components are called sub-units. After soldering the electronic functions of the sub-units are checked and preliminary adjustments are made.

Independently of this production line, a team of operatives make the cable forms which will interconnect the various sub-units.

The assembly of the chassis consists of fitting the required sub-units and making the necessary interconnections. The chassis then passes to an inspection point where it is checked and adjusted.

Final Assembly

Tubes and cabinets are supplied to the assembler by an overhead conveyor system. The assembler mounts the chassis and the tube in the cabinet and passes the completed set to a test area where it is adjusted to obtain the final picture.

The television is then packed and handed over to the marketing division. The schematic diagram of the factory shown in Figure 1 indicates the work flow through the factory.

A breakdown of the labour requirements and material costs for typical models is shown below:

Black and White Sets (about 300 different components per set)

	Direct Labour (hours)	Material Cost (francs)
Circuit Boards		
(1) Video		
Component positioning	1.22	103.00
Sub-unit test	0.28	
(2) Intermediate Frequency Unit		
Component positioning	0.52	62.00
Sub-unit test	0.25	
(3) Power Supply Unit		
Positioning	0.10	
Test	0.15	15.00
(4) Sweep Unit		
Positioning	0.40	
Test	0.18	30.00
Chassis sub-assembly 1 + 2 + 3 + 4	3.00	210.00
Final Mounting		
Tube		90.00
Cabinet and sound		100.00
Chassis mounting in cabinet	0.67	
Start-up test	0.33	
Total	4.00 h	400.00 F
Average selling price per set		500.00 F

Colour Sets (about 1,200 different components per set)

	Direct Labour (hours)	Material Cost (francs)
Circuit Boards		
(1) Colour Control	1.52	153.00
(2) C.A.G.	0.23	18.00
(3) Sweep	0.73	48.00
(4) Focalization	0.30	27.00
(5) Horizontal Scanning	0.43	100.00
(6) Power Supply	0.34	20.00
(7) Dome	0.52	17.00
(8) Cushion	0.85	36.00
(9) Convergence	2.47	140.00
(10) Intermediate Freq.	1.62	55.00
(11) Base Freq.	0.22	15.00
(12) Tube Base	0.16	3.00
(13) Ocillator	0.61	7.00
Chassis sub-assembly	10.00	639.00
Final Mounting		
Tube		630.00
Cabinet and sound		120.00
Chassis mounting in cabinet	1.35	
Start-up test	0.50	
Inspection	1.15	
	13.00 h	1,389.00 F
Average selling price per set		1,950.00 F

A steady flow of production is difficult to establish because of the diversity of models produced and the level of work in process.

Labour cost is about 8.50 F/hr overall, with overtime at 11.0 F/hr.

In general, employee turnover has been substantial in this industry which is based on a female labour force.

Turnover rate is about 5% per month on average. This is usually replaceable but it is difficult to actually increase the work force rapidly. No more that a 5% overall increase can be attained in any one quarter.

Interview with the Production Manager

Question: Can you reduce your material costs?

Answer: I oversee every requisition myself: not one component, pair of pliers, work cloth, or supply of solder reaches the assembly line without my signature on the order form; I don't want to have any waste.

Question: Could you reduce your manufacturing time?

Answer: I make a colour set in 13.60 hours and a black and white set in 4.20 hours — that's 10% below the times of our competitors and only 5% above standards.

Question: Do you ever have any slow-downs or work-stoppages on the assembly line?

Answer: I have two or three work stoppages per year. These are due to materials shortages. When this happens I make use of the time to do a general cleaning operation. Last year, for example, I never had a work stoppage exceeding a half day, and even then on only one assembly line at a time.

Question: And the slow-downs?

Answer: Our models differ according to screen size and cabinet design. The Marketing Division sometimes misjudge demand and have to switch cabinet types. In this case I'm forced to slow down a little in order not to produce too many of a certain model in advance of actual demand. This causes the assembly line to become unbalanced and when the new cabinets arrive I have to go onto overtime at the cabinet-mounting stage in order to do the extra work and return to the usual balance.

Question: How could you reduce your costs?

Answer:

(1) Prevent the Marketing Division from changing its mind every three days.

(2) Prevent the technical department from incessantly modifying the components, which upsets both assembly habits and the parts supply system.

(3) Ask the buyers to seek better prices from their suppliers.

Question: What are your main problems?

Answer: I employ a relatively unskilled labour force and to achieve acceptable productivity it is important to level the workload as much as possible. Otherwise we experience constant stockouts, it is not unusual to have 10 in the same day. The production programme for the day then has to be modified and the model changed. Instead of producing one or two models a day I have to make 4, 5, 6 or even 8 different models. Each time the model changes the labour force have to get used to a new job and productivity drops.

In general terms I think that we have too many different sub-units and switching production several times a day does not help.

In addition, I am not informed of forthcoming stockout conditions, often only learning of them at the time they occur. Using the components we do have available we improvise the best programme we can which will in any case probably be changed within a few hours. Truly, production is very long-suffering. If only I could know a few days in advance what stockouts were going to occur!

Even when I have the right components in the right quantity it doesn't stop there. There are frequent quality problems, I often have to oversee the control of external cabinets myself. The metal base plates for the printed circuits often do not conform to standards and I have to use production labour to carry out the necessary modifications. Similarly the location holes in the printed circuit boards have to be redrilled.

Question: In your opinion, what should be done about these problems?

Answer: First, we should have fewer models so that the operators can become more experienced with particular jobs. Secondly, production should be in large batches. Finally, in order to achieve this, we should establish a stock of components which would guarantee supply to production.

Operations Planning:

Annual Forecast

The annual forecast is made annually to cover the complete year.

Export sales and sales to the specialist markets in France are known from the sales forecasts supplied by customers. Sales through the distribution network are forecast partly on the basis of preceding years data and partly from the forecasts of trade organizations. The sales forecast is broken down month by month by export sales, network sales and sales to special outlets.

Sales show a very strong seasonal variation: the majority of sets are sold in the last three months of the year. Production is not geared to follow such fluctuations and therefore uses forecast sales to maintain a more constant production level during the eleven months of operation. (See Figure 2.)

Thus stock is built up during the slack season (up to July) for later sales through the distribution network. Part of this stock of completed items is kept at the factory and part of it is distributed to the regional agents. It is, however, important to ensure that the distributed stock will be in line with eventual customer demand.

Monthly Forecast

At the beginning of each month (m) the sales forecast is specified by model up to month $m + 3$.

From this forecast the production programme is specified for the next three months. In practice, production usually run quantities of 1300–2000 of a particular model before changing a line or aim to run a line for four days before changing (producing about 1000 sets).

The Production programme for month m dictates the quantity of materials to be issued to production. For month $m + 1$ it defines a level of production requiring little modification. This is important to the purchasing department for the marshalling of stocks prior to issue. Deviations from forecast are greater in month $m + 2$ and purchasing use this as a basis for their orders. The forecast for month $m + 3$ is used to reserve provisional capacity with suppliers.

Monthly Issues

The Scheduling Department breaks down the production programme for the month into the different sub-assemblies required (a printed circuit board constitutes a sub-assembly, as does a tuner or the specific items which define the model, i.e. the cabinet and accessories).

In addition to the requirements for sub-assemblies for building finished televisions provision must be made for sub-assemblies supplied as spares through the service network and for replacements needed to cover losses during the previous month.

Many sub-assemblies are common to several models. For example, only 35 different sub-assemblies are used in the production of the 15 SECAM models and overall there are about 100 different sub-assemblies.

The sub-assemblies for which stores issues are required are grouped by Works Order Number (WON), see Figure 3. The WON defines the production requirements and while an order is being processed it carries the same WON through the shop.

The Purchasing Department

Outside purchases account for almost 90% of the direct cost of a television set.

The purchase department establishes an annual programme and reviews this each month for the subsequent four months. The development department maintain an up-to-date parts list which specifies the detailed make up of each sub-assembly in terms of its individual components. Purchasing use this to break down manually the annual requirements for components. Subsequently these component requirements are regrouped by the supplier. Altogether the stores identify some 1800 different components, 1200 of which are only used on colour sets.

Modifications are a continuing problem (200 during the last three months of 1972) and purchasing do not maintain their own parts lists for this reason. While any part of the organization can request a modification, only the laboratory can implement one.

For the smaller components an open order is placed covering the expected annual requirements. Monthly delivery is equal to one eleventh of the total amount and the purchase order specifies the following clauses:

(1) The supplier must always hold one to two months supply of components in stock.
(2) If Sonimage cancel an order they must accept the quantity due in the next month plus the supplier's stock. This will be on average about 1.5 months stock.
(3) Increases or decreases in demand must be covered by the supplier within 15 days of notification.

Certain very specialized components may have a delivery delay of up to 6 months and are not therefore covered by these rules.

The Purchasing Department aims to carry a minimum stock of 3 weeks usage. However, practical problems frequently prevent achievement of this aim.

For more expensive components, such as the external cabinet, the tubes or the tuners, the Purchasing Department makes provision to cover the production forecast up to month $m + 2$.

At the beginning of 1973 the delivery problems of tubes resulted in a stock of 4 months usage. This causes problems as the tube is the most expensive component in a colour TV. In total, stock had built up to a three month usage and certain components have very low turnover. Some items had not moved since early 1972. (Figure 4 shows a typical stock record.)

(1) Colour sets

Model/Market	Feb	March	April	May	June	July	Sept	Oct	Nov	Dec	Jan	Total
COLOUR NETWORK												
JACYNTHE	430		2,000				2,000				570	5,000
DAHLIA	125	375				180		650				1,330
ROSE	1,000		400	2,625	200			125	800	1,050	800	7,000
TULIPE	150	1,500						1,050			300	3,000
PIVOINE	130	220	100	60	480	400			480	220	310	2,400
MYOSOTIS						50	80	50		180		360
TOTAL NETWORK	1,835	2,095	2,500	2,685	680	630	2,080	1,875	1,280	1,450	1,980	19,090
EXPORT												
PAL SECAM	100	200		100	240	560			300	300	200	2,000
PAL 56 cm 90°		100	1,125	1,500		700	1,250	750		1,000	500	7,000
PAL 66 cm 90°		1,500					750			450	400	3,000
PAL 66 cm 110°	875	750	1,375	625	1,375			2,100	810		200	8,110
TOTAL EXPORT	975	2,550	2,500	2,225	1,615	1,260	2,000	2,850	1,110	1,750	1,300	20,110
SPECIAL OUTLETS												
56 PARSIPHAL						300						300
66 PARSIPHAL		300				300						600
SECAM 110 PARSIPHAL	100							100	200		100	500
66 SIEGFRIED	180			160	910							1,250
PAL SECAM SIEGFRIED	50	30	100		230						30	440
66 FLAINE					550				800	150		1,500
66 FONT ROMEU			100		450		100		350			1,000
PAL SECAM WALKYRIE	90				225	350			125			790
56 WALKYRIE				50	750							800
67 WALKYRIE	500				200	300			250	350		1,600
PAL SECAM HAMLET	500						100			200		800
SECAM 110 HAMLET	150							200	200	300		850
PAL SECAM LOCAVIS				100			100	100			150	450
TOTAL SPECIALS	1,570	330	200	310	2,175	2,390	300	400	1,925	1,000	280	10,880
TOTAL ALL COLOUR	4,380	4,975	5,200	5,220	4,470	4,280	4,380	5,125	4,315	4,200	3,560	50,080

(2) Black and White sets

Model/Market	Feb	March	April	May	June	July	Sept	Oct	Nov	Dec	Jan	Total
BLACK AND WHITE NETWORK												
EDELWEISS	1,000	700	2,000			2,000		600	1,400	1,500	800	10,000
GENTIANE	1,800	1,700	2,000		4,000		800	2,370	2,530	2,800	2,000	20,000
BOUTON D'OR		840		1,000		760		600	600	800	400	5,000
61 CROCUS	200	1,000				600		200	200		200	2,400
51 PENSEE				650								650
TOTAL NETWORK	3,000	4,240	4,000	1,650	4,000	3,360	800	3,770	4,730	5,100	3,400	38,050
EXPORT												
51 cm T K'		300		700								1,000
61 AS K'		500			500							1,000
61 DP K'	250		210	890			550					1,900
61 GP K'	1,000		750	1,050		1,000		1,200			1,200	6,200 –
TOTAL EXPORT	1,250	800	960	2,640	500	1,000	550	1,200			1,200	10,100
TOTAL ALL B AND W	4,250	5,040	4,960	4,290	4,500	4,360	3,850*	4,970	4,730	5,100	4,600	50,650

*Includes additional 2,500 made to order special.
N.B. No August production planned.

Figure 2 (Sonimage)   Annual production programme 1973/74

W.O Issue Date 18/02/73	For .../.../..		Date .../.../..	W.O. No. 669
Establish by: Release to Shop				
Distribution Order Colour			Special Order PAL 110°	

QTY	Production Requirements		Comments
1300	BLOC alimentation	ref. 301803	
1400	CI culot	ref. 301804	
1400	CI alimentation	ref. 301807	
1400	CI o/c mise en formiez	ref. 301808	
1400	CI o/c focalisation	ref. 301809	
1400	CI varidop RTC—COIR	ref. 301801	
1400	FI CCIR	ref. 301802	
1300	CI o/c demagnetisation	ref. 301806	
1400	CZ convergences	ref. 301820	
1300	platine connecteurs	ref. 301810	
1400	Balayage lignes	ref. 301812	
1400	Base de temps	ref. 301823	
1300	Bloc de regulation	ref. 301825	
1300	ensemble support connecteurs	ref. 301828	

Figure 3 (Sonimage)   A manufacturing order

Stores Operations

Stores receives orders from manufacturing which indicate the number and type of sub-assemblies to issue (see Figure 3). The works order numbers are classed according to priority by the scheduling department.

Stores obtain the correct component specification (parts list) for each sub-assembly from the development department. They then determine the total quantity of each component required by multiplying the sub-assembly requirement by the 'quantity off' per sub-assembly. The appropriate quantities are then issued. Eight storemen are engaged in this work each of them covering a particular set of components, e.g. one issues condensers, another resistors, another transistors, etc.

The sub-assembly specification is passed from hand to hand until all the requirements have been covered. Every component is listed on the specification right down to the nuts and bolts and electric wire. All the different components which make up a Works Order are collected together on a palette and transferred to the preparation department. There, the main task is the fitting of connecting leads to the components as required by their eventual use. Finally, the prepared components pass to the Works Order Stores to await issue to production. Issues necessary to cover scrap, modifications to the parts list or changes in the production programme are made by special orders. All stock transactions are

CASSETTE						
D84	CONDENSER			N750/831		15 pF
Dates	Order No.	Details	Deliveries	Issues	Stock	On Order
5. 9.72		Stock			81000	
7. 9.72		41824		2600	78400	
8. 9.72		211814		1500	76900	
8. 9.72		81842C9		4600	72300	
8. 9.72		81842		2500	69800	
11. 9.72		171804		65	69735	
15. 9.72		BL1347	6000		75735	
15. 9.72		BL1864	16000		91735	
15. 9.72		BL1824	3000		94735	
3.10.72		BL2008	8000		102735	
3.10.72		BL1825	3000		105735	
3.10.72		BL1346	6000		111735	
4.10.72		41824		600	111135	
5.10.72		41820		4000	107135	
14.10.72		41820		50	107085	
17.10.72		81842		4500	105585	
17.10.72		41820		2000	103585	
20.10.72		41824		5400	98185	
25.10.72		1345	6000		104185	
25.10.72		2009	3400		107585	
27.10.72		81842		9500	98085	
31.10.72		81831		3200	94885	
2.12.72		1344	6000		100885	
14.12.72		2615		10990	111875	
14.12.72		2635		3810	115685	
			MAXI		MINI	

Figure 4 (Sonimage)   Stock card

recorded on the stock cards. The Stores process 100 to 140 (average 115) parts lists each month. This work takes up all the available time and it is not possible to check in advance that sufficient components are available to cover the subsequent months' issues. If an item is unavailable for issue against a parts list the Stores raise a 'shortage note' which is passed to purchasing. Purchasing attempt to obtain the component on a top priority order. There are between 50 and 150 shortages each month.

Apart from the main activity of the stores in servicing manufacturing orders it must also cater for the needs of the preparation department. This employs about 25 people and particularly towards the end of a month there can be insufficient issues to keep them busy. Some work on the more standard sub-assemblies can be started in advance of requirements (to cover the subsequent month's usage) and this often happens. While this helps considerably to smooth the work load on the preparation department it does disrupt the smooth running of the stores.

DESIGNATION :

SUPPLIERS :

MIN STOCK	QUANTITY OFF	
	BSW	C

DATE	ORDERS	ORDER NO.	IN	OUT	STOCK		SUB ASSEMBLY				QUOTA :
							B &W		C		
							N°	C.	N°	C.	

REQUIREMENTS											
JAN.			AVR.			JUIL.			OCT.		
FEV.			MAI			AOUT			NOV.		
MAR.			JUIN			SEPT.			DEC.		

ORDER RECORD		

Figure 5 (Sonimage) Allocation stock card

The Development of the System

Both stores and stock control became service functions to the scheduling department. Mr. Poulin, the scheduling manager, had the idea of installing allocation stock cards (see Figure 5). For the major components these would show not only the physical stock as on the existing stock cards (Figure 4) but also the sub-assemblies using the component, the forecast requirements month by month and the details of purchase orders. A comparison of requirements and stock would generate an order to be passed to the purchasing department.

To aid the storekeepers the sub-assembly parts lists would be sorted by issue type. Thus for each sub-assembly there would be a parts list for resistors, one for condensers and so on. Each storekeeper would have only the details of his own issue requirements.

These allocation stock cards should make it easier to avoid stockouts because there would be a central Kardex file of all the information on components including details of the sub-assemblies which they are used on.

This new procedure was not implemented because it seemed easier to install a data processing system. During 1971 an implementation study was undertaken. The stages were as follows:

(1) Establishment of a part number file covering all components and including:

	Example
Part number and control letter (see Note)	1B
Description	Condenser 10p
Supplier 1	RTC
Supplier code	C010
Supplier 2	Telefunken
Supplier code	MA 074 010
Lead time (weeks)	2
Minimum stock	1000
Maximum stock	3000
Stores location code	EZ52

Note: The control letter is obtained by dividing the part number by 19: if the remainder is 0, letter A; if the remainder is 1, letter B; etc. e.g. 19=A; 52=0; 123=J. This allows a check on punching errors.

This file was set up in its entirety.

(2) Establishment of the breakdown of final products into their component sub-assemblies. Each sub-assembly had to have a unique identification. The presence of a sub-assembly in a finished product could be designated by 1, and the absence by 0. The breakdown appeared thus:

	Sub-Assembly								
Model	*1*	*2*	*3*	*4*	*5*	*6*	*7*	*8*	*....*
JACYNTHE	1	1	1	0	0	1	1	0	....
DAHLIA	1	1	0	1	1	0	1	1	....
ROSE	1	1	0	1	0	1	0	1	.... etc.

This breakdown was not fully achieved in 1971. It would have allowed the finished product programmes to be broken down into sub-assembly requirements.

(3) The establishment of sub-assembly parts list records. In order to define a sub-assembly it is necessary to specify the component by the part number defined in (1) above and to indicate the quantity of that component required. Thus:

Colour
Control   SA   80
Circuit

Component Code	*Quantity Required*
1B	3
52O	1
123J	2

This work was partially completed but only at the expense of current operations. In order to avoid more short term disruptions it was abandoned. The installation of a data processing system had stopped there.

(4) In parallel with the establishment of sub-assembly parts lists, it had been anticipated that all entries into and withdrawals from stock should be noted under the part number concerned:

	entry	*withdrawal*
1B	1,000	
52O		500

This registration would have allowed the stock to be known by part number at all stages of processing.

Outline of the anticipated processing steps:

Production programme of finished products

     ↓   Sub-assembly processing: First stage breakdown

Sub-assembly programme

     ↓   Component processing: Second stage breakdown

Gross requirements for components

     ↓   Comparison with stock

Net requirements for components

In the course of time it was anticipated that orders would be raised to cover outstanding net requirements which were not covered by current orders.

The Special Chemical Co (SCC)

Company Background

SCC is a medium-sized chemical company. It operates a number of manufacturing divisions.

SCC maintains its competitive position by producing bulk speciality products for which there are a limited number of producers. This specialization has helped SCC to avoid direct competition with the giants of the chemical industry such as ICI and BP. However, as markets for the basic specialities increase, the larger companies have moved into these markets, either directly or through subsidiaries.

Because of this potential challenge, SCC has concentrated on producing chemicals that have been 'tailored' to individual industrial applications. This has meant using additives and special treatment processes based on development research carried out by SCC.

Case Background

This case is concerned with a development in one of the major manufacturing divisions of SCC.

The division produced highly refined raw materials, for use in the chemical, packaging and paint industries, from basic raw materials. The refined raw materials were produced in a wide range of grades to cater for individual product applications. They were supplied directly to a wide variety of manufacturers.

The main speciality product of the division was also produced by a major competitor in the UK, who held over 50% of the market in 1965. The division also marketed on an international basis and there were about thirty overseas producers.

Demand for the main product was expanding but subject to fluctuation depending on the general economic situation.

A New Process

In 1965 SCC decided to go ahead with an ambitious project to increase the division's total production of the main speciality by 70%. The increased production was to be made by a new process which would provide new, superior quality grades. The project required an investment equal to 18% of the assets employed by the company.

The process in use in 1965 took low grade feedstock through an 11-stage system. This was slow and required a considerable amount of equipment such as grinders, tanks, filter plants and reactors. It also produced a large amount of pollution.

The new process offered the possibility of rapidly producing a high quality product through a five-stage system with little or no pollution problems. The new process was also very efficient and one of its prime advantages was its ability to recycle one of the main reactants for reuse. This was not possible with the old process.

The only disadvantages of the new process were the higher cost of the high grade feedstock required and the difficult technology. High grade feedstock was required as some of the impurities present in lower grade feedstock could both physically foul the plant and contaminate the final product. The technology was difficult because the process involved the use of extremely corrosive reactants and intermediate products at high temperatures.

The principle of the new process had first been patented about 30 years previously but the difficult technology had prevented its exploitation on a wide scale.

In the late 1940s SCC had studied the process, and in the late 1950s, in conjunction with a foreign chemical company, had developed the technology to the pilot plant stage. By the early 1960s the foreign partner had built a modest sized commercial plant which eventually operated successfully.

SCC's plans for a prestige plant using this process called for construction on twice the scale of the foreign plant. This was considered necessary to achieve economic viability. Capital costs were to be lowered by replacing the multiple units used in the foreign plant by single large units and by having only a few parallel items. The plant would also incorporate numerous improvements devised since the construction of the foreign plant. These improvements had been tested in research laboratories but not on an operating plant.

The New Plant

By mid-1966 the Chairman announced to the shareholders that all was going well, the project was within budget and it was expected to start commissioning in 1966, building up to full production by 1967.

By the spring of 1967 commissioning was under way, but 'teething' troubles were holding the plant back. By mid-summer the Chairman was mentioning difficult technical problems due to operating at high temperatures in a corrosive environment. These were the very problems that had held up the widespread development of the process for about 30 years from its first inception.

SCC's original plans called for full operation of the new process by mid-1967 and £½ million was allocated for commissioning. The Chairman announced in his mid-summer speech that output was increasing and profitable operation was expected in the second half of the financial year.

The Introduction of Reliability Modelling

In January 1968 all was still not well with the plant and a member of SCC's Mathematical Services Department was called in to take an independent look at the problems. The commissioning team was proving too small to do other than 'firefight' problems. The mathematician was instructed to report back within one month. He commenced by examining the failure data that was available.

The data on failures proved to be unsatisfactory on several counts. Safety shutdowns on reactors due to a blockage in the chemical flow some distance away were reported as reactor failures, not blockages. If unit A failed, resulting in its shutdown and the rest of the plant being placed on standby, and 4 hours later unit B failed, causing the shutdown to continue for a further 8 hours, then the lost time would be arbitrarily allocated between the two units. The 12 hours of failure time would be recorded as 6 hours per unit, whereas unit A might have been in a failed condition for 10 hours, and unit B failed for 8 hours.

To overcome these problems the data was split to show the failure times for various units on two bases, one optimistic and one pessimistic. The optimistic failure data was produced on the basis that 'if no one says its failed, then it's running'. The pessimistic data used the basis 'if no one says it's working, then it's failed'.

From this data the mathematician decided to construct a simple model to find the reliability of the total system by considering the failure probabilities for each unit. The form of the model is shown in Appendix 1 of this case, except that the probabilities are shown in terms of the probability of the plant working. The original model followed the mathematical tradition of working in terms of failure. The mathematician thought this approach was useful in that it challenged the undue optimism which, he felt, prevailed after every failure was corrected. This original model had also to be produced for both optimistic and pessimistic data.

The construction of this model gave an insight to the fundamental problems of the plant. Because the process was very quick, taking only a few minutes from start to finish, and a main reactant was recycled for re-use, without effective decoupling storage, every piece of equipment had to run at the same time. If there was any break in flow through the plant, the flow of recycled reactant was interrupted and the process stopped. Although the process only had five stages, when vital controls, pumps, etc. were considered some 30 items of equipment needed to function simultaneously. When considered as independent items these pieces of equipment seemed reliable, but when the 30 independent reliabilities, or probabilities of working, were multiplied together the whole plant was insufficiently reliable.

The initial model produced substantial values for the probability of failure of the plant. Calculations based on paralleling items indicated that work should be concentrated on improving the individual items to achieve greater reliability. The figures were also presented in terms of potential output, derived from planned output multiplied by the probability of the plant working.

These initial findings were reported within the month, but did not find ready acceptance amongst the designers and engineers on the plant.

The designers had incorporated equipment in the plant which was regarded as reasonably reliable when operating as single units. The calculations for economic viability had been based on the plant running continuously between relatively brief annual overhauls. The findings presented to them were so at variance with expected design performance that they were not credible to the designers. The foreign plant was also known to be operating successfully and the only major design differences were considered to be improvements. These improvements had not come up to the same performance in the plant environment as under research conditions, but were responding to modifications in the light of operating experience.

Although the mathematician's findings were not accepted at this point he continued his research into the problems. The engineers and designers began searching for differences between their plant and the foreign plant.

Throughout 1968 the pressure to get higher production from the plant increased. As a first move a Director was appointed to take charge of the new process in February and a firm of chemical engineering consultants were called in by March.

In the company's annual report it was stated that the adverse divergence from the output forecasts for the new process could have severe financial implications for the company and the budget had been exceeded. The same report also mentioned that the delay in bringing the plant to profitable operation was not long when compared with some similar plants. A forecast of 60% of rated capacity was made for the financial year.

The Development of Reliability Modelling

In parallel with these events the mathematical work continued, entering a second phase. In this phase the effect of adding additional plant in parallel was considered using a static model based on updated reliability data. This model still showed the system to be unreliable because cost factors resulted in only a limited amount of paralleling being feasible. From this work the mathematician reaffirmed that work should be concentrated on improving the individual items.

The model then entered a third phase. A simple dynamic simulation was carried out by hand, prior to trying a more complex computer simulation, to assess the impact of storing the recycled reactant before returning it for re-use. As an intermediate product was already stored at a testing point mid-way through the plant, this additional storage for the recycled reactant would uncouple the plant into two halves.

Although the model suggested it would be cost effective up to a fairly high level of plant reliability the idea was never implemented.

Implementation of the storage concept was prevented due to doubts over some of the technical problems involved in storing the reactant. The reactant was known to be contaminated by the product when it was recycled, and grossly contaminated during periods of failure. It was suspected that this contamination would require the use of complex separation equipment before the reactant could be stored conveniently.

At about this time the chemical engineering consultants made an important point about the model. Although it did not directly concern them, they suggested that the model should be rewritten so that it reported in terms of probable success rather than in terms of failure. The consultants suggested that this might increase the enthusiasm of the engineers working on the plant as morale had fallen to a low level by this time. On the basis of this suggestion the model was rewritten.

At mid-summer 1968 the Chairman had to make a further annual statement. This was largely restricted to the comment that the budget had been exceeded but that output was continuing to increase.

During this same period a firm of management consultants were brought in by the Chairman, and shortly after this, project teams were recruited from other divisions of SCC to tackle plant problems.

By this time the mathematician had commenced a more rigorous analysis. The management consultants were able to confirm that the approach was correct and provide encouragement through their specialist knowledge of this type of analysis.

Failure patterns were drawn for each unit including concurrent failures. The failures were examined for randomness and only the first and last vessels were found to have linked failures. This linking of failures was attributed to contamination of the recycled reactant. The failure data was still unsatisfactory at this point, partly due to failures becoming 'planned shutdowns'. Attempts were being made to shutdown items before they failed. Also during shutdowns caused by failure, unfailed items were serviced to extend their lives. These practices tended to distort the data.

The company's interim report in September brought further bad tidings to the shareholders in the form of a decline in profits, attributed to the plant, and a statement that the plant would not reach the previously forecast capacity in that year. However the problems 'were considered to be responding to technical effort'.

The Acceptance of Reliability Modelling

October 1968 brought a breakthrough in acceptance of the reliability model when the Mathematical Services Department and the management consultants jointly presented a report on possible alterations to the plant and their effect on reliability and throughput. This report was accepted by the plant engineers and designers as it corresponded closely with new data obtained about their foreign partners' earlier development.

It was now apparent that the main difference between the SCC plant and the foreign plant was SCC's reliance on single large items of plant. The foreign plant used up to four, oversized, items in parallel. The foreign plant could have 50% of its equipment failed at each stage of the system without interrupting production, although the output would be reduced. This ability to continue production in spite of a substantial failure rate, also helped the morale of plant personnel, since they seldom faced a total plant shutdown.

In fact a similar situation had existed with the old process used by SCC. Up to eight pieces of equipment were used in parallel, with storage between items. Thus failure of several pieces of equipment did nothing more than produce a minor reduction in output. This plant had been designed prior to the availability of single 'jumbo' units. The data from the model then began to be used from this point to monitor the campaign on the plant to improve reliability.

Commenting over a year later on the part played by the management consultants in assisting the acceptance of the model, the mathematician stated that 'they were a catalyst and a smoothing agent'. Their experience and freedom to communicate with all personnel while reporting directly to board level had been a considerable asset.

The model continued to be developed. Attempts were made to predict future plant output from the monthly failure analysis. Effort on the main model was directed to producing better data from the plant. A new information system was devised by the Mathematical Services Department. Its outline is shown in Figure 1. Two new record sheets were required. The failure event report required comment from up to six members of the plant staff on the cause of failure. It replaced a report which merely classified faults as mechanical, process faults requiring mechanical help, or process failures which could be rectified by process personnel.

The second sheet divided the plant into 19 blocks, related to units of the model. An hourly indication of whether the block was producing, at standby, not working or failed was required. This sheet was to be summarized by each shift and totalled on a weekly basis.

The operating personnel rejected this system as they felt it involved too much paperwork. Instead they devised their own system which used the old failure report, a new failure record sheet covering 39 items, and a reliability analysis sheet with the 39 items reduced to 16 blocks for analysis purposes. The new failure record sheet was completed on a weekly basis by the plant statistical clerk. He also had access to sufficient information to complete the reliability analysis sheet. Failure details, availability for each unit (that is the time left after deducting planned shutdowns), throughput data, and plant managers' comments on why 100% rated capacity was not achieved while the plant was operating, were to be recorded.

The summary sheet carried monthly, cumulative and quarterly data showing actual probabilities and targets for the quarter. The original targets were set on an arbitrary basis and were reappraised monthly in the light of experience. Weekly meetings were held by the plant manager with the maintenance staff and selected technical staff. They studied performance versus targets and filled in the necessary action comments. Effort was directed to rectifying consistently unreliable plant and major breakdowns.

This new information system was put into operation in December 1968. This marked the point at which the reliability model had become a working tool, as the calculations were now carried out on the plant and the results used to direct project

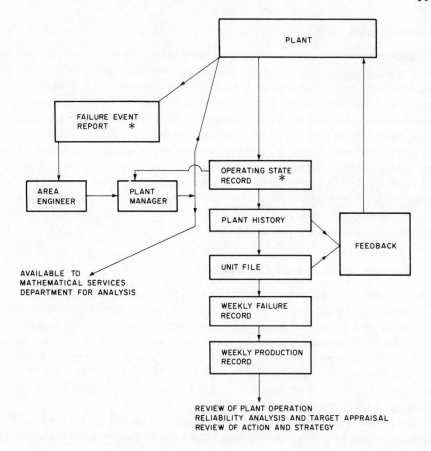

* INDICATES A NEW SHEET REQUIRED

Figure 1 (SCC)   The proposed information system (simplified)

effort and assess performance. The relatively simple form of the static model, for example:

$$A \times B \times [1 - (C \times D)] \times E \ldots$$

meant that the plant statistical clerk could insert the probability values he had calculated and produce the overall plant figure without supervision.

The data produced by the statistical clerk was also used by the Mathematical Services Department for predicting output for the period ahead and as a basis for computer simulation of possible changes to the plant.

From this point reliability on the plant started to improve. There was a cautious statement to the shareholders in January 1969 that output at the end of 1968 was considerably above that in 1967, but still well below design capacity. In mid-summer 1969 an increased dividend was announced on the basis of the improving plant performance.

Industry Trends

By mid-summer 1969 several competitors had also built variants of the new process and were attempting to operate them with varying degrees of success. All manufacturers were experiencing increases in both raw material and wage costs at this time. With stable prices, profitable operation was even harder to achieve. SCC were becoming increasingly worried about the price they might have to pay when their medium term contract for raw materials expired.

In the meantime the old process had been developed and plants had been rebuilt by several competitors, including some using the new process. These refurbished plants using the old process route, with some small changes, were making product grades equivalent to the new process and at greater efficiencies than had been known or thought possible prior to the introduction of the new process. However, the pollution problem still remained to be solved.

Further Applications of Reliability Modelling

The success of the reliability model led to interest by other departments of SCC, and simulation models were used to assess various new plants under consideration. These included a new process, which SCC had just patented, that could upgrade low grade feedstock from the old process to the high grade required by the new process.

Reliability data for use in these simulations was mutually agreed by the designers and maintenance engineers. It was stated by the staff involved on these projects that one of the major impacts of the model was in encouraging new ways of thinking and cooperation at the design stage.

The simulations led to considerable changes in design, and it was found that the addition of storage between process stages could considerably improve the reliability of these designs. This in turn increased the output for a stream of equipment of given rated capacity. The cost of tanks, hoppers, etc. in these designs proved to be low in comparison to the cost of using higher rated equipment or parallel streams. Although the reliability data could not be precise at the design stage, now that the implications had been seen by the designers, they were able to make better decisions on the size of storage and equipment that would be required. They were also able to leave sufficient room in the design for any increase in storage capacity that might later be found to be necessary.

By the end of 1969 it was widely acknowledged in SCC that reliability modelling was a useful design tool and a great help in deciding where to direct effort to increase reliability. It was felt that the model had shown that problems related to the total plant rather than individual items. There was still concern over whether the analysis was sufficiently detailed to pinpoint key areas.

Problems also remained over how to separate cause from effect and how to increase motivation towards improving reliability when a plant had been unreliable for a long period. Consideration was being given to the choice between the use of project teams drawn from other SCC plants, the use of contract labour or the use of incentive payments based on plant availability, in the drive to achieve reliability.

APPENDIX 1

The following are examples of the application of probability theory to simple process plants. The probability values have been chosen for illustrative purposes and would normally be expected to range from 0.950 to 0.999.

Plant A

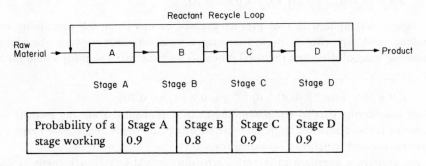

Probability of a stage working	Stage A 0.9	Stage B 0.8	Stage C 0.9	Stage D 0.9

The model form is $P(A) \times P(B) \times P(C) \times P(D)$
Total probability of the plant working
$= 0.9 \times 0.8 \times 0.9 \times 0.9 = 0.583$

Plant B

In plant B the least reliable stage of Plant A, stage 2, has been duplicated, with each stream of stage 2 sized to keep the plant operating satisfactorily without the other.

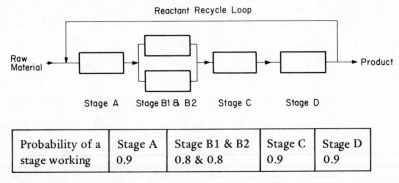

Probability of a stage working	Stage A 0.9	Stage B1 & B2 0.8 & 0.8	Stage C 0.9	Stage D 0.9

The model form is

$$P(A) \times \{1 - [(1 - P(B1)) \times (1 - P(B2))]\} \times P(C) \times P(D)$$

Total probability of the plant working

$$= 0.9 \times [1 - (0.2 \times 0.2)] \times 0.9 \times 0.9 = 0.700$$

The change in the probability of the plant working, or expected reliability, from

0.583 to 0.700 illustrates the advantage of adding a parallel stream at the least reliable point.

Having parallel plant also gives a choice as to where to direct the maintenance effort. For example stage B1 might be raised to a 0.9 probability of working whilst B2 is allowed to fall to an 0.7 probability. The total probability of the plant working would then be:

$$0.9 \times [1 - (0.1 \times 0.3)] \times 0.9 \times 0.9 = 0.707$$

If stage B was built with four parallel streams, each with an 0.8 probability of working, and any two of these four stages were sufficient to keep the plant operating successfully, then the total probability of the plant working would then be:

$$0.9 \times \{1 - [4(0.2)^3(0.8) + (0.2)^4\} \times 0.9 \times 0.9 = 0.709$$

When considering parallel equipment the main considerations are the amount of increased revenue available from the more reliable plant versus the increased capital, maintenance and sometimes, operating costs.

An alternative approach to increased reliability would be to instal storage tanks between each process stage and in the reactant recycle loop. Sometimes this provides a cheap alternative to parallel streams, but it may not always be technically possible. The sizing of the tanks for such an installation is often carried out by dynamic simulation.

APPENDIX 2

Analysis of Failure by the Weibull Distribution

Figure 2 shows a very common pattern of equipment failure as a probability distribution of failure density. Failure density is defined as the number of failures (expressed as a fraction of all failures under consideration) per unit time. The pattern is known as the 'bathtub curve', its features being that:

(1) AB represents early failure or infant mortality, characteristic of the debugging stages.
(2) BC shows random failure at a constant rate.
(3) Beyond C failure increases due to wearing out. A single item of equipment will fail ever more often, so that the curve rises continuously (CE), but with a population of components a few will have abnormally long lifetimes so that the failure rate falls before the last component fails (CD).

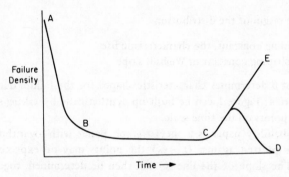

Figure 2 (SCC) Typical pattern of failure density with time

A cumulative survival rate as shown in Figure 3 can also be defined. This is simply a different representation of the pattern shown in Figure 2. At time 0, the origin of the distribution, nothing has failed so that the cumulative survival rate is 1: similarly at some time nothing survives. Thus, a cumulative failure rate at any time

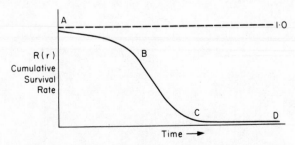

Figure 3 (SCC) Cumulative survival rate curve corresponding to the failure density curve in Figure 2

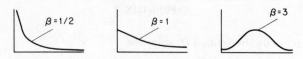

Figure 4 (SCC)   Failure density curve corresponding to
various values of the Weibull curve

can be defined as:

1 — cumulative survival rate

Then by successive subtractions a table of failure densities for individual time
periods may be constructed.

The Weibull distribution is exponential in form and describes cumulative survival
rate as

$$R(t) = e^{([\,t-t_0\,]/\alpha)^\beta}$$

where t_0 is the origin of the distribution

α is a scaling constant, the characteristic life
β is the shaping constant or Weibull slope

The value of β determines characteristic shapes for the failure density curve, as
shown in Figure 4. Figure 2 can be built up synthetically by taking suitable values
of β at various points on the time scale.

Weibull probability paper is a special graph paper with logarithmic axes, such
that if $R(t)$ is plotted against $(t - t_0)$ the points may be expected to lie on a
straight line. The slope of the line (β) can then be determined, together with the
characteristic life (x). Ancillary scales are available from which mean times between
failures can be calculated together with appropriate confidence limits.

Trans World Airlines

The Crepes Suzette Decision

TWA was one of the major US airlines. It operated extensive routes in the United States and to major cities in Europe, Asia and Africa. Competition was keen on all of these routes. The Company's officials firmly believed in providing service that was in all respects at least as good as that offered by the competition — and a little better if at all possible.

When TWA began jet operations in 1959, it was able to provide a higher degree of schedule reliability than did its competitors. TWA's marketing officials believed that in order to be successful an airline must first have a good product, i.e. excellent equipment, good schedules, on-time performance, and well-run operations. Realistically they knew that competitors could have identical equipment and identical flight schedules. They also knew that, at least in the long run, any competitor could copy a successful innovation and share in some of the traffic that was attracted by such device.

Since TWA flew to Paris and Rome, it seemed quite natural to adapt certain European ideas to its domestic service in the US. It began to serve a good French wine with dinner followed by a vintage champagne. Passengers reacted favourably and the competition reacted accordingly; they too began to serve wine and champagne, at least on the competitive runs.

Not content with the status quo, TWA pioneered with freshly brewed coffee, a choice of salad dressing, hot hors d'oeuvres, freshly baked hot rolls and other gourmet touches. While each additional service involved certain costs, TWA management believed that additional expenditures were justified as long as they continued to produce more business. The fact of the matter was that TWA's traffic continued to grow. By 1963 it was outstripping its rivals in terms of percentage growth and in absolute terms in certain markets.

In 1961, TWA pioneered with in-flight movies. The passenger response was good. A few months later it introduced its internationally famous Royal Ambassador menu on its coast to coast domestic flights. It introduced French pastries, attractive parfaits, assorted cheeses, and fresh fruits. Since no service innovation could be protected by patent, there was nothing to keep the competition from following suit. TWA management felt that its future lay in pioneering more new ideas and in staying ahead of the pack.

In April of 1965, TWA was interested in adding another feature that would help to distinguish its service from that of its competitors. After making a detailed canvass for ideas, TWA's Vice President — Customer Service concluded that there would be marketing appeal in serving crepes suzette dessert. These French delicacies were served on several flights. Passenger reaction was enthusiastic and seemed to indicate that crepes suzette could become another TWA 'first'.

Before he made final plans for their introduction, the V.P. — Customer Service advanced the idea at the President's staff meeting, inviting comments and suggestions. The reaction there was mixed.

The chief hostess was apprehensive. She took the position that before any additional service features were added, a careful study should be made to determine whether the present cabin force could realistically be expected to provide the service without risking a deterioration in quality. It was her belief that on certain coast to coast flights, when most of the seats were occupied, the hostesses had no 'slack' time and that on some flights they did not have adequate time to perform all their tasks in a gracious, leisurely manner.

The Vice President — Industrial Relations also expressed some concern over the idea. He pointed out that as the level of service had increased, the demands on the hostess had likewise increased. Because the jets flew much faster than had piston driven aircraft, hostesses made more round trips per month than they had made in the older craft. There were several indications of hostess dissatisfaction, and he was reluctant to have anything done which might lower their morale or disrupt the course of impending contract negotiations.

All of the executives were conscious of the fact that the hostess was a very important employee, generally having more passenger contacts than any other. A good hostess could do much to encourage repeat business — and the contrary likewise was true.

While the executives wanted to institute any innovation that was promising, they did not want to plunge into a programme without adequate study. Accordingly they requested a study that would indicate precisely how much work was presently expected from hostesses on the coast to coast flights and how the crepes suzette service would affect that work load. There was general agreement that crepes suzette might well have marketing appeal and that it would be difficult for the competition to copy, because TWA's 707s were equipped with a special type of oven that was not in general use. Should crepes suzette prove to be popular, it would be expensive for the competition to install the ovens, and the installation would take some time.

A staff assistant was assigned to the crepes suzette feasibility study. The following material is drawn from his report.

This report concerns the possibility of serving crepes suzette for dessert in the first class section of coast to coast Royal Ambassador Flights. At the present time, these flights have four hostesses on board. Two hostesses are assigned to the first class section and two to the coach section. There presently are 38 seats in the first class section of most of the 707s in this service and 83 coach seats. Coach passengers are provided liquor service on these flights followed by attractive hot meals. The hostesses customarily offer each passenger a hot beverage at least twice during the flight.

Movies are also provided in both sections. This requires a hostess in each section to install the screen and to provide head sets for the passengers. An earlier study indicates that two hostesses can adequately serve the coach section even when it is full. When there are more than 50 passengers in this section both hostesses are very busy and must serve some meals during the movie. Average movie duration is 90 minutes. When there are fewer than 40 passengers in the coach section, the hostesses in coach have free time and generally offer to help the hostesses in first class.

Time requirements in the first class section are more critical. The result of time studies taken in the first class section on several coast to coast flights are shown in Figure 1. (All times are in terms of the efforts of one hostess.)

It should be pointed out that these are *average* times. On occasion any item may require more time because of turbulence, the inexperience of hostesses, or for other reasons. On occasion some hostesses adequately perform all these duties in somewhat less time. But the times quoted are normally accurate, considering the nature of the work.

If crepes suzette service is instituted, preparation will require ten minutes

Activity	Time (minutes) Per Passenger	Per Flight
Checking, hanging and returning of coats	0.5	
Taking cocktail orders	0.5	
Serving cocktails	2.0	
Heating hors d'oeuvres		10.0
Serving hors d'oeuvres	2.0	
Preparing salads	1.0	
Serving salads	1.5	
Serving wine	2.0	
Preparing entree		10.0
Serving entree	2.0	
Baking rolls		5.0
Serving rolls	0.5	
Serving coffee	2.0	
Serving dessert	1.0	
Serving cordials	0.5	
Picking up dishes, glasses, etc.	2.5	
Heating (or chilling) towels		5.0
Serving and picking up towels	1.0	
Installing and removing movie screen		5.0
Passing out movie head sets	0.5	
Miscellaneous service	0.5	
Totals	20.0 min/passenger	35.0 min/flight

Figure 1 (TWA)   Hostess time requirements — first class section

Origin	Destination	Number of Flights	Scheduled Flying Time
Los Angeles	Boston	1	4:55
Los Angeles	New York	8	4:26
Los Angeles	Philadelphia	1	4:30
Los Angeles	Baltimore	1	4:25
Los Angeles	Washington	2	4:38
Boston	Los Angeles	2	5:25
New York	Los Angeles	6	5:20
Philadelphia	Los Angeles	1	5:00
Baltimore	Los Angeles	1	4:50
Washington	Los Angeles	1	4:58
San Francisco	Boston	1	4:55
San Francisco	New York	5	4:55
San Francisco	Washington	1	4:45
Boston	San Francisco	1	5:40
New York	San Francisco	4	5:35
Washington	San Francisco	1	5:15

Last summer in our heavy traffic months (May, June, July, and August) coast to coast on-time performance was as follows:

>15 minutes over schedule	<1%
15—10 minutes over schedule	3%
10—5 minutes over schedule	5%
5 minutes over—5 minutes under schedule	72%
5—10 minutes under schedule	10%
10—15 minutes under schedule	5%
15—20 minutes under schedule	3%
>20 minutes under schedule	<1%
	100%

Figure 2 (TWA)   Daily schedule — non-stop coast to coast flights

additional time (working) per flight, and one minute serving time per passenger more than is presently required for less fancy desserts. That would effectively mean an increase in hostess work load. Assuming that we wish to maintain our high standards of service, this may mean that an additional hostess will be required on some flights. The work load generally will be more critical on the east bound flights because of westerly winds and consequently faster flights.

This summer we have scheduled daily coast to coast flights as shown in Figure 2. The best meteorological data available would indicate that we can expect about the same type of winds this summer and approximately the same in-flight time.

Typically coast to coast fares are, for example, Los Angeles—New York one-way:

First Class $160
Coach Class $145

At the present time we require a load factor (the ratio of the number of fare paying passengers to the number of seats available) of 39% to cover our full costs on coast to coast jet flights. This means that each additional passenger that we can attract will contribute materially to our profits, since the incremental cost of carrying an additional passenger is small — perhaps ten dollars per first class passenger, and somewhat lower in coach.

Our hostesses are presently paid according to the following schedule:

1st 6 months	$323.87
2nd 6 months	341.22
2nd year	364.35
3rd year	381.70
4th year	393.27
5th year	404.84
6th year	416.40
7th year	427.97
8th year	433.76

These pay schedules are per month, for flying up to 70 hours. The present contract with the Air Line Stewards and Stewardesses Association provides that for every hour of flying per month above 70 hours hostesses will receive additional compensation at the following hourly rates:

1st 6 months	$4.63
2nd 6 months	4.87
2nd year	5.21
3rd year	5.45
4th year	5.62
5th year	5.78
6th year	5.95
7th year	6.11
8th year	6.20

The agreement further provides that cabin attendants may be scheduled for a maximum of 78½ flying hours per month, exclusive of ground time, en route station time, and time spent at lay over stations.

While the composition of the labour force changes from time to time, the following seniority breakdown is fairly accurate at the present time.

6 months seniority	5%
6 months—1 year seniority	10%
1 year—2 years seniority	20%
2 years—3 years seniority	20%
3 years—4 years seniority	15%
4 years—5 years seniority	15%
5 years—6 years seniority	10%
6 years—7 years seniority	2%
7 years—8 years seniority	2%
More than 8 years seniority	1%

On March 1, we had approximately 1,600 domestic hostesses. Fifty hostesses were on sick leave or otherwise unavailable, making a total of 1,550 domestic hostesses available for flight duty. Hostess turnover was of sufficient magnitude that the company found it necessary to hire some 800 new hostess trainees in 1964. Average monthly hostess utilization in 1964 was approximately 65 flying hours per month. That calculation takes into account vacations, sick leave, and the fact that every domicile must maintain some 'reserve' hostesses to be available when regular 'bid' hostesses are not available for any reason.

There are definite industrial relations implications in any decision here. For several months many hostesses have been talking about a reduction in flying hours. Others have been requesting that we put a fifth hostess on all coast to coast flights.

Some of these requests have been made via the company suggestion plan. Many of these appear to be thoughtful suggestions to improve our service. Some remarks have been written in the hostesses' regular post-flight reports. There have been many notes and letters to various supervisors and company officials. Recently the union has taken up the cry, and some questionable materials have been distributed in some of our terminals and near some of our sales offices.

Some of these materials have urged passengers to write to the president of the airline asking that a fifth hostess be placed on all flights. Others have asked passengers to write the Federal Aviation Agency to urge that the Civil Air Regulations be amended to require a fifth hostess on all flights. Some of these materials are almost in the nature of the type of materials that would be distributed on a strike picket line. Of course, we have no accurate way of measuring the impact of these materials on our customers; nor do we know whether they have been sanctioned by the officers of the International Union. But it is obvious that the existence of such materials is another factor which we must consider.

It is difficult to determine how much of this activity represents a real concern over work load and how much represents union pressure. We are, of course, approaching contract sessions with the union. It would not be unrealistic to look for a demand for sizeable wage increases coupled with a reduced work load.

Nonetheless, there is a work load problem. If we add crepes suzette, or any other item that requires more time to serve, we will have to add a fifth girl, at least on some flights.

We analysed the loads on coast to coast flights in May, June, July, and August of 1964, taking a sample consisting of every fifth day on a representative flight pairing between Los Angeles and New York and return (see Figure 3). The Los Angeles based crew that flies the east bound trip would normally return home on the west bound flight after a lay over in New York.

As I see the alternatives, we can:

(1) do nothing in the hostess complement question and hope that the problem does not become serious,
(2) add a fifth hostess for all coast to coast flights,
(3) calculate the probablilities and carry a fifth hostess on only those flights for which the work load would warrant the additional expense.

Date	FLIGHT 102 EAST BOUND Coach	First Class		FLIGHT 101 WEST BOUND Coach	First Class	
			58.33			
May 1	83	38*	*12.67 + 35'*	52	19	*6.33*
6	60	20	*6.67 + 35*	83	38	*12.67*
11	42	19	*6.33*	60	19	*6.33*
16	51	22	*7.33*	75	21	*7*
21	75	23	*7.67*	76	32	*10.67*
26	48	16	*5.33*	81	16	*5.33*
31	35	15	*5.*	69	14	*4.67*
June 4	62	4	*1.33*	72	25	*8.33*
9	83	38	*12.67*	83	36	*12*
14	83	34	*11.33*	83	37	*12.33*
19	82	13	*4.33*	81	19	*6.33*
24	81	33	*11*	83	24	*8*
29	80	14	*4.67*	82	34	*11.33*
July 4	22	4	*1.33*	16	3	*1*
9	65	31	*10.33*	64	31	*10.33*
14	66	14	*4.67*	38	16	*5.33*
19	75	18	*6*	74	19	*6.33*
24	76	21	*7*	78	19	*6.33*
29	75	19	*6.33*	72	30	*10*
Aug. 3	73	21	*7*	69	19	*6.33*
8	76	14	*4.67*	75	24	*8*
13	78	34	*11.33*	55	18	*6*
18	79	33	*11*	53	21	*7*
23	65	29	*9.67*	52	23	*7.67*
28	62	28	*9.33*	49	16	*5.33*

*All regular seats plus four lounge seats occupied.

Figure 3 (TWA)   Passengers carried on a sample of flights between Los Angeles and New York

Should we elect alternative (3) we would inevitably have some stand-by costs for hostesses called out for possible fifth girl duty and not used. Call out pay is at the rate of two (flying) hours pay per call out, but this is a wage cost only. It is not deducted from the girls' available flying hours.

Flight crews normally return on specific flights in accordance with established turn-around patterns, but it would be possible to hold the fifth hostess awaiting a flight that required her services. Hostesses can be deadheaded, but deadhead rates are the same as flight pay rates; however, deadheading does not count against a hostess's monthly maximum flying time.

Whitehaven Steel Section Co.

In the early 1960s a major company, specializing in rerolling and stocking steel, decided to build a small steelworks in the Northwest. A new subsidiary, the Whitehaven Steel Section Co., was formed to construct and operate the works. Construction started in October 1966 at a site on the edge of the Cumberland Coalfield near Whitehaven.

The new steelworks was designed to roll special steel sections from steel made by the electric arc process. A feature of the project was to be a new power station, sited close to the steelworks, which would supply all the power required.

Two arc furnaces were to be erected, each designed for an average output of 150 tons per day. There were also to be reheating furnaces and a twin rolling mill.

The rolling mill was to be split into two sets of stands to increase its flexibility. One set was expected to deal with high volume products, and the other was to handle the smaller orders.

The power station was to have three boilers and three 120 MW turbogenerators. Two generators were to supply the full load and the third was to be a standby. In operation it was expected that each generator would feed one arc furnace and half the rolling mill.

The complete project was expected to cost £52 M of which £21 M would be spent on the power station. However, the project was located in a regional development area which provided strong financial inducement to the steel company in the form of government grants and tax concessions.

The site in the Northwest had also been selected as it fulfilled most of the primary needs for steelmaking. There were good port facilities, and coal could be obtained at an attractive price from local collieries. One of the major influences in the decision to incorporate a power station had been the advantageous coal contract that had been negotiated with the NCB. In addition the area also offered local supplies of semifinished steel, and ample reserves of electricity were available from the National Grid.

The local region was a traditional ship building, steel and mining area, apart from the Calder Hall nuclear power station. Virtually all the local industry was of a heavy character and Whitehaven expected no problems in recruiting suitable labour.

The Organization of Construction

The constructional plan required the project to be completed in two phases. The first phase covered all the civil engineering work, installation of the rolling mill, one arc furnace and half the generating capacity. The rest of the work was scheduled to be completed six months later, in phase two.

The size and complexity of the works posed a major problem in coordination and timing. The first task of the civil engineering contractors was to prepare the site, install site services and build foundations. When this work was sufficiently advanced steelwork and plant erection could commence. The remainder of the installation and roofing would follow the structural steelwork, but with overlapping tasks. The electrical contractors could only start after much of the mechanical plant had been partially completed. Over the greater part of the construction period all the contractors would be on site at the same time, and their progress would be dependent on each other. The construction schedule for phase 1 is shown in Figure 1.

The Whitehaven Steel Section Co. had employed a consultant to design and supervise the construction of the works. Whitehaven was to award the construction contracts and allow the consultants to manage them. Under this system it was traditional to leave industrial relations in the hands of the contractors.

The consultants had specialist experience of power station construction, and they coordinated the design for the project around the company's design requirements for the rolling mill. They prepared the contract document, called tenders, managed and inspected for the company. They were excluded from responsibility for industrial relations but were responsible for site welfare facilities, security, canteens and safety.

	YEAR															
	1966				1967				1968				1969			
	1	2	3	4	1	2	3	4	1	2	3	4	1	2	3	4
Start on Site and Preliminary Site Works			⊢	—	—	⊣										
Main Foundations (Steelworks and Power Station)				⊢	—	—	—	—	—	⊣						
Steelwork (Steelworks and Power Station)					⊢	—	—	—	—	⊣						
Boiler						⊢	—	—	—	—	⊣					
Rolling Mill and Furnace Erection						⊢	—	—	—	—	⊣					
Coal, Ash and Steel Handling Equipment							⊢	—	—	—	—	⊣				
Electrical Work (Steelworks and Power Station)							⊢	—	—	—	⊣					
Turbo Generator							⊢	—	—	⊣						

Figure 1 (Whitehaven Steel Section Co.)   Construction schedule for Phase 1

Contractor	Contracted to	Work Involved	Type of Contract	No. of Subcontractors
W. Deep	Whitehaven	All civil engineering	Fixed price + CPA	1
Northern Steel Erectors	Workington Boiler Co.	Supply and erection of boiler house steelwork	Fixed price + CPA	1
	Whitehaven	Erection of steelwork for rolling mill	Fixed price	0
Furness Bridge and Engineering	W. Deep (Nominated)	Supply and erection of steelwork for furnace area, turbine hall and coal bunkers	Fixed price + steel adjustment	0
Workington Boiler	Whitehaven	Manufacture, supply and erection of steam generating units	Fixed price + CPA	10
Bolton Turbo Electric	Whitehaven	Manufacture supply and erection of turbo generators	Fixed price + CPA	0
Nottingham Mechanical Handling	Whitehaven	Supply and erection of coal, ash and steel handling equip.	Fixed price + CPA	1
Stott Rodgers	Whitehaven	General mechanical erection for rolling mill and furnaces	Reimbursable	0
C. G. Henderson	Whitehaven	General electrical services	Reimbursable	1

Note: CPA = Contract Price Adjustment

Figure 2 (Whitehaven Steel Section Co.)   Main contracts

Contract Policy and Contractors

The Whitehaven Steel Section Co. decided to use several direct contractors rather than let the work to a single contractor or consortium. This decision was taken in the belief that more competitive prices could be obtained. The work content of each contract was based on normal practice. However, the company found it necessary to split the steelwork contract as no contractor would undertake the complete contract within the time and price required. The company planned to have phase 1 of the construction plan completed within three years of construction commencing.

The civil engineering contract was let to W. Deep and Co.. In turn W. Deep nominated Furness Bridge and Engineering as a steelwork subcontractor for the turbine hall, coal bunkers and furnace area. The boiler house contract was let to the Workington Boiler Co.. The boiler house steelwork was then subcontracted by Workington to Northern Steel Erectors. A further contract, for the rolling mill, was also obtained by Northern Steel Erectors. Mechanical erection was let to Stott and Rodgers, and the mechanical equipment was to be purchased by Whitehaven under a number of contracts. Most of the electrical work was contracted to C. G. Henderson. These and other main contracts are detailed in Figure 2.

Many of the contracts were fixed price with firm completion dates. Some contained a contract price with adjustments to compensate for any rise or fall in the cost of materials and labour. This adjustment was to be calculated by using a recognized formula of the relevant trade association. Other contracts included an adjustment for an increase in steel prices. Most of the contracts contained clauses in respect of liquidated damages for delay in completion. All of the contracts reflected Whitehaven's preference for placing responsibility for performance on the contractor.

The Contractors' Workforce

The average workforce of the non-civil engineering contractors is shown in Figure 3. These figures were subject to wide variation at different stages in the contract. The labour force of Stott Rodgers is shown as an average of 154 men. However, in Figure 4, it can be seen that the labour force for Stott Rodgers was 330 during the period of peak activity. Similar patterns are apparent for other contractors.

Figure 4 shows that only a small proportion of the craftsmen were permanently employed by the contractors. Similarly the semiskilled and unskilled workers were temporary employees. The service lengths for all three groups are detailed in Figure 5.

Although unskilled labour could be obtained locally, skilled and semiskilled workers had to be drawn from a wide area. Figure 6 shows the number of workers living in lodgings or camps.

	Fitters	Welders	Plumbers	Erectors	Electricians	Pipe Fitters	Semiskilled	Labourers	Others	Total
Northern Steel Erectors				41			5	3		49
Furness Bridge and Engineering			2	59				6		67
Workington Boiler	6	5		22			27	2	3	65
Bolton Turbo Electric	5	1			2	2	4	3	1	18
Nottingham Mechanical Handling	2	1		6			5		2	16
Stott Rodgers	14	14	22	35	4		50		15	154
C. G. Henderson					77		43			120
										489

Figure 3 (Whitehaven Steel Section Co.)   Average number of men employed by main contractors

	Constructional Steelwork %	Electrical Engineering %	Boiler %	Other %	Average No. of Workers*
Northern Steel Erectors	10.6				52
Furness Bridge and Engineering	26				38
Workington Boiler			11.7		131
Bolton Turbo Electric			50.1		39
Nottingham Mechanical Handling				21.9	10
Stott Rodgers				0.0	330
C. G. Henderson		40.1			280
1970 National Survey by NEDO	42.1	55.8	32.2		

*Average number of workers differs from Figure 3 due to different basis of calculation.

Figure 4 (Whitehaven Steel Section Co.)   Percentage of craftsmen permanently employed by the contractors

	CRAFTSMEN				SEMISKILLED				UNSKILLED			
	Less than 6 months	6 mths. 1 year	1–5 yrs.	Over 5 yrs	Less than 6 months	6 mths. 1 year	1–5 yrs.	Over 5 yrs	Less than 6 months	6 mths. 1 year	1–5 yrs.	Over 5 yrs.
Northern Steel Erectors	28.3	40.0	23.9	7.8	14.0	50.8	35.2	0.0	10.7	50.5	38.8	0.0
Furness Bridge and Engineering	17.8	23.9	37.6	20.7	–	–	–	–	7.9	26.3	65.8	0.0
Workington Boiler	40.3	27.3	21.2	11.2	48.1	26.2	25.7	0.0	44.0	45.1	10.9	0.0
Bolton Turbo Electric	48.0	6.5	14.6	30.9	63.1	21.4	5.8	9.7	100.0	0.0	0.0	0.0
Nottingham Mechanical Handling	33.4	23.7	35.4	7.5	57.1	33.0	9.9	0.0	–	–	–	–
Stott Rodgers	60.1	30.3	9.6	0.0	60.1	31.6	8.3	0.0	–	–	–	–
C. G. Henderson	63.4	19.3	16.6	0.7	62.4	32.5	5.1	0.0	–	–	–	–
NEDO Survey all Companies	21.2	27.1	34.0	17.8	–	–	–	–	–	–	–	–

Figure 5 (Whitehaven Steel Section Co.)   Length of service with contractor

	Craftsmen	Semiskilled	Unskilled
Northern Steel Erectors	19.1	14.1	0.0
Furness Bridge and Engineering	48.9	0.0	0.0
Workington Boilers	7.1	0.0	0.0
Bolton Turbo Electric	19.4	12.1	0.0
Nottingham Mechanical Handling	23.4	0.0	0.0
Stott Rodgers	5.7	1.1	0.0
C. G. Henderson	40.1	0.0	0.0
Average for Site	26.2		
Average for 1970 NEDO Survey	38.6		

Figure 6 (Whitehaven Steel Section Co.)   Percentage of manual employees living in lodgings or camps

Contractors' Personnel Policies

Contractors' policy varied widely in the degree of responsibility and autonomy given to site agents at Whitehaven. All the contractors were engaged on contracts on other sites, and this limited the autonomy that could be given to the agents. In some firms the site agent was given little direction from headquarters and made his own decisions on discipline, pay and recruitment. In other firms the site agent had to work within his company's personnel policy. Bolton Turbo Electric had the only personnel policy incorporating a company agreement negotiated with full-time union officials.

Most of the contractors had personnel or industrial relations specialist at their headquarters. However, Stott Rodgers was the only firm with an industrial relations adviser on site. Only Stott Rodgers, Workington Boiler and C. G. Henderson employed personnel officers in senior managerial positions.

All the contractors used the national agreements as the basis of their personnel policies. These agreements, apart from the electrical contracting agreement, set the minimum rates of pay and allowances. The electrical agreement set standard rates and allowances with no unauthorized additions. This meant that the contractors were free to devise their own bonus schemes for all except the electricians.

The contractors who maintained a more permanent workforce (see Figures 4 and 5) tended to have well developed policies for personnel and industrial relations. They also provided training, pension schemes and systems of promotion. Only C. G. Henderson trained their shop stewards in industrial relations. C. G. Henderson and Stott Rodgers also trained their site agents and foremen in industrial relations.

The type of labour force also affected other company policies. To maintain a permanent workforce, pay systems were selected which encouraged mobility and

TRADE	LOWEST FIRMS MEDIAN* PAYMENT AS A % OF HIGHEST MEDIAN			
	Weekly Earnings	Hourly (No overtime)	Incentive Earnings	Overtime Earnings
Fitters	46	78.4	20.7	41.9
Welders	44	73.9	15.0	10.7
Plumbers	69	62.9	18.9	100
Erectors	45	52.6	19.3	14
Electricians	64	60.9	21.6	36.9
Semiskilled	47	42.6	17.6	25.8
Labourers	60	72.2	22.6	29.1

*Medians for 1968

Figure 7 (Whitehaven Steel Section Co.)   Comparison of earnings for men in the same trades in different companies

long service. Where casual labour was used, the contractors had developed good central recruitment systems.

Bonus Schemes

All the companies except C. G. Henderson introduced bonuses or conditions money above the basic rate. Northern Steel Erectors paid a bonus based on the number of steel bays erected. Furness Bridge and Engineering devised a tonnage bonus scheme in which targets were specified as the contract progressed. Workington Boiler used a system of target times with bonus for time saved, though the system was modified during the contract period as a result of disputes.

Stott Rodgers paid a bonus, but used no incentives due to the problem of work measurement. Similarly Bolton Turbo Electric paid bonuses, but did not use incentives as a matter of company policy.

Figures 7, 8 and 9 show the variations in earnings between contractors, and between weeks with the same contractor.

Union Membership and Recognition

The non-civil engineering workers belonged to four main unions:

(1) The Amalgamated Society of Boilermakers Shipwrights Blacksmiths and Structural Workers (ASBSBSW).
(2) The Electrical Electronic Telecommunications Union/Plumbing Trade Union (EETU/PTU).
(3) The Amalgamated Union of Engineering and Foundry Workers (AUEW).
(4) The Constructional Engineering Union (CEU).

	Fitters %	Welders %	Erectors %	Electricians %	Semiskilled %	Labourers %
Northern Steel Erectors	–	–	40	–	21	10
Furness Bridge and Engineering	–	–	47	–	–	8
Workington Boiler	33	28	30	–	30	–
Bolton Turbo Electric	29	35	–	29	18	20
Nottingham Mechanical Handling	27	31	28	–	32	–
Stott Rodgers	39	35	40	37	36	–
C. G. Henderson	–	–	–	0	0	–

Figure 8 (Whitehaven Steel Section Co.)   Proportion of incentive in the median weekly wage excluding overtime

	Fitters £	Welders £	Erectors £	Electricians £	Semiskilled £	Labourers £
Northern Steel Erectors	30.9	–	–	–	6.65	11.1
Furness Bridge and Engineering	33.6	21.4	–	–	–	6.46
Workington Boiler	20.8	18.5	19.8	–	17.8	4.84
Bolton Turbo Electric	–	7.92	5.57	1.76	3.52	3.08
Nottingham Mechanical Handling	15.0	15.8	15.0	–	20.0	–
Stott Rodgers	15.1	27.6	20.0	25.8	14.5	–
C. G. Henderson	–	–	–	5.68	4.27	–

Figure 9 (Whitehaven Steel Section Co.)   Range between minimum and maximum weekly earnings excluding overtime

	CEU	AUEW	EETU/PTU	ASBSBSW	Number of Shop Stewards
Northern Steel Erectors	X				1
Furness Bridge and Engineering	X				3
Workington Boiler	X	X		X	3
Bolton Turbo Electric		X	X		1
Nottingham Mechanical Handling	X	X		X	1
Stott Rodgers	X	X	X	X	5
C. G. Henderson			X		2

Figure 10 (Whitehaven Steel Section Co.)   Unions with members in the companies on site

| | EEF AGREEMENTS FOLLOWED | | | | | ELECTRICAL CONTRACTORS ASSOCIATION | |
| | | | Steam Generating Plant Agreements | | | | |
	EEF Fed.	Outside Steel Erection	CEU/ TGWU/ GMWU	ASBSBSW	AEU/ PTU/ H & D	ECA Fed.	Follows Agreement
Northern Steel Erectors	X	X					
Furness Bridge and Engineering	X	X					
Workington Boiler	X		X	X	X		
Bolton Turbo Electric	X				X		
Nottingham Mechanical Handling	X		X	X	X		
Stott Rodgers	X		X		X		
C. G. Henderson						X	X

Figure 11 (Whitehaven Steel Section Co.)   Agreements followed on the site, and contractors' membership of employers' associations

Figure 10 shows which contractors had employees belonging to these unions, and the total number of shop stewards in each contractors' workforce.

Most of the shop stewards had some contact with officials of their union, but only the CEU regional organizer maintained regular contact. There was very little contact between site members and the local union branches.

There were several attempts by the CEU regional organizer to coordinate bargaining on the site. Early in 1967 he tried to promote regular meetings for all CEU stewards on the site. This joint CEU stewards committee was never recognized by the employers, and after a number of meetings it was abandoned.

The next year the CEU regional organizer approached the employers to obtain recognition of a site convenor and shop stewards' committee. This was rejected, and the employers refused to support any coordination of union activity on site fearing that union coordination could increase the pressure on management.

The regional organizer also made several approaches to the site coordination committee (the employers' joint body) for a site agreement and negotiating structure for unions and contractors. Following the first approaches the organizer was asked to submit proposals, but his first proposal in April 1967 for a joint discussion of holiday dates was rejected. The employers felt this should be discussed on an individual basis.

In 1968 the general secretary of the CEU tried to arrange a site meeting with the steel erection firms to negotiate minimum rates. The coordination committee declined to participate

Following a strike later in 1968 the major contractors agreed to meet full-time officials of the CEU, AUEW and ASBSBSW. However this meeting failed due to disagreements over the agenda. No further joint meetings were attempted.

The agreement followed by the employers, and their membership of employers' associations is shown in Figure 11. Early in 1967 the contractors formed a coordination committee under the auspices of the EEF. Only Northern Steel Erectors, Workington Boiler and Bolton Turbo Electric were represented at the first meeting, but they produced the constitution and policy, shown in Figures 12A and 12B, which was circulated to all contractors. Membership of the committee was restricted to 'executives of managerial status with contract responsibility' in an attempt to ensure the committee's status and authority. Thus site agents were excluded. This level of membership made frequent meetings impracticable and first hand knowledge of site issues was not available.

The committee did not succeed in leading a coordinated approach to issues of pay and conditions. The first major dispute over pay and bonus was settled without reference to the committee. When prior consultation did occur a coordinated approach on pay issues seldom emerged.

Industrial Relations

No major disputes occured on site between the time work started in October 1966 and the arrival of the steelwork contractors in the Spring of 1967. From that time

(1) All employers were to supply the coordination committee with full information on their intended pay rates, bonus payments and conditions of employment before they start on the site. If any rates, bonus payments or conditions of employment were out of line, then the employers were to be advised not to start any employees before approval had been given by the committee.

(2) Firms were not to make any changes in pay rates, bonus payments or working conditions, which would affect the level of take-home pay, without consulting the site coordination committee. Where such changes could have repercussions on other contractors, a meeting of these contractors was to be convened.

(3) Firms were not to engage labour currently or latterly in the employment of another firm on this site without reference to the other firm. No firm was to engage workers without the verification of references. All firms were to avoid action likely to embarrass another and be prepared to help any firm faced with an unreasonable claim or direct action by their workers. Threats of industrial action were to be reported to the committee.

(4) Membership of the committee was to be restricted to executives of managerial status with contract responsibility. Members were also to ensure that subcontractors followed the principles of the constitution.

Figure 12A (Whitehaven Steel Section Co.)   Main points of the constitution of the site coordination committee

(1) Federated employers were only to deal with site stewards specifically appointed to represent their own workers.

(2) Convenors of site stewards were not provided for in any of the procedure agreements and were not to be recognized.

(3) Site stewards committees should not be recognized and stewards should not be allowed time off to attend them.

(4) Unpaid time off for a site stewards meeting was only to be allowed if a full-time union official requested it for an approved reason.

Figure 12B (Whitehaven Steel Section Co.)   The site coordination committee's policy on shop stewards

on the site was continually disrupted by strikes, resulting in the loss of 37,116 man days. Phase 1 of the construction plan was completed nearly one year late.

The civil engineering contractor, W. Deep, was the first contractor to start on the site, and suffered no major industrial relations problems during the full period of the contract. This could possibly be attributed to the different unions and national agreements involved in the civil engineering work. Of the non-civil engineering contractors only Bolton Turbo Electric managed a strike free contract period.

A summary of the stoppages between the Spring of 1967 and the completion in late 1970 follows:

Company	Number of Stoppages	Days Struck	Man days lost
Northern Steel Erectors	33	91.5	2,634
Furness Bridge and Engineering	10	58	2,022
Workington Boiler	20	106	6,300
Bolton Turbo Electric	0	0	0
Nottingham Mechanical Handling	18	44	556
Stott Rodgers	12	31.5	7,960
C. G. Henderson	4	68	17,644
			37,116

The early disruptions took the form of overtime bans and go-slows in support of pay claims from the steel erectors. Both pay and industrial action increased, and this influenced further strikes in support of the parity claims by other workers. Further disruptions were also caused by a number of short strikes over safety, discipline and dismissals.

Site Disputes

The contract proceeded smoothly without any disputes until the steelwork contractors started work in March 1967. Employees of both steelwork companies began a campaign to increase their general level of earnings to 87½p per hour within days of starting work. Pressure was applied to the companies by means of go-slows and overtime bans. This pressure resulted in Furness Bridge and Engineering conceding a pay rise from 55p to 60p per hour in July. Whitehaven's consultants then began to urge Furness Bridge to keep up to the construction schedule. This resulted in Furness Bridge introducing a tonnage bonus scheme which could raise earnings to £1 per hour. Both these increases in earnings were made without reference to the site coordination committee or other employers.

Northern Steel Erectors followed the lead of Furness Bridge and increased its workers' earnings in 1967. In early 1968 both companies found they were under pressure to increase earnings by improving the bonus and guaranteed minimum payments. Several short strikes occurred in support of the workers' claims, and the CEU met both companies separately. Neither company could reach an agreement with the CEU and the dispute was referred to statutory conference.

In the statutory conference the claim for a minimum rate of 60p per hour was rejected. However, it was suggested that the CEU and employers continued an information discussion on a local basis while working continued. The employees of both companies rejected the proposals and went on strike.

All the strikers were threatened with dismissal. When this failed to gain a return to work, the strikers were given notice. Three weeks later the EEF, CEU and the steelwork companies reached an agreement to pay a minimum of 62½p per hour. Work was resumed two weeks later.

Over the next two months there were a series of disputes over bonus and guaranteed payments. These resulted in a number of short strikes and concessions. In June both companies held a joint, informal, meeting with the CEU. The unions' application for a site agreement was rejected, but the minimum rate was increased to 65p per hour. Overtime bans and short stoppages still continued throughout the remainder of the contract period, and both steelwork companies had to make further concessions.

Workington Boiler established itself on site in mid-1967 and it was soon suffering from serious industrial unrest. Owing to the hold-ups created by the steel erecting disputes, Workington's labour force was not built up from a token presence until December 1967. Prior to this date the token labour force had received a 10% lieu bonus, but an incentive bonus scheme had been agreed with union delegates for when work started. The new workers, and subsequently their elected representative, had the incentive bonus scheme explained to them and appeared to be satisfied.

In early 1968 the labour force of Workington Boiler were unable to proceed with boiler erection due to the steelworkers' disputes. However, they were found alternative work and were retained on site. During this period the steward requested a bonus other than the 10% lieu bonus that was being paid. This was rejected on the grounds that boiler erection had not commenced. Following the steel erectors' strike and 62½p settlement, the site steward requested a lieu bonus increase to 100%. This would have raised earnings from 40p + 4p to 40p + 40p per hour. This claim was rejected, and after further talks with site stewards, at which a measured incentive bonus was offered, a ½ day token strike ensued.

A claim for a 70p rate of earnings was then pressed in March. This was rejected as it exceeded the bonus payable on other Workington Boiler sites. Over the following two months a series of strikes occurred. The longest of these was for three weeks. A site conference was held, but this registered 'failure to agree'. It was not until the end of June that agreement was reached on a one month trial of a bonus scheme which was expected to yield a minimum of 65p per hour.

A series of minor disputes involving CEU members then occurred up until September. In September the CEU members held a short strike in support of a steward, sacked by one of the steel erection companies. There then followed a series of CEU meetings and an overtime ban. This resulted in a shortage of work for other employees, who consequently withdrew their labour for an afternoon to discuss the matter. The CEU members then held a series of strikes over safety matters. However, none of the claims of unsafe working conditions were substantiated by the Factory Inspector called in by the CEU organizer. The CEU organizer urged a return to work without success. Eventually he expressed his sympathy for his members and this resulted in an unconstitutional strike lasting nearly four months.

The CEU procedure for dealing with disputes could not be used as an unconstitutional strike was already in progress. Several informal meetings took place between CEU and EEF officials and the management of Workington Boiler. During these discussions a claim for earnings of 87½p per hour emerged as the main issue. The dispute was only resolved by the introduction of a bonus scheme which gave the opportunity to earn 90p per hour or more for a reasonable performance.

Nottingham Mechanical Handling suffered its first strike in June 1968. Its men came out in support of Workington Boiler's men, and stayed out after Workington's settlement. The strike was ended by the introduction of an incentive scheme without a guaranteed minimum. The men continued to come out in sympathy with Workington Boiler's men and these strikes were resolved by domestic negotiations. Eventually in February 1969 Nottingham Mechanical Handling declared the site steward and another man redundant. There was a strike and sympathetic action by other companies' workers, but the men were not reinstated.

Stott Rodgers were only affected by the sympathy strike in favour of the steward, sacked by one of the steel erection firms, until December 1968. There then followed a number of strikes by welders over working conditions. The welders claimed 5p an hour, but the company rejected this and provided additional safety equipment. The welders then reduced the claim to 2½p per hour. The dispute was finally resolved at a site conference in July 1969, at which an extra 2½p was awarded. During the renegotiation of the fixed bonus in July 1969 all Stott Rodgers employees struck for two weeks. This dispute was resolved by a 10% increase in bonus rates, awarded at statutory conferences in August.

The electrical contractor, C. G. Henderson, suffered a four week strike for parity of earnings in October 1968. The claim was rejected by the Joint Industry Board and the union ordered a return to work. Work was finally resumed after the company threatened to dismiss the strikers.

In August the electricians tried to claim parity by approaching the JIB with a complaint of poor working conditions. The JIB refused to investigate the claim as it believed that it represented a hidden wage claim precluded by their national rules. This resulted in Henderson's labour force of 360 going on strike.

At this point in time C. G. Henderson was short of work on the site as a result of other contractors' problems. Henderson was also aware that supplies of special steel sections had increased, the market was now fiercely competitive, and that Whitehaven only wished to operate one furnace and one set of rolling stands. Henderson was therefore only under pressure to proceed with the phase 1 electrical work, although it had hired enough labour to proceed with phase 1 and 2.

Initially the JIB, the union and Henderson tried to persuade the workers to return to work. After six weeks the company dismissed the strikers and recruited about 50 new workers in the face of fierce picketing. However, Whitehaven were not satisfied with this step.

Shortly before the strike had commenced Whitehaven had appointed a new chief executive. This man was a Harvard graduate with a strong interest in adopting a 'human relations' approach. He reversed Whitehaven's policy of non-intervention and appointed specialist industrial relations advisers.

The new chief executive then intervened in the C. G. Henderson dispute, persuading Henderson to concede 12½p per hour in breach of the JIB agreement. In turn this led to further claims from local electricians employed on the site.

Henderson rehired approximately half the strikers at the new rates. The men who were rehired were carefully selected, and C. G. Henderson rapidly completed phase 1 to Whitehaven's satisfaction. Henderson then took its time over phase 2 and was the only contractor to make a satisfactory profit.

Whitehaven's new chief executive succeeded in improving the industrial relations climate, and phase 1 was completed in September 1970. Phase 2 was completed five months later and the whole project cost 26% over budget.

The Winton Shirt Company

In late 1963, top management of the Winton Shirt Company was approached by a consulting firm which proposed the use of statistical sampling to replace Winton's 100% inspection of shirt parts and assemblies. A brief study of the quality of shirts leaving the company's main plant in Wellwood had revealed considerably more defects passing undetected through the 100% inspection procedures than management had realized. The consultants recommended a statistical quality control system (SQC) geared toward improving quality and reducing operating costs. Eager to augment their quality image, which had been recognized by numerous industry association awards, and hoping to reduce costs, Winton's management installed the proposed system in the Middletown plant on a trial basis. In October of 1966, Mr. R. Harris, plant manager of the Middletown operation, received a phone call from corporate headquarters. Top management was considering the extention of SQC to the eleven other Winton plants, and asked Mr. Harris to prepare a report evaluating SQC's effectiveness in Middletown.

History of SQC

Middletown had been selected for the trial because it was considered one of the company's best managed plants. In addition, its union had already accepted an SQC application in another company, and the union president was known to be enthusiastic about the concept. Mr. Harris, then Middletown's industrial engineer, was assigned to work with the consultants on the installation.

Initial discussions with the union paved the way for a preliminary survey which required each inspector to record the number and nature of every critical and major defect found[1] and to identify the responsible operations. (A summary of the survey data is presented in Figure 1.) Piece rate earnings of inspectors and stitchers were monitored throughout the four-week period and revealed no change from the presurvey levels. (Stitchers averaged $1.70 per hour and inspectors, $1.65.)

The survey identified a number of problem operations. The work stations at which these operations were performed were designated as 'primary stations', and

---

[1] Critical defects would result in a customer return if not repaired. Major defects would not result in a return but might be noticed by a customer. Minor defects were those which the customer probably would never discover.

Defects Caused By	Found in Process by Inspectors (Defects/ Hundred)	Found by Audit Conducted by Consultants Immediately After Final Inspection		'Total' (Defects/ Hundred)
		(Defects/ Hundred)	(% of Total Defects/ Hundred)	
Collar operations	6.4	—	—	6.4
Cuff operations	.8	.3	27	1.1
Front operations	1.7	2.8	62	4.5
Back operations	.3	2.3	88	2.6
Sleeve operations	.1	.5	83	.6
Assembly operations	10.2	12.0	54	22.2
Bad material	—	.4	100	.4
	19.5	18.3	48.4	37.8

The Survey recorded data for each operation in the shirt making process (see Column 1 of Figure 9). The figures given here are the sums for each of the operations pertaining to collar making, cuff making, etc.

Figure 1 (Winton Shirt Co.)   Summary of data collected on critical and major defects (four-week consultants' survey, 1963)

all sampling was to be done at these points. A statistical quality control system was then formulated consisting of three distinct elements: a sampling plan to determine if output was meeting quality standards; a quality audit procedure to act as a check on the system; and reporting procedures which included a quality rating for operator performance.

The Sampling Plan

The consultants provided a sampling plan based on Middletown's basic unit of production: the bundle. Each bundle contained four dozen identical shirt parts and was moved as a unit through a sequence of operations (see Column 1 of Figure 9) until, at final assembly, the bundles were matched and the shirts put together (see Figure 2). The plan operated as follows:

(1) Every fourth bundle completed by an operator at a 'primary station' would be sampled (sampling interval = 4).

(2) A sample, the size to be determined by Middletown's management, would be drawn from each bundle selected (sample size = N) and each item in the sample would be inspected.

(3) If no defects were found in the sample, the bundle would be accepted (acceptance number = 0). If one or more defects were found, the bundle would be rejected and returned to the operator for sorting and rework, with no additional compensation. (Rejection number = 1 or more.)

(4) If a bundle was rejected, two consecutive bundles out of the next three

produced by the operator would have to be acceptable for the operator to obtain clearance (clearance number = 2) and for normal sampling to resume. If the operator could not be cleared, the matter would be referred to the foreman.

To enable Mr. Harris to select the sample size, the consultants provided the operating characteristic (OC) curves for various sample sizes which are presented in Figure 3. From these Mr. Harris constructed the average out-going quality (AOQ) curves[2] for the plan, using various sample sizes (Figure 4). (The formula he used to derive these curves is presented in Figure 5.) Middletown's management assumed the 'process average per cent defective'[3] to be 4%. From an examination of the AOQ curve at this point, Mr. Harris selected a sample size of 15, based on the fact that a move from the N = 8 curve to the N = 15 curve resulted in a large improvement, while an additional step up to the N = 18 curve resulted in only a small gain which he believed was not worth the extra effort required. The use of the N = 15 curve provided an average outgoing quality limit (AOQL) of 3.61 defects per hundred.

Quality Audit

The plan included a 100-shirt quality audit procedure, which was coupled with an index of SQC effectiveness. The one hundred shirts were randomly selected each week and inspected according to a standards book which had previously existed but had not been used rigorously. (Figure 6 presents one of the standards contained in the book.) Defects were classified as critical, major, and minor and were assigned weights of 1.0, 0.5, and 0.1 respectively.

The quality effectiveness rating was derived by multiplying the total number of each type of defect found by the corresponding weight, totalling the weighted figures, and subtracting the sum from 100. Based on the initial survey, Mr. Harris estimated the plant's 1963 quality effectiveness rating to be 80. Since the company was already content with its over-all quality performance, and since quality standards would now be enforced more stringently, he decided to use the attainment of 80 or above as an indication of effective quality control.

Reporting Procedures

Reporting procedures were relatively simple. Operator rating forms were prepared by the quality control personnel to summarize weekly quality records for each operator. These indicated the number of rejected bundles and the sequence of bundles accepted or rejected, the total number of items examined, and the number of defects discovered per hundred items sampled. The operators were then rated as follows:

[2] The number of defects passing undetected through an inspection point expressed as a percentage of the total volume of parts.
[3] The number of defects generated by each production operation expressed as a percentage of the total volume of parts.

Standard or Above:	Excellent	0.0–0.99 Defects/Hundred
	Good	1.0–1.99 Defects/Hundred
	Fair	2.0–2.99 Defects/Hundred
Substandard:	Poor	3.0–4.49 Defects/Hundred
	Unsatisfactory	4.50 Defects/Hundred and over

The rating scale had been supplied by the consultants, but Mr. Harris had attached the labels to the scale. 'Since a 3.61 AOQL was the goal of SQC, I decided to designate the range which contained this figure as "poor",' he explained.

Quality audit summaries were prepared weekly for distribution to Middletown's plant manager and the corporate office. These reports listed, by responsible operation, the number of defects discovered in process and at quality audit, indicated the quality effectiveness rating and contained back-up sheets showing the nature and distribution of critical and major defects by responsible departments.

Installation of SQC

The biggest problem according to Mr. Harris, was finding the people needed for SQC and freeing them from the union. 'On the whole', he explained, 'the group of inspectors we had were not versatile enough nor oriented sufficiently towards human relations for the job. The work calls primarily for the exercise of tact and judgement, and little technical skill is required to identify defects'.

The job of 'inspector' was replaced by a position designated 'quality control supervisor', paying an hourly rate of $1.65. The union, after receiving guarantees that any inspectors who were not absorbed as QC supervisors would be retained for production jobs which would maintain their earnings, endorsed the SQC plan in its entirety.

Only one of the 28 inspectors was selected for the new position. (According to Mr. Harris, inspection had been used as a dumping area for girls who could not make out on production jobs.) The rest of the QC supervisors were selected from the production operators, many of whom took reductions in hourly earnings; however, better sick leave benefits, combined with some increased security against loss of time due to reduced workloads on any given day, tended to reduce differentials in take-home pay. Mr. Harris believed that the job was desirable because of the increase in status and prestige (e.g. signing their own time cards rather than punching the clock), the authority which went with the job, and the elimination of piece rate pressures.

SQC was introduced in the collar and cuff department in December of 1963. This was considered the best managed department and was the only one which adhered to the company's long stated policy of paying only for good work by returning defective work to the operators. The system was gradually extended to other departments, covering all except packaging by April of 1965.

QC supervisors were provided with tables which contained racks to hold operator rating cards, measuring equipment, and the book of inspection standards. Except in the assembly department, where inspection was performed at the manufacturing stations, all bundles were taken to the tables for inspection. A ticket listing the sequence of operations accompanied each bundle, and each operator who worked on the bundle wrote her number on the ticket beside the operation she performed. Bundle tickets were removed just prior to assembly.

Early Results of SQC

According to Mr. Harris initial foreman and worker reactions to the system were negative. The foremen, each of whom had been briefed about the plan prior to its installation in his department, objected to the paperwork. The operators objected both to the 'report cards' and to the fact that they would have to sort entire bundles and rip out defective work. Management maintained that inspection was merely a service function to insure maintenance of quality standards, that the operators were responsible for quality, and that it had long been an established policy to pay only for good work. The improvement in earnings to be expected as a result of the quality of parts reaching each operator was also stressed, and assurances were given that the company would enforce only the already existing standards, making no changes in the quality standards themselves.

Production dropped approximately 5% in each department upon introduction of SQC, but in all cases except one, levels returned to normal within a month. The 20 workers on 'pocket attach' presented the only major challenge to the system, according to Mr. Harris. When SQC was introduced, the defect per hundred rate ranged between 30 and 50 for failure to meet a three-stitch bar requirement (see Figure 6). The operators began to stitch by hand-turning the wheel on the sewing machines, and production dropped by 20%. Shortly thereafter, the operators filed a grievance stating that the standard had been changed and that a rate increase was required. Management contended that the standard had always been a three-stitch count, and it presented time studies to demonstrate that the standard was attainable and the piece rate fair.

According to Mr. Harris, the 'pocket attach' operation had always been one of the most troublesome in the plant. He said: 'There was a great deal of bitterness within the group at the time of the SQC installation, and much of this has carried over and remains even today. In spite of continual general increases in the wage rate structure, take-home pay for this group has hardly changed. Average group earnings were $1.57 per hour in 1963 and are now (1966) only $1.60, although several of the newer members of the group are earning $2.00.

We could not give the girls special consideration without jeopardizing the entire programme. Instead, we put them all on day-work and began a major retraining operation. Our union agreement specified that, when we introduce changes, we must maintain the average earnings for the group, not the individual. We pooled the total average earnings for the group and then distributed the money according to output. Several of the old timers began receiving the minimum wage, while some of the newer girls were taking home very good money. About half of the girls came up to standard within six to eight weeks. The others held out. We applied a great deal of pressure and a few problem workers left the company. We did not fire them, but we let them know that they were not wanted.

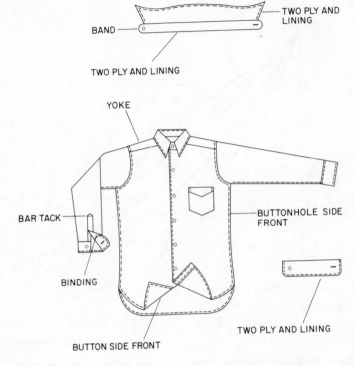

BAND — TWO PLY AND LINING

TWO PLY AND LINING

YOKE

BAR TACK —

BINDING

BUTTONHOLE SIDE FRONT

TWO PLY AND LINING

BUTTON SIDE FRONT

Figure 2 (Winton Shirt Co.)   Basic parts of an assembled shirt

In addition to the training efforts (we had a supervisor working full time with the group), we re-examined our standard. We decided that we really wanted a bar which was 2/16" − 3/16" long, and that, depending on such operator-introduced variables as tension and speed, three stitches plus or minus one could yield this measurement. Since it was easier for the operator to judge distance than number of stitches, we changed the standard.

It took four months to do the job, and during this period, some of the girls were close to rebellion. The only thing which stopped them was our firm policy to fire anyone who walked off the job. Our time studies had convinced us that our position was correct. By the end of the fourth month, the group finally reached standard, and we took them off daywork. The union, which had not pressed hard on the grievance, withdrew the action. This was the only grievance which was ever filed in regard to quality control. We have since made it quite clear that quality standards are not a subject for negotiation, although we are willing to negotiate on any matter relating to piece rates.'

During the course of the installation, it became evident that more supervisory time was required. In addition to their old duties, the foremen were required to spend more time dealing with paperwork, training, and the QC supervisors. As a result, another level of shop supervision was added. The job of foreman was upgraded to 'general foreman' and each general foreman was given one or more

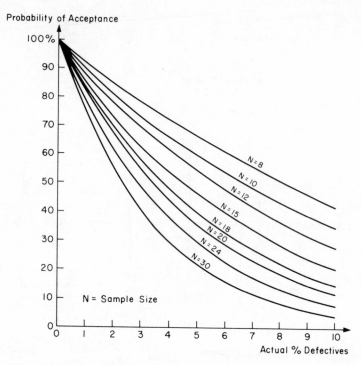

Figure 3 (Winton Shirt Co.)   Operating characteristic curves for single sampling plans with acceptance no. = 0

foreladies. 'Forelady' was a management position, at the same level in the organization as QC supervisor but at a slightly higher hourly wage rate.

A change in the structure of work stations was required for the introduction of SQC. Previously, the inspectors had performed production operations such as trimming loose threads, buttoning the two halves of the fronts together for felling[4], counting to insure that bundles were complete, etc. Since the QC supervisors were now examining only a small portion of total output, it was necessary to change some production methods to eliminate these steps (e.g. to fell separate shirt halves) or insert these operations in the manufacturing sequence. Production people, drawn from the old group of inspectors, were added for this purpose.

In July 1964, the consultants conducted a follow-up survey. Brief excerpts from their survey report are presented in Figure 7.

Present Status of Quality Control at Middletown

Only minor modifications have been made in the SQC system since 1963. The basic sampling plan has been altered for a number of operations by changing both sample

---

[4] Stitching operation which closes the shirt, starting at the end of the sleeve, running up to the armpit, and down the side of the shirt.

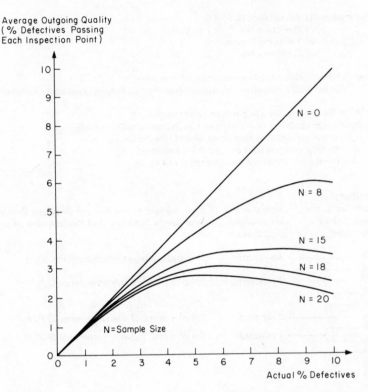

Figure 4 (Winton Shirt Co.)   Average outgoing quality curves for SQC sampling plan

size and interval. According to Mr. Harris, this takes process characteristics into consideration. For example, 'buttonsew collar' (placement of the collar button on the end of the band) is inspected in sample sizes of 10 and at intervals of 12 bundles. Mr. Harris explained the innovation: 'The buttonsewing machine is either good or bad, depending upon its setting. The operator can spot bad work easily, and it is not necessary to look at the operation as frequently or to take as large a sample to find out how well quality standards are being met. This is essentially equivalent to assuming a much lower process defect average, and it is therefore possible to achieve the same AOQ with a looser inspection plan.'

The actual numbers were not selected on a statistical basis but represented Mr. Harris' best estimate of what would do the job.

Figure 8 depicts the Middletown plant organization as it appeared in October 1966. Mr. Harris had reorganized the plant in December of 1965 to place all production operations under his direct control and free himself from staff functions, in accordance with his belief that 'the most important aspect of operations is the control of the volume of shirts going out the door. The former quality control manager had left the company's employ in August and Mr. LaFond had recently been assigned responsibility for quality control and training, in

Plan Parameters: 1) Acceptance No.   = 0
2) Rejection No.   = 1 or more
3) Sampling Interval = 4
4) Clearance No.   = 2

Assume: Uniform distribution of defects within bundles
Perfect 100% inspection of rejected bundles (all defects repaired or replaced)

Let p' = the process average per cent defectives
P_a = the probability of acceptance (taken from the OC curves)
P_r = the probability of rejection (taken from the OC curves)
R = bundle which would be rejected if inspected
A = bundle which would be accepted if inspected

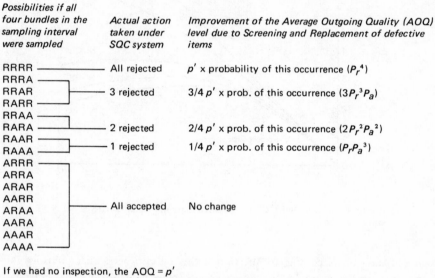

Possibilities if all four bundles in the sampling interval were sampled	Actual action taken under SQC system	Improvement of the Average Outgoing Quality (AOQ) level due to Screening and Replacement of defective items
RRRR	All rejected	p' x probability of this occurrence (P_r^4)
RRRA / RRAR / RARR	3 rejected	3/4 p' x prob. of this occurrence $(3P_r^3 P_a)$
RRAA / RARA / RAAR	2 rejected	2/4 p' x prob. of this occurrence $(2P_r^2 P_a^2)$
RAAA	1 rejected	1/4 p' x prob. of this occurrence $(P_r P_a^3)$
ARRR / ARRA / ARAR / AARR / ARAA / AARA / AAAR / AAAA	All accepted	No change

If we had no inspection, the AOQ = p'
With inspection, the AOQ = p' — savings due to screening.

$$AOQ = p' - p'P_r^4 - 3/4 p'(3P_r^3 P_a) - 2/4 p'(2P_r^2 P_a^2) - 1/4 p'P_r P_a^3$$

$$= \frac{p'[4 - P_r(4P_r^3 + 9P_r^2 P_a + 4P_r P_a^2 + P_a^3)]}{4}$$

Figure 5 (Winton Shirt Co.)   Mr. Harris' derivation of the AOQ curves

addition to his duties as second-shift foreman. (The company had recently established a small training laboratory to break in new workers and retrain old employees.)

Mr. LaFond devoted approximately 25% of his time to quality matters, most of which was spent compiling data and completing quality reports, since he had no clerical help. He was responsible for data collection and reporting, rotation of QC supervisors from department to department (every three months), and overall analysis and modification of the SQC system; however, in keeping with Mr. Harris'

Inspect for:

(1) Mismatched stripes or patterns where applicable
(2) Make sure that no Fold Down exists (creased edge at top of pocket showing)
(3) Position correct:

Size	Dimension
13½–14	3¹/₁₆" in from front edge
14½	3³/₁₆" in from front edge
15–15½	3⁷/₁₆" in from front edge
16–16½	3¹³/₁₆" in from front edge
17–17½–18–18½	4¹/₁₆" in from front edge
19–19½–20–20½	4⁵/₁₆" in from front edge

9" ± ¼" down from shoulder point on all sizes

(4) Correct Finished Pocket Dimensions: 5³/₈" by 4⁵/₈"
(5) Pocket Bar: The width of the triangular stitching on either end of the pocket opening should be a maximum of ³/₁₆" and a minimum of ²/₁₆" and run to the junction of the fold-back (See Diagram)

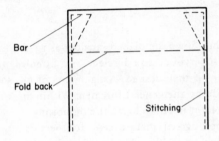

(6) Stitching:

Material	Stitches Per Inch
A	13 ± 1
B	14 ± 1
C	16 ± 1

Note: In addition, the inspector was supposed to look for material defects, wrinkles in the seams, cleanliness, loose or torn stitches, or any defect which would adversely affect the appearance of the pocket.

Figure 6 (Winton Shirt Co.)   Standard for inspection of pockets

desire to consolidate all staff functions under one man, rating and promotion of QC supervisors was handled by the supervisor of staff functions. Since Mr. LaFond was not available during most of the first shift, and since their working relationships were entirely within the departments, the QC supervisors reported, functionally, to the general foremen.

Mr. Harris viewed quality control as a function to assist rather than to control production. He stated that 'the responsibility for producing quality products must rest with the responsibility for production', and he believed that 'giving quality

(1) During the period, several operations have been changed, combining or altering manufacturing process steps. There had not been the improvement in process quality which we desired and expected, although the shifts were made without losing control over the quality and without any increase in the defects/hundred process rate. Perhaps, considering the changes which have been made in the organization and structure of manufacturing operations, holding our own could be considered an improvement.

(2) Initially, 41 people were employed as Foremen, Inspectors, Repair Operators, and Match-up Cutters. Now there are only 38. Although these savings cannot be attributed to the QC program, it is important to note that we have accomplished many of our objectives without increasing the number of personnel.

(3) There have been a small but significant number of major successes shown by SQC in controlling process defects. One such example occurred at 'trim top' in collar making. When we first introduced SQC in that department, we were running 17.4 defects per hundred at 'band and examine'. Only three out of eleven workers had excellent ratings, and three had unsatisfactory ratings. We carefully analyzed the operation and found that the problem came from poor trimming. Defective work on the 'trim top' operation is hidden in the 'band and examine' step. We spent time training the operators and made adjustments to the machines at 'trim top'. The net result was that, in a few weeks time, our defects/hundred rate at 'band and examine' had dropped to 1.1, and all but three of the 'band and examine' operators had excellent ratings, with only one poor rating in the group.

Figure 7 (Winton Shirt Co.)   Excerpts from the consultants' follow-up survey of SQC, July 1964

control the right to shut down the plant is analogous to the tail wagging the dog'. Thus, although QC supervisors could reject any bundles, the general foremen overruled the rejections if they desired. Assignments of QC supervisors within the departments were made by the general foremen. Within most departments, the QC supervisors swapped jobs at noon, to break the monotony.

The general foremen agreed that, except for personality problems, the SQC system was functioning smoothly. The initial resistance to the system and the 'report cards' on the part of the operators had long since diminished, but considerable conflict centered around particular QC supervisors. Typical of the comments made by the general foremen were the following:

(1) 'They get too chummy and start playing favourites. They tend to go easier on their friends.'

(2) 'Many of the QC supervisors have a bug about a particular operation and tend to be overly strict when they inspect at that station. This is especially true if the QC supervisor used to perform that operation, or if she performed a subsequent step which was dependent upon the quality of that particular operation.'

As an example, the general foreman of the parts department described a recent occurrence in the 'trim collar' operation: 'This trimming operation has a tolerance of plus or minus $1/32''$ according to the inspection standards. It is a critical operation in regard to 'collar band and examine', which is the most highly skilled in the plant. Poor trimming makes the difference between making out on the piece rate and just getting by. The particular QC supervisor had been a former banding operator and began inspecting the trimming operation very critically. The operator and the QC supervisor got into conflict and the QC supervisor tightened

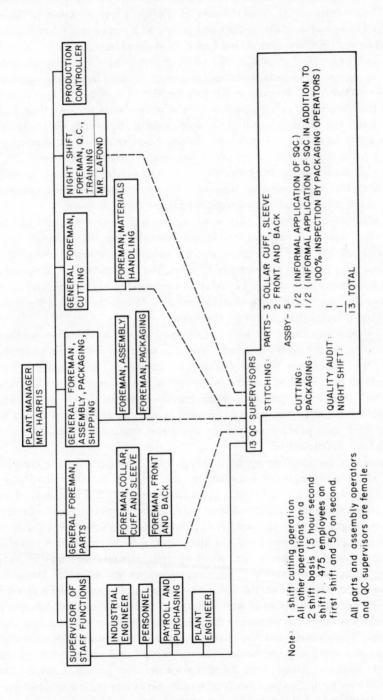

Figure 8 (Winton Shirt Co.)   Organization of the Middletown operation and its quality control function, October 1, 1966

PLANT MANAGER MR. HARRIS

SUPERVISOR OF STAFF FUNCTIONS

GENERAL FOREMAN, PARTS

GENERAL FOREMAN, ASSEMBLY, PACKAGING, SHIPPING

GENERAL FOREMAN, CUTTING

NIGHT SHIFT FOREMAN, Q.C., TRAINING MR. LAFOND

PRODUCTION CONTROLLER

INDUSTRIAL ENGINEER

PERSONNEL

PAYROLL AND PURCHASING

PLANT ENGINEER

FOREMAN, COLLAR, CUFF AND SLEEVE

FOREMAN, FRONT AND BACK

FOREMAN, ASSEMBLY

FOREMAN, PACKAGING

FOREMAN, MATERIALS HANDLING

13 QC SUPERVISORS

STITCHING: PARTS – 3   COLLAR CUFF, SLEEVE
             2   FRONT AND BACK
             ASSBY – 5

CUTTING: 1/2 (INFORMAL APPLICATION OF SQC)
PACKAGING: 1/2 (INFORMAL APPLICATION OF SQC IN ADDITION TO
                  100% INSPECTION BY PACKAGING OPERATORS)

QUALITY AUDIT: 1
NIGHT SHIFT: —
              13 TOTAL

Note: 1 shift cutting operation
       All other operations on a
       2 shift basis (5 hour second
       shift). 475 employees on
       first shift and 50 on second.

       All parts and assembly operators
       and QC supervisors are female.

up even more, rejecting work for all possible reasons. (There are many such reasons which QC supervisors can find. In the case of sewing, a typical reason is "loose stitching".) The operator finally complained to me. As it turned out, I felt that the QC supervisor was being too critical, and I ok'd the rejected bundles.

'These problems come up frequently. Unfortunately, there are time delays in straightening things out. Several bundles are usually rejected before the operator comes to me. Then I may be busy and it may be half an hour before I get to her, and all of this time she is performing rework and screening on her own time. This leads to a great deal of friction within the shop. I think that we should rotate the QC supervisor at least once a month, and I strongly believe that no QC supervisors should be hired from within the company. It just creates too many problems.'

Several QC supervisors commented that the SQC system was working well, especially with the newer operators. However, they reported that a large number of 'screened' bundles came back with unrepaired defects. Since they usually knew the operators who 'played the game', they would re-examine these 'screened' bundles, although they were not required to do so. Also, to prevent operators from concentrating on the two subsequent bundles to obtain clearance following a rejection and then reverting to poor quality work, the QC supervisors did not take the next two consecutive bundles, but selected two bundles at random, later on in the day. For the same reason, they randomly selected 25% of the bundles produced by each operator rather than take every fourth one.

The QC supervisors frequently added or dropped inspection operations on their own, depending on the problems which arose. For example, they often inspected the 'collar trim' operation because defects were covered up after handling, and because defects discovered at banding might necessitate major repair work. These 'unscheduled' inspections generated some friction between operators and QC supervisors. Occasionally the general foremen would assign QC supervisors to inspect at other than primary stations, in which case friction was minimized and SQC procedures were followed.

The procedure for handling operator ratings had become much more complex than Mr. Harris had originally intended. At the time of the SQC installation, operator ratings had been established, but no firm procedure had been devised for their use. Over the years, a method had evolved whereby substandard operator ratings were assigned points, the number of points depending upon the sequence in which the ratings were received and the time interval between them. A complex warning and disciplinary procedure, involving four separate meetings between management, the worker, and the union representative was based on the point system and could take a worker through a 13-week preprobationary and a 13-week probationary period. An operator who maintained poor performance throughout the 26 weeks was subject to transfer or dismissal. The procedure had been endorsed by corporate headquarters and Mr. Harris accepted it. According to Mr. LaFond, 'all the foremen are going bug-house over the setup', and at least 30% of the substandard operator ratings were being voided by the general foremen. No operator had ever been dismissed for poor quality performance, and few had ever been transferred or disciplined. In addition, the time period (26 weeks) was so long that frequently the operator had moved to another job as a result of seasonal changes in the product line long before 26 weeks had elapsed.

Minor model changes occurred frequently, but basic changes were introduced only twice a year when the plant shifted from short sleeves to long, and back. Quality suffered somewhat from these transitions, but usually bounced back after a few weeks. In addition to weekly production schedules which were issued from the Wellwood headquarters two weeks in advance, a three-month forecast was provided to facilitate training of workers for new jobs which would be created. Mr. Harris believed that the improvement in the quality effectiveness rating which was evident over the previous few years was largely the result of more efficient scheduling, since the number of models manufactured and the frequency of changes had been reduced. Production averaged 4,000 dozen shirts per week.

A small quality control group at corporate headquarters was responsible for coordinating procedures throughout the company, although they had no direct authority over the plants. They received copies of all quality control reports, but the only report issued by them was a monthly summary of the reasons for customer returns. Since it was not broken down by plant, Mr. Harris always asked the general foremen to double-check the manufacturing operations which might be responsible for the types of defects reported, to insure that Middletown was not contributing to the problems. He believed that Middletown was responsible for few of these returns. Most were for defects at felling, where the chain stitch came loose and started to rip back.

Union relations were characterized as excellent. Middletown had never experienced a strike and Mr. LaFond said that the recent upward revision of the wage structure in anticipation of the $1.40 minimum wage level, without any union pressure, was typical of plant management's attitude. He said that the union had not become involved in the procedure for setting standards and piece rates since 1959, when major revisions were made. Standards for new jobs were set by time study. Every job was classified into one of four 'skill ratings' and each such rating had been assigned a job value in 1959. New jobs were assigned ratings by the supervisor of staff functions. The job value ($/hour) was then divided by the standard (pieces/hour) to yield a piece rate. Since 1959 there had been few changes in standards, and piece rates had changed only in proportion to general wage increases which affected job values. In October 1966, stitchers averaged $1.91 and QC supervisors received $1.87 per hour.

Mr. LaFond, who had been a member of the union executive board prior to his appointment as nightshift foreman in 1964, stated that the union's positive attitude towards SQC had been maintained throughout its history at Middletown and that there had been no difficulties regarding the administration of the operator rating system. He explained: 'Although the system was never really explained to the union in detail, everyone had agreed on the meaning of "poor" and "unsatisfactory" and the concept has been accepted. The union's presence at all meetings pertaining to warnings or disciplinary action leads to a cooperative and understanding attitude.'

Furthermore, the company preferred to avoid involvement in disciplinary action and instead of firing a girl, had found it very effective to let her know that

Operation	Average of Defects/Hundred Reported by QC Supervisors Each Week — By Responsible Operation		Average % Coverage*
	Found in Process	Found at Audit	
COLLARS:			
Run Top	0.80	0.32	
Trim Point	1.21		30
Fuse Stay	0.53		
Turn Top	0.81	0.34	
Stitch Top**	(4.21)	(1.39)	95
Trim Top	0.48	0.08	23
Stamp Band	0.40	0.09	
Hem Band	1.52	0.08	30
Band and Examine	1.04	0.20	
Turn Band Ends	0.02	0.06	
Stitch Band**	(4.72)	(0.89)	61
Trim Band	0.69		
Buttonhole Collar	0.36	0.06	
Quartermark	0.01		
Buttonsew**	(1.43)	(0.12)	119
Press	0.20		
Miscellaneous***	(1.46)	(0.69)	
TOTAL	11.82	3.09	
CUFFS:			
Hem Cuffs	1.38	0.14	
Run**	(3.17)	(0.26)	69
Turn	1.26	0.06	
Press	0.03		
Top Stitch**	(2.66)	(0.47)	127
Buttonhole Cuff	1.08	0.06	89
Buttonsew Cuff**	(2.14)	(0.09)	53
Miscellaneous***	(0.03)	(0.33)	
TOTAL	8.00	1.15	
FRONTS:			
Hem	0.49	0.09	11
Buttonsew**	(1.27)	(0.18)	82
Overedge Front	—		
Press	0.03		
Buttonhole**	(0.43)	(0.22)	
Overedge Pocket	—		
Crease Pocket	0.19	0.37	
Pocket Attach**	(1.32)	(2.17)	99
Miscellaneous***	(0.70)	(0.67)	
TOTAL	3.72	3.24	
BACKS:			
Fuse Label	0.33		
Yoking**	(0.97)	(0.69)	121
Miscellaneous***	(1.46)	(0.13)	
TOTAL	2.43	0.82	
SLEEVES:			
Binding	3.10	0.33	113
Bar Tack**	(3.77)	(0.87)	64
Miscellaneous	(1.55)	(0.43)	
TOTAL	5.32	1.30	

Operation	Average of Defects/Hundred Reported by QC Supervisors Each Week — By Responsible Operation		Average % Coverage*
	Found in Process	Found at Adult	
ASSEMBLY:			
Joining**	(0.44)		
Run on Collar**	(0.44)		105
Stitch Down**	(0.96)	(0.26)	69
Sleeve Insert**	(0.82)	(1.09)	73
Felling**	(0.51)	(0.83)	72
Bottom Hem	0.87	0.78	82
Cuff Attach	1.10	1.73	
Trim Thread**	(3.90)	(5.51)	124
Loose Thread#	2.66	31.66	
Miscellaneous***	0.22	8.26	
TOTAL	9.95	47.61	
GRAND TOTAL	41.24	57.21	

Quality Effectiveness Figure:		
	1966	84.4
	1965	80.1
	1964	75.6

1966: Breakdown of average defects/hundred found at quality audit

	Critical	Major	Minor	
Collar	1.5	1.2	3.9	
Cuff	.4	.4	1.2	
Front	.3	1.0	3.5	
Back	.4	.4	.5	
Sleeve	1.7	.7	1.5	
Assembly	2.9	3.6	32.1	
TOTAL	7.2 +	7.3 +	42.7	= 57.2

Average % of output classified as seconds (1966)

Found in process	1.31
Found at audit	1.8

Notes: Figures in parentheses are total defects per hundred found at each primary inspection station.

*Percentage of bundles actually sampled in comparison to the number which should have been sampled under SQC, based on that week's production (data for five weeks, beginning with the fourth week in August 1966).

**Primary station.

***Unusual defects or defects pertaining to short sleeve shirts and special models only.

#Unattached threads which should have been removed by a blower during packaging but still cling to the shirt.

Figure 9 (Winton Shirt Co.)   SQC data: January–September 1966

management would be happy if she looked elsewhere. 'Most people do not want to work in a place where they are not wanted,' Mr. Harris stated.

Mr. Harris was pleased with the results of SQC. He said: 'I believe the SQC system has made a much greater contribution than the figures indicate. For example, although the initial survey showed a quality effectiveness figure of 80%, I think we are doing a better job. We are enforcing our standards more firmly, and I think our present figure would be 90 to 92 if we were inspecting the same way as we did in 1963. Then we were examining only critical dimensions. Now we inspect all, because even though a 1/8″ variation in the width of the shirt (especially if it is oversize) won't be noticed by the customer, it could result in a manufacturing process getting out of control if we let it go too long.

'Another reason which makes it difficult to evaluate the contribution of SQC is the fact that we have changed methods as a result of the change to SQC. Overall, the resultant change in number of employees has been negligible, but quality has improved. Our rework and match-up[5] costs are now running at 8.7¢ per dozen each, as compared to 9½¢ and 15¢ respectively in 1963, and during this period our production has increased by a third.'

'On the other hand, we cannot really identify all of our defects, and this tends to cloud the figures. Defects which escape the system are hidden in the process as subsequent operations cover them up. Also, operators tend to informally screen production from preceding operations and return defective parts to their friends. None of this goes through the recording procedures.'

'Another plus for SQC is the fact that we have very few seconds,[6] and we have virtually no output below second quality. Our greatest and only major mistake in this programme has been the fact that we did not provide a good management orientation for the QC supervisors. They have never lost the union viewpoint. It has hurt us, not so much quality-wise, but in regard to obtaining people who can eventually assume higher managerial responsibility. At the moment, I have a forelady position to fill and I cannot find a single QC supervisor who I can consider. I will have to promote someone from below.'

'The problem is that the QC supervisors are the bottom step of management. The job is low in importance in regard to participation in major management decisions. The QC supervisors have to be on the floor eight hours a day, performing very specific functions, and we don't have the time to bring them into decision making sessions.'

'We are hampered by the close ties they still maintain with the union and the possibility that they may leak information to union people. As a result, we cannot

---

[5] Match-up work involves recutting material to replace unrepairable or lost parts. Rework costs are incurred when defects cannot be traced back to operators, as when defective parts are found in the assembly department.

[6] Seconds are shirts with critical defects which cannot be repaired but can be sold at substantially reduced prices. All other shirts found in process or at quality audit are returned for repair unless they contain only minor defects such as 'trim threads' which can easily be corrected by the QC supervisor.

regard them completely as management personnel. In addition, there are too many conflicts among the group. If one girl starts doing too much, or thinking along managerial lines, the others who think of themselves primarily as inspectors exert pressure; however, I believe they are happy with their work. Although their absenteeism rate is the same as the 15% plant average, turnover has been nil, whereas the plant averages about 40% per year.'

Figure 9 presents data generated by Middletown's SQC system for 1966, through September. Mr. Harris planned to study this information before finalizing his report. He knew that top management was very eager to receive not only his evaluation of the Middletown experience but any suggestions which would be helpful in their deliberations on the extension of SQC to the other plants.

Index

414